D1016510

MASKED MEN

ARTS AND POLITICS OF THE EVERYDAY

Patricia Mellencamp
Meaghan Morris
Andrew Ross

MASKED MEN

Masculinity and the
Movies in the
Fifties

Steven Cohan

Indiana University Press
Bloomington and Indianapolis

© 1997 BY STEVEN COHAN
ALL RIGHTS RESERVED

No part of this book may be reproduced or
utilized in any form or by any means,
electronic or mechanical, including
photocopying and recording, or by any
information storage and retrieval system,
without permission in writing from the
publisher. The Association of American
University Presses' Resolution on Per-
missions constitutes the only exception to
this prohibition.
The paper used in this publication meets
the minimum requirements of American
National Standard for Information Sciences—Permanence of Paper for
Printed Library Materials,
ANSI Z39.48-1984.

Manufactured in the United States of America

Library of Congress Cataloging-in-Publication Data

Cohan, Steven.
Masked men : masculinity and the movies in the fifties /
Steven Cohan.
    p.   cm. — (Arts and politics of the everyday)
Filmography: p.
Includes bibliographical references and index.
ISBN 0–253–33297–4 (cl : alk. paper). —
ISBN 0–253–21127–1 (pa : alk. paper)
1. Men in motion pictures. 2. Masculinity (Psychology)
—United States—History—20th century.
I. Title. II. Series.
PN1995.9.M46C65   1997
791.43'652041—dc21
 96-29965

1 2 3 4 5 02 01 00 99 98 97

CONTENTS

ACKNOWLEDGMENTS

I am one of those baby boomers lucky enough to have been raised on movie culture. Sure, we had television, but my parents were of the generation that still went to the movies every week, and they continued this habit after I was born. I am told they took me as an infant, so I cannot even remember the very first film I ever saw. My mother's favorite star was William Holden, with Doris Day a close second. Their new films were always major events in my house. My father's favorite star was John Wayne, and his favorite genre was the Western, though he liked musicals a lot, too. There never seemed to be a time when the movies weren't important in our home, when we weren't talking about them or reading about them or going to see them. I went with my parents together, with each of them separately, with them and their adult friends, and later with my younger sister. My parents' unqualified love of the movies is, without doubt, the source of inspiration for this study.

Returning to the present, I have many people to thank for helping me. I am grateful to Constance Penley, Sharon Willis, Annette Kuhn, Andrew Ross, Patricia Mellencamp, and Susan Jeffords for their enthusiastic support of this project as it began to take shape. At professional conferences, colleagues helped to hone my ideas in subtle, probably indiscernible ways: particularly Sabrina Barton, Dennis Bingham, Henry Jenkins, Peter Lehman, Alan Nadel, and most of all, Virginia Wright Wexman, who always asked me tough questions that I needed to think about; even when we disagreed, her viewpoint has been crucial to my understanding of the fifties. I owe a debt to friends and acquaintances who spurred my thinking at points in the writing process: Gaylyn Studlar, Barbara Klinger, Laura Mulvey, Jane Hendler, Mark Jancovich, Frank Krutnik, Sari Champagne, Susan Edmunds, Bennet Schaber, Bill Readings, Diane Elam, Beatrice Skordili, Uli Knoepflmacher, Steve Melville, Gael Sweeney, Matthew Tinkcom, and Ina Ferris. Your influence can be felt in the pages of this book in ways that I cannot possibly footnote. I must also single out Adrienne McLean for sharing fan magazine articles as well as her knowledge of fifties stars, and Allen Larson for urging me to think about Montgomery Clift, for leading me to some valuable resources, and most of all, for just listening as I talked on and on. Pat Moody and Richard Fallis provided institutional assistance, and the staff of Bird Library's Interlibrary Loans was enormously helpful in finding sources of fan magazines. I am also grateful for the assistance I received while working at the Margaret Herrick Library in Los Angeles. Linda Shires read a portion of the manuscript in draft, and her comments gave me some direction when I needed it; her friendship gives me needed direction, too, and I value it greatly. The two anonymous readers for the Press offered sound criticism as well as praise; the book is better for what they had to say. I also thank Joan Catapano, my editor at Indiana University Press, for her support and her patience.

Portions of this book were previously published in different form. A short version of chapter 1 appeared under the title "The Spy in the Gray Flannel Suit: Gender Performance and the Representation of Masculinity in *North by Northwest*" in *The Masculine Masquerade,* ed. Helaine Posner and Andrew Perchuk (Cambridge: MIT Press, 1994); and a portion of this same chapter is drawn from an article, "Cary Grant in the Fifties: Indiscretions of the Bachelor's Masquerade," in *Screen* 33, no. 4 (Winter 1992). An early version of chapter 5, "Masquerading as the American Male in the Fifties: *Picnic,* William Holden, and the Spectacle of Masculinity in Hollywood Film," appeared in *Camera Obscura* 25–26 (1991). A highly abbreviated version of chapter 7, "So Functional for Its Purposes: Rock Hudson's Bachelor Apartment in *Pillow Talk,*" was included in *Stud: Architectures of Masculinity,* ed. Joel Sanders (Princeton: Princeton Architectural Press, 1996). I thank the edtiors for giving me permission to include this material.

Finally, I want to thank my sometimes collaborator and longtime movie buddy, Ina Rae Hark, who has seen me through this book at every stage of its composition. I treasure her input, and her friendship—well, that goes without saying. She, too, loves the movies of the fifties, and once commented that, when it comes to the era's stars, her fifties was not exactly the same as mine, although we do meet on common ground with Charlton Heston in *The Ten Commandments.* I dedicate *Masked Men* to her.

INTRODUCTION

Most popular accounts of the fifties look back at this period as a kind of long, comforting sleep, an era of affluence and complacency nestled between the war years of the early forties and the political activism of the late sixties. There is some justification for this nostalgic picture. According to historian J. Ronald Oakley, the fifties was "a time of consensus," notably at mid-decade, when "America was becoming homogenized" (314–15). "[F]or most white, middle-class Americans, and particularly white, middle-class males," he concludes, "the fifties was perhaps the best decade in the history of the republic" (434). When it came to representing the masculine contentment that Oakley alludes to, however, American culture in the fifties was more deeply conflicted than has been remembered. Perhaps nowhere are those tensions in greater evidence, this book argues, than in the era's movies.

Before going any further, I should explain that I do not take "the fifties" to refer, in a strictly chronological sense, simply to the years 1950–59. The actual demarcations of any momentous historical era do not follow the calendar, and what I am calling "the fifties" more accurately describes the years of postwar demobilization and the onset of cold war hostility, the span of time measured by the Truman and Eisenhower administrations. (For purposes of clarity, then, when I refer to "the fifties" I mean this historical era, and when I refer to "the 1950s" I mean the particular years inclusive of the chronological decade.) Historically, the fifties began with the United States' emergence at the center of global politics and the world economy after World War II. As Thomas J. Mc-Cormick recounts in his history of twentieth-century U.S. foreign policy, "the American economy by 1946 was the workshop, the bakery, and the banker of the postwar world" (47). Taking advantage of its economic position and pursuing the agenda that had determined its wartime strategies in the Pacific Rim and the Ruhr valley in Germany, the United States quickly solidified its hegemony over both the world market and global politics, "presid[ing] over the integration of Europe into a North Atlantic community, the integration of Japan into a North Pacific community, and the Cold War isolation of the Soviet bloc." From this portentous beginning, the fifties saw closure once "American hegemony reached its pinnacle and simultaneously commenced its decline in 1958," for at this point "the first signs were perceived that America's inflated postwar trade balance might eventually become a trade deficit." Just as ominously for the future, "these first cracks in the economic edifice coincided with the first cracks in America's overseas political-military imperium" (238–39). The 1960 election of Kennedy—whose administration accelerated U.S. involvement in the Vietnamese Civil War, intensifying the militarization of the nation's economy, and whose youthful, virile, aristocratic, and intellectual persona set a different tone for what I shall be calling the culture's hegemonic masculinity—marks the end point of the era that I examine in this book.

Within this completed first act of what would become a forty-year-long cold war, most Americans were divided in their responses to the nation's economic prosperity at home and military power abroad. According to Oakley, "[t]he period that most of the nostalgic feelings have centered upon is the time sandwiched between the end of the Korean War in the summer of 1953 and the launching of Sputnik in October of 1957" (434). Before then, he points out, the nation was traumatized by one international crisis after another, each having immediate reverberations on the domestic front (the Soviets' testing of the atomic bomb, Chiang Kai-Shek's retreat from mainland China to Formosa/ Taiwan, the spy scandals, HUAC, the outbreak of war in Korea, Truman's firing of MacArthur, and so on). Likewise, the "peace and prosperity" of mid-decade were quickly followed by an erosion of "national prestige and confidence," which resulted in a "period of self-examination. . . . The nation was criticized for its conformity, materialism, complacency, apathy, dull homogeneity, and confusion about its national purpose and goals" (413). The cultural mentality of the fifties, however, was not as neatly segmented as it appears in this retelling. Sputnik increased apprehension about the arms race in 1957, but anxiety about the bomb was as intense throughout the period. More to my point in this book, while the crisis in national confidence that Oakley attributes to the late 1950s was, as part of the culture's self-examination, directed at the imperiled state of American manhood, widespread apprehension of a masculinity crisis began right after World War II and, though its inflection changed, it remained strong during the entire decade.

In *Masked Men*, I examine the postwar masculinity crisis as depicted by some of this era's most popular films. Paying close attention to the slippages that occurred within cinematic representations of the so-called typical American male, I follow contemporary gender theorists such as Judith Butler in claiming that sexed identities, desires, and bodies are performative, the effects of a masquerade that is neither singular nor continuous; but as importantly, my study of masculinity intends to bring a frequently overlooked historical dimension to this theoretical perspective. The "Masked Men" of my title summarizes both aims. The title refers to the way that a normative masculinity functioned on screen to mask the social differences that stratified U.S. society during the fifties, while it recognizes, too, how films of this period highlight the multiple masquerades that constituted masculinity in its representation. Although this double focus shapes the entire book and determines my argument in each chapter, structurally speaking, chapters 1, 2, and 3 concentrate more on the first sense of masquerade; chapters 5, 6, and 7 on the second; and chapter 4 pivots around both to mark the transition from one thread to the other.

The advantage of undertaking a historical analysis of masculinity in fifties films from the vantage point of contemporary gender theory should be immediately apparent: it challenges the culture's own impression that the typical American male, presumed to be coherent, stable, and equivalent to the national character, actually existed outside of representation. What seemed homogenous about American men in the fifties, at least according to the discourses about masculinity in widespread circulation then, was actually specific to the normative social position of some men within the culture, namely, the white, heterosexual, corporate, WASP, suburban breadwinner as personified by the ubiquitous figure of The Man in the Gray Flannel Suit, the logo of the age which still represents it four decades later. While this norm was repeatedly invoked, as the movies readily illustrate, it was just as often subverted. Viewing masculinity as a masquerade helps to articulate more precisely why a hegemonic representation like the fifties' Man in the Gray Flannel Suit could dominate the culture and yet be subject to change (because of its location in history as a social position); why such a normative standard of masculinity is never stable or coherent or authentic (because of its location in representation as a mask); and why it has to exist alongside a range of alternative forms in representation (because of its location in a hierarchy of competing masculinities, even though this plurality has the effect of making masculinity multiple in its incarnations). Fittingly reduced to a logo of mass production and consumption, the fifties' standard of normative masculinity was an incoherent portrait of the typical American male, not fully aligned to the social interests it authorized. In registering this incoherence, representations of the middle-class breadwinner made it all the more visible and problematic as a gender "crisis," what *Look* magazine called, with great solemnity, "The Decline of the American Male."

Such a crisis in masculinity was by no means unique to the fifties, the twentieth century, or American culture, to be sure. As Tania Modleski points out in *Feminism without Women,* "male power is actually consolidated through cycles of crisis and resolution, whereby men ultimately deal with the threat of female power by incorporating it" (7). A culture's representations of masculinity in crisis thus often reflect a perceived "feminization" of men, as it did in the fifties. However, it does not follow, as Modleski suggests, either that a culture's apparent loss of faith in masculinity does not illuminate major disturbances in the traditional structures of patriarchy, or that the rhetoric of a "masculinity crisis," which implicates men and women alike in representations of sexual difference, is not without its significance for feminism. In the fifties, the widespread apprehension of a national crisis caused by the "declining" state of American manhood was clearly responsive to some special historical circumstances, just as it was represented on screen in some very distinct, often very troubling, always very revealing ways.

A number of factors contributed to the culture's perception of a masculinity crisis, and they did not go without notice at the time. Demobilization required restoration of the gender relations that World War II had disturbed both in the home and the workplace, while anxiety about the mental stability of returning veterans exaggerated the danger their ungovernable masculinity posed to the social order. After the war, too, the first Kinsey report on men, published in 1948, challenged many traditional assumptions regarding the normality of male sexual practices, revealing the surprising number of American men who had had homosexual encounters or were not monogamous, for example; and the 1953 follow-up volume on female sexuality gave equally disconcerting evidence about the asymmetry of male and female sexualities, underscoring the physical instability of men, in comparison to women, as they matured into their breadwinner positions to serve the American family.

Masculinity was jeopardized at work as well as in the bedroom. The initial postwar economic boom gave apparent evidence of America's transformation into a seamless middle-class society, with the ability of working men to buy a refrigerator, car, even a house apparently signaling their rise in social status. But the dominance of an emerging upper middle class, identified through a man's corporate or professional employment, was confirmed by the culture's equation of normative masculinity with white-collar labor. This corporate setting ended up relocating masculinity in what had previously been considered a "feminine" sphere, primarily by valuing a man's domesticity (and consumption) over his work (and production) as the means through which he fulfilled societal expectations of what it took to be "manly." Whether on the assembly line or in an executive office, corporate culture also prized conformity over individuality. It therefore uncannily resembled the repressive ethos of communist societies, disclaiming what the diversity of the U.S. economy, churning out a vast and seemingly endless array of consumable products, was supposed to connote to the world at large about Americans' freedom of choice. Cold war politics further complicated the picture by projecting contradictory ideals for American manhood, requiring a "hard" masculinity as the standard when defending the nation's boundaries, yet insisting upon a "soft" masculinity as the foundation of an orderly, responsible home life.

I elaborate upon these historical circumstances in the following chapters. Taken together, they all point to an even more profound and, at the time, less discernible transformation in the culture's understanding of the masculine gender in relation to male sexuality. As historian George Chauncey puts it, "the hetero-homosexual binarism," which organizes sexual categories around object choice and not gender status, is "the sexual regime now hegemonic in American culture," but it in fact "is a stunningly recent creation" (13). In the late nineteenth and early twentieth centuries, masculinity was generally understood to be legible through a man's gendered behavior, not his sexuality, primarily in working-class culture, where "gender governed the interpretation of sexual practices and manliness was self-consciously performative" (127). An effeminate male who had sex with other men, for example, was called a "fairy"

to designate his "'woman-like' character" as much as for "his solicitation of
male sexual partners" (13). Likewise, a man who did not deviate from accepted
gender norms could have a same-sex encounter without impugning his virility
so long as he took "the 'man's part'" just as he did with women (100). This gender ideology, which did not make heterosexuality "a precondition of gender
normativity" (97), defined masculinity in terms of differences among men according to their outward appearance and behavior, and it permeated the fabric
of American society, Chauncey claims, until some time in the mid-twentieth
century, as evident in the complex social ordering and visibility of diverse gay
male subcultures in his case study, New York City from 1890 through 1940.

Chauncey points out, however, that it was during this same period that the
now axiomatic hetero-homosexual binarism did become crucial to the masculinity of "normal middle-class men[, who] increasingly believed that their virility depended on their exclusive sexual interest in women" (100). He attributes this different, class-specific perspective to the rise of corporate labor in
the late nineteenth century. In revising "the character and meaning of the work
performed by many middle-class men," the economic reorganization of
American businesses into large corporations displaced white-collar employees
from the culture's traditional supports of masculinity, particularly in comparison to their working-class counterparts, who appeared more manly, thereby
intensifying the middle class's apprehension of a gender imbalance in their
own lives (111). Exclusive heterosexuality provided middle-class men "with a
new, more positive way to demonstrate their manhood" (117), and it was inconceivable without reference to "homosexuality" as a category designating the
negation of manhood.

Historian E. Anthony Rotundo draws the same conclusion from his analysis of nineteenth-century masculinity. He documents how the binary logic
characterizing bourgeois culture in the late nineteenth century, "dividing all
things (including the male sex) into male and female" (278), revised even the
language that the middle class used to describe manliness. Whereas in the
mid-nineteenth century the male's "base nature," his "appetites" or "passions,"
had needed to be civilized by femininity, it was now understood to form the
core of a robust, vital masculinity in contradistinction to femininity. Middle-
class men thus "began to sort themselves out into hardy, masculine types and
gentle, feminine types" (265). In compliance with the resulting belief that
"one's sexuality defined one's identity and one's true inner self" (276), the locus
for absorbing and stigmatizing all that was not manly in male nature was
"homosexuality," which, toward the end of the century, began to acquire its
currency as "a category of persons who could represent men's unacceptable
feminine impulses" (278). Since this new appreciation of virility made it
inseparable from a "heterosexual" nature, intense romantic friendships between men, which Rotundo shows had been relatively common for the middle
class at mid-century, were likewise devalued, their energies redirected into

competitive sports and business pursuits. As a consequence, middle-class men had to deny any affective, let alone erotic, component in their interactions with other men (Chauncey 100).

Starting sometime in the 1880s and 1890s, then, middle-class masculinity began to be governed by a sexual ideology that interpreted the gendered attributes of men as either normal or deviant expressions of their sexuality. While this mentality certainly influenced the discourses about masculinity circulating through the culture during the first decades of the twentieth century, from psychoanalysis to the advice manuals that defined male desire as "active, insistent, quickly aroused, and genitally focused" (D'Emilio and Freedman 267), it did not dominate American society as a whole until after World War II, when the middle class achieved a hegemonic standing it had not previously held. The war—with its disruption of class divisions, atmosphere of sexual deprivation, and deflation of traditional heroism—was a significant catalyst in breaking down ideological walls that had previously differentiated working- and middle-class men, in effect, bringing "gendered" and "sexual" conceptions of masculinity into greater contention. On one hand, the institutions of wartime laid the groundwork for the eventual absorption of working-class men into a middle-class outlook. An ideology celebrating "home" and "nation" motivated patriotism by equating a single normative masculinity with the American character, setting the terms for the working class's identification with middle-class hegemony (and with it, conformity to middle-class beliefs about masculinity) after the war. On the other hand, the war repositioned men of all classes in a same-sex environment that challenged the middle class's presumption of heterosexual normality in opposition to homosexual deviance. Officially, the military pathologized homosexuality, defining it as the inversion of heterosexual masculinity (the "sissy") and basing the diagnosis on the outward effeminacy of potential soldiers; but at the same time, the military permitted camp entertainments featuring men in drag, officially endorsed the close, passionate bonding of men in buddy relations, and tended to look the other way when men engaged in homosexual activity in the barracks or on ship. Men who had same-sex encounters to relieve sexual deprivation, moreover, did not necessarily have trouble thinking of themselves as "normal" or "heterosexual" afterward.

The virulent repression of homosexuality following the war is a rather telling index of the entire culture's conversion to a middle-class sexual ideology. "[S]ex was seen as perhaps the most important thing in life in fifties America," Richard Dyer comments (*Heavenly* 24). Since he is speaking of perceptions about the entire culture, this has to be understood as a dramatic shift in thinking about gender, distinctly signaled by the public's fascination with the first Kinsey report in 1948, which became an immediate best-seller. As perceived by its readers, the book projected a readily identifiable "American male" characterized by his sexuality. After Kinsey, the anxieties of a working man, such as one of psychologist Helen Mayer Hacker's patients in the 1950s, a "mechanic who feared listening to Caruso records" would be interpreted even by nonprofessionals as a clear-cut sign that he was worried about his manhood, which automatically translated to "a fear of homosexuality" (232), not to his apprehensions about what such taste in music might connote to others regarding his gender status or social nonconformity.

As Hacker's mechanic illustrates, in the postwar reconfiguration of masculinity the middle-class ideology of a uniform sexuality did not simply replace a working-class ideology of variable gender performativity but intersected with it, and the resulting contradictions were volatile. In trying to account for what she called "the new burdens of masculinity," Hacker herself pointed out at the time that the culture defined normative masculinity in conflicting terms: as a question of social responsibility, with a man expected to perform his duty as the family breadwinner, and, simultaneously, as a question of sexual potency, with a man expected to perform in bed with vigor (and with a woman, that should go without saying). The era's ideal of companionate marriage meant to bring these two definitions together in a coherent package. However, the unease with which this reformulation of masculinity took place, the disturbances it produced, and the instabilities it made evident, motivated the perception of a gender crisis that assumed national proportions and accounts for its continued significance four decades later. For while the fifties marks the historical conjuncture when the hetero-homosexual binarism governing the way our culture now interprets gender distinctions and maintains sexual conformity achieved its hegemonic standing, this era also records, especially in predominantly middle-class entertainment such as the movies, how gender and sexuality did not easily or securely meld together as the coordinates of a normative masculinity committed to heterosexuality and applicable to all men everywhere.

In *Masked Men*, I place American films of the fifties in their historical context with the intention of examining how they contributed to but also resisted and problematized the postwar articulation of masculinity as a universal condition, the automatic effect of a man's inborn nature, his being "male" in his identity, his desires, and his body. It may now seem impossible to "think about sexuality without taking into account gender," and vice versa, because the two are "inextricably linked" in our culture's understanding of masculinity and femininity (Weeks 45). But what this means, as Judith Butler puts it, is that gender is a cultural masquerade replacing the biological determination of sexuality: "If gender consists of the social meanings that sex assumes, then sex does not *accrue* social meanings as additive properties but, rather, *is replaced* by the social meanings it takes on" (*Bodies* 5). Gender is performative, in her view, because it "enacts or produces that which it names" (13)—sexuality—and in the process "regulates and constrains" the object of its production (2). As I emphasize throughout the course of this book, particularly when focusing upon the male body's visibility in cinematic representation, an understanding of how masculinity functions in performative terms as a masquerade can begin to sort out the vexing relation between gender and sexuality. Since gender deviance was a conventional way of referring to homosexuality on screen without mentioning it, a requirement of the Production Code's restrictions, fifties American films generally made the two comparable, so the representations of male gender trouble in movies of this period invariably raise problems of sexuality, too. The "Masked Men" of my title therefore also summarizes the gendered *and* sexualized masquerades underlying the performative dimensions of masculinity in the movies, which serves to remind us all the more how *any* figuration of manliness can never be separated from its ground in representation.

Film makes it especially difficult not to think of masculinity as a masquerade. Because, as both a medium and an institution, Hollywood cinema depends so greatly on making the sexually differentiated bodies of stars visible to an audience, it invariably brings the performativity of gender to the forefront of representation. The musical, which does not generically follow the conventional strategies by which Hollywood cinema has routinely naturalized gender on screen, takes the performativity of male and female stardom as its very premise. Indeed, because of the musical's great popularity during the years covered by this book, its absence might seem odd. But it became clear when writing *Masked Men* that the carnivalesque gender play and erotic male spectacle characterizing the era's major male musical stars (Fred Astaire, Gene Kelly, Danny Kaye, Bob Hope, not to say Elvis Presley) deserves a separate book in itself. As a result, I decided to exclude the musical and its stars from the scope of this study.

While I regret having had to postpone discussion of masculinity in the postwar musical for the time being, it nevertheless turned out to be easy enough to bracket off consideration of the problematic status of the era's song-and-dance men. The open acknowledgment in musicals that masculinity and femininity are equally performative, and that this performativity has spectacle as its intent, is a crucial effect—you might even call it the fundamental insight—of the Hollywood star system in general. A male star may play manly roles in his films, but the apparatus of stardom turns him into a spectacle, valuing him for his whole body as well as his good looks even more than for his impersonation of agency. Produced in an era of widescreen technologies and genres that exploited but also problematized the male body's status on screen, and reflective of a culture that read everyday life through its visibility, looking at the material world of consumable products with "a scrupulous, pleasurable regard for both shape and surface" (Marling 15), fifties films made the spectacularity of actors the central dimension of their stardom—and a focal point for assessing the masculinity they projected, in an open violation of the widely held presumption that the typical American male was defined through his invisibility as a man in a gray flannel suit.

To demonstrate further the unstable position of masculinity in Hollywood cinema of the fifties, I read the era's stars themselves as highly charged and conflicted social constructions, considering what they bring to a given film and, as importantly, how a given film revises their significance. As John Ellis states, "The basic definition of a star is that of a performer in a particular medium whose figure enters into subsidiary forms of circulation, and then feeds back into future performances" (91). In the fifties, while the discourse of stardom brought together all venues of press coverage from the various media— including news releases from the studios' publicity departments, radio and television interviews and appearances, articles in the daily press and large-circulation magazines—the fan magazines, which featured the same writers (Sidney Skolsky, Hedda Hopper, Louella Parsons) whose bylines appeared in newspaper columns and mainstream magazines, were the most important, both in constructing the aura of a star's offscreen "personality" and in situating it in relation to screen roles as a means of determining his or her charismatic presence. According to *Variety*, despite the noticeable fall-off in movie attendance following the boom period of the war and immediately thereafter, the fan magazine industry actually prospered during the postwar years, resulting in the continuing strength of publications like *Photoplay*, which led the field with a circulation of over 1,440,000 in 1954. "As one publisher explained it: 'Maybe our readers didn't go to the movies as often as before, but they still maintained their loyalty to the stars'" ("Fan Mags" 7). Encouraging their readers to respond to stars as if they transcended and yet embodied the films that created them, fan magazines fostered what Dyer calls "a rhetoric of sincerity or authenticity, two qualities greatly prized in stars because they guarantee, respectively, that the star really means what he or she says, and that the star really is what she or he appears to be" (*Heavenly* 11). Stardom does not just oppose an actor's charisma to the theatricality of cinema, it makes the opposition central to a star's persona, casting it in gendered terms, so that what a star authenticates is the apparent naturalness of his or her sexual difference.

As mediated through the fan magazines of the period, the fifties star system brings out numerous contradictions arising from the positioning of actors as gender models and sexual objects, all underscoring the comparable performativity of masculinity and femininity, so it provides a fundamental link between my historical research and my analyses of film texts. For a similar reason, I am equally interested in setting films against their marketing, at times paying as close attention to poster art and trailers as to the films themselves. Put somewhat simply and without intending to be flippant, what we academic scholars take pains to interpret today as the underlying *ideology* of cinematic representation was in fact often displayed as plain as day: it was called *publicity*. Having said that, I do not mean to imply that the ideological content of fifties films was any more transparent to moviegoers of that time than it is to critics today. Publicity, like stardom, helps to locate a film in its historical moment, identifying the range of meanings offered for it through its exhibition. Of course, no film ever simply reproduces a single ideology in a pure form, since other ideologies invade, complicate, and often disturb its representational field, disallowing certain types of meaning and enforcing others to determine the materiality of what can—and, as importantly, what may not—be represented on screen. I therefore approach the films of this era as historical objects embedded in a network of cultural discourses, and I rely heavily on the popular press of the time to establish the discursive currency of screen masculinity in its multiple representations.

Because I seek to examine masculinity in movies of the fifties from various angles, all the while having to remain within the boundaries of a very mainstream—and white, middle-class, heterosexual—institution of popular entertainment, I have not organized this book chronologically to develop a linear argument about masculinity, the movies, or the fifties. Nor do I maintain the same type of critical focus in each chapter: some pivot around a specific film, some around a star persona, some around a specific issue of representation. The subject of masculinity itself requires me to deviate from the more conventional chronological organization of most period studies because, as sociologist R. W. Connell cautions, "The history of masculinity, it should be abundantly clear, is not linear. There is no master line of development to which all else is subordinate, no simple shift from 'traditional' to 'modern'" (*Masculinities* 198).

Respecting this warning, I structure my historical analysis of the masculine masquerade in movies of the fifties around a representational field characterized by what it obscures (homosexuality) and outright excludes (race) and openly includes (class, ethnicity, age) in determining the coordinates of normality. *Masked Men* begins by centering my discussion around a specific socially inflected and historically motivated persona of white masculinity: The Man in the Gray Flannel Suit, discussed in chapters 1 and 2. As I have already indicated, this figuration of the middle-class breadwinner achieved its hegemony in representation—so that it was readily identified as the typical American male—because of its position in a hierarchy of competing masculinities. Within this hierarchy, alternative masculine personae were made complicit with the interests served by this norm (as in the cases of the epic and Western heroes discussed in chapters 4 and 6, respectively); or they were subordinated to it (as in the cases of the psychopathic criminal discussed in chapter 3, the racialized alien in chapter 4, and the rebel boy in chapter 6); or they were marginalized (as in the cases of the drifter discussed in chapter 5 and the bachelor in chapter 7). Each of these alternative personae is not an "image" or stereotype of masculinity, as my cursory description here might imply, but a social position for masculinity; each interacts with the others within the larger, hierarchically ordered field of power relations; and each has its own discursive history, which became imbricated in its cinematic representation.

Even though I risk oversimplifying the arguments of each chapter, in order to elaborate upon the framework I have just described, and as a means of being even more precise about the overall contours of this book's structure, let me explain further how the seven chapters of *Masked Men* interlock. Dispensing with the rules of Classic Hollywood Narrative myself, I open *Masked Men* by moving immediately to the close of the fifties with an analysis of *North by Northwest*, produced in 1959. Using this well-known Hitchcock film to raise both the historical and theoretical issues informing the entire book, in chapter 1, "The Spy in the Gray Flannel Suit," I examine the heterogeneous ground of this film's depiction of masculinity in crisis: the cold war framework determining the conjunction of marriage and espionage in its thriller narrative, the performance ethic arising from the protagonist's identification with the hegemonic formation of a new postwar professional class, and the masquerade elements accruing around the star persona of Cary Grant—all of which, I argue, locate masculinity in representation while revealing its place there to be highly problematic.

The next two chapters unfold from points introduced in the first. Chapters 2 and 3 examine the fifties' construction of normative masculinity within the historical context of postwar domestication. The second chapter, "The 'Paradox' of Hegemonic Masculinity," concentrates on three films depicting the breadwinner in crisis (*Pitfall*, *The Seven Year Itch*, and *The Man in the Gray Flannel Suit*) in order to trace the historical pressures operating upon this representation of normative masculinity. My purpose here is to document how the discourse of masculinity crisis registered as a problem of gender what were, more subtly, social contradictions pressuring the ideological function of "the new American domesticated male," as *Life* named the middle-class breadwinner in confirmation of his typicality. Offering the other side of this argument, the third chapter, "Tough Guys Make the Best Psychopaths," follows the shifting inflections of Humphrey Bogart's tough-guy star persona in order to historicize the fifties' revision of the virility he epitomized in his film noir roles: from the positioning of his persona in both the aggression and, more crucially, the homoeroticized male bonding consistent with a wartime ideology of masculinity (in *Dead Reckoning*); to an ambiguous redefinition of that persona according to the postwar revaluation of male anger and enforced heterosexuality required of domestic ideology (in *In a Lonely Place*); to its complete reconstruction as a portrait of social deviancy, the outcome of postwar sex crime laws serving to regulate social and sexual conformity through the category of the criminal psychopath (in *The Desperate Hours*).

Chapter 4, "The Body in the Blockbuster," may appear to change my focus somewhat dramatically but only because, in turning to the era's popular biblical epics, I move away from the domestic preoccupations of chapters 2 and 3. Here, I examine the numerous ways in which *The Ten Commandments* became embedded in contemporary global politics, which supplied a timely historical context for the reception of this film's representation of heroic masculinity, Charlton Heston's Moses standing on Mount Sinai with the West's laws in his hands. Like other epics of this period, *The Ten Commandments* incorporates the various antinomies of cold war ideology into its biblical narrative, with its ready-made parallels to both U.S.-U.S.S.R hostility and American interests in the Middle East. But even more importantly, DeMille's epic capitalizes upon the racial opposition personified by its two stars, Heston and Yul Brynner, visualizing both the American/alien binarism of cold war ideology and its incoherence in the very spectacle of their bodies.

Taking up the issue of male spectacle raised by chapter 4, the last three chapters more explicitly treat the erotic value of male stardom in the fifties, stressing its potential for disturbing the gender norms epitomized by the seemingly effaced body of The Man in the Gray Flannel Suit. In chapter 5, "The Age of the Chest," I examine *Picnic* and its visual exploitation of star William Holden in terms of fifties conventions for displays of male beefcake, which make a mask out of the body and multiply the possibilities of a sexualized gaze. *Picnic* implicates its leading man along with its protagonist, the drifter Hal, in a masquerade that is sexual as well as gendered in its performativity, and Holden's star persona brings to the film a means of containing what that spectacle of virility reveals about the movies' investment in the male body. Chapter 6, "Why Boys Are Not Men," takes this issue further, demonstrating how the erotic screen imagery of the fifties' new generation of stars was mediated by the fan magazines' response to sexy young actors such as Montgomery Clift and Marlon Brando. Interpreting their visibly different masculinity as a gender subversion, the fan discourse portrays them as boys who are not men, in direct contrast to more traditionally "virile" stars like John Wayne. In this chapter I examine at length the related dimensions of gender performativity and bisexuality that characterize Clift's star persona as such a boy in *Red River* and *A Place in the Sun*. I then look at Brando's comparable boyish persona, primarily as determined by the spectacle of his body in *A Streetcar Named Desire*, and conclude by documenting how the industry's censorship of the boy in *Streetcar* and *Tea and Sympathy* conflates gender and sexuality in a manner that reproduces the same confusion of man/boy, heterosexual/homosexual categories, which structures the transgressive personae of both Clift and Brando.

Finally, in chapter 7, "The Bachelor in the Bedroom," I discuss the antithesis of the fifties breadwinner, the bachelor playboy personified by Rock Hudson as a series of masquerades in *Pillow Talk*. Drawing on *Playboy* magazine's promotion of the bachelor's hyperactive heterosexuality to start with, I follow the intricacy with which *Pillow Talk* brings out the *Playboy* discourse's strong undercurrent of male performativity and closeted homosexuality, with both attributes informing the spatial meaning of the 1950s bachelor apartment (in the pages of the magazine as well as in this film) to characterize the single man's marginalized status—and his potentially subversive desires. In *Pillow Talk*, this becomes particularly evident in the film's masquerade plot, which narra-tivizes the performativity of playboy bachelorhood, and in the process alludes in some very specific ways to Hudson's own problematic position in the star system as the fifties' exemplar of desirable masculinity, the quintessential but fabricated heterosexual bachelor. *Pillow Talk* returns me full circle to concerns raised in my opening chapter. In much the same way that *North by Northwest* does, this film uses its narrative, social setting, and leading man to call explicit attention to the gender and sexual masquerading that, I demonstrate through-out *Masked Men*, underlies the representation of masculinity in movies of the fifties.

MASKED MEN

The Spy in the Gray Flannel Suit

The poster for *North by Northwest* (1959), reproduced as figure 1, offers an arresting image of male vulnerability: Cary Grant suspended helplessly in space. Although he stretches out his arms as if ready to break the fall with his hands, Grant's bent legs and flung feet indicate an utter inability to support himself were he to reach the ground. What's more, the expression on his face—his mouth agape, his eyes closed—testifies to, if not fear, then horror at his plight. The inclusion of Eva Marie Saint in the background behind Grant—where she stands, gun in hand, as the apparent cause of his danger—encourages us to read the poster as a reference to an actual moment in the film: when Eve Kendall (Saint) pretends to shoot Roger O. Thornhill (Grant), who is posing as the nonexistent American spy, George Kaplan, in order to convince her lover, Phillip Vandamm (James Mason), that she has not wavered in her affection or loyalty. The choice of this scene for the poster was obviously a calculated one on the studio's part. Those who hadn't yet seen the film would presumably interpret Eve's shooting of Roger much as Vandamm himself does, deducing that Eva Marie Saint plays the part of a treacherous siren who puts Cary Grant's life in jeopardy. The theatrical trailer for the film uses voice-over narration to instruct uninitiated spectators to view the relation between Grant and Saint in just this fashion. It begins by addressing the star himself: "You can't fight it, Cary. Someone's out to get you . . ." And it closes by promising audiences: "It's one surprise after another. Adventurous Cary, romanced by the kind of blonde that gets into a man's blood, even if she has to shoot her way in." To illustrate, the trailer then shows the shooting scene.

The publicity instructs audiences to watch for a crucial scene in *North by Northwest*, the turning point in fact, since it results in Roger Thornhill's recuperation as a full-fledged hero who acts rather than reacts.[1] George M. Wilson maintains that the false shooting scene constitutes "the death of Roger Thornhill" (65), but it would be more precise to say that this scene achieves the demise of George Kaplan, that fictional identity which has been serving as an

Figure 1.
The poster for *North by Northwest*: Cary Grant
hanging helplessly in space.

effective masculine persona for Roger. After the phony shooting, for the first time in the film Roger takes charge of the story. Defying the command of the Professor (Leo G. Carroll), he changes his clothes and escapes from the hospital, where "George Kaplan" has been sent for safekeeping, to go after Eve in his own name and on his own authority, signaling his concealed presence in Vandamm's house by tossing his monogrammed matchbook in front of her. Needless to say, while Eve's shooting of "Kaplan" may be nothing more than a put-up job, the heroic masculinity Roger displays in rescuing her afterward is meant to be read as the genuine article.

Whereas the poster gives the impression that Eva Marie Saint's gun has launched Cary Grant's body into space, when Roger performs his phony fall in the film, he hits the ground immediately after Eve fires the gun, landing with so much force that he gets a bruise on his side, which he shows to the Professor in the hospital room. Perhaps the poster's image of the star posed helplessly in midair stands out because the climax of the film on Mount Rushmore—when Eve loses her footing and falls, only to be caught by Roger—plays on the similar danger which ends *Vertigo* (1958), the film Alfred Hitchcock made right before *North by Northwest*. More likely, because *North by Northwest* ultimately averts the very catastrophic fate which concludes the earlier film (Cavell 775), the poster evokes the scene of falling that opens *Vertigo,* when Scottie (James Stewart), in pursuit of a criminal, loses his footing and hangs onto the roof of a building. Dialogue in *Vertigo* later gives contradictory accounts of Scottie's terrifying vulnerability on the roof, on one hand explaining his fear of heights as the effect of his trauma, which remains to haunt him through the recurring symptom of vertigo, while on the other considering it an inherent debility which, predating his trauma, caused his paralysis when he lost his footing. "What a time to find out I had it," Scottie reflects of his acrophobia to Midge (Barbara Bel Geddes). *North by Northwest* raises this same fear of falling and with the same implication of emasculation, and, like the last moments of *Vertigo,* it also alleviates that anxiety through the mediating figure of a more vulnerable woman.[2] The climax puts Roger on relatively firm footing on the monument while Eve dangles helplessly below him, prevented from plummeting to her death (as Judy/Kim Novak does in *Vertigo*) only by the grip of his hand—which invites Vandamm's sadistic henchman, Leonard (Martin Landau), to grind his heal on Roger's other hand. The poster, by contrast, pulls the ground out from under Cary Grant's body, leaving him without any observable means of support whatsoever, much the same way that the opening of *Vertigo* strands Scottie on the rooftop, visualizing a state of emasculation that is at once circumstantial and inherent.

Although an image of vulnerability may seem incongruent with the power normally projected by male American movie stars throughout the tenure of the studio system, it is highly appropriate that MGM used it to advertise *North by Northwest.* The studio's publicity department even went so far as to reproduce the poster at the start of the theatrical trailer. In putting the danger back into

the hero's phony fall, as it were, the poster exploits the very fear of emasculation at the hands of an armed and dangerous female which, in its closure, *North
by Northwest* makes every effort to resolve—indeed, to erase, since in the
diegesis of the film itself she shoots with blanks. As depicted by the poster,
Cary Grant's "fall" is a rather haunting image of masculinity in crisis, and the
film itself cannot completely exorcise this anxiety even though its closure on
Mount Rushmore gives every appearance of doing just that.

   Prompted by its advertising campaign, I want to examine how *North by
Northwest* depicts masculinity in crisis. To be sure, at the time of its release in
July 1959, *North by Northwest* was extremely popular with critics and audiences
alike because of its adventure and comedy, not for its social currency. Praised
as the director's return to form after the box-office failures of *The Wrong Man*
(1956) and *Vertigo*, *North by Northwest* stills stands out today as "the quintessential Hitchcock film" (Kapsis 56): thrilling, romantic, and adult escapist entertainment which appears to have little sense of history, no concern at all with
real social problems, and, unlike *Rear Window* (1954) or *Vertigo*, an unproblematic portrait of masculinity as constituted in a patriarchal culture. As the
climactic setting on Mount Rushmore makes clear, however, *North by Northwest* is by no means that ideologically innocent or emptied of history. Whatever other purposes Hitchcock and screenwriter Ernest Lehman may have had
in mind when creating "Roger O. Thornhill," this character was a commer-
cially shrewd intuition of what fifties America wanted to believe, for better *and*
worse, about masculinity in its contemporary setting.

Marriage Makes the Man

Starting with Robin Wood's 1965 auteurist appreciation of the art with which
Hitchcock takes Roger Thornhill on his breathless journey toward his final
union with Eve Kendall, the social and sexual conservatism of *North by Northwest* has been demonstrated repeatedly. As he works his way through the three
faces of this film's Eve (first she is his seducer, then his betrayer, ultimately his
mate), Roger reconciles his dependency on his mother, mistrust of women,
and fear of commitment.[3] It is therefore tempting to agree with Leslie Brill's
claim that the film is a mythic quest originating out of "Roger Thornhill's
search for identity and a proper mate—two aspects, it usually turns out, of a
single goal" (8). The film's motivation, however, is much more timely than
that, since it also follows the culture in believing that "marriage—and, within
that, the breadwinner role—was the only normal state for the adult male"
(Ehrenreich, *Hearts* 15). *North by Northwest* thus puts the question of its hero's
maturation explicitly in terms of his getting married. If he is to revitalize the
patronizing, insincere, manipulative, and self-absorbed masculinity he displays in the first scene on Madison Avenue, Roger must learn the difference

between a "proposition" (what he calls Eve's intention when she confesses that she bribed the waiter to seat him at her table in the dining car) and a "proposal" (what he names his invitation, while they are still on the monument, to take the train back to New York City together).

As it does in scores of other films produced during this decade, then, in *North by Northwest* the male breadwinner ethic motivates a seemingly straightforward narrative trajectory toward marriage and maturity for the hero. But until that closure, for much of the film Roger's behavior actually parodies the breadwinner ideal. "I'm an advertising man, not a red herring!" he exclaims to the Professor when the latter requests that he accompany him to Rapid City to help put Vandamm's mind at ease about Eve. "I've got a job, a secretary, a mother, two ex-wives, and several bartenders waiting for me, and I don't intend to disappoint them all and get myself slightly killed." While phrased as if to emphasize the many economic dependents he has taken on in his private life, Roger's flippant declaration actually indicates his irresponsibility. Psychiatrist Abram Kardiner's diagnosis of "momism" summarized fifties thinking about masculinity in a manner that describes Roger at this moment to a tee:

> The attachment to a strong, dominant mother can have various characterological outcomes. Thus we have the case of a man of thirty-five who is an only child and who complains that he has difficulties with women. There is no disturbance of orgastic potency or performance, only difficulties in adjusting to females. He has had many affairs without much tenderness. His difficulties arise from his wanting only to *take* from a woman and to give nothing. . . . [His mother] was his protector but a tyrannical one. He now seeks a life situation in which he can reproduce the situation with his mother, in order to be the exclusive object of his wife's attention and to be supported by her. Were it not for the ease with which women are currently available for "affairs," he would never consort with them at all. (28)

With Roger exhibiting this very pattern of behavior in his relations with women, including his flighty mother, his characterization encourages audiences to identify him with "[t]he increasing emotional immaturity of the American male," a syndrome of postwar life one expert traced back to the inability of many men to adapt to a military environment during World War II. "Most of them were emasculated males," this psychiatrist stated. "They wanted to depend on somebody else. Instead of giving and protecting, they wanted to be protected. They had never learned to accept responsibility—somewhere they had lost the male image" (qtd. in Coughlan 114). As Roger's immaturity appears to confirm the prevailing psychiatric opinion of arrested male development, it evokes the ideology of cold war global politics alongside that of the breadwinner ethic. His characterization all too readily confirms the assumption that emotional deficiencies in the American male (as implied by Roger's failed marriages and drinking problem), which led to his social as well as personal irresponsibility (as Roger reveals in his speech to the Professor), in turn made him unduly dependent upon a strong woman (his mother) and consequently susceptible to pernicious influences (communism).

As I mentioned in the introduction, the suspicion that attractive, middle-class American men like Roger had "lost the male image" and become "emasculated males" was part of a "decline in national prestige and confidence" generally during the latter part of the decade (Oakley 413). Bewilderment about the proper masculine role reached such a pitch that in 1958 *Look* published a series analyzing what it named "The Decline of the American Male."[4] The first article set the tone for this examination, commenting: "[S]cientists worry that in the years since the end of World War II, [the American male] has changed radically and dangerously; that he is no longer the masculine, strong-minded man who pioneered the continent and built America's greatness" (Moskin 77). Each piece in the series concentrated on a different symptom of the nation's masculinity crisis: that men let themselves be dominated by women, that they worked too hard for their own physical and spiritual good, and that they conformed to the values of the crowd much too readily. With the allusion to Gibbon and falling empires in the wording of its title, *Look's* series clearly meant to have ominous implications about ebbing U.S. strength in world politics:

> For all the wear and tear on his nervous system, the American male has provided himself and his family with goods and services unmatched in any other country. . . . (The danger, of course, is that we will become too soft, too complacent and too home-oriented to meet the challenge of other dynamic nations like China and the Soviet Union.) . . . The answer—if there is to be one—is for the American male to grow up emotionally so that he can learn to live with the pressures of this society and balance the demands of job, community and home without ruining his health and disposition. (Attwood, "Why" 74–75)

North by Northwest makes several casual references to the cold war setting in which Roger Thornhill rehabilitates himself through his marriage to Eve Kendall. The Professor remarks after the phony shooting scene, for instance, that the United States has already lost a few cold wars, and he is clearly worried about ceding additional ground. Particularly when glossed through the Professor's concern about America's waning strength against communists, audiences in 1959 would no doubt have seen the film's initial characterization of Roger as momma's boy, womanizer, and alcoholic, like its ultimate recuperation of him as a responsible breadwinner through marriage, as a representation of the decline and renewal of the national character. Collapsing manhood into nationhood, this representation was a commonplace of the era:

> The logic went as follows. National strength depended upon the ability of strong, manly men to stand up against communist threats. It was not simply a matter of general weakness leading to a soft foreign policy; rather, sexual excesses or degen-

eracy would make individuals easy prey for communist tactics. According to the common wisdom of the time, "normal" heterosexual behavior culminating in marriage represented "maturity" and "responsibility"; therefore, those who were "deviant" were, by definition, irresponsible, immature, and weak. It followed that men who were slaves to their passions could easily be duped by seductive women, who worked for the communists. Even worse were the "perverts" who, presumably, had no masculine backbone. (May 94)

What's particularly notable about the cultural paranoia which Elaine Tyler May describes here is the way such representations of the national interest so blatantly imagined the political differences between the Soviet Union and the United States in gendered terms, picturing cold war conflict as a battle between masculinity and femininity, with perverse sexuality serving as the dominant trope for representing perceived imbalances of power.

This metaphoric logic operates throughout *North by Northwest*. Roger's easy sexual manner allows him to be duped by a *femme fatale* (one named Eve, no less!) working for communists. Just as importantly, an association of communists with emasculation and perversion—a homophobic imagining of the feared enemy as the inversion of the male breadwinner and everything he stood for in U.S. society—explains Vandamm's effeminate characterization, as encoded in his diffident and haughty British manner, his expensive tastes and interest in antiques, and his close association with a homosexual sadist, his secretary-companion, Leonard. Indeed, it is probably coincidental, but what should we make of the fact that Roger's identity crisis begins when he is "picked up" by Vandamm's men in the Oak Room of the Plaza Hotel? According to George Chauncey, it was a "well-known rendezvous among gay men . . . where men were expected to dress well and carry themselves with discretion" (350). In any event, when Roger bests the effete Vandamm by getting away with Eve *and* the figurine containing the stolen microfilm, our hero's triumph equates the revived health of his masculinity with that of his nation.

While the film's closure confirms Roger's maturation as a man through his redemption as a lover and hero, it is still the case that he does not defeat Vandamm and Leonard on his own but must depend upon the help of the Professor—who arrives at the very last minute with a park ranger, armed this time with *real* bullets. Rather than diminish or undercut Roger's status at the end of the film, curiously enough, the Professor's timely intervention seems only to enhance it. Because Roger has acted entirely on his own authority when he left the hospital room to go after Eve Kendall, the Professor's help at the end now reestablishes the state's authority over Roger by making their interests identical. Michael Rogin points out that cold war narratives typically close with the free man triumphing over communist agents while remaining, paradoxically, dependent on "the armed might of the state." Such a resolution ends up making the United States and its communist enemies comparable in their techniques of state power (militarism, espionage, surveillance). In order to evade this ideological contradiction, a false antinomy "between motherhood and communism" appears to resolve the contradiction by raising the Red Scare one notch to a higher level of cultural paranoia, the fear that absorption by the communist empire is like engulfment in femininity (240). *North by Northwest* achieves closure on Mount Rushmore in just this fashion, equating the two most potentially disruptive and overwhelming forces needing masculine containment, communism on the international front and female sexuality at home. As Robert J. Corber concludes, singling out *North by Northwest* as the fifties Hitchcock film which delivers the most straightforward reproduction of the postwar consensus supporting cold war politics, once the spy and romance plots converge to align the successful realization of Roger's masculinity with the active performance of his patriotic duty, "gender and nationality [function] as mutually reinforcing categories of identity" (191). The fate of the nation consequently appears to depend upon the strength of American manhood, and vice versa. What this also means, though, is that *North by Northwest* can reach its recuperative ending only by making femininity, *not* masculinity, its primary site of gender disruption in the narrative, and for this reason the film's ameliorating closure is not quite as unproblematic as Corber maintains.

The Meaning of "Togetherness"

Evoking the cold war mythology of endangered masculinity in its spy plot, *North by Northwest* responds by proposing a solution through its romance plot: the maturity implied by Roger's new willingness to accept responsibility for a woman. With this gesture toward the personal, the film recasts Roger and Eve's sexual relation through an ideology of domestic containment, cold war global politics as played out in the suburban household. "Containment," the term coined by George Kennan in 1947 to propose an effective U.S. foreign policy regarding the Soviet bloc, dominated American culture's understanding of domestic security too, fostering the belief that "[a] home filled with children would create a feeling of warmth and security against the cold forces of disruption and alienation" (May 23). Home was supposed to provide married couples with a buffer against the hostile outside world, functioning to protect its inhabitants much as the nation itself did when holding the communist empire at bay. With the single-dwelling house celebrated as the space "that would fulfill virtually all its members' personal needs through an energized and expressive personal life" (May 11), this expectation then took tangible form in the development of suburban tract housing and the layout of ranch homes, as well as in the appliances and automobiles that served as the status symbols of a breadwinner's financial success (Clark, Spigel). In reinforcing cold war domestic ideology, the national obsession with the heterosexual couple further

Figure 2.
Roger Thornhill (Cary Grant) and Eve Kendall (Eva Marie Saint)
toast to their "togetherness."

helped to contain male and female sexuality within a relatively new form of social union, "eroticized marriage" (May 133–34). As the only legitimate site for finding emotional and sexual fulfillment, the representation of marriage in such highly idealized terms—the companionate couple finding their unity in a mutual orgasm—served as an effective means of sexual regulation.

North by Northwest allu es to the ideology of domestic containment at a most unexpected moment in the story: when Roger believes that he has been set up by Eve. In Eve's room at the Ambassador East Hotel after the crop-dusting sequence, Roger makes it plain that he will not let her out of his sight again, presumably in order to follow her to his unnamed, unseen nemesis. "Wouldn't it be nice if my problems and your plans were somehow . . . connected?" he asks. "Then we could stay close to each other from here on in and not have to go off in separate directions. Togetherness. Know what I mean?" A far cry from a world of foreign agents and their *femmes fatales,* the term "togetherness" first appeared in the 1954 Easter issue of *McCall's* (Oakley 119). Referring to the married couple who spent time together and shared equally in what had hitherto been familial duties determined by gender (e.g., women washing dishes versus men mowing lawns), the idea of "togetherness" was central to cold war domestic ideology. It implied a husband who was home oriented, who took seriously his responsibility for child rearing, and who viewed his wife as his primary companion.

When Roger mentions "togetherness" to Eve he does so ironically, since he now believes that she "could tease a man to death without really trying." He chooses his words carefully to indicate that he is on to her sinister game and to get back at her for her apparent perfidy. The ambiguity of Roger's verbal play, though, also suggests that his guarded banter should be taken at face value as an honest expression of his growing feeling for Eve. Ernest Lehman's published script makes this subtext explicit, stating that, as Roger delivers his "togetherness" speech, Eve's "quick glance finds his face smiling softly, nay, lovingly" (81). While watching this scene, as he taunts Eve with his talk of "togetherness," most of us probably read more hostility and bitterness than tenderness and affection into Roger's tone, but his very last line in the film helps to revise that impression more in accordance with Lehman's description. As they embrace in the upper berth of a train, Eve says "this is silly," to which Roger replies, "I know. But I'm sentimental." His sentimental gesture in recreating their courtship effectively restores what he had mocked earlier in the hotel, namely, the meaning of "togetherness" as the code word for the culture's regulation of sexuality through domesticity.

With its emphasis on making home life a partnership, "togetherness" justified the gender division (male breadwinner, female homemaker) which domestic ideology sought to perpetuate. Roger thus *has* to go sentimental on Eve at the very last moment in the film in order for her sexuality to be contained by marriage as the ground for defining his. To use the film's own terms, he offers her a "proposal" as the only sure way of countering her ability to take the sexual initiative by making him a "proposition." For although she introduces herself to Roger by explaining she is twenty-six and unmarried—"Now you know everything"—there is in fact much more to know about Eve Kendall, who is, when you think of it, not just a spy but a single working woman with an active and unconventional sexual life. While Eve tends, after the phony shooting, to be increasingly passive before all the men (the Professor and Vandamm as well as Roger), this is not the state of affairs at the start of the film, when she is actually as all-knowing about George Kaplan and Vandamm as Roger is clueless. Thus his proposal to Eve on Mount Rushmore ("if we ever get out of this alive, let's go back to New York on a train together") revives his sagging masculinity by bringing *her* back home, where he can more safely contain that disturbing implication of an active feminine sexuality which has arisen because of her agency in the story.

Just how did Eve, a woman, fall into a position of such power in the first place, doing a man's job for the U.S. intelligence agency? When Roger asks after the phony shooting, she guesses that "maybe it was the first time anyone ever asked me to do anything worthwhile."

> *Roger:* Has life been like that? . . . How come?
> *Eve:* Men like you.
> *Roger:* What's wrong with men like me?
> *Eve:* They don't believe in marriage.
> *Roger:* I've been married twice.
> *Eve:* See what I mean.

When they reviewed initial drafts of the script, officials at the Production Code Administration appeared to agree with Eve. Worried about the references to Roger's two ex-wives, the PCA twice urged the studio to drop the detail from the dialogue.[5] In addition, the censors were just as concerned about the representation of Eve's sexuality in the film. They wanted dialogue inserted that denied she was ever Vandamm's mistress (the finished film never does supply that open denial, as it turns out); and they also insisted, with more success, that, to suggest marriage in the end rather than "an implicit illicit sex affair," Roger and Eve had to be "dressed for day, not night" so as not to give even the barest hint of consummation, a command that forced Hitchcock to film and then use in the final print a cover shot of the last scene on the train (Leff 112–13).

North by Northwest diminishes Eve's considerable power as both narrative and political agent by confining all her future activity to the marriage bed. As Eve's retort ("See what I mean") makes clear, if Roger's rehabilitation requires him to believe in marriage, then with two strikes against him he needs the proper sort of mate to keep him in line, which is why the film transforms Eve from vamp to tramp to Girl Scout. Once the film discloses that Eve is neither helper nor vixen but the double agent, then she represents both the cause of masculinity's crisis and its means of cure. She has been acting as the Cold Warrior in Roger's place, although his ability to perform that task better than she is made evident by his discovering what she has been unable to do, namely, the secret of how Vandamm has been smuggling microfilm out of the country (through his antique purchases). What began as a crisis of mistaken identity for Roger turns out to be a drama of significant political dimension: he shows the American government's own agents how to outwit the enemy and win a cold war battle, thereby demonstrating the importance of a "hard" masculinity demanded by foreign affairs; and he redeems the tarnished breadwinner virtues of honesty, commitment, and fidelity through his marriage to Eve, thereby demonstrating the importance of a "soft" masculinity needed to handle domestic affairs. Because Eve herself is the figure marking the integration of the romance and spy plots, the film's closure uses her to avoid recognizing that these two vastly different ideological constructions of masculinity are in fact irreconcilable.

Beware of the Blonde

With her real purposes regarding Roger concealed by an expressionless face and provocative talk, Eve Kendall seems perfectly formed in the mold of the Hitchcock blonde, her personality radiating the "ice-cold" sexuality epitomized for the director by Grace Kelly, whose "indirect" sensual appeal meant to suggest, as François Truffaut interpreted it, "the paradox between the inner fire and the cool surface" (224). This particular type of icy sexual persona serves what Sabrina Barton has aptly named "the blonde-function" of the typical Hitchcock film (76). As the female whose body commands the spectatorial gaze, the Hitchcock blonde signifies feminine spectacle in cinema, the radiant blondeness of her fetishized image offering the viewer a specularization of male desire much as the shimmering whiteness of the cinema screen itself does. This powerful way of conceptualizing the effect of the Hitchcock blonde finds its fullest realization in *Vertigo*, Barton notes, with its transformation of the dark-haired Judy back into the platinum Madeline.

Why does blondeness have that spectacular effect upon masculinity, particularly as exploited by Hitchcock? It's no accident of history that, with the exception of Madeleine Carroll in the early British films, his blonde actresses all date from the 1950s: Grace Kelly, Doris Day, Vera Miles, Kim Novak, Eva Marie Saint, Janet Leigh. His most celebrated 1940s stars, Joan Fontaine and Ingrid Bergman, while light-haired, were not marked or marketed as blonde (in the manner of Betty Grable, say). "We're after the drawing-room type," he told Truffaut about his casting of blonde actresses such as Kelly, "the real ladies, who become whores once they're in the bedroom. Poor Marilyn Monroe had sex written all over her face, and Brigitte Bardot isn't very subtle either" (224). Just as there have always been blonde female stars, so too has there been a long tradition of light and dark heroines in Western sexual mythology, as in the historical fiction of Sir Walter Scott in the early nineteenth century or 1940s film noir. But in contrasting two types of *blonde* stars, those with sex on their faces and those without, Hitchcock's remarks help to place blondeness, in whatever incarnation, in its historical setting as the fifties' primary trope for female sexuality. During this period female stars became increasingly blonder while their male costars steadily remained, as the formula went, tall, dark, and handsome.

Representing the most desirable form of femininity, blondeness obviously reflects the supremacy of white masculinity. This meaning was what, to cite Hitchcock's passing remark about the most famous fifties blonde, the "sex" in Monroe's face (actually her whole body) signified. "To be the ideal Monroe had to be white," Richard Dyer comments, "and not just white but blonde, the most unambiguously white you can get" (*Heavenly* 42–43). In Monroe's case, he points out, blondeness anchored her femininity in a social position which connoted wealth as well as racial superiority. Particularly when viewed in the wake of the United States' military defeat and occupation of both Nazi Germany (itself fostered by an ideology of male blondeness) and Japan (a war driven in large part by white racism), the preference for blonde women in the fifties signified the superiority of the American men who possessed them. The craze for becoming blonde on screen and off during this period reflected the increased value of WASP identity for a nation beginning to see white supremacy challenged at home (with the Montgomery, Alabama, bus boycott beginning the civil rights movement in 1955 and crystallizing fears about the sporadic blockbusting starting to happen in white neighborhoods) as well as abroad (with the United States' global power becoming increasingly enmeshed in the unpredictable politics of newly independent, nonwhite nations of Asia and Africa).

Because it was so overly determined by cultural codes of the period, isn't there also something uncanny about the extremely white look of some fifties Hollywood blondes, particularly in retrospect when the look now seems all the more dated and artificial? Pauline Kael goes so far as to remark that Eva Marie Saint's blonde look in *North by Northwest* turns her face into "an albino African mask" (418). While not meant as a compliment to the actress, the image evoked isn't all that far-fetched because her hair color and makeup, emphasized by bright lighting and dark costuming, do connote the unnaturalness of whiteness, the way the color signifies an absence, as in bleached fabric or a face drained of color. As Dyer remarks, "when whiteness *qua* whiteness does come into focus, it is often revealed as emptiness, absence, denial or even a kind of death" ("White" 44). This is, of course, the meaning of whiteness which so appalled and yet fascinated Ishmael in *Moby Dick*—and it is also, I believe, why fifties *femmes fatales* like Eve Kendall tend to be blonde.

For all its apparently fixed ideological function, blondeness turns out to be a highly volatile symbol of white patriarchy. On one hand, the contrived look of the fifties blonde, which Hitchcock justifies through the double standard of the lady/whore, is, as his comparison testifies, perhaps the ultimate form of disavowing sexual, social, and racial differences. On the other hand, if blondeness, especially those platinum shades so popular during the fifties, is, as Dyer says, the most unambiguously white a woman can get, it is also for most women the most unnaturally white they can get. Few American women ever successfully pass as a natural platinum blonde, and not many even want to do so. Paradoxically, the more the blonde stands out as an unnatural construction of female beauty, the more successfully she naturalizes the economic and racial supremacy of the white male she is designed to attract.

This paradox arises because the blonde acquires her cultural purchase precisely by drawing excessive attention to the manufacturing of female whiteness as the primary means of disavowing the basis of white male patriarchy itself in a symbolic system; while, at the same time, that very attention to her blonde-ness subjects the meaning she symbolizes to great risks, bringing the whole system of representation to the point of possible collapse. Too much attention to whiteness as a symbolic construction can expose the inscription of blonde-ness on the female body for the forgery it is, as in *Vertigo;* or it can go to the other extreme, consuming the female figure so totally in blondeness that she evokes the blank or absent surface connoted by the color white, an effect which, if not recuperated as the dumb blonde stereotype enacted by Monroe in her films, then materializes as the *femme fatale:* "the kind of blonde that gets into a man's blood, even if she has to shoot her way in." In this last formula-tion the blonde is impenetrable, whereas the male, significantly, is not. With her blondeness functioning as the blank façade serving to defeat his scrutiny, "her sex" is *not* in her face, which simply refuses to perform its proper specular function, presenting to the male gaze—well, it *is* the best phrase for it—"an albino African mask," suggesting how blondeness can collapse the light/dark racial opposition it means to construct.

The symbolic function of blondeness explains why Eve Kendall remains inscrutable for much of the film, in contrast to the men in *North by Northwest,* who turn out to have the more legible faces. Not only do the familiar counte-nances of four presidents hover in the background of the final scenes to evoke the reassuring presence of patriarchy, but Roger's face is itself instantly recog-nizable from the moment he meets Eve on the train:

> *Roger:* I know, I look vaguely familiar.
> *Eve:* Yes.
> *Roger:* You feel you've seen me somewhere before.
> *Eve:* Yes.
> *Roger:* Funny how I have that effect on people. Something about my face.
> *Eve:* It's a nice face.

As their exchange continues on in this vein, the dialogue resonates with irony because of Eve's success in reading Roger's face, all the while keeping him deceived as to both her identity and her intentions. When he goes on to say, "Honest women frighten me" because "they put me at a disadvantage," Eve surmises that is because *he* isn't being "honest with them," showing how she can size him up with speed and accuracy. Her comment not only reflects ill on his character but it also indicates how inadequately he reads women; she is sparring with him here with a seriousness that he does not sense. Despite his smug response, Roger really has no idea what Eve is up to, which in effect is to show him that he has much yet to learn about being put at a disadvantage by a *smart* woman.

Several critics have noted how Eve's hidden agency in the narrative of *North by Northwest* reveals a far greater range of emotion than she ever lets on to, since she is passionate enough to sleep with Roger on the train, ruthless enough to send him off to his death the next morning, expressive enough to show her relief when he survives, and caring enough to feel wounded by his insults when he unexpectedly turns up at the auction house (R. Wood 139, G. Wilson 75). However, the film's concentration on Roger pushes her subjectivity to the margins of the narrative action so that the drama in *her* story appears to happen solely off screen. This placement further intensifies the ambiguity of her character because it means that her motives can be read only indirectly, made all the more difficult by her restrained manner. When I mentioned earlier that Eve has three faces, which the narrative lineates into a sequence of apparent transformations, I somewhat overstated the case, referring to the effect that the film's closure gives in appearing to manage her mystery so totally. It is more accurate to say that her three personae continually intersect in the film, generating the disturbance to masculinity that she embodies as a blonde.

Her complexity makes Eve very different from the film's villain—the unseen agency displacing Roger's identity—insofar as, Hitchcock told Truffaut, he and Lehman "split this evil character into three people: James Mason, who is attractive and suave; his sinister-looking secretary; and the third spy, who is crude and brutal" (107). Appropriately, these men are all dark, while the character who resists splitting, Eve, is blonde, her lightness reflecting not moral goodness, but the opacity resulting from her successful manipulation of multiple personae. The ambiguity created by Eve's masquerading, in contrast to the clarity achieved by the splitting of villainy into separate personalities, marks sexual difference in the film, with the transparency of dark-haired men opposed to the impenetrability of a blonde woman. The phony shooting scene causes the turning point in Roger's relation to Eve's femininity by turning her inscrutable female agency into controlled male play: his performance then subordinates her activity as a narrative agent to his, containing her female sexuality within the terms of his own masquerade as George Kaplan. But this is also precisely why Eve causes Roger so much trouble as a blonde. For when, in her "blonde-function," she mirrors his own performativity, Eve ends up revealing what the blonde is supposed to disavow: the extent to which white masculinity itself is premised on a gender masquerade, too.

He's an Advertising Man, Not a Red Herring

While we should not discount how the cold war ideologies of the breadwinner ethic, global politics, domestic containment, and whiteness all intertwine in *North by Northwest*'s closure, to read Roger's masculinity solely through that framework makes the film appear more somber and humorless than its screenplay and direction actually warrant. After all, *North by Northwest* is a funny as well as thrilling adventure, characterized by continual tongue-in-cheek wit.

Wryly, often outrageously, as it wends its way toward that conservative closure on Mount Rushmore, when Roger proposes to Eve and saves the nation from its communist enemies, *North by Northwest* keeps placing the familiar cultural idiom of fifties America in highly inappropriate contexts, in effect defamiliarizing terms, such as "togetherness," which by 1959 had already been ground in the mill of conventionality. The crop-dusting sequence works this way, too, making the banal Indiana cornfield turn sinister, just as the film's many jokes quote clichés at inopportune moments to give them an unexpected edge, as when the unflappable Mrs. Thornhill (Jessie Royce Landis) calls out to her forty-something son, as he flees from Vandamm's men at the Plaza Hotel: "Roger, will you be home for dinner?"

The gags reenact on a verbal or visual level what the film itself does to Roger by pulling the rug out from under his identity when Vandamm's men mistake him for Kaplan. This mistake occurs, not through any resemblance on Roger's part to the person of Kaplan, but because of the former's accidental proximity to the name. Not only does Roger get mistaken for "George Kaplan," himself just a contrivance of superficial clues, metonymies of masculinity (a hairbrush, business suits, a name) left by the Professor's cohorts to convince Vandamm of this decoy's existence, but in the process of trying to prove his innocence, Roger learns just how easily the conventional signs of his own masculinity (i.e., his relation to business affairs, social drinking, women, and the Oedipus complex—all sketched out in the film's opening conversation between Roger and his secretary) can be quickly disassociated from his very ordinary identity. As I began to imply with my comments about Eve's blondeness, in the last analysis Roger's identity is a persona or mask much like the identity made up for Kaplan. Only when he realizes this fact himself can Roger then begin to overcome his troublemakers by beating them at their own game: *performance.*

Clothes Make the Man

In an important book reprinted in paperback the same year as the film's release, sociologist Erving Goffman claimed that performance actually constituted the ground of identity, "the presentation of self in everyday life." Originally published as a shorter academic monograph in 1956, Goffman's analysis of various professional as well as personal forms of interaction as instances of "impression management" well describes the role-playing that occurs repeatedly in the diegesis of *North by Northwest.* When Roger claims that "in the world of advertising there is no such thing as a lie . . . only the Expedient Exaggeration," the comment prepares the way for the film to link him to both Vandamm and the Professor. Goffman showed that this axiom was not limited to the advertising profession or espionage but characterized the games and gambits of social relations generally: "[I]n everyday life it is usually possible for the performer to create intentionally almost any kind of false impression without putting himself in the indefensible position of having told a clear-cut lie. Communication techniques such as innuendo, strategic ambiguity, and crucial omissions allow the misinformer to profit from lies without, technically, telling any" (62).

The phony shooting scene in *North by Northwest* marks the apparent end of such identity play for the film by bringing the curtain down on the performativity that has been occurring as the catalyst of its narrative action. Afterward, Vandamm learns who the double agent really is, Roger goes to rescue her in his own name, the Professor shows up with real bullets, and all the deceit and feigning necessary for cold war espionage appear to be securely marshaled off from the private life to which Mr. and Mrs. Thornhill return. But the film actually takes a more complicated stand toward the playacting of cold war spy games. Consequently, while outwardly committed to resecuring the most orthodox representation of masculinity, as critics from Wood to Corber have argued, in its social setting *North by Northwest* also recognizes, with just as much conviction, the basis of meaningful representation in performance, with identity displaced from its moorings in the gender-nationalism equation and understood instead as a dynamic and unstable social production involving the continual deployment of masks, role-playing, and theatricality.[6]

Given the film's proposal that *all* identities may be realized only through performances of what Goffman called a "sign activity" (2), one has to ask, what makes one identity (Roger's, say) any more real than another (Kaplan's)? I suppose the answer is: whichever one wears better. All the time Roger's faith in his identity is challenged, and all the while a first-time viewer's confidence in him as an innocent bystander may even be shaken when Vandamm's men mistake him for George Kaplan, there is one constant, unyielding and intractable given throughout his many sincere professions of innocence and accidental performances of guilt. I am referring to the seemingly indestructible gray business suit Roger wears almost without exception until after the phony shooting, when his change of clothing signifies that he is finally taking charge of the narrative action.

Until he retires his suit along with the persona of George Kaplan, Roger looks fastidiously neat at all times. His clothes appear clean and freshly pressed regardless of circumstances, both to suggest the hero's cartoon-like indestructibility and to reflect the presence in that role of Cary Grant, who was celebrated for both his fashion sense and his fastidiousness when it came to his tailored clothes. According to a press release at the time:

> His shirts, also always tailor-made, have fly fronts concealing the buttons. He never folds his jacket pocket handkerchief in points, always folds it square and just tucks it in carelessly. His ties are never pointed, always have rounded edges. He prefers monotone ties, or a sombre-colored tie with small, sparse print. He never wears bright ties, bright colors of any kind in any part of his apparel.
>
> His favorite daytime or informal suit is dark gray, pin-striped, single-breasted,

and he always wears cream-white shirts. He prefers a gray tie, a shade darker or lighter than his suit. With this he wears silk-and-wool mixture socks, sometimes plain, sometimes with a black clock. Extremely dark brown shoes, almost gunmetal brown, are his preference.[7]

As this description of Grant's signature wardrobe also implies, the well-tailored and seemingly imperishable gray suit worn by the hero of *North by Northwest* inflects his identity through an instantly recognizable marking of social class. "The hero is an advertising man (a significant choice of profession)," Lawrence Alloway noted at the time of the film's release in 1959, "and though he is hunted from New York to South Dakota his clothes stay neatly Brooks Brothers. That is to say, the dirt, sweat, and damage of pursuit are less important than the package in which the hero comes . . . the urbane Madison Avenue man" (Alloway, *Long*). In its review, *Daily Variety* similarly saw Roger as "a Madison Avenue man-about-Manhattan, sleekly handsome, carelessly twice-divorced, debonair as a cigaret ad" ("Powe"). *North by Northwest* celebrates this packaging of masculinity as one of its running gags about the star power of Cary Grant, not the least of those times when Roger's suit should

Figure 3.
Roger Thornhill in his seemingly indestructible gray suit.

appear the worse for wear, as when Eve packs it in her overnight case so that he can get off the train disguised as a Red Cap, or after the crop-dusting sequence when he decides to get it sponged and pressed, giving her an opportunity to lead him to Vandamm. The copy in another one of the advertisements for the film made no bones about the comic indestructibility of Roger's clothing, exclaiming: "The spies come at you from all directions . . . run from the cops, killers, secret agents, beautiful women . . . and see if you can do all this without wrinkling your suit!" (Pressbook).

Why is Roger's suit so important that it should not—and in fact *does* not—escape notice?[8] It is revealing that the published screenplay pictures his suit a bit differently than viewers tend to recall: he is "tall, lean, faultlessly dressed (and far too original to be wearing the gray-flannel uniform of his kind)" (Lehman 2). Fair enough, particularly since the gray suit Cary Grant wears for most of the film varies in its chromatic tones according to the light and location, so that sometimes it seems more blue than gray, at other times more gray than blue. But while Roger's suit may not be your run-of-the mill flannel uniform purchased off the racks at Brooks Brothers—it was actually tailored personally for Grant by Quintino of Wilshire Boulevard (Higham and Mosely 273)—through most of the film (until after the phony shooting, in point of fact), the characters surrounding Roger are dressed in darker colors (charcoal, navy, black) to emphasize the gray color of his clothing. Visually, this is to say, he even exemplifies that exquisite contradiction of fifties conformity described by Lehman's screenplay. In his designer suit Roger Thornhill is instantly recognizable as the "original" representative of "his kind," the middle-class professional, whose values had come to dominate the entire culture during the postwar era.

Roger's affiliation with this particular segment of the middle class is his most salient, most stable, most incontestable characteristic. The one crucial measurement of continuity for him throughout the film, this identity remains clear enough to invest his character with a social if not moral authority no matter what happens to him or what he does. As *North by Northwest* keeps placing this man in a gray flannel suit before an audience's eyes, it has the effect of repositioning his masculinity in another, less transparent political context, one representing gender to America with just as much historical currency as the various cold war ideologies motivating the closure. Much of the significance of The Man in the Gray Flannel Suit as a pervasive cultural figure had to do with the way that advertising, increasingly directed toward male shoppers as well as female, revised what had been presumed to be an absolute gender divide: masculine production versus feminine consumption. The launching of *Playboy* and *Sports Illustrated* magazines in 1953 recognized the growing and potentially diverse market of male consumers, as did the burgeoning "do-it-yourself" industries. The Man in the Gray Flannel Suit was perceived as the agent of this unorthodox—but also, everyone recognized at the time, economically advantageous—absorption of masculinity into consumerism.

Moreover, since he was viewed as both a producer and product of the advertising industry, he came to personify the conflation of production and consumption.

As an advertising executive, Roger Thornhill exemplifies the postwar transformation of the disreputable and disheveled radio huckster—the type played by Clark Gable in *The Hucksters* (1949)—into the respectable, well-dressed public relations man. "You're an advertising man, that's all I know," Eve tells Roger on the train between kisses. "You've got taste in clothes. Taste in food . . . you're very clever with words. You can probably make them do anything for you. Sell people things they don't need. Make women who don't know you fall in love with you." Although her rhetoric may make it seem as if she has been dipping into Vance Packard's *Hidden Persuaders*, Eve says all of this in a tone meant to be excited rather than disapproving. Despite the instant criticism of Roger's masculinity implied through his association with Madison Avenue hucksters, it is still the case that he generates considerable sympathy in audiences as well as in Eve from the moment the film opens and puts his life in jeopardy. Cary Grant's relaxed and confident performance contributes to his character's attractiveness, but so does the film's insistence—for all of Roger's immaturity and insincerity, not to mention his own resemblance to the spies as a fellow manipulator of masks and performance—upon his *ordinariness* as a harried businessman thrust into the duplicitous world of foreign intrigue and CIA machinations. Truth to tell, the ordinary man or woman in the audience would not have had the economic power and social position which Roger takes for granted in the opening scene on Madison Avenue; but it is nevertheless the case, particularly once *North by Northwest* begins to correct his arrogance and dishonesty, that the film encourages audiences to identify with Roger as, in Robin Wood's phrase, "a modern city Everyman" (134).

Speaking more precisely, though, wouldn't it be more correct to describe Roger not as every man, but as the fifties' most exemplary type of man? His profession immediately links him to the emerging power base of postwar America, in historian Jackson Lears's words: "a hegemonic historical bloc . . . formed by the groups often characterized as a 'new class' of salaried managers, administrators, academics, technicians, and journalists—people who manipulated symbols rather than made things, whose stock in trade consisted of their organizational, technical, conceptual, or verbal skills" (50). Analyzed during this period as "the other-directed character" (in David Reisman's phrase), "the organization man" (in William H. Whyte's), and "the diploma *élite*" (in Vance Packard's), these college-trained professionals were, to use Packard's description, "the big, active, successful people who pretty much run things," in contrast to "the supporting classes contain[ing] the passive non-big people who wear both white and blue collars: the small shopkeepers, workers, functionaries, technical aides" (41). As Packard saw it in 1959, the new allegiance between the "real upper class" (i.e., old money) and the "semi-upper class" (i.e., corporate managers and educated professionals) actually stratified the seemingly homogeneous middle class, with far-reaching consequences for U.S. society. Because of this "revolutionary blurring of the boundary line between white- and blue-collared people" (36), the lower middle-class was living out the consequences of a historical reorganization of social affiliations that it did not perceive, continuing to identify with the economic and political interests of their employers without recognizing any incompatibility in their vastly different class positions.

Technically, the new grouping of educated media and managerial professionals lacked the coherence and unity of a "class" in the strictest sense of the term, but it nevertheless possessed real power and yielded palpable influence as a "historic hegemonic bloc, [which] identifies its own problems and interests with those of society and indeed humanity at large." As Lears points out, this was "a coalition of groups which differed in many ways but which were bound together (up to a point) by common interests, common experiences, and a common worldview" (51). Although this coalition then began to break apart during the 1960s, its consensus unraveling over issues of civil rights and the Vietnam War, some social historians now refer to it and its successive reformations in the 1970s and 1980s simply as "the professional middle class" in order to name that particular social grouping which (1) is distinguished by an "economic and social status . . . based on education, rather than on ownership of capital or property," and (2) "uses consumption to establish its status, especially relative to the working class" (Ehrenreich, *Fear* 12–14).

Even at the time of its formation in the immediate postwar years, this new professional-managerial class was already perceived to be reflecting the United States' transformation from an economy organized around production to one increasingly driven by consumption. For example, writing in 1954 to answer the question posed on its cover, "What is the American character?" *Time* called attention to the consequences of this radical turn in the U.S. economy, going on to read the nation through the hegemonic lens of those men who made consuming their business:

> Increasingly, businesses group themselves in trade associations and businessmen look to their competitors, rather than to their own accounting department, for the signals that mean success. Their attitude toward their own work is not that of producers, but of consumers. Morale is bucked up when a business decision meets the approval (and imitation) of the "antagonistic cooperators" of the adult peer group. ("Freedom" 23)

These comments appeared in a lead article on David Reisman's *Lonely Crowd*, published four years earlier. By 1954, that hugely influential book had already introduced into the popular idiom the standard term for characterizing the personality of the new middle-class, consumer-driven, professional business man: the "other-directed" conformist, who personified the twentieth-century organization man as a *consumer*, as opposed to the "inner-directed" individualist, who personified the nineteenth-century captain of industry as he used to be, a *producer.* Following Reisman, *Time* describes how the postwar consumer economy transformed the masculine "business mind" to the point of reorienting its epistemology around the exchange of what Goffman would soon analyze as performance signs: the communication skills required for success in business demanded sensitivity to outer appearances and also considered social identity a persona or mask. By mid-decade no single professional figure epitomized American deployment of capital solely in the interest of selling consumerism more vividly than The Man in the Gray Flannel Suit, the advertiser whose business was literally the manipulation of signs and who himself blended seamlessly into the crowds of nameless, similarly dressed professional men filling up downtown streets in every U.S. city—the scene, in fact, which *North by Northwest* evokes in its opening shot of Madison Avenue. Singling Roger Thornhill out from this crowd, the film then immediately dramatizes his quickness to "the signals that mean success" because it shows how readily this professional man takes to performance in response to his own "antagonistic cooperators," Vandamm and his men.

From the moment that Vandamm accidentally sets the stage for Roger to think of his identity as a performance, this spy in a gray flannel suit turns out to be the epitome of both the other-directed professional man *and* the cold war ideologies sustaining the hegemony of his class by confirming the value of his masculinity. In its first scene, *North by Northwest* gently satirizes Roger as a Madison Avenue type; in the second scene, it abruptly challenges his identity; and from that point on, the film seeks to restore his affiliation with the professional-managerial class as a means of legitimizing its cultural hegemony in American society. In the process of saving both the woman he loves and the state's stolen secrets, Roger lives out the romance of the postwar armchair adventurer, winning the prize (the blonde) and returning to Madison Avenue. The urgency of this romance, the film proposes through Roger's affiliation with the new professional-managerial class, arises from the need to validate his masculinity, which his job more than Vandamm actually imperils. "The typical 'manly' or masculine vocations are rapidly disappearing . . ." remarked psychiatrist Henrik M. Ruitenbeek: "If masculine occupations are decreasingly important in a technological economy—and one largely oriented to finance and public relations rather than to production at that—the masculine role in the family has also changed" (86). An ideologically overdetermined event, to say the least, Roger's victory at the end of *North by Northwest* means to recuperate the endangered masculinity of the *professional* middle-class male.

Performing Genders

Because the film's closure seems so wholeheartedly committed to equating Roger's revived manhood with the national interest, it is important to appreciate that *North by Northwest* also dramatizes how the performance ethic of the professional-managerial class could easily cause the representation of gender and nationalism to go out of alignment as each other's mirror image. The other-directed persona of this new class severely undercut the stability and singularity of "identity," projecting in its place a heterogeneous field of social types, what sociologist Orrin E. Klapp described as the "cafeteria style" of personality formations in U.S. society (98). Looking back on American social life of the fifties after the close of the decade, Klapp noted that, contrary to the American ideology of individualism, "in our society we do not have, as one might at first suppose, freedom *from* typing but a *choice* of type" (2). Significantly, he characterized the diversity and confusion of self-presentation in American society by metaphorically equating the performance of an identity with the consumerist economy that underwrote it: "Americans find themselves in a kind of bargain basement with a bewildering variety [of roles] to choose from—the models may not all be equally becoming, but nothing prevents us from trying them on" (96).

Roger epitomizes what Klapp, in a modification of Reisman's other-directed personality type, analyzed as "the audience-directed hero of today [who] may play with ease parts from men-about-town to pillar of the church. He is at home anywhere, has 'stage presence,' and always manages to land on his feet" (107). Roger's skill in performance, which enables him to survive one dangerous predicament after another as he moves across the map of the United States from the Northeast to the midwestern hinterlands, redefines his personality as a site of repeated identity displacements. These occur over time and across a range of overlapping but not identical ideological contexts, and each performance theatricalizes his personality according to different masculine personae (Madison Avenue executive, kidnap victim, alcoholic, momma's boy, murderer, fugitive, lover, Red Cap, and so on). The same is true of Eve. Each time she readjusts her mask to suit the particular scenario of the moment, she also reveals her lack of a stable core identity transcending the circumstances that require her to adapt one feminine persona or another for her own survival. This blonde is dangerous, not because she wields a gun, but because she shoots with blanks in more ways than one. She exemplifies how every social identity is, to borrow Goffman's phrase again, a "sign activity" requiring adeptness in theatricality, flexibility in handling her multiple personae, and attention to the demands of a constantly shifting audience. Like Roger's masculinity, her feminine identity is not *expressive,* in the sense of referring back to a coherent, continuous self beneath the layers of masquerade (the "real" Eve), because it is *performative,* continually being reconstituted in a theatricalized representation.

In showing how the social act of self-presentation destabilizes the continuity of a single identity, *North by Northwest* calls into question the authenticity of *any* representational activity. The professional-managerial class relied on controlling representation for its social dominance and for much of its income, but it also mistrusted representation in principle. From the spy scandals at the beginning of this period to the quiz show scandals at the end, apprehensions about the dangers of professional misuse of representation made both the advertiser and his occupation persistent objects of criticism within the new class itself. Functioning as scapegoats for the insincerity and conformity of the dominant corporate mentality, the advertising industry and its gray-suited practitioners were accused of equating substance with its packaging—and then suspected (as in *Lover Come Back*, 1961) of doing even worse: selling an empty package to an unsuspecting public. As *North by Northwest* imagines it, the U.S. government itself resorts to this cynical extreme with its invention of George Kaplan. Although "Kaplan" is no more than an ensemble of empty gender signs, both Roger and Vandamm believe in his existence for most of the film. Hitchcock and Lehman nonetheless inform the audience about the fictive status of Kaplan early on in order to persuade viewers that a convincing representation, far from needing to refer to its origin in reality, actually stands in for the source as its substitution—to the point of easily faking its own referential ground.

The instability of representation in *North by Northwest* has particularly disruptive consequences for the seemingly stable position of masculinity in its various ideological settings. For if a social identity displaces the "real" person with a persona, then don't genders, sexual inflections of "identity," involve the same degree of imitation and fakery? In asking this question, I have in mind Judith Butler's theorization of gender as an ongoing performance, "the repeated stylization of the body, a set of repeated acts within a highly rigid regulatory frame that congeal over time to produce the appearance of substance, of a natural sort of being" (*Gender* 33). She goes on to explain:

> The distinction between expression and performativeness is crucial. If gender attributes and acts, the various ways in which a body shows or produces its cultural signification, are performative, then there is no preexisting identity by which an actor or attribute might be measured; there would be no true or false, real or distorted acts of gender, and the postulation of a true gender identity would be revealed as a regulatory fiction. (141)

From this perspective, "masculinity" does not refer to a male nature but instead imitates a "regulatory fiction" of normality that authorizes the continued representation of certain types of gender performances for men (such as the breadwinner), marginalizing others (such as the momma's boy), and forbidding still others (such as the effeminate homosexual). By the same token, Butler models her argument about gender not on the regulatory fictions of straight masculinity and femininity, but on their subversion: gay and lesbian drag. "The replication of heterosexual constructs in non-heterosexual frames brings into relief the utterly constructed status of the so-called heterosexual original. Thus, gay is to straight *not* as copy is to original, but, rather, as copy is to copy" (31).[9] Gender is a symbolic representation perceived in culture as a mimetic one; it always involves some element of masquerade, which is why drag, with its crossed and parodic references to the binarism of sex, functions so well to expose the regulatory fiction of heterosexual gender norms in Butler's account.

To be sure, in the 1950s public criticism of The Man in the Gray Flannel Suit's masculinity by popular and academic writers was directly aimed at his social behavior (in being passive before women, in conforming too whole-heartedly, in working too hard for his body's own good), not his sexual identity as a male. The masculinity crisis heralded by *Look* as "The Decline of the American Male" was by no means talked about as an instability in or disrup-tion of the category of "gender" itself. However, the identifying characteristic of the other-directed professional was nonetheless a gender attribute—he was, after all, a *man* in a gray flannel suit. Butler's theorization of gender as a performance helps to articulate what was not stated directly during the fifties but continually suggested by this period's anxiety about a masculinity crisis. For instance, in another of its articles on masculinity, *Look* magazine recog-nized that, since "masculinity . . . is what his society expects the male *to do and be*" (Frank 53, emphasis in original), then the ongoing engendering of men as "masculine" also meant that *being* male was not necessarily the same as *doing* what a man's gotta do. "[G]ender is always a doing," Butler states, "though not a doing by a subject who might be said to preexist the deed" (*Gender* 25). If masculinity were indeed performative, as *Look* implied, then it was a socially determined fiction, a representation of manly attributes without an origin beyond the act of representation itself. The performance of gender required men and women alike to engage in masquerades of the sort that Roger and Eve undertake in *North by Northwest*, doing what the culture expected of men and women in order for them to appear to be properly "masculine" or "feminine."

By now there is a tradition in feminist film and cultural studies of analyzing femininity as a masquerade along the lines set out by Joan Riviere's famous case study of 1929, which associated femininity exclusively with the masquerade and posited that the feminine mask covered up a female's theft of the phallus. "Womanliness therefore could be assumed and worn as a mask," she explained, "both to hide the possession of masculinity and to avert the reprisals expected if she was found to possess it." Riviere's conclusion that there is no difference between "genuine womanliness and 'the masquerade'"—"whether radical or superficial, they are the same thing" (38)—has dominated examinations of the feminine masquerade in cinema, particularly as it concerns female specta-torship and subjectivity.[10] The masquerade has recently been applied to men as well, but because it has been invoked so often to explain the cultural construc-tion of femininity, it is still believed to result in the male's implicit feminization (as in Riviere's own examples in passing of gay men putting on the mask of heterosexual virility).[11] Even Marjorie Garber's impressive study of the cultural function of the transvestite in *Vested Interests* takes nearly four hundred pages to conclude that the masquerade argument about gender leads one to realize "that 'man'—the male person—is at least as artifactual as 'woman'" (374).

With my own analysis of the masculine masquerade in *North by Northwest*—as well as in all the films discussed in this book—I am more interested in picking up its theatrical rather than phallocentric implications, so I am using the term in accordance with Butler's theorization of gender as "performative—that is, constituting the identity it is purported to be" (*Gender* 25), an effect achieved by treating the expressions of a gendered identity as if they were its causes as well as its results.[12] A gender masquerade of this sort does not conceal the secreted theft of the phallus, as in Riviere's formulation, so much as it defines identity in terms of opposing—and also shifting—planes in order to establish the impression of dimensionality: an outside in relation to an inside, surface to depth, figure to ground, performance to authenticity. Far from raising questions of concealment and dissembling in order to imply a hidden, more real, if still lacking, identity, what a gendered persona—the mask itself—signifies is the mark or playing out of those differences.

This understanding of a gender masquerade is especially pertinent to cinema because of its institutional reliance upon stardom. The movie star—whose screen personality is, not accidentally, termed a *persona*—brings to the foreground of popular representation the epistemological problems that Butler describes in her deconstruction of sexual identities. On one hand, a star bears a seemingly fixed and authentic relation to a referent in the real world, as epitomized by the photographic still, used extensively by the industry to promote films and their leading players (Dyer, "*Star*" 135). But on the other hand, the star is also an "image" in more than a purely visual sense. As Dyer explains in *Stars*, the "star image" is an institutional product, a construction resulting from a complex, often overdetermined, sometimes underdetermined, interplay of biographical details, film roles, body codes, and media coverage, and extending, often in contradictory ways, across the duration of a performer's career. Far from reproducing the original person, a star image on film is itself always a copy of a copy, a mask or persona meant to authenticate a social, racial, and sexual type in the theatricalized settings of a movie and its promotion.

In their performances of gender, Hollywood stars produce an effect akin to drag insofar as they too cross seemingly rigid binarized categories, such as the oppositions seeming/posing, natural/artificial, sincere/deceptive, which themselves carry a secondary gender inflection of masculine/feminine. According to Dyer, "star images function crucially in relation to contradictions with and between ideologies, which they seek variously to 'manage' or resolve"—or even subvert because of the way a star image can set up a "clash of codes" (*Stars* 38). While, as Dyer observes, all stars embody "values that are under threat," some stars are extremely popular at certain times in their careers because their screen personae vividly stage or at least provoke ideological rupture (32). That Cary Grant, voted the most popular male movie star of 1958, could so well represent heterosexual American masculinity speaks volumes about the ambiguous and unfixed status of "masculinity" in the culture at this time. Consequently, as *North by Northwest* unfolds and makes repeated and quite self-conscious allusions to the presence of its star player in the hero's part, the star persona of "Cary Grant" supplies Roger Thornhill with another important layer of gender performance, one which has to be taken seriously when understanding the full significance of his masculinity crisis in the film.

The Familiar Face of Cary Grant

Although a popular Hollywood star since the 1930s, Grant experienced a comeback of sorts during the late 1950s, returning to box-office prominence with the successes of *An Affair to Remember* (1957), *Indiscreet* (1958), and *Operation Petticoat* (1959) as well as *North by Northwest*. Unlike other stars of his generation (John Wayne, Humphrey Bogart, Gary Cooper, James Stewart, for example), whose fifties roles altered their screen personae in recognition of their age (Biskind 252–53), during this period Grant not only seemed to hold the clock still, but his star persona acquired even *more* glamour and appeal as "an authentic American hero" (Rothman 177) or "a national monument" (Cavell 769). In 1958, when *Photoplay* included Grant, dubbed "Hollywood's epitome of romance," in a pictorial spread featuring a number of male stars in swimming pools, it did not at all seem surprising—or inappropriate—to find the 54-year-old actor placed alongside such younger heartthrobs as Tony Curtis, Rock Hudson, George Nader, and Hugh O'Brian ("6 Ways" 95). Nor was it odd, following the success of *North by Northwest*, to see "debonair" Grant pictured between "no square" Dwayne Hickman and "campus man" Troy Donahue as part of the magazine's 1960 guide to bachelor types ("Leap" 47).

Despite his legendary status in the fifties as Hollywood's quintessential leading man, Cary Grant was something of a paradoxical romantic hero for this period. His biographers explicitly call his fifties screen image "his mask," by which they mean, with reference to his "sexual problems," "his false image, so carefully sustained, of unequivocal masculinity and strong emotional security" (Higham and Moseley 248). While successfully personifying an image on and off screen of eternal youthfulness, Americanness, heterosexual attractiveness, bachelorhood, and sartorial elegance, Grant was actually middle-aged, British, bisexual, married (he was not yet divorced from Betsy Drake), and a secret cross-dresser (apparently wearing women's nylon panties underneath his expensively tailored suits).[13] The star's postwar screen persona, in short, refashioned his own age, class, nationality, sexual orientation and marital status to represent something else entirely: the ever youthful American bachelor

Figure 4.
Cary Grant, "Hollywood's epitome of romance" in 1958 according to
Photoplay. A fuller version of this uncredited photograph
appeared in the magazine.

businessman, the role that Hitchcock and Lehman tailored expressly for him in *North by Northwest* (Spoto, *Dark Side* 436).

In the late fifties, this manufactured persona of "Cary Grant" was so widely accepted as a paragon of romantic American masculinity that Billy Wilder could have Tony Curtis imitate the star's well-known speaking style, and audiences at *Some Like It Hot* (1959) immediately recognized this joke as a citation to Hollywood's exemplary leading man. "Where did you get that phony accent?" Jack Lemmon asks Curtis after watching the latter pose as a bachelor oil heir to catch Marilyn Monroe's attention: "Nobody talks like that." But everyone watching Wilder's film knew who *did* speak that way— for one thing, most of the reviews identified Cary Grant by name as the joke's referent—though audiences at the time were divided over whether the point was tribute, satire, or just plain gossip about the star's private life.

Released just a few months before *North by Northwest, Some Like It Hot* still offers the most acute reading of the Cary Grant star persona in its fifties setting. More than a simple reference to a famous cultural icon of romantic seduction, the clever allusion to Grant represents his celebrated persona as a performance, specifically designed as a masquerade, constructing "masculinity" out of voice, clothes, bearing—all, as the Wilder film plays it out, borrowed from someone else to cover up a fundamental failure of male sexuality. "I'm harmless," Tony Curtis confesses to Marilyn Monroe in Cary Grant's voice; and while the male's disguise in this scene is nothing but a decoy for his own heterosexual aggression (the pretense of impotence lures Monroe into making all the moves in Curtis's seduction of her), Wilder's reference to Grant recognizes the disturbing underside of the star's image. Most obviously, it implies that this famous screen persona of charm and elegance is actually covering up the *other* Great Fear that preoccupied fifties American culture when it came to thinking about masculinity: not communist subversion or atomic war but impotence, which the culture equated with emasculation, particularly in the light of the two Kinsey reports and the widely circulated revelation of the second volume that female sexuality peaked late in life while male sexual performance petered out much earlier in the game.[14]

The allusion to "Cary Grant" in *Some Like It Hot* goes beyond a simple suggestion of phallic imposture, however, because it so fully equates the actor's star persona with his self-conscious performance of masculinity. Far from just making a joke about the sexual potency of a legendary Hollywood leading man, the allusion tries to account for Grant's highly mannered but also enduring romantic style. When, within the diegesis of *Some Like It Hot*, Tony Curtis plays a man who disguises himself as a woman and then, while still pretending to be her, also passes himself off as a generic version of "Cary Grant," Curtis's impersonation of the star implies that Grant's similar and equally successful manipulation of performance signs (voice, bearing, looks) continues to produce this quintessential leading man for the benefit of

American movies. What lies beneath that consummate performance of romantic masculinity, the Wilder film suggests, is the mask itself: a potential subversion of the stable, binarized terms by which American culture in the fifties represented masculinity as the automatic, unchanging, and natural continuum of gender, sexuality, and anatomy. That debonair American lover Cary Grant that *Some Like It Hot* teases may be harmless, like a gun with blanks, but he is irresistible all the same—possibly for that very reason.

One explanation why Grant's fifties star persona implied that the basis of his appeal lay in performance and masquerade has to do with the apparent agelessness of his face, which he seemed to borrow from the picture of Dorian Gray. From the start of his career as Mae West's costar in the 1930s, Grant's value as a leading man had derived from his male beauty; in the postwar era he then became legendary for his eternal youthfulness—ever tanned, ever handsome, ever the same. As Richard Schickel puts it, "some time in his fifties, while he still looked as if he were in his forties—happily combining an elegant and easeful maturity with an undiminished capacity for playfulness—he simply ceased to age. Just plain stopped. As far as we in the audience could see" (9). Grant's irresistible good looks never coarsened with age but continued to attract the gaze of the female spectator, on screen as well as in the audience, often making her and not him the sexual aggressor, no matter what their difference in ages. The seduction scenes in the two 1950s Hitchcock films starring Grant—*To Catch a Thief* (1955) as well as *North by Northwest*—when the cool, sophisticated, and younger blonde becomes aroused enough by his good looks to break with convention, putting the moves on him, exemplify the extent to which "Cary Grant" signified desirable maleness and, hence, active sexual excitement in women.

Grant's postwar films self-consciously acknowledge this important dimension of his star persona through both verbal and visual references to his famous looks. Often giving Grant the kind of glamorous build-up usually reserved for female stars, his films of this period play up his desirability as a male through the close-ups that introduce him and make his face comparable to the female lead's. His recognizable face, moreover, even became something of a regular in-joke, as when Roger and Eve discuss the familiarity of his face on the train in *North by Northwest*. The wit in their banter clearly arises from the interplay of extradiegetic references pressing against the diegetic immediacy of this scene. As well as establishing the fact that Eve has identified Roger from the photograph of him in the newspapers, and so has to reckon with the potential danger he might pose to her as a suspected murderer, the dialogue alludes to what the reassuring *and* exciting sight of Cary Grant's familiar face means in a romantic movie like this one. Eve's comment that Roger can make strange women fall in love with him likewise acknowledges Grant's status as the consummate screen lover, and the significance of this reference is then compounded when Eve, as if recognizing the commodification of the actor's famous face, goes on to equate his star power with his selling power. An even more self-conscious allusion to Grant's iconic status as the quintessential leading man occurs much later in the film, when Roger sneaks through a woman's hospital room, and she *twice* tells him to stop, the second time after she has gotten a better look at him with her glasses on, so that the repetition of "stop" now means "stay." In contrast to the way that Tony Curtis has to gull Marilyn Monroe into being the aggressor in *Some Like It Hot*, Grant himself doesn't need to trick a woman into acting upon her desire for him; in his films, he simply has to let her look at him.

North by Northwest also takes note of Grant's famous face in the editing of his performance through close-ups, which direct repeated attention to his apparently ageless face. *The Hollywood Reporter*'s description of Grant's performance in the film takes for granted that his appearance on screen is designed to be watched: "He delivers a marvelous series of closeups . . . he keeps you enthralled by doing nothing at all . . . [in the crop-dusting scene] he arouses more fear than a dozen movie Joan of Arcs being burned at the stake. The women will be attracted to him every minute, particularly in a hospital scene when he strides about clad only in a bath towel" (Moffitt). Along with the camera's attention to his good looks, the highly mannered idiom of Grant's acting relies, in *North by Northwest* as in his other films, upon an ensemble of predictable (which is not to say unpleasurable) theatrical effects as a performer.[15] As a consequence, Grant's celebrated diction, smile, double-takes, and pratfalls—all featured prominently in *North by Northwest*, as when Roger escapes from Vandamm in Glen Cove—like his famous clothes sense, play up the theatricality of his masculine persona over its authenticity without in any way belittling the star's sexual appeal or his cinematic value as a leading man.

With his star persona as the suave, consummate, and ageless lover resulting from the construction of an attractive male identity out of artifice and theatricality, Cary Grant was ideally suited for the identity play and gender performativity that characterize the narrative action in *North by Northwest*. In one way or another most of Grant's films of the postwar era have him undertaking some form of disguise, however flimsy the pretense, innocent the motivation, and transparent the mask. Grant masquerades in some of his earlier films, to be sure: in *Bringing Up Baby* (1938), for example, he has to hide his identity from Katharine Hepburn's aunt; and in *Mr. Lucky* (1943), his character first adopts the name of a dead Greek crony in order to avoid the draft and then goes on to double his masquerade by trying to con a socialite (Laraine Day). But such disguises become even more of a routine feature in his later films. As well as being mistaken for a spy in *North by Northwest*, for a variety of reasons, most of them rather far-fetched to emphasize the self-consciousness of his role-playing, Grant poses as a teenager in *The Bachelor and the Bobby Soxer* (1947); as a bride in *I Was a Male War Bride* (1949); as an adolescent and child in *Monkey Business* (1952); as a businessman from Oregon in *To Catch a Thief*;

as a married man in *Indiscreet;* and these various impersonations culminate in the multiple masks his character wears before Audrey Hepburn in *Charade,* his final romantic leading role in 1963.

The frequency of masquerading in Grant's fifties films has a great deal to do with the growing disparity between his age and the romantic roles that he continued to play. However, rather than concealing, as *Some Like It Hot* implies with its joke about his impotence, some form of male lack (i.e., the diminishment in sexual capacity that, Kinsey showed, accompanies a man's maturity), the masquerading in these films renews the gender mobility of his 1930s screwball comedies, such as *The Awful Truth* (1937) and *Bringing Up Baby.*[16] By the late 1950s, the fluidity with which Grant's postwar star persona could still successfully move back and forth between seemingly rigid binaries—not only feminine/masculine but also British/American, genteel/common, youthful/aging—made them appear more contradictory than ever: on one hand, he represented gentility and social bearing without, as did many comic actors of lesser rank, seeming effete or elitist; on the other, he traded upon his eternal good looks as a screen lover without, as did many other foreign leading men, sacrificing his ability to connote the combination of virility and middle-class Americanness that ranked him alongside the likes of Wayne, Stewart, Cooper, and Bogart.

In contrast to those other male stars, Grant's star persona always runs the implicit risk of crossing that symbolic line that, for the popular imagination of the fifties, polarized virility against effeminacy in an effort to authenticate masculinity, to push it beyond representation as the origin of all other gender impersonations. This playful celebration of theatricality over authenticity grounds his appealing star persona as Hollywood's consummate dreamboat in a performance of masculinity no different from Roger Thornhill's—or George Kaplan's for that matter. Thus, when *North by Northwest* has Cary Grant engage in a masquerade as part of its plot, with Roger assuming the persona of Kaplan, it reproduces in the diegesis the very signs of the star's own performing, blurring the boundaries separating his character's acting from his own. Indeed, since "Cary Grant" is also a made-up name attached to a fabricated persona, Archie Leach's rise to stardom in Hollywood mirrors the invention of George Kaplan perhaps even more closely than the star's theatricalized image resembles the role-playing of Roger Thornhill.[17] "George Kaplan" and "Cary Grant" are both personae that signify all the more powerfully and credibly in being complete *and* successful fabrications.

Masculinity on the Rocks

The comparability of "Kaplan" and "Grant" helps to clarify how the invention of the imaginary spy functions for *North by Northwest* much as the invention of "Madeline Elster" does for *Vertigo*. To paraphrase Scottie in the final scene of that film, the "Madeline" of his desire turns out to be the first "fake" or "counterfeit" that exposes the basis of gender itself in masquerading. As *Vertigo* pulls the veil away from Madeline's blondeness to expose her position in a chain of forged copies, it confirms what Kim Novak's star persona implies, that femininity is a performance of womanliness that the Hollywood star system celebrated as female glamour. When *North by Northwest* lets Roger be mistaken for Kaplan, this chain of forged male copies results in a similar revelation, but, because it involves masculinity, it is much more unsettling. Roger Thornhill's masculinity—no less than George Kaplan's *or* Cary Grant's—is as much a performative masquerade as femininity; his masculinity, like Eve's femininity, is a gendered persona lacking an origin beyond representation and repeatedly needing to be reconstituted in one. The depiction of masculinity crisis in the film's poster—with the image of Cary Grant falling in space, the ground pulled out from under him—epitomizes the unstable position of "masculinity" in such a chain of "forged" representations of gender. Significantly enough, Grant's point of reference in the poster is itself another representation, a copy of a copy, reproducing the scene in the film that happens to bring out Roger's most willing complicity in performance: the phony shooting scene. Representation, as the transparency of George Kaplan dramatizes within the film, provides masculinity with a very unsteady ground indeed.

Crisscrossed by so many levels of masquerades and identity play, *North by Northwest* calls into question whether masculinity can *ever* be assumed to be a coherent and singular, not to say authentic, condition in culture. This is ultimately why the film then has to work all the harder to restore the period's dominant ideologies of gender in its closure. But because that effort exposes the complex ideological machinery driving Roger on his road to marriage, maturity, and manhood, the ending of *North by Northwest* can also be viewed as one more gender performance. In its famous parting shot of the train speeding through the tunnel on its way back to Grand Central Station, the film winks all the more boldly at the many ideological imperatives motivating its closure. In drawing this inference, I do not mean to suggest that *North by Northwest* seriously challenges or revises the hegemonic status of Roger Thornhill's masculinity; this film is not utopian or revolutionary in its intent by any means. But I am claiming that, in its subtle historical understanding of the performance ideology motivating the personae of its hero, his fictive nemesis, and its leading man, *North by Northwest* encourages our perception of the masquerading that forms the basis of gender identities in culture, masculinity as well as femininity. I take this premise as the starting point of my study of fifties Hollywood cinema, just as I see Roger Thornhill's relation to George Kaplan—and to Cary Grant—as being fittingly emblematic of the status of masculinity in movies throughout this period.

The "Paradox" of Hegemonic Masculinity

> But remember that a man in a gray flannel suit is also a man and that for two or three years he was away from you in one or another war. For two or three years he lived as undomesticated men do live: without the bills and taxes perhaps, living among other men and not inhibiting man's natural impulse to obscene language and obscene storytelling, seeing men die and perhaps expecting to die himself, free in the sense that he often had no idea what the next day would bring. And free, if he wished, to lie on his bunk evenings, to think and dream.
>
> There are certain deep and perfectly normal masculine drives that were "permitted" during a war as they are not permitted in a suburban back yard. They are an inborn attraction to violence and obscenity and polygamy, an inborn love of change, an inborn need to be different from the others and rebel against them, a strong need for the occasional company of men only and an occasional need for solitude and privacy.
>
> Certainly all men do not feel these drives to the same degree. And certainly these drives shouldn't all be permitted in that clean, green, happy back yard. But if they are always and completely inhibited—the man in the gray flannel suit will stop being a man. (Lyndon 107)

In this conclusion to an article entitled "The Paradox of the American Male," appearing in *Woman's Home Companion* in 1956, writer Louis Lyndon displays the confidence with which cultural commentators of this era felt they could represent masculinity in singular terms. The several paragraphs quoted above simply assume not only that The Man in the Gray Flannel Suit personified masculinity of every caste and color in U.S. society, but that he came equipped as well with a standard biography common to all adult American men: their experience first as soldiers on the battlefield in World War II (or Korea), then as heads of a middle-class household upon their return. According to Lyndon, married men now have to adopt a docile persona that is fundamentally at odds with their inherent masculinity. The writer asks his (presumably) female readers to realize that home life is built upon the repression of "certain deep and perfectly normal masculine drives," which meet their match in a feminine reality principle that threatens married men with emasculation. For "if [these drives] are always and completely inhibited," Lyndon warns, "the man in the gray flannel suit will stop being a man."

As it seeks to explain this paradoxical portrait of the American male, Lyndon's article reflects upon the displacement of one dominant representation of masculinity by another that occurred after the end of World War II. However, the writer's universalizing claims about an "inborn" masculinity allow him to evade the implication of what he observes, namely, that masculinity is a social position rooted in historical circumstances. Such evasion typifies how the era's most commonplace representation of masculinity, which linked gender (manhood) and male psychology (maturity) to a heterosexual goal (mating) and economic obligation (breadwinning), functioned to secure the cultural hegemony of the professional-managerial class in the face of other, older as well as marginalized and excluded, social interests: men who did not live in the suburbs or even in single-family dwellings, who held down blue-collar jobs or ran business empires, who supported family members in addition to their wives or were not even married. "The ability to impose a particular definition on other kinds of masculinity is part of what we mean by 'hegemony' . . ." explain sociologists Tim Carrigan, Bob Connell, and John Lee. "It is . . . a question of how particular groups of men inhabit positions of power and wealth and how they legitimate and reproduce the social relationships that generate their dominance" (179).

The hegemonic masculinity of a historical era does not define a proper male sex role for all men to follow so much as it articulates various social relations of power as an issue of gender normality. "At any given time," Connell observes in a separate study, "one form of masculinity rather than others can be defined as the culturally exalted. Hegemonic masculinity can be defined as the configuration of gender practice which embodies the currently accepted answer to the problem of the legitimacy of patriarchy, which guarantees (or is taken to guarantee) the dominant position of men and the subordination of women" (*Masculinities* 77). This definition should not be taken to imply that hegemonic masculinity operates simply by perpetuating a patriarchal system of gender governance through a male/female binarism that allows for the essentialization of "men" and "women," although, as Lyndon's article illustrates, that is its rhetorical effect in popular discourse. Clearly, the men who comprise a living culture have more diverse experiences of masculinity than any hegemonic norm can represent. Thus, as it underwrites positions of power and wealth, a culture's hegemonic masculinity has to appear to accommodate competing masculinities, too, with the purpose of maintaining "a particular variety of masculinity to which others—among them young and effeminate as well as

Figures 5a and 5b.
The standard biography of hegemonic masculinity that all American
men were assumed to have shared, first as soldiers (left) and then
as head of the house (right). Gregory Peck as Tom Rath in
The Man in the Gray Flannel Suit.

homosexual men—are subordinated" (Carrigan, Connell, and Lee 174). In order to regulate these variations, hegemonic masculinity organizes itself at the top of a hierarchy of power relations "created with at least three elements: hegemonic masculinity, conservative masculinities (complicit in the collective project but not its shock troops) and subordinated masculinities" (Connell, *Gender* 110).[1]

In his own commentary on gender and power, Connell, like his collaborators Carrigan and Lee, describes the hegemonic masculinity of American culture by calling upon well-known icons of virility from the movies. "Indeed, the winning of hegemony often involves the creation of models of masculinity which are quite specifically fantasy figures, such as the film characters played by Humphrey Bogart, John Wayne and Sylvester Stallone" (*Gender* 184–85).[2] Viewed historically, this generalization more accurately depicts the cultural status of Bogart and Wayne in the years following the fifties (as their revisionist association with Stallone implies) than it characterizes their star value during this period. In the fifties, the domesticated breadwinner, commonly identified by the media as The Man in the Gray Flannel Suit, was responsible for legitimating the hegemony of the professional-managerial class. The tough-guy movie hero epitomized by Bogart, the subject of my next chapter, and the Western hero by Wayne, discussed in the sixth, moved increasingly into the background as a conservative partner in the social consensus. The subordinated masculinities suggested in films via references to homosexuality, ethnicity, and race were either subordinated to the hegemonic authority of the domesticated breadwinner, often in direct opposition to his "tough" conservative partner, or not represented on screen at all. As an institution whose business was the production of representation for popular consumption, Hollywood cinema of this period was obviously a participant in the culture's reconfiguration of masculinity along such lines after the war. Fifties films as a whole are complicit, as Peter Biskind's book *Seeing Is Believing* has shown, in the consensual politics empowering the professional-managerial class. At the same time, though, Hollywood cinema was not simply a propaganda machine for the corporate interests that had put its hands on the operation of the major studios more directly than ever before following the 1948 Paramount consent decree. As I will be demonstrating in all of the following chapters, there were major deviations from hegemonic masculinity in the movies and these are of considerable significance; but they still occurred with reference to the formidable ideal of the middle-class breadwinner, that typical American Male who had traded in his 1940s khaki regulation uniform for a 1950s gray flannel one.

The breadwinner described by Lyndon was thus a central fixture of Hollywood films of the fifties. As the movies told it, the hegemonic masculinity of this typical American male—identified with middle-class domesticity, white-collar employment, and the national character—seemed to fall into place almost as soon as World War II was over. In illustration, I pay close attention to three films that make the "paradox" of the breadwinner's normality central to their narrativizations of hegemonic masculinity: *Pitfall* (1948), *The Seven Year Itch* (1955), and *The Man in the Gray Flannel Suit* (1956). Each film takes the normality of its breadwinning protagonist for granted, yet each also stages a crisis for his home life that calls his manhood into question. While all three films ultimately vindicate their protagonists' hegemonic stature, their narratives lead one to ask why, given the breadwinner's supposed position of dominance, was this normative figure used to represent masculinity as a condition of discontent? What did his masculinity crisis put at issue, particularly when set in a domestic context? And how did that crisis change in its inflection over the course of the decade? Although the man and his suit appeared to be uniform in 1956, the postwar era records the process by which this particular formation of hegemonic masculinity attained its dominance over other masculinities, and the domestic narratives constructed by Hollywood to rationalize the breadwinner's dominance cannot be viewed apart from the historical conditions that determined his hegemony in representation and supplied his masculinity with a discursive setting that made its normality legible.

Pitfall: "A Little Man with a Briefcase"

A relatively unknown film produced by an independent company for United Artists in 1948, *Pitfall* registers the ambivalence with which the hegemonic masculinity of the forties, defined to serve the militarism of World War II, was first made to conform to domestication in the years following demobilization. While the film itself, as contemporary reviewers recognized, concerns an average American husband's discontent with the regulation and boredom of his domestic life, the studio's publicity focused instead on its "story of sex, violence and shady characters,"[3] marketing it as a film noir thriller rather than as the male melodrama it really is.

The lobby card, for instance, reprinted as figure 6, promises a sexual adventure with ominous implications for the hero's masculinity: "A man can be strong as steel . . . but somewhere there's a woman who'll break him!" In support of its explosive tag line, the poster exploits the well-known star personae of the film's lead players (Lizabeth Scott with the weapon triggered and concealed by her side, Dick Powell in a shootout, the couple in a clinch) in order to situate the masculinity crisis evoked by the ad copy within the generic framework of a thriller. This advertising art alludes to the tough-guy image of Dick Powell from *Murder My Sweet* (1944), where he personifies private eye Philip Marlowe, and the *femme fatale* persona of Lizabeth Scott from *Dead Reckoning* (1947), where "The Threat," as she was called, almost "breaks" the hardest of all forties men, Humphrey Bogart. It turns out, though, that neither star plays such roles in the film itself, which stages a masculinity crisis for its

Figure 6.
The lobby card for *Pitfall* promises a sexual adventure with
ominous implications for its hero's masculinity.

hero precisely by playing against the conventions of film noir and the star
personae of its leading players.

Pitfall tells the story of a breadwinner fed up with the domestic routine of
his postwar life. A claims adjuster at the Olympic Mutual Insurance Company in Los Angeles, John Forbes (Powell) meets Mona Stevens (Scott) while
attempting to recover property purchased with embezzled funds by her fian-
cé, Bill Smiley (Byron Barr), who is serving time for the theft. Johnny and
Mona begin an affair, which ends as soon as she discovers that he is married.
They cannot make a clean break, however, because J. B. MacDonald (Raymond Burr), a private investigator whom Johnny used to track down what
Smiley purchased with the stolen money, is obsessed with Mona and jealous of
Johnny. When Mona rejects him, MacDonald tries to blackmail her, threatening to go to Johnny's wife, Sue (Jane Wyatt), with news of her husband's
infidelity. Frightened, Mona goes to Johnny for help instead, and he momentarily stops MacDonald's harassment. Or so it seems. For taking advantage of
Smiley's helplessness while in prison, the detective plays Iago to the convict's

Othello, taunting him with thoughts of what Johnny has appropriated from him: the money *and* the woman. After Smiley's parole, MacDonald gets him drunk and armed and, as a means of eliminating both rivals, goads him into trying to murder Johnny in the latter's home. Almost immediately after Johnny kills Smiley in self-defense, MacDonald tries to force Mona into going off with him; feeling trapped and defenseless, she shoots him twice. In the end, while a police matron takes Mona away to jail, Johnny—himself officially cleared of any blame for shooting Smiley—returns to his wife, who agrees to take him back.

If there is a woman strong enough to break the wayward husband of *Pitfall*, it may well be not the blonde with the gun, but the nurturing brunette wife with the small child. The film begins with its hero complaining about the responsibility of providing for his wife and young son, Tommy (Jimmy Hunt). Recalling that he was voted the boy most likely to succeed and Sue the prettiest girl in their high school class, Johnny wonders aloud at breakfast what happened to "those two people who were going to build a boat and sail around the world." "I had a baby," his wife replies. "I don't know about you." As Sue drives her husband to work, he continues to voice dissatisfaction with his life as a breadwinner, and she asks, "Old Man Routine getting to you again?" Her question indicates that the couple have had this conversation before.

> *Johnny:* No, I don't know. Sometimes I get to feeling like a wheel within a wheel within a wheel.
> *Sue:* You and fifty million others.
> *Johnny:* I don't want to be like fifty million others.
> *Sue:* You're John Forbes. Average American. Backbone of the country.
> *Johnny:* I don't want to be average American, backbone of the country. I want somebody else to do that and hold me up.
> *Sue:* You've been reading Tommy's geography book again. Glamorous Borneo. Rubber plantations. And dusty dames.
> *Johnny:* It sounds a lot better than glamorous Olympic Mutual Insurance, Inc.

Failing to take seriously Johnny's boredom or his sense of home as a confining space, with her reference to their son's geography book, Sue, like the wives mentioned in the *Woman's Home Companion* article a decade later, cuts short her husband's complaint by dismissing it as boyish daydreaming. Later, when Johnny meets Mona, her hostile reaction functions like a tape recorder, repeating back to him what he himself has been thinking: "You're a little man with a briefcase. You go to work every morning and you do as you're told." "You know, I'd shoot myself if I thought I was turning into the guy you describe," he replies, asking her out for a drink in a sudden—if still vague—show of sexual interest. Mona's confirmation of what he himself dislikes about his life spurs his desire, not for the woman herself so much as for the transgression of patriarchal duty—disruption of "Old Man Routine"—which she enables him to perform; after all, as if in direct response to his complaint at breakfast, Mona takes Johnny out for a ride on her boat, allowing him to play hooky from his job and to sail, if not around the world, then at least in circles around Santa Monica Bay. Afterward, when Mona asks if he has to be somewhere for dinner, Johnny says, flatly, no (though we know from earlier dialogue that his wife is in fact expecting him to be dropped off by his car pool at "exactly five-fifty"), adding a defiant note: "I don't *have* to be anywhere."

There is some justice to Johnny's complaining about Old Man Routine getting him down. Married life fails to provide him with a proper site for realizing his masculinity according to the conventions of gender representation in thrillers of the late 1940s—the sort of film noir evoked by this film's poster and crystallized in its lead actor's style of performance and previous association with such roles. Though a product of postwar Hollywood and responsive to demobilization in its own way, film noir still represents masculinity in the militant terms of a war culture, opposing both femininity and domesticity to specific standards of "tough" male prowess (e.g., physical endurance, loyalty to a male partner, heterosexual desire, freedom from marital obligations, social mobility), which it plots through a thriller narrative. *Pitfall,* by contrast, gives home life and marriage much more prominence than one usually finds in film noir of this period. For this reason Frank Krutnik reads *Pitfall* as failed film noir, a male fantasy of sexual transgression which has little chance of ever being realized because "the hero's castration is far too evident" from the very opening (*Lonely* 147), with his life at home and at work "characterised by self-delimitation and self-sacrifice" (148). Johnny's attempt to transgress in the manner of other noir heroes—like Walter Neff (Fred MacMurray) in *Double Indemnity* (1944), say—is therefore doomed to mediocrity to start with. As Krutnik points out, as part of his duties at the insurance company Johnny gets to handle large sums of money while lacking direct access to it; yet rather than steal money from the corporation he works for to finance an adventure and break free of the domesticity which circumscribes his life, he retraces the path taken by money that somebody else has stolen (148). Likewise, the film contrasts Johnny's half-hearted desire for Mona to the more intense and overwhelming obsession of both Smiley, who commits embezzlement to buy her things that he mistakenly assumes she desires, and MacDonald, who plots a murder by remote control, as it were, to eliminate his rivals.

Of all the characters in *Pitfall,* MacDonald—both a private eye and an ex-policeman just like Dick Powell's character in *Murder, My Sweet*—most resembles the typical tough guy populating 1940s film noir. MacDonald, who even poses as Forbes at one point in the film, serves as Johnny's double, which is to say that the detective's figure is made to take responsibility for the bread-winner's transgression (Krutnik, *Lonely* 151). During their initial conversation about the whereabouts of Smiley's money, MacDonald adds that he has an

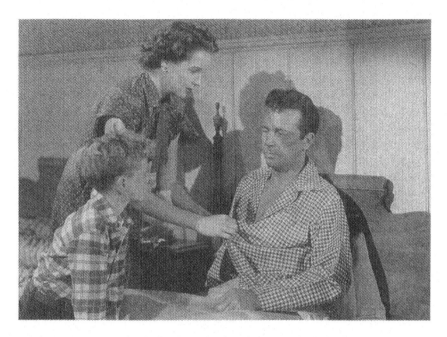

Figure 7.
Johnny Forbes (Dick Powell), beaten, bruised, and strapped in a corset
of bandages after MacDonald sends him home where he belongs.

interest in Mona, so he in effect introduces Johnny to the idea of desiring her. Then, after Johnny acts on that desire, breaking his marriage vows, Mac-Donald punishes him for it. MacDonald waits for Johnny to return from a tryst with Mona and, catching him off guard, soundly beats him up outside his own house. Walking away unharmed himself, MacDonald calls back sarcastically: "Maybe this will keep you at home where you belong for a few days." The next morning reveals a pathetic sight. Beaten, bruised, and now strapped into a corset of bandages, Johnny sits in bed; a doctor examines him and advises several days of additional bed rest; his wife ministers to him as if he were a child; and his adoring son asks, "There were two of 'em or you would have handled him, couldn't you dad?" Well, probably not. In the fight scene between Johnny and MacDonald, the rogue detective's larger, more burly body conveys a physical substance and power lacking in Johnny's leaner frame. True, when Mona seeks his help in keeping MacDonald in line, Johnny later returns the pleasure with an attack of his own; but that earlier sight of helpless Dick Powell in bed hangs over the rest of the film as a visual reminder of Johnny's vulnerability at the hands of MacDonald.

Far from representing the middle-class home as the site of Johnny's castration, as Krutnik contends, *Pitfall* fully endorses the domesticity which requires the exclusion of violent men like MacDonald, who endangers the security of the family. MacDonald's beating does not emasculate Johnny so much as set up the terms by which the film can differentiate between their masculinities. The beating exposes Johnny's lack of potency but it also supplies the circumstances for Mona's discovery that he is married, for her ending the affair, and, most importantly, for his renewed commitment to domesticity. "What happens to men like you, Johnny?" Mona scolds when, following his recovery from the beating, he admits the truth about his marital status. "If I had a nice home like you did," she continues, "I wouldn't take a chance with it for anything in the world." Later that evening, while Johnny and his wife wash the supper dishes, Tommy apes his father in complaining that he is "tired of this town." In his response to the boy, Johnny repeats what Mona told him. "That's the trouble with your generation," Johnny lectures Tommy. "You don't appreciate the things you have. You got one of the nicest houses on the block. Security." Surprised by her husband's abrupt turnabout, Sue can only express amazement at his paradoxical behavior. "What's come over you?" she asks. "Contentment," he replies. "And that's the secret of happiness."

This conversation occurs midway through the film, and it allows Johnny to recover his position in the home through his son and not through his wife. Ultimately, paternity, not desire, is what will keep this wandering breadwinner home where he belongs, which is why the many tender exchanges between father and son repeatedly generate more affect on screen than do the conversations between husband and wife. "Sometimes I'm awfully proud of myself," Sue tells her husband, "for giving my son such a wonderful father. He thinks you're the greatest thing on earth."

Sue pays Johnny his due after listening to him comfort Tommy, who has awakened screaming from a nightmare apparently caused by his reading scary comic books at bedtime. Johnny calms his son by explaining how a bad dream works:

> *Johnny:* The mind is like a very wonderful camera. Do you know how a camera works?
> *Tommy:* Sure, it takes pictures.
> *Johnny:* That's right. And that's the way the mind works. Evidently, from the day you were born the mind takes pictures and stores them away. Now and then one of those pictures come loose in our sleep and that becomes a dream. So, the trick is to take only good pictures and have only good dreams.

Johnny's ability to ease his son's fears testifies to the truth of what Sue says. But what's striking about his explanation, which owes an obvious debt to the currency of psychoanalysis in the 1940s, is that it does much more than exhibit his considerable skill as a parent. For at the same time that *Pitfall* authenticates the value of Johnny's domesticated masculinity through his persona as a father, the language he uses in his parenting recalls the film's own apparatus of representation: the camera. At this moment, *Pitfall* lays bare the objective of its crisis narrative and, in a manner of speaking, goes on to display its recognition that this objective is ideological in its intent.

The timing of this disclosure is far from coincidental. With the adoring gaze of his young son compensating for the adventurous life that Johnny has to give up to accept his responsibility as a family breadwinner, this is the point when *Pitfall* puts forward the new social persona—fatherhood—which fully vindicates its hero's hegemonic masculinity against the implicit charge of emasculation. And at this point, too, through Johnny's language, the film openly equates its own activity of representation with the ideological censorship of history, showing how it functions much as psychoanalysis explains the mechanisms of repression in a dream. Although "the trick is to take only good pictures," Johnny says, every so often some "bad" pictures "come loose" to reveal, in the very texture of a representation, what the "good pictures" have repressed.

Johnny's explanation is as good a description as any of the way that *Pitfall* operates in its representation of the breadwinner, superimposing ideology ("good pictures") over history ("bad pictures") as a means of discouraging a fuller recognition of the social circumstances that, while motivating its crisis narrative, also call into question the terms by which its closure universalizes the breadwinner's domesticated masculinity through fatherhood. *Pitfall* participates in what was, historically speaking, the postwar culture's own struggle to redefine hegemonic masculinity in the light of demobilization; but in order not to acknowledge that Johnny's masculinity is a historically determined social position, *Pitfall* has a strong investment in *mis*representing the historical conditions that motivate its endorsement of the domesticated breadwinner over the noir tough guy. We can still find traces of what the film censors, however, by examining how *Pitfall* incorporates the war into its diegesis.

On the face of it, *Pitfall* appears to be very conscious of its setting in postwar America. In fashioning its plot out of Johnny's discontent with domestic life, the film resonates with the sense of anticlimax that many men felt following their return to civilian life after demobilization, particularly as exacerbated by a veteran's nostalgic memories (fantasized or real) of freedom and adventure—of limitless masculine experience first exemplified by the war and now belied by the responsibilities and confinements of peacetime. When interviewed by Studs Terkel, one veteran of WWII recalled: "As I see it, at that young age, we hit the climax. Everything after that is anticlimactic" (55). Another elaborated: "In a short period of time, I had the most tremendous experiences of all of life: of fear, of jubilance, of misery, of hope, of comradeship, and of the endless excitement, the theatrics of it. I honestly feel grateful for having been a witness to an event as monumental as anything in history and, in a very small way, a participant" (46). *Pitfall*, however, does not cite Johnny's own wartime experience to explain his sense of "anticlimax" upon returning home, and this omission is hard to ignore since it turns out that Johnny's life has always been regulated by Old Man Routine, even in wartime. "What did you do in the war?" Tommy asks his father, who replies, "Anything I was told." "I mean, what were you?" the boy persists, and Johnny then explains: "Most of the time I was stationed in Denver, Colorado." Not only did he never fight abroad (in contrast to the decorated father of Tommy's best friend), but it further appears that, unlike most married men of the period, Johnny also spent those war years in Denver, Colorado, with his wife. "After all, nothing's too tough for us," Sue reassures her husband when trying to persuade him to confess his troubles. "We won the war together. You brought Tommy through pneumonia."

Important in this brief allusion to their early marital history is Sue's statement that war was something they fought together, like any other storm which every married couple has to weather. As viewed in 1948, then, Johnny's wartime background would have appeared markedly different from that of "fifty million others." This "average American" did not have the same kind of military service that most American men had, nor did he suffer from their problems of readjustment to civilian life. But by placing Johnny in the States with his wife during the war, *Pitfall* can ask its viewers to imagine the hegemony of his domesticated masculinity as already inherent in wartime, conveniently forgetting the more disruptive history of the veteran's return to the kind of average life that Johnny is supposed to represent in his domesticity.

"Few remember today that the prospect of the World War II veterans' demobilization and reintegration was a cause for widespread concern, indeed, alarm long before V-J Day," writes historian David Gerber (547). The representation of the veteran, whether in films such as *The Best Years of Our Lives* (1946) or official governmental publications and the popular press, viewed his return to home life with ambivalence. "On the one hand, the veteran's heroism and sacrifices are celebrated and memorialized and debts of gratitude, both symbolic and material, are paid to him. On the other hand, the veteran also inspires anxiety and fear and is seen as a threat to social order and political stability" (546). In the years 1945–46, as the various governmental and professional experts prepared Americans to receive the millions of men returning home, "the discourse of the veterans problem served to cast doubt on the mental stability of every demobilized man, able-bodied or physically disabled. Every veteran was a potential 'mental case,' even if he showed no symptoms" (549). This picture turned out to be an exaggeration, of course. Nevertheless, particularly in news stories in the years immediately after the war, the angry vet was depicted either as "an excess of masculinity," a brutal killing machine set loose on the city streets, or as "its paucity," a shell-shocked bundle of nerves, unable to hold down the responsibilities of breadwinning (Fischer 78).

While no deranged veterans populate the diegesis of *Pitfall* to threaten the social order, the film recalls this perceived fear through the menacing figures of Smiley and MacDonald, who manifest the aggression required of wartime but which a breadwinner like Johnny now has to repress in order to occupy his new position in the home. Much like the vet played by Dana Andrews in *The Best Years of Our Lives*, Smiley returns from prison only to discover his girl's infidelity. As he becomes more determined to understand what happened while he was away, and to fix blame upon Johnny, he becomes more uncontrollable, more angry and agitated, his potential for violence inflamed by alcohol and explicitly directed at the Forbes family. Indeed, while Tommy's parents attribute his nightmare to comic books, since at this point we know that Smiley is threatening to go to Johnny's house with a gun, and since what the child imagined was a face at his bedroom window, Tommy may not have been dreaming at all. The "bad picture" may in fact have been a real one.

Even more than Smiley, MacDonald's unruly behavior, as he stalks both Mona and Johnny, exhibits the same degree of violence and manifests the same kind of psychosis that postwar culture associated with the vet who could not be readily integrated back into home life. "That was quite a boy you sent to see me yesterday," Mona tells Johnny on their first meeting, when he goes to her apartment to recover the things Smiley bought her. "I've met some weird ones in my life, but that one nearly scared me to death." "I'm sorry he annoyed you," Johnny replies, and Mona reiterates how much MacDonald has disturbed her: "He shouldn't be let loose without a keeper." Mona is not alone in responding to MacDonald like this; Maggie, Johnny's secretary, calls the detective "Gruesome." MacDonald's menacing presence in the film arises from his disturbing sexuality, from the way he looks at Mona, objectifies her, disregards her feelings; that is why she implies he is not only "weird" but an animal who needs to be caged. MacDonald, moreover, does more than simply "annoy" Mona. He harasses her at the department store where she works and waits outside her apartment until she finally has to ask one of the floorwalkers to accompany her home. Later, when he thinks he has blackmailed Mona into going away with him, as MacDonald packs her clothes, he fondles her undergarments and caresses her shoes, further suggesting his perverse sexuality.

In its diegesis *Pitfall* does not attribute MacDonald's deranged behavior to the war but his "gruesome" and "weird" figure nevertheless provokes in the two female characters who describe him the same apprehension of menace that, in the late 1940s, clustered around the veteran whose failure to be reintegrated into family life posed a threat to the social order. Furthermore, as a catalyst of the events on which the plot of the film hinges, MacDonald forces this repressed history to make itself visible in the diegesis if only fleetingly and obliquely: because MacDonald beats him up, Johnny appears bandaged and weak, just as if he were a wounded soldier in a scene from a war movie; because

MacDonald arms Smiley, gets him "hopped up" on alcohol and sends him over to the Forbes house, Johnny can kill a man in self-defense to make up for his unexciting tour of duty in Denver during the war.

MacDonald and Smiley focus attention upon *Pitfall*'s virtual erasure of the historical conditions motivating its endorsement of what was, after the war, a new formulation of hegemonic masculinity. Because even World War II was a family affair for him, Johnny lacks a history of *ever* being released from domesticity. Sue and he fought the war together as a married couple while, in another of the film's modifications of traditional gender positions, she credits him alone with nursing their son through childhood illness. By the film's end, it appears that even "the Big One," WWII, has receded into the background as part of the simple but endurable tableau of this couple's domestic history. Instead of the war, what threatens to tear their marriage apart is Johnny's infidelity, which was motivated, not by the couple's separation (as happened in wartime), but by his boredom. As Sue says, in explaining why she has finally decided not to press for a divorce, "If a man has always been a good husband except for twenty-four hours, how long should he be expected to pay for it?" It is equally clear that Sue decides to remain with her husband for the sake of their son. When she tells Johnny that she will try to forgive him, she also asks him to arrange for a transfer to another city, presumably, since she has pulled Tommy out of school, in order to avoid the scandal that would tarnish the boy's respect for his father. Paternity, in short, and not a revival of the "good husband's" desire for his wife, repairs this marriage, restoring Johnny to the position of "average American, backbone of the country."

The film's advertising campaign, which gives no indication that *Pitfall* is a drama of marital infidelity, is just as crucial an indication of how its endorsement of domesticity works to project a "good picture" of Johnny's masculinity through fatherhood. In a manner of speaking, as a consequence of his brief affair with Mona, Johnny brings film noir, and with it the social history noir encodes, into the home; as this happens, he endangers the family by becoming as far from the poster's monolithic "man of steel" as one can imagine. The affair envelops his masculinity in masquerade, making it appear more discontinuous, situational, and performative. He begins lying to Sue—about where he was all night, how he was beaten up, why he is worried about Smiley—just as he lies to Mona in not telling her that he is married. The results of Johnny's infidelity forge a gap between the breadwinner and the man, and he conceals it by wearing a mask, pretending to be the loving husband with Sue and the tough guy with Mona. The contrast between Johnny's performativity and Dick Powell's own emotionally flat acting style, which does not vary from scene to scene, then underlines the character's masculine masquerade even when the diegesis does not accent it.

More than just dissembling to cover up a momentary fling with another woman, Johnny's masquerading implies that the role of family breadwinner does not essentialize his masculinity but instead constitutes it as a series of performances, the discontinuity of which is apparent every time the film noir elements of *Pitfall* disrupt his home life. Home offers him, not continuity, but repetition, the same kind of repetition that, at work, turns him into "a little man with a briefcase." Although he claims that, if he were the kind of man Mona describes, he would shoot himself, he *does* go to work every day and *does* do as he is told, performing his part by rote much as he does at home (just as he did during the war). However, while work calls Johnny's manhood into question, as Mona's remark indicates, the narrative directs the consequences of his discontent on the home, not the office. As I have pointed out, he does not transgress professionally, scheming to rob the company, say, but strays from his marriage; and after Mona sends him back to his wife, Johnny voices his relief by reversing the position he took in the opening scene, causing Sue's surprise. His avowal of domesticity in this crucial scene gives only the appearance of reversing himself, though: whereas he originally complained about the drudgery of working for Old Man Routine, he now validates his domesticity, reminding his son of all the advantages of their home life, so the reason for his discontent has not changed. What *has* changed is that fatherhood compensates for the anomie he feels as a white-collar worker; and as fatherhood revives Johnny's hegemonic masculinity, it also renews his economic subjection. Fatherhood simply relocates the setting of his masculinity from the public sphere of work to the private one of home, where Johnny can more readily identify with Old Man Routine.

The Domestic Mystique

After confessing to his friend—and boss—Ed Brawley that he has had an affair, Johnny is about to leave the office when he asks Ed: "How does it feel to be a decent, respectable married man?" A sarcastic aside on the character's part, the question is no throwaway line. Johnny's own sense of exclusion from the breadwinner ethic at this point in the film indirectly highlights the very terms—"decency," "respectability," "marriage"—through which postwar society had already begun to renegotiate the status of hegemonic masculinity for "fifty million others" as well.

Although it is by now a cliché of the period that "[t]he fifties were a time of unprecedented sentimentalization of marriage and family life, and young men and women were going to the altar in unusually large numbers and unusually tender ages" (Oakley 117), all clichés have some basis in truth to start with, and the fifties' glorification of domesticity very much determined what most Americans, men and women, came to expect of adult life. During the 1950s, "Americans married at earlier ages, produced more babies, and divorced less frequently than during and just after World War II or in the 1960s and 1970s"

(Bremner 3). In noting this well-known fact, I do not mean to make it seem as if the postwar era, positioning the middle-class male in the home as the family breadwinner and thereby reconfiguring the terms of hegemonic masculinity in the light of this new setting in domesticity, was the very first time that U.S. culture had struggled to undertake "the redefinition of manliness to include some traditional female functions," such as the maintenance of family life. Anxiety over the domestication of middle-class men had also been prominent at the turn of the century, when the new virtues of "manliness," challenged by the feminist movement, were rigorously defended by Teddy Roosevelt's cult of masculinity; at the same time, the middle class migrated to the suburbs to escape the congestion and crime of industrialized cities, just as in the fifties, further encouraging, because of the changing material conditions of family lives, masculine domestication (Marsh 180–81).

What *was* "new" about hegemonic masculinity in the fifties was its full absorption into what Peter Filene calls, with reference to Betty Friedan's book, "the domestic mystique" (169). Domesticity pervaded the entire culture as the standard of normality, not just the middle class, resulting in a new definition of the family's role that crossed social divisions, and it extended to men as well as women, as indicated by the male's position in the family as its moral and psychological leader. As Filene points out, "Father's Day had begun merely as an afterthought—a commercial afterthought—to the moralistic proclamation of Mother's Day. Following the Second World War, however, it acquired a genuine meaning of its own" (172).

Historians agree that, prior to the war, the family had performed an "institutional function" harking back to the agrarian context of American domestic life in the nineteenth century. The family served as the crucial site where food and clothing were produced, informal and formal education took place, and children were introduced to the world of work and adult responsibilities. Furthermore, no doubt manifesting the economic effects of the Great Depression, the distinguishing feature of American families before the war was their great variety. Individual families differed from each other according to size, income, class, ethnicity, religion, region, and so on. This diversity still characterized the American family after the war's conclusion. In 1948, the year in which *Pitfall* was produced, one sociologist claimed, "Never before in human history has any society been composed of so many divergent types of families" (qtd. in Bremner 3). However, in response to profound social changes that had occurred during the war years—greater urbanization, industrialization, and geographic mobility—the family's role in America's cultural life was significantly revised to fulfill more of a "personality function." The family now provided the proper conditions for character development, not only to maintain good physical and mental health, but to supply the nurturing environment of affection, sympathy, and comradeship as well (Bremner 5).

Needless to say, the family's new "personality function" also recorded its ideological value in legitimating the cultural hegemony of the professional-managerial class. At the same time that the American character was becoming nationalized through "the emergence of a popular culture more homogeneous than Americans had previously known" (Marchand 164), representations of the family became increasingly modeled on a uniform standard that was specific to the new social formation of the professional-managerial class. The diversity of American families consequently ceased to be a dominant characteristic of U.S. society, if not in actual fact then at least in popular representations of home life. If Johnny Forbes was an "average American" in 1948, his life situation mirroring that of fifty million others, the same was believed to be true of his family as portrayed on screen.

The attention paid to the male's role in particular helped to promote the family's important "personality function" through the father's position as breadwinner. In contrast to the previous two decades, when "critics noted and often deplored the American tendency to make women responsible for nearly all aspects of home life and parenthood while men concentrated on work and matters outside the home" (Bremner 6), the fifties breadwinner found continual external reinforcement—whether through the admonishment of experts such as anthropologist Margaret Mead, or the numerous feature articles in popular magazines such as *Parents* and *McCall's,* or in the movies—to take his position at the head of a family, and to take it seriously.

An early Fred Zinnemann film, *Teresa* (1951), for instance, which at first appears to be portraying the inability of an obviously shell-shocked veteran to readjust to life as a civilian, turns out to be an attack on momism. In the opening scene, Philip Cash (John Ericson) bolts in panic once he has reached the front of a seemingly endless line at the unemployment office, and a voice-over identifying him adds that "his occupation is running away." What he runs away from is his responsibility as a breadwinner. Though the film uses a flashback narrative to locate Philip's condition in his memories of the war, its ultimate revelation is that his many psychological problems—timidity, alcoholism, migraine headaches, radical mood swings—are the result of an overbearing momma, who has already emasculated her husband. In order to keep her son home with her after he returns from the war, momma breaks up his marriage to his Italian war bride, Teresa (Pier Angeli), and openly discourages him from finding work. Internalizing his mother's debilitating influence through a series of symptoms that evoke the psychological wounds of a veteran, Philip is just one step away from the serial killer in *While the City Sleeps* (1956), whose violence against women externalizes his rage at an adopted mother who has tried to turn him into a girl ("Ask Mother," the gender-confused killer writes in lipstick on the walls of his victims' apartments). At the end of *Teresa,* Philip finds deliverance in fatherhood: with his own father's belated support, Philip finally leaves the nest to get a job, rent an apartment, and establish his own home with his estranged wife—that is, as soon as she has their baby. Paternity confirms his maturation and, apparently, solves all his problems.

The domestication of men through marriage meant to counteract the growing anxiety that women, primarily responsible for raising the nation's children during the World War II years, were producing a generation of sissies like Philip Cash.[4] In the movies especially, fatherhood was shown not only to serve an important "personality function" for the family, but, as in *Teresa*, to be psychologically crucial to a male's maturation. Even in the period's family comedies, which typically made the head of the house seem out of synchrony with the rhythms and preoccupations of home life, primarily because his role as breadwinner regularly required him to leave the house to go to work, by the time the end titles rolled father's hegemonic masculinity was neither out of place in the domestic sphere nor irrelevant to its daily operation; far from it, since narratives of family life routinely made home, and not work, the site through which the breadwinner most fully realized his masculinity.

In *Father of the Bride* (1950), the most famous ruffled father of this period, Stanley Banks (Spencer Tracy), feels that his role in his daughter's nuptials is simply to pay the ever-increasing costs run up by his wife, Ellie (Joan Bennett), thereby financing female consumerism through his own production of capital as an attorney. Many comic set pieces of this film underscore Stanley's ineffectualness with, bewilderment at, and alienation from the wedding at each stage of its planning. But these jokes do not detract from the film's premise, which is that fatherhood serves to identify this breadwinner's masculinity so deeply with his middle-class domesticity that the family cannot function without him as its psychological leader. Thus, while the jokes in *Father of the Bride* may all be at Stanley's expense, they actually work to engender his position in the home as a properly "masculine" one and to establish his authority over the family as its guiding light despite his alienation from each stage of the wedding.

According to James Naremore, the wedding in *Father of the Bride* is "a kind of domestic show business," geared to the conspicuous consumption of women, who know how to play their assigned parts to a tee (*Films* 96). Stanley, by contrast, is "a bad actor ... a man who mistimes his entrances, misjudges his speeches, and messes up his costumes" (98, 101). However, even though Stanley's "bad acting" may set his masculine authenticity against the performativity of women, his masculinity has its own performative dimension. As moments of crisis occur, when his role as psychological leader of the family counts, nothing seems to faze Stanley, as daughter Kay (Elizabeth Taylor) says, because of the ease with which he slips on the persona of "father." He reasons Kay through her prewedding jitters, but, since he himself has just had a nightmare because of his own anxiety, this calm demeanor is a pose, showing how the mask of "father" is something he puts on and takes off (in much the same way that another Tracy character, Adam Bonner, demonstrates to his wife that he can turn his tears on or off at will to manipulate her in *Adam's Rib,* 1949). Something similar happens at each crisis. Stanley cannot fall asleep, worrying about Kay's financial future after she announces her intention to marry, but sleeps like a baby once he tells Ellie about his fears, causing her to have the restless night. Exasperated with the bickering over the wedding plans, he offers Kay money to elope and then, when his wife appears, pretends that he has been trying to talk their daughter out of the idea.

That fatherhood demands performativity of Stanley is just as apparent in the sequel. *Father's Little Dividend* (1951) is a virtual remake of the first film, with the birth of a grandchild substituting for the wedding as the ritual which defines Stanley as a "bad actor" when it comes to feminine spectacle and consumerism, in contrast to his "good acting" as a parent. The climax of *Father's Little Dividend* occurs when Stanley loses his six-month-old grandson while baby-sitting. At last discovering that the police have the child, Stanley must convince the desk sergeant that he is an attentive, responsible, and loving grandparent—all of which he is not—while hoping that the baby will not burst into tears at the sight of his grandfather, as the infant has done every other time the two have looked at each other. Humiliated by the police sergeant's threat to call his daughter and expose his irresponsibility, Stanley approaches the child, thinking in voiceover: "I dreaded the moment that he'd see me. I knew if he started crying, I was cooked." Instead, his grandson smiles, gurgles, and reaches out to him, which Stanley interprets, not as affection, but as the baby's going along with his masquerade. They bond through this performance: "From that time on I was his pigeon."

Father of the Bride and *Father's Little Dividend* conclude in similar fashion. After Stanley's "bad acting" brings him to a point of crisis that indicates his alienation from the family's feminine world, his daughter's affirmation immediately brings him back into the fold. In each film, the conclusion reiterates the breadwinner's centrality to the family, not as a husband (though Stanley's close relation with Ellie is never called into question by either film), but as a father. In each film, too, his renewed intimacy with his daughter, which crystallizes both his importance to home life and its value for him, follows a demonstration that fatherhood is performative, an ongoing process of acting out his masculine position as head of the family in the setting of home life, not work.

"The New American Domesticated Male"

It is not too difficult to see how the fifties' domestic mystique extended the "good picture" of the American home that World War II had glorified as an idealized representation of the nation itself. John Hersey wrote in 1942: "Perhaps this sounds selfish. It certainly sounds less dynamic than the Axis slogans. But home seems to most marines a pretty good thing to be fighting for. Home is where the good things are—the generosity, the good pay, the comforts, the democracy, the pie" (60). Variations of this simplistic appreciation of "home" were inserted into many Hollywood films made during the war years, and the movie cliché is significant now for its irony, since the war resulted in the extensive relocation of American men and women both domestically and abroad, effacing what had previously been strong regional and class values regarding family life and gender roles. Of course, not all these changes were immediately apparent on every Main Street in every small town throughout the United States. But as *Time* pointed out in 1954, "In a generation of change so rapid that the pace cannot be appreciated, the American self-picture has gone out of focus. . . . U.S. society today [is] very different from the picture of it that Americans carry in their heads" ("Freedom" 22). Because the society in which Americans actually lived was no longer synchronous with the one they imagined as "America," home acquired renewed value after the war as the metonymy of the nation. The uniformity of home life in popular representations of domesticity conveyed the unity and coherence that U.S. society itself lacked; and with home serving this function, its domestic mystique reinforced the breadwinner's similar role in representing a coherent and unified national character: the American male.

A 1954 humor piece in *Life* depicted "the new American domesticated male" by name, using a series of cartoons that purport to show how the breadwinner is, like Stanley Banks during the preparations for his daughter's wedding or his grandchild's birth, ill-suited for the domestic sphere because of his male nature. As in the two *Father* films, this article actually proves just the opposite, however, since its jokes demonstrate that the breadwinner fits into the home more comfortably, even more productively, than the homemaker herself, and with greater theatrical flair, too. For example, one cartoon hits an easy target in mocking the male's fascination with gadgets. "Lawn mowing," the caption reads, "now that it can be accomplished behind a noisy engine, gives a man a sense of power and a gadget to tinker with. He spends almost as much time fussing over his mower as he does mowing his suburban plot" (43). But turn the page, and we learn that the new American domesticated male actually brings a modern, technical mastery to the home, one contrasting to his wife's ineptitude with technology. "Cooking in an outmoded kitchen is possible for a woman, but it riles the efficiency expert that every man imagines he is. He wants convenience, and the latest laborsaving devices." In much the same way, "[t]esting when buying furniture might not occur to a wife, but a husband insists on quality, so he is a tester, label reader and comparative shopper" (45). For that matter, because of his professional life outside the home, the domesticated breadwinner cannot help but modernize his habitat: "Going modern involves educating his wife to a new point of view. He is accustomed to modern buildings in the city and to modern offices so that he is more receptive to mobiles and functional furnishings than she is likely to be" (42). The breadwinner, these cartoons show, not only realizes his masculinity through his domestication, but in his domicile represents his culture's modernity, while his wife stands for the opposite of modernism, his culture's traditionalism. The fifties male thus compares more than favorably to his wife as a consumer as well as a homemaker. He is, *Life* trumpets in its subtitle, "a boon to the household and a boom for industry."

The domestic male's expertise with machines and technology was an oft-repeated characteristic of the breadwinner when at home, and it helped to obscure the varying economic positions of real breadwinners within corporate America and their political subjection to a federal government that was growing increasingly larger, and getting more intrusive and paranoid as it did so. Even though many still considered their jobs "the mirror of their identity," in much the same way that "the family was for their wives" (Filene 169), fifties American men increasingly turned their sights inward to domestic life in reaction to the growing impersonality of the large corporations that employed them, whether in production lines or at desks. As *Life* reported: "Probably not since pioneer days, when men built their own log cabins, have they been so personally involved in their homes" ("New" 43).

Defining themselves through their position in domestic space gave breadwinners a sense of achievement and power as their family's provider, compensating for the anomie they experienced while working under the watchful eye of Old Man Routine (May 88). The home workshop in particular functioned as an escape from the dissatisfaction and alienation of corporate labor, as *Time* noted with a cover story in 1954:

> [T]he whole character of U.S. life has been undergoing a complex change. As mass-production techniques have broken jobs into smaller and smaller parts, the average American worker has often lost sight of the end product he is helping to build.... In the same way, the meaning of the tasks performed by white-collar employees and executives often becomes lost in the complexities of giant corporations; it is hard for them to see what they are really accomplishing. But in his home workshop, anyone from president down to file clerk can take satisfaction from the fine table, chair or cabinet taking shape under his own hands—and bulge with pride again as he shows them off to friends. ("Shoulder" 63)

As well as recognizing the extent to which home had successfully incorporated the masculine sphere of work, this passage suggests another reason the domestication of masculinity became so important. The do-it-yourself industry, like all the mass-consumption industries emerging in the fifties, brought out the homogeneity of the American character. "Americans, more than any other people," *Time* observed, "have always been a nation of how-toers, of putterers, tinkerers and inventors" ("Shoulder" 65). Conforming to the national profile, every breadwinner sawing and hammering away in the private space of his own home workshop on Sunday afternoon testified to the uniformity of—if I may pressure *Time*'s phrasing a bit by shifting its emphasis—"the *whole* character of U.S. life." In *Time*'s account, home functioned for men as a social leveler, eradicating the differences between clerks and executives, which *did* matter in very real economic terms, at least in the workplaces of corporate America, like General Motors, IBM, or Time-Life.

The era's hegemonic masculinity helped to foster the misleading impression of the United States' coherence after the war as a socially unified nation populated by an ever-growing, ever affluent middle class of average Americans like Johnny Forbes and Stanley Banks, thereby effacing the considerable difference in their economic status. Despite the actual division of the middle class, the fifties was dominated by the belief that, in Studs Terkel's words, a "new middle class had emerged" in the late 1940s with the end of World War II, insofar as "the great many" no longer "had to scuffle from one payday to the next," as they had done by necessity before the war (10). As one of the men Terkel interviewed puts it: "There came this great burst after the war, a very prosperous time. The working man got his own house, his car, his refrigerator, and became middle-class" (319). Spoken by a New Dealer turned Navy man turned lawyer, this view of a monolithic middle class getting bigger and richer after the war until it embraced the "whole" of America drastically oversimplified the composition of as well as the power relations within the U.S. class system, to be sure; but the enormous growth of the American middle class was perceived as the great social accomplishment of postwar life, and the male breadwinner personified that democratic achievement in his domesticity.

The Domestic Mistake?

At the same time that the breadwinner came to personify the national character, justifying that "good picture" of social entitlement for all, a "bad picture" of his eviscerated manhood kept erupting in representations of the culture's hegemonic masculinity to call its optimism into question. Fifties America exalted domesticity, equating *any* form of deviation from that norm with emasculation, but also worried that domesticity itself had resulted in, as *Look* put it, the "decline" of the white middle-class American male. In the first article of this series, one of the magazine's writers asked, "How did the American male get into this pit of subjection, where even his masculinity is in doubt?" (Moskin 80). The question was by no means rhetorical. Mounting evidence of the American male's "decline" could most readily be found in a doctor's office. High blood pressure, ulcers, alcoholism, boredom and depression, and heart disease all testified to the dangers of job-related stress or, as many writers interpreted it, to the breadwinner's debilitation caused by his pushing too hard to satisfy his wife's ambition and finance her consumerism.

References to the heavy physical toll breadwinning made on successful professional men abound in films produced in the middle of the decade. In *Executive Suite* (1954), Tredway president Avery Bullard dies from a stroke at age 56; he leaves his company's future direction uncertain because he has not yet designated a successor, his vice-president himself having but recently died at age fifty. In *The Man in the Gray Flannel Suit*, the president of the United Broadcasting System, Ralph Hopkins (Fredric March), has already had one "warning," so he now has his heart and blood pressure monitored regularly. In the same film, the head of public relations, Gordon Jenkins (Arthur O'Connell), is under doctor's orders to rest but, rather than cut down on his busy schedule, he installs a lounger in his office so that he can recline at his desk while working. And in *Patterns* (1956), corporate executive Bill Briggs (Ed Begley) suffers from an ulcer, "a pesky stomach disorder," as well as a bad heart, which kills him by the end of the film.

Such ailments are not limited to the upper echelon of big business but characterize the more typical American male, too. In *The Seven Year Itch*, book editor Richard Sherman (Tom Ewell) tries to stop smoking and drinking because of two different doctors' orders (one for each vice, no less), and in *It's Always Fair Weather* (1956), TV advertising executive Doug Hallerton (Dan Dailey) has an ulcer, requiring him to watch what he eats and drinks with fastidious care. Even schoolteacher Ed Avery (James Mason) in *Bigger than Life* (1956), who drives a cab part-time in secret in order to maintain his family's middle-class status, suffers from a mysterious, debilitating pain which turns out to be caused by "inflammation of the arteries." First reduced to a defenseless, pain-wracked body monitored and tested in the hospital, Ed is soon transformed, by overdosing on the drug cortisone, into an arrogant, self-absorbed big shot, and his drug abuse makes him psychotic, to the point where he tries to murder his family. It also takes little stretch of the imagination to include in this group of suffering breadwinners another advertising exec, Scott Carey (Grant Williams), the eponymous *Incredible Shrinking Man* (1957), who falls victim to a kind of anti-cancer, an illness resulting from his exposure to a lethal mixing of atomic radiation and DDT. Instead of causing malignant cells in his body to reproduce, this disease makes them radically diminish in size.

As these films illustrate with their sickly men, the breadwinner's much publicized physical malaise underscored the fragility of the male body in comparison to the female, the more so since "[w]hat had been defined as masculine maturity and understood as 'success' began to look, in the light of new findings, like a hazard to men's health" (Ehrenreich, *Hearts* 68). Men may have larger and stronger bodies, *Look* cautioned in a 1955 article, "[b]ut despite these superiorities, men are actually weaker than women—in health, longevity and other ways" (Frank 52). Attention to the American male's precarious situation was not confined to the popular press, either. Helen Mayer Hacker's 1957 article in the academic journal *Marriage and Family Living* claimed, with obvious understatement, "there are objective indices that all is not well with men" (228). Noting various expressions of discontent among her male patients, Hacker attributed their distress signals to the imbalance arising from the disparity between their actual lived experiences and the culture's norms. In her view, "[t]he urgency of the problem of impotence," always the implication of the media's and Hollywood's anxiety about the emasculated American male, arose from the widespread equation of virility with monogamous (and genital) heterosexuality as "an alternative to economic success in validating manhood." "Virility used to be conceived as a unilateral expression of male sexuality," she explained, "but is regarded today in terms of the ability to evoke a full sexual response on the part of the female" (231).

Hacker's observation about the popular definition of virility was clearly informed by the Kinsey reports on male and female sexuality. The findings of Kinsey's first volume on men, published with a modest first printing run in 1948, were highly publicized, quickly entering the public idiom as "the great topic" (Ives) and turning into a national best-seller. *The Nation* described the first book's influence with an obvious if undaunted metaphoric aptness: "It has stimulated a frank discussion of sex that has had the character of an explosion and has provided a wholesome release" (Gumpert 471). Men, the Kinsey Institute in Bloomington, Indiana, showed America, had active and varied sex lives. Among other moral and legal transgressions, they masturbated, had homosexual encounters, were promiscuous before marriage, adulterous afterward. So widespread was public interest that *Newsweek* even reported the moment "the Kinsey report had its network debut" on radio when Jack, a thirty-one-year-old male character on the venerable soap opera *One Man's Family*, cited Kinsey's confirmation of his own sexual awakening when a teenager: "I've never had such driving urges, such overpowering hungers, and such curiosity concerning girls as I had along about that age [16–19]. That was the very Vesuvius of my emotional needs, and I've just discovered that I'm not alone—the Kinsey report comes right out and confirms it" ("Kinsey" 52, brackets in original). If he had bothered to pause for a moment to ponder what Kinsey was *actually* telling him about his teenage experience, however, that character on *One Man's Family* would have realized, much to his chagrin, that it had been half a lifetime since he had experienced those volcanic eruptions, and that their ashes were now starting to cool, to say the least.

Recognition of the waning trajectory of male sexual ardor did not become fully apparent until Kinsey's companion volume on female sexuality appeared in 1953. The findings of the second report were even more widely publicized by the mainstream press, which stressed this unexpected difference between men and women according to Kinsey: the sexuality of men peaks in their late teens, *Time* reported, which was consequently "the height of their physical power for sexual activity," and then "the man's curve keeps on dropping, *i.e.*, his need for sexual activity generally declines while the woman's stays fairly high" ("5,940" 54). In its coverage, *Newsweek* even italicized the point so that no one would miss its troubling implication about male sexuality: *"Females are most sexually responsive in their late 20s and early 30s, and their capacity remains more or less constant into their 50s and 60s"* ("All" 70). *Newsweek*, in fact, considered Kinsey's report on women as explosive as a bomb dropped on the American public since the magazine went on, in the next issue, to compare it to the successful testing of the H-bomb by the Soviets during the same week ("Bombs" 57).

Brought to public attention by Kinsey and underscored by the experts' revelation that female sexuality outdistanced male performance in the same way that, physicians confirmed, the female body outlasted the male's, male sexual inadequacy became increasingly visible throughout the decade as the obvious problem of the modern American male's psychological plight. "In the United States," commented *Hush-Hush* magazine, an imitation of the notorious *Confidential*, "Kinsey found that all males—a total of 100 percent—not only had some sexual experience at the time of marriage but had by then actually passed the peak of sexual capacity" (Reed 58). This is the same kind of thinking that director Elia Kazan invoked, in his effort to protect *Baby Doll* (1956) from PCA cuts, when he defended Archie Lee Meighan's (Karl Malden) "sex frustration" as a point of pathos, not eros: "[E]very middle aged man," Kazan wrote, "is familiar with the sudden slump of ALL his powers that come (dismayingly) in his late forties."[5]

Although Hacker herself did not specifically refer to either of the two Kinsey reports, their findings had much to do with giving the new, more fully sexualized definition of virility its currency. The widely publicized publication of the second Kinsey volume's unsettling view of sexual difference raised the stakes of manhood, as Hacker indirectly observed when she noted that "masculinity is more important to men than femininity is to women, and that sexual performance is more inextricably linked to feelings of self-worth than even motherhood is to women." In response to this inflated and yet narrow ideal of masculinity, Hacker proposed that "homosexuality may be viewed as one index of the burdens of masculinity"—a "flight from masculinity" that indicates the confusing multiplication of cultural definitions of a "real man" (231).

That American men failed the test of manliness because of American women was a complaint repeated in the popular press again and again. The first article in *Look*'s series on the decline of the American male mentioned Hacker by name but missed the whole point of her analysis. "Today's American male," author Thomas J. Moskin claimed, "if the experts are right, has even lost much of his sexual initiative and control; some authorities believe that his capacity is being lowered" (78). Taking to task "women's new aggressiveness and demand for sexual satisfaction" (78) as the reason for "[t]he decline in male sexual potency," Moskin then turned around the implications of Kinsey's findings, arguing that the male's "withdrawing from sex relations" is not due to a biological clock but is another symptomatic defense—like "bachelorhood" and "homosexuality"—against the female-dominated society that fifties America had become following World War II (80). With a woman now regulating sexual contact, repressing "the male's recognized biological nature, which impels him to seek the company of a variety of females" (77), and then demanding that he direct his own pleasure toward her total satisfaction—for "she cannot accept compromises" (78)—it is small wonder that men were said to be suffering from "fatigue," "passivity," "anxiety," and "impotency" (78–79) or that, one expert warns, "our younger generation shows signs of being fagged out and of having lost 'the hunting instinct'" (78).

Given such a dismal picture, how could the hegemonic masculinity of "the new American domesticated male" make *any* claim to be representing the norm of the national character? Hacker's analysis helps to explain why representations of hegemonic masculinity, particularly when positioned in this new discursive setting of gender crisis that was excited by the popular press's widespread dissemination of Kinsey's findings, could easily incorporate ample reference to the "burdens" of breadwinning without in any way jeopardizing its centrality or diminishing its authority. Hacker argued that the culture's competing demands on men to be passive *and* aggressive, emotional *and* stoic, made masculinity a site of contradiction, with its incoherence felt in every area of a man's life. Far from standing in for all humankind to characterize "the general human condition," she pointed out, masculinity is variable for men because "their interpretation of the masculine role varies according to individual personality needs and social situations." It is also multiple in its social forms because "the norms of masculinity . . . (and, conversely, those of effeminacy) may vary among social groups, and multiple group participations may set up contradictions and inconsistencies in outlook" (227). What then unifies and gives coherence to masculinity, she concluded, is not a male's inborn nature but the socioeconomic role of men as the family breadwinner: "Everyone thinks he knows what is masculine, and how to recognize a 'real man,' but no one can give an adequate definition. It is neither money nor muscles. A woman sociologist offered this one: 'A real man is one who can take responsibility for a woman and their children.' While not probably in the forefront of men's consciousness, this definition is no doubt the traditional one" (233).

While Hacker ultimately turned to the era's hegemonic masculinity to find a "traditional"—and standardized—definition of manliness, her commentary nevertheless indicates why, if "neither money nor muscles" signify "a real man," representations of the breadwinner did not need to translate his hegemony into a healthy, powerful body. A weak body masked by the bland uniform attire of gray flannel suit, white dress shirt, and fedora was the primary visual index of the breadwinner's social position, in contradistinction to the exposure of the male body in representations of conservative and subordinated masculinities, especially in the movies, where muscles, more than money, functioned to mark deviations from the norm. For this reason, when incorporated in representations of home life, the experts' and the journalists' warnings about the damaging physical, psychological, and sexual consequences of the breadwinner's economic ambition on his body only characterized the ordinariness of hegemonic masculinity all the more—and functioned all the better in directing attention away from the social incoherence that commentators such as Lyndon could only explain as a "paradox."

The Seven Year Itch: Performance Anxiety

With its title supplying the name for the midlife crisis which, in Hacker's view, was symptomatic of the heavy burdens imposed upon masculinity, *The Seven Year Itch* outwardly plays upon the ambivalence informing the era's hegemonic masculinity. Just a few months before the film's premiere in 1955, for instance, *Look* complained: "Boys and men growing up today are much more confused about what they should and should not do to fulfill their masculine roles. Being uncertain, men face many conflicts, trying to be both tough and tender, successful but not ruthless, strong but not dominating, virile but not 'wolves'" (Frank 54). Richard Sherman, the hapless hero of *The Seven Year Itch*, is similarly unable to walk the fine line separating virility and wolfish behavior, and director Billy Wilder exploits Richard's midlife crisis to satirize the culture's domestication of masculinity, underscoring this breadwinner's emasculation while directing attention away from the economic premise of the film's plot. In charge of advertising for a press which specializes in using sex and violence to sell its twenty-five-cent paperbacks, Richard cannot convince his boss to give him vacation time because summer is the firm's busy season as it prepares the fall book list. Richard must therefore remain in New York City while his wife and son vacation without him in Maine. When asked by her small son why his father cannot accompany them to their summer cottage, Helen Sherman (Evelyn Keyes) replies matter-of-factly: "Your daddy has to stay in the hot city and make money."

Wilder and his cowriter George Axelrod use this situation as the basis for poking fun at the overactive and underworked libido of a "typical Manhattan husband" (as an anonymous voiceover identifies Richard Sherman in the film's prologue). With the cat away, mousy Richard dallies with fantasies of seducing his upstairs neighbor, an unnamed blonde referred to only as "The Girl" (Marilyn Monroe). In Axelrod's original Broadway play, Richard and The Girl finally do spend the night together, after which he renews his commitment to his wife and their marriage. The play's setting in 1952 means that the Shermans were married in 1945—presumably very quickly upon Richard's return from fighting in WWII—so his "itch" seven years later specifically indicates the "paradoxical" masculine discontent which followed upon the postwar rush to get married and settle down. Filmed three years after the play's premiere, and extensively revised to conform to the requirements of the Production Code, which forbade humorous treatment of adultery, the film version of *The Seven Year Itch* turns the original play on its head by recounting Richard's *failure* to have sex with The Girl.

As a consequence, the film represents his masculinity in a complete state of domestic containment, with his desire to stray from the conjugal bed relegated to the kind of daydreaming described by Lyndon's article in *Woman's Home Companion*. When first alone in his apartment, Richard has three fantasies which he addresses to his absent wife because they make him the object of uncontrollable female desire. In one he recounts to an imaginary Helen how his secretary, Miss Morris, is so infatuated with him that she ripped open his shirt in the office, and his exposed back appears to give him the same sex appeal that a torn T-shirt gave Marlon Brando in *A Streetcar Named Desire* (1951); in another, how the night nurse, Miss Finch, had to be pulled off him by doctors and orderlies the time he was in hospital, evoking the sex scenes of Hemingway's novel *A Farewell to Arms* (remade as *Force of Arms* in 1951); and in a third, how even Helen's best friend, Elaine, tried to seduce him on the beach in imitation of the famous love scene between Deborah Kerr and Burt Lancaster in *From Here to Eternity* (1953). All three fantasies allow Richard to imagine illicit sexual frenzy while repudiating it himself. "Although I have tremendous personal magnetism," he concludes for Helen from these self-serving daydreams, "I also have tremendous character."

By contrast, after he invites The Girl downstairs to his flat for a drink, Richard engages in a fantasy that puts him in a more active sexual role. He does not visualize this daydream for Helen's benefit, but, like the earlier ones, it still carries the implication that his fantasy life is a series of gender performances drawn from the movies. He imagines himself with The Girl at the piano, stimulating a scene of sophisticated seduction in his mind which has him dressed in a smoking jacket like a suave Rex Harrison while speaking in the style of the potboilers that his firm publishes for two bits: "Now I'm going to take you in my arms and kiss you, very quickly and very hard." When he tries to act out this scene in real life, though, he and The Girl are playing an impromptu duet of "Chopsticks," and he makes his sexy-Rexy move only to push her off the piano bench. Embarrassed by his ineptitude as well as frightened by his desire, he asks her to leave; as she goes out, The Girl turns back to say sweetly, "I think you're very nice." Once she is gone, Richard ruminates on his guilt: "Nice? You're not nice. You're crazy, that's what you are. You're running amuck. Helen's gone for one day and you're running amuck! Smoking. Drinking. Picking up girls. Playing 'Chopsticks.' You're not going to live through the summer. Not like this, you're not." As he ponders the decadence from which his body is already starting to suffer, Richard stares into a mirror where he fantasizes that he looks just like the picture of Dorian Gray. This terrifying image of his body dissipating before his very eyes causes him to shudder in horror, concluding what is effectively the film's first act. The next day, even though nothing actually happened with The Girl, he guiltily imagines her going public about his sexual aggression, revealing on television for the whole world to hear that he attacked her while they played "Chopsticks": "Suddenly he turned on me," she says to the TV camera in his fantasy. "His eyes were frothing at the mouth, just like the Creature from the Black Lagoon!"

With its satire of the breadwinner's libido revised to meet the demands of PCA censorship, the film's gags require Richard to be completely inept as a seducer, making one wonder just how strong his desire (or ability) to stray really is. His failure to bed The Girl, however, does not automatically make the film version of *The Seven Year Itch* an "emasculation" of an original sexier text, as trade reviews complained.[6] Rather, the censorship heightened the film's own historical location in mid-fifties debates about hegemonic masculinity, particularly as prompted by the two Kinsey reports on male and female sexuality. In both play and film Richard is reading for publication the scholarly work of psychiatrist Ludwig Brubaker (Oscar Homolka), whose tome *Of Man and the Unconscious*—with chapter titles such as "The Repressed Urge in the Middle Aged Male: Its Roots and Its Consequences" and "The Sporadic Infidelity Pattern in the Married Male, or The Seven Year Itch"—clearly means to situate the "new American domesticated male's" masculinity crisis within the context of Kinsey's research on male sexuality. The play makes the reference explicit, since Richard's office has mocked-up a cover for Brubaker's book—its title changed to *Of Sex and Violence*—with the tag phrase "Hotter than the Kinsey Report" (Axelrod 337). In the film Richard keeps the new title but drops the overt Kinsey reference in favor of a graphic picture of what he describes as "a man terrorizing a young and beautiful girl." However, awareness of Kinsey still permeates the film in numerous other ways, as when Richard reads brief passages aloud from Brubaker's lofty volume, based on a survey of 18,000 marriages, or talks to him about case studies mentioned in the book. Richard's reading of Brubaker's book, for that matter, also frames each of the fantasy sequences preceding The Girl's arrival in his apartment for drinks.

The film's recurring reference to Kinsey shapes its satire of domesticated masculinity by exerting another highly productive censoring force upon its representation of the breadwinner's midlife sexual crisis. In its difference from the play, the film version of *The Seven Year Itch* does not exactly capitulate to the industry's censors so much as engage in ideological collusion with the culture at large: by transforming the "seven year itch"—originally, as in *Pitfall*, an urge in the domesticated male to shake loose of the binding ties of middle-class marriage—into male anxiety about virility and, even more importantly, about aging. The two Kinsey reports on male and female sexuality thus provided the crucial impetus for Wilder's reinterpretation of Richard Sherman's seven year itch as a satire of fifties hegemonic masculinity. The Broadway play clearly had in mind the Kinsey report on men, and the film version went into production after the publication of the more notorious companion volume on women. On the face of it, though, as Bruce Babington and Peter Williams Evans note, the film seems totally indifferent to the second Kinsey report (*Affairs* 220). While it not only follows the play in having Brubaker's research encompass only men and not women, truth to tell, the film also seems even *more* uninterested in female sexuality than the play, primarily in order to accommodate Marilyn Monroe's dumb-blonde screen persona.

Where the film's recognition of the Kinsey report on women makes itself felt is in the revised characterization of Richard Sherman, who now registers, in the very gesture of denying it through his active fantasy life, the effects of Kinsey's revelation about the asymmetrical curve of male and female sexuality. "Women have been throwing themselves at me for years," Richard boasts to a fantasized Helen, assuming that this state of things is testimony to *his* sexual vitality, not to *theirs*. He can boast about his restraint all he wants, but the crick in his neck every time he looks up at The Girl is a continual reminder of his middle-aged body (though he is only thirty-nine) sagging under the burden of breadwinning. However, he projects this realization onto Helen and interprets it as a biological fact of sexual difference. Why is Helen worried enough to telephone him at ten o'clock in the evening?

> She probably figures she isn't as young as she used to be. She's 31 years old. One of these days she's going to wake up and find her looks are gone, and then where will she be? Well, no wonder she's worried, especially since I don't look a bit different than when I was twenty-eight. It's not my fault that I don't. It's just a simple biological fact: women age quicker than men. Yeah, I probably won't look any different when I'm sixty. I have that kind of face. Everyone'll think she's my *mother*.

In the play, The Girl is the one who compliments Richard on his youthful-looking appearance, remarking that he looks twenty-eight, whereas on film what attracts her is his marital status because that means he won't harass her with a proposal, which, with the innocent logic characteristic of Monroe's dumb-blonde persona, she considers worse than being hit on. "You look married," The Girl observes. ". . . I think it's wonderful that you're married. . . . With a married man it's all so simple. I mean, it can't possibly get drastic." And Richard replies, "I'm probably the most married man you will ever know," without realizing, in his effort to please The Girl, that his confession reveals a more significant reason for the sexual incompatibility between the unattainable blonde and the aging lothario, namely, that he *likes* being married—perhaps because his domicile makes *him* feel safe and secure. "I like this house," Richard announces to himself at the start of the film, when he returns home for his first night of summer bachelorhood. "Why does Helen talk about moving? It's peaceful with everyone gone. It sure is peaceful. No Howdy Doody; no Captain Video. No smell of cooking or 'What happened at the office today, darling?' What happened at the office? Well, I shot Mr. Brady in the head, made violent love to Miss Morris and set fire to three thousand copies of *Little Women*. That's what happened at the office. What *can* happen at the office?"

In their unsympathetic analysis of Richard's domesticity, Babington and Evans claim that the Sherman household represents more of a trap than a home for him. They cite his speech about liking his home in particular to show that, with its series of negative statements, Richard's welcoming of peace and quiet actually indicates "disenchantment with his roles as husband and father" (*Affairs* 222). However, they fail to mention the rhetorical question which Richard asks at the end of his paean to his own domesticity. "What *can* happen at the office?" sets up the contrast between the uneventful passivity of Richard's life as a Man in a Gray Flannel Suit, which gives evidence of his failure to find support for his masculinity at work, and his expectation of achieving something more fulfilling at home. To be sure, Richard imagines the liberation of his masculinity from domesticity through the most conventional of sexual scripts, as his fantasy of what *could* happen at work, like his movie-inspired daydreams of sexual frenzy, bears out. But regardless of his decided lack of originality, home clearly functions for the film as the primary site of male fantasy. As Babington and Evans more rightly observe, the arrangement of the brownstone itself maps out "a kind of polymorphous world that Sherman cannot escape: in the basement the lustful janitor, the household's own 'Creature from the Black Lagoon'; on the top floor two interior decorators (the usual code for homosexuals); and renting the Kaufmann's [*sic*] place above him, the overwhelmingly sensuous Girl" (224).

More than just laying out a landscape of the repressed male unconscious as the fifties imagined it to be, the brownstone maps out the social contours of Richard's hegemonic masculinity. The building's obvious reproduction of a social ladder of occupations supporting domesticity—working-class janitor at the bottom, professional decorators at the top—fashions a hierarchy of masculinities which supports Richard Sherman's position as "a typical Manhattan husband." The janitor, Krahulic, another invention of the film, not only helps to maintain the material comforts of the Shermans' middle-class life, but, with his own dallying while his wife is away, crudely copies Richard's summer bachelorhood, implying the ethnic working-class man's willing conformity to a middle-class construction of masculinity—and his greater skill at perfecting it, since Krahulic, not restricted by the breadwinner's marital ethic, succeeds in having a summer fling. Likewise, "the two guys on the top floor," as Richard refers to them, "interior decorators or something," are never seen, indicating their banishment, because of their homosexuality, to the uppermost floor of the building: out of sight, out of mind, out of the question.

And The Girl? Subletting the Kaufmans' flat one story above, because of the structural history of the building (their two flats were once joined together) she has the most direct and private access to Richard's flat (and, hence, to his fantasy life) through the boarded-up staircase. Richard's close proximity to her sexuality surely helps to privilege his masculinity over both Krahulik's and the gay couple's. But Richard and The Girl actually bond most intimately over popular culture (when they go to the movies to see *The Creature from the Black Lagoon*) and consumerism (she performs in a television commercial, while he directs the promotion of twenty-five-cent paperbacks), not sex. Moreover, what draws The Girl down to the first-floor flat is not Richard's virility as an older man, as in the play, but his air-conditioning, which he displays as a proud consumer and which she covets because of the oppressive summer heat. The absent Kaufmans themselves, by contrast, see no need to buy an air-conditioning unit for their flat. They travel to Europe for the summer and invest in art, not mass-produced commodities. By way of their association with high culture and good taste, as well as their probable coding as Jewish or Germanic, the Kaufmans disdain ordinary consumerism to imply their important social difference from the Waspish, middle-class Shermans as an old-moneyed (and absent) upper class controlling capital. When The Girl appears in the Kaufmans' place, that difference gets effaced and along with it, the implication that the Shermans' domestic life on the first floor structurally supports and so ideologically enables the Kaufmans' good taste on the second. Because her eroticized figure allows the film to represent Richard's seven year itch solely as an effect of biology, the midlife crisis that sets in when the male's ability to perform sexually begins to wane, The Girl deflects attention away from the cultural support of his hegemonic position as the typical middle-class, middle-aged husband: the fact that Richard's authority as a "normal" male depends on his obtaining the implicit endorsement of other, different men like Krahulik, Kaufman, *and* those two interior decorators.

To make this point even more obvious, the prologue, set among the Native American population of Manhattan island, depicts the seven year itch as a universal condition of married men going back to a time prior to the founding of the nation. The prologue invites audiences to view Richard's midlife crisis through the presumption that virility is tantamount, as Hacker suggested, to sexual potency, thereby obscuring the film's more implicit revelation that masculinity is a historical social position. Setting up this imaginary universal norm, the prologue allows the film to draw its currency from the culture's anxiety about the debilitating effects of domesticity on the middle-class breadwinner's sexuality, while simultaneously detaching his position as "a typical Manhattan husband" from its social setting in a politicized structure of masculinities.

From this safer vantage point, *The Seven Year Itch* can then audaciously confirm the emasculation of America's breadwinners by the culture's domestic mystique. However, while made the object of satire, Richard's castration anxiety also erupts in unexpected outbursts of anger as well as in his highly theatricalized sexual fantasies, and these are hard to ignore. In his recent book on 1950s comedy, Ed Sikov does not analyze *The Seven Year Itch* at length but he touches on Richard's anger, mentioning a moment early in the film. As Richard slips on one of his son's roller skates and hits his head on the floor, Sikov explains, "His reaction is especially strong . . . he growls murderously, as if his anger and frustration toward his son [have] been building for some time. Throughout the film, Sherman's reactions toward his wife and child are much more extreme than their behavior toward him" (127).

The climax of *The Seven Year Itch* makes Richard's anger even more apparent. After fantasizing that his wife has been unfaithful with family friend Tom MacKenzie (Sonny Tufts), Richard imagines that Helen, dressed in film noir regalia, comes back to their flat to shoot him ("five times in the back and twice in the belly") because she suspects he has slept with The Girl. Actually, though, Richard believes that he is not attractive enough to give his wife reason to be jealous. "Let's face it," he tells The Girl. "No pretty girl in her right mind wants me. She wants Gregory Peck." In a speech written for the film, The Girl replies with a ringing endorsement of Richard's hegemonic masculinity:

> You and your imagination. You think every girl's a dope. You think a girl goes to a party and there's some guy, a great big lunk in a fancy striped vest, strutting around like a tiger, giving you that "I'm so handsome, you can't resist me" look. And from this she's supposed to fall flat on her face. Well, she doesn't fall flat on her face. . . . But there's another guy in the room. Way over in the corner. Maybe he's kind of nervous and shy and perspiring a little. First you look past him. But then you kind of sense he's gentle and kind and worried, and he'll be gentle with you, nice and sweet. That's what's *really* exciting. . . . If I were your wife, I'd be very jealous of you. I'd be very, *very* jealous.

Then, who should arrive at the Sherman apartment while Richard is recovering on the couch from his imaginary wounds but MacKenzie himself, and the big lunk is even wearing a striped vest! Wrongly assuming that his imaginary rival has come with Helen's request for a divorce, Richard exclaims that she still loves *him:* "And you know why she loves me?" he screams. "She loves me because I'm sweet and gentle and worried and nervous and shy and tender!" That avowal of gentle masculinity out of the way, in another deviation from the play, Richard punches MacKenzie, knocking him out cold.

This surprising display of violence on Richard's part brings the film to its conclusion. It substitutes for the forbidden sexual transgression with The Girl, just as it externalizes his rage at Helen—which his film noir daydream initially internalizes when he imagines his wife shooting him—without directing it at her. The effect of this double displacement seems positively liberating for Richard since, after flexing his muscles to prove his manhood, he then makes what is, for this film, a much more daring move than going to bed with The Girl: he decides to demand a two-week vacation from his boss so that he too can go to Maine. However, as he runs out of the apartment in his stockinged feet, hurrying to make the train that will take him to his wife and son, Richard asks The Girl to call his office for him, thereby avoiding a direct confrontation with his boss over the latter's refusal to let him take a vacation.

Pumping up his ego, Richard's display of fisticuffs may give the appearance of resolving his midlife crisis, since it returns him to his wife and son, but actually it allows him to disavow, through his performance of "virility," the economic subjection which caused his emasculation in the first place, and which the film encourages us to attribute to his family, not to his boss, who is himself enjoying his own freedom from domesticity as another summer bach-

Figure 8.
Richard Sherman (Tom Ewell) clutches his stomach in pain after fantasizing that his
wife has shot him, as The Girl (Marilyn Monroe) looks on.

elor. The "paradox" of Richard's middle-class status, which gives him the
position of social power without making it material, drives his sexual fantasies
and anger alike, which is why they are comparable as performances of sex
and violence; but his performativity is not liberating (certainly not in the way
transvestism is in Wilder's later *Some Like It Hot*) because, confined to the
home, it cannot disturb the social hierarchy which the structure of the brownstone reproduces. As *The Seven Year Itch* imagines it, hegemonic masculinity
does all the work in stabilizing the social order but cannot enjoy any of the
dividends.

The Man in the Gray Flannel Suit: A Recipe for Success

The social incoherence masked by the era's hegemonic masculinity is made
even more pronounced in the character who gave a fictional body to The Man
in the Gray Flannel Suit: Tom Rath (Gregory Peck), the hero of the 1956 film
by that name. While *The Man in the Gray Flannel Suit* outwardly works to
reconcile what are, in effect, the class imbalances underwriting Tom's identification with hegemonic masculinity, it dramatizes his exemplary position by
placing him in a state of moral paralysis, the origin of which the film's narrative

attributes to the Second World War. Like *Pitfall*, *The Man in the Gray Flannel Suit* draws on the same biography for hegemonic masculinity which Lyndon's article in *Woman's Home Companion* puts forward as the norm of American men everywhere: the postwar family man whose domesticated masculinity in the present can be understood only when set against the historic event of the war in his past. However, because they were produced at different points in the culture's ongoing renegotiation of hegemonic masculinity after World War II, these two films also register significantly different inflections of the breadwinner's crisis. Released in 1948, when the culture's need to assimilate the returning soldier into home life was still of pressing concern, *Pitfall* obscures its postwar setting in order to project the continuity of domestic ideology as the ground of masculinity, even in wartime. By contrast, released in 1956 when domestic ideology had come to dominate the representation of hegemonic masculinity, *The Man in the Gray Flannel Suit* makes the war experience of its protagonist more prominent in order to dramatize the discontinuity between the burdens of masculinity in wartime and afterward as its primary means of marking out the difference between Tom Rath's complex psychological interior and his relatively straightforward social exterior as the exemplary gray-flannel worker.

Following its source in the best-selling novel by Sloan Wilson, published the year before, the film version of *The Man in the Gray Flannel Suit* shuttles back and forth in time between the present (1955) and the past (1945), using this flashback structure to dramatize how the war appears to have effected an unbreachable chasm between Tom and Betsy Rath (Jennifer Jones), which manifests itself in their home life. Betsy does not believe "the war is over—forgotten," as Tom assures her it is for him, because "ever since the war," she insists, ". . . I don't know. It's just that you've lost your guts and all of a sudden I'm ashamed of you." In a reversal of the expected gender roles, Betsy fuels Tom's ambition, while he prefers to remain in what he calls "an absolutely safe spot," the unnamed foundation where he works for $7,000 a year. Tom fears taking undue chances with his career, justifying his caution, he admits, in the interest of loving his family perhaps "too much." Betsy therefore has to prod him into taking action every step of the way. For example, she hates their house because it smells of "defeat," but he does not have the confidence in his earning potential to finance a new one with a mortgage. So she takes the lead herself. Selling the house, she moves the family into the antiquated and mortgaged home bequeathed to Tom by his grandmother, and schemes to get the land rezoned so that she can break up the estate into lots for a housing development.

Likewise, Betsy goads Tom into accepting a new job in public relations at the United Broadcasting Company, and then has to press him into asking for a higher salary than the one offered. Once there, he has to deal with the arrogance of his superior, Bill Ogden. Threatened by Tom's rapport with the company president, Ralph Hopkins, Ogden repeatedly humiliates Tom, accusing him of doing "awful" work on a speech he has been assigned to write and preventing Hopkins from seeing it. When Hopkins gives Tom a version of the same speech that he and Ogden have been drafting, Tom wants to safeguard his new position in the corporation by saying exactly what he thinks Hopkins wants to hear. "This is a loaded situation with all kinds of angles to it," Tom tries to explain to his wife. "I didn't want to get in this rat race and I'd be a fool not to play it the way everyone else does." "I wanted you to go out and fight for something again—like the man I married," she returns. "Not to turn into a cheap, slippery yes-man. . . . Because with a decent man there isn't any peace of mind without honesty." Betsy is, her husband realizes, braver than he: "Nothing ever scared you, did it?" he asks her at another point in the film. "Only you," she replies.

Betsy has reason to be scared. Tom worries about his children's obsession with violence and death without realizing that they reflect his own morbidity. At the same time that it recounts Tom's distance from Betsy and his attempts to negotiate the power relations of his new job in public relations at UBC within the limits of his moral integrity, *The Man in the Gray Flannel Suit* also follows his reveries, which obsessively return to events that occurred at the end of World War II, when he fought on both the European and Pacific fronts. Betsy is correct; the war is not yet over for Tom. Wartime appears to be the point in time when he experienced the emotional intensity lacking in his present life. Tom remembers the war as a moment of uncontrollable desire, in the form of his illicit affair with Maria (Marisa Pavan), but also as a period of unrelieved and unrelenting violence, in the form of seventeen senseless and brutal killings that he committed in the name of duty. Not only did he knife a young German soldier in order to steal a coat to keep from freezing to death, but Tom also accidentally blew up his best buddy with a hand grenade. What Tom represses in the present, then, are not memories of the war—he vividly remembers them in these flashback sequences—but their affect, particularly the anger which remains as the residue of his war experience, a time of adultery and murder.

When coupled with the plot contrivance of Tom's discovering that Maria bore his illegitimate son after he left her to go fight in the Pacific, the flashback narrative then persuades us to conclude that the war explains his present anxiety about taking risks. "I was what we have to have in our country, what they call a citizen soldier," Tom tells Betsy when she finally gets him to talk about the difference she has sensed in him since his return. "One day a man's catching the 8:26 and then suddenly he's killing people, and then a few weeks later he's catching the 8:26 again. It'll be a miracle if it didn't change him in some way." Later, when confessing and trying to justify his infidelity during his time away, he elaborates about the violence required of him by the war.

> *Tom:* I don't know how to make you realize the way things were then. Nobody knows who wasn't in the war. I killed seventeen men I was actually looking at.

Looking right straight at them. Not enemies at a distance that I couldn't see but persons. Persons like you see on the train and the elevator. I cut a German boy's throat to get his coat. I killed my best friend with a grenade. It was an accident, but he was blown open down the front just the same. Was having a child worse than things like that?

    Betsy: I don't know. Only the child has happened to me.

    Tom: And when I met this girl I was sure that I'd never see you again. I was certain that I'd be killed in the next action. And I was scared. More than you can imagine. I can't tell you the terror and the hopelessness that I felt.

The dialogue here differentiates Tom's and Betsy's war experiences according to their gender. "Only the child happened to me," she says. A woman like Betsy stayed home, able to evade the truth of what happens to a man like her husband, who had been sent away to do battle with "the terror and the hopelessness." The brutality required of him during the war appears to be Tom's prime excuse for his infidelity, just as repression of that violence, committed not in acts of valor but in the normal mixed-up course of events, motivates his present passivity. In 1955, his life as husband and father are neatly compartmentalized according to an opposition of the past (with its emotional intensity) and the present (with its boredom regulated by Old Man Routine) because Tom has never fully adjusted to returning home, although he goes through all the right motions so as to convince his family and his employer that he has done so. He is now so repressed—an effect exaggerated all the more by Peck's stiff, uncomfortable performance—that, appropriately enough for a man who lives in his memories, the site where his anger appears to reveal its masking is, symptomatically, his own surname: *(w)rath.*

    In calling attention to his repressed anger, I don't mean to turn Tom Rath into an Americanized version of the angry young men noisily pushing their way to the forefront of British drama and fiction at about this same time. Tom's anger lacks their passion as well as their motivation in "class hostility[, which] was suppressed and twisted into new forms of sexual hostility" (Segal 82). But while The Man in the Gray Flannel Suit comes across as every bit the stuffed shirt in comparison to the volatile, brutish Angry Young Man exploding in rage on the other side of the Atlantic, his own anger is no less a register of the social tensions which this figure served to embody and to give every appearance of resolving.

    The Hollywood Reporter's trade review, a good indication of how the studio directed *The Man in the Gray Flannel Suit* to its audience, helps to articulate the terms by which the film was received upon its release as effective social commentary. Comparing the film favorably to *The Best Years of Our Lives,* the review observes:

Like that film, it is filled with disturbing and thought provoking social comment (though with no political propaganda) and its situation will come close to home to almost every person in the audience.... In its larger sense, the film shows America (in very personal terms) standing at the moment of crisis where all great organizations have stood at their climax. Has it become so organized that only the professional yes-men, the courtiers and the unprincipled robots can happily adapt themselves to it? ... [T]he film concludes that human decency is more important than success in this era when either has been difficult to maintain. (Moffitt, *Man*)

Perhaps one forgets today that, while The Man in the Gray Flannel Suit exemplified the average white-collar worker, he was also no paragon of integrity but a man who had sold out for the sake of a buck, "someone who was sacrificing his individuality to become a part of the new more faceless middle class" (Halberstam 526). The film version of *The Man in the Gray Flannel Suit* tries to have it both ways, though, valuing Tom for his representativeness as the typical breadwinner, which implicates him in the careerism signified by his gray flannel uniform, while distinguishing him from the pack of corporate yes-men by virtue of his moral singularity. He is, after all, played by Gregory Peck, the star who could still project, in the words of a *Look* magazine cover story appearing a few months after the film's premiere, a "tall, dark, and dignified" persona, even after he had left his wife for a younger woman. The film takes pains through its three plot lines—one involving his marriage, one his career, one his inheritance, with all three pivoting around the same question of his honesty—to establish Tom Rath's decency as the hallmark of his individuality. At the same time, the film has him bear the standard of suburban commuters everywhere, so that he can be instantly legible as the quintessential American man of the fifties: "the young white-collar hero who must meet the challenges that confront nearly every man" ("Man," *Look* 104).

Even more so than in the novel, on film *The Man in the Gray Flannel Suit* invests Tom Rath with his connotation of ordinariness as a suburban commuter trying to make ends meet by contrasting him with other male characters whose ethnicity functions to marginalize any impact they might have as alternatives to Tom's hegemonic position as "a young white-collar hero." During his first day on the job at UBC, when he runs into his old army pal, Caesar Gardella (Keenan Wynn), the man who introduced him to Maria in Italy, Tom comments, "We're working for the same management again," without pausing to notice the difference in their positions either within the firm or their society. (Nor, for that matter, does Tom consider the implications of his glib comparison of the U.S. government to a national broadcasting system.) Gardella is an elevator operator who, with his wife Gina, Maria's cousin, has been supporting Tom's former mistress and illegitimate child; but they can no longer afford to continue doing so, and this financial exigency prompts Gardella to breach the implied caste system of the company and approach Tom in order to take advantage of an old familiarity which no longer applies to either man's life in the present.

Similarly, when Tom deals with Judge Bernstein (Lee J. Cobb) about his grandmother's estate and asks him to look into the dispute over her will, the film turns the complex, introspective Semitic intellectual of the novel into a folksy and sentimental Jewish wise man, complete with Yiddish inflections and indigestion. Acting on Tom's behalf when his grandmother's former retainer, Edward Schultz, claims to have a later will leaving him the house, the judge uncovers Schultz's fraud and confirms Tom's honesty, which Betsy has challenged when she berates her husband for trying to play all the angles at work. Bernstein and Tom bond over their triumphant exposure of Schultz, who is, significantly enough, not only another ethnically identified male, but also the only character in the film who incites Tom into expressing his anger. When Schultz insults his late grandmother after the Raths arrive to occupy her house, Tom grabs Schultz by the lapels, throws him out, and then quickly calls Bernstein to get legal advice about the will.

As is the case with Gardella, Bernstein's deference to Tom validates the latter's moral *and* social position. Just on the basis of a simple phone conversation with him about the contested will, when Tom exclaims, "I hope nobody else dies and leaves me anything," the judge concludes, "He must be quite a character!" At the end of the film, after agreeing to handle the legal side of Tom's financial arrangement for the illegitimate son in Italy, the judge goes so far as to exclaim what a privilege it has been to meet the Raths. He does not say why exactly, but presumably it is because of Tom's integrity in not deserting the Italian waif and Betsy's resolution not to divorce her husband because of his ten-year-old infidelity. "It must have been on such a day as this that the poet was moved to sing, 'God's in his heaven, all's right with the world,'" Judge Bernstein concludes to his secretary right before the film cuts to its closing shot of the Raths leaving together, secure once again in their marriage. The film lets this allusion to Browning's *Pippa Passes* go by without awareness of any irony in that famous and oft-quoted line, and the omission stands out all the more because in the novel Tom himself thinks about this very quotation, engraved on a stone bench on his grandmother's property, still remembering the "bitterness" in his mother's voice when she read the verse aloud to him thirty years before (S. Wilson 17).

The ethnicity of Gardella, Bernstein, and Schultz places them at the margins of the film's social field, and this subordination helps to authorize Tom's hegemonic position over them. More significantly, the film also contrasts Tom with powerful Ralph Hopkins—the president of UBC, a character reportedly modeled on Roy Larsen, a founder of Time-Life (Halberstam 524), though he is just as likely to evoke David Sarnoff of RCA—with the apparent aim of subordinating the businessman's drive to the breadwinner's domesticity. Hopkins's failure in his domestic life vindicates Tom's own success in that area, although to make this comparison stick, the film has to condense the many arguments between Hopkins and his wife and daughter that occur in the novel, focusing their conflict more single-mindedly around the issue of the business tycoon's irresponsibility as parent and husband. "She's your daughter, too," Helen Hopkins (Ann Harding) reminds her husband when begging him to intercede in their daughter Susie's reckless existence, "and you've got to give her the same attention you give to a business deal or new station or Sunday night program." Then Hopkins gets the same criticism from the other side of the generation gap. "It's really stupid the way you live," his daughter arrogantly informs him. "Working all the time ever since I can remember. You must either have a guilt complex or you're a masochist." Such a double-barreled attack on Hopkins does not play fair with the character but it is crucial to the film's strategy of using the business tycoon to validate Tom's integrity as a domesticated breadwinner, one who takes his responsibilities as husband and father much more seriously than Hopkins has done.

Rather than confront the social, political, and moral differences between Tom and Hopkins, the film version of *The Man in the Gray Flannel Suit* tries to turn the latter into an apostle of the former's hegemonic masculinity. In the novel Hopkins hires Tom, planning to groom him for a position of power in the company; in the film, the elder man's mentoring of the younger quickly turns into surrogate fathering because Tom reminds Hopkins of his own estranged son Bobby, who died in the war: "the same eyes and mouth, the same kind of smile." Hopkins boasts several times in the film that Bobby refused to take advantage of his privileged social position, turning down a guaranteed commission and instead joining up as an enlisted man like everyone else, including Tom. This detail further associates Tom with Hopkins's son, thereby enabling a paternal relation between the tycoon and his younger employee to obscure their class difference all the more. After he witnesses the disintegration of his own family, Hopkins orders Tom to spend time with the kids, even to kick in the TV to get their attention: "Don't let anything get in the way of spending time with your family." The elder man elaborates:

> You know where I made my mistake. And yet . . . somebody's got to dedicate himself to it. Big successful businesses just aren't built by men like you, nine to five and home and family. You live on them but you never build one. Big successful businesses are built by men like me, who give everything they've got to it, and live it, body and soul, lift it up regardless of anybody or anything else. Without men like me there wouldn't be any big successful businesses. (*Pause.*) My mistake was in being one of those men.

At the end of the film, after his reconciliation with Betsy, Tom backs off from following in Hopkins's footsteps, refusing to leave his distraught wife for an important business trip to Los Angeles.

> *Tom:* I have to be home with my family this evening. Remember those nine-to-five fellows you were talking about? I'm afraid I'm one of them.
> *Hopkins:* I see. No, no need to be sorry. . . . We have to have both kinds, you know.

One can't do anything without the other. And if I had my choice again, I have a feeling that's what I'd be. Nine-to-five, home, family.

Incredibly, Tom's boss—the president of a national broadcasting company, remember, a man who does not hide his political ambitions—not only accepts at face value an underling's refusal to obey him, but he goes on to tell this employee that putting family first over the organization (and its product) is the far, far better thing to do for the company!

In actuality, while Hopkins appears to validate Tom's priorities of home and family life over career advancement, he himself steadfastly remains one of those old-fashioned inner-directed business giants, "who give everything they've got to it, and live it, body and soul." His long speech quoted above seems to confess that if he had to do it again he would be more like Tom, but it actually celebrates Hopkins's single-minded drive and ambition. Representing the ideal of what the tycoon would like to be, "nine-to-five, home, family," Tom vindicates the domestic values which Hopkins himself has steadfastly abjured. The film may therefore give Tom's hegemonic masculinity all the moral points but it does not disguise the fact that Hopkins's conservative masculinity still retains and exercises what this domesticated breadwinner lacks: real social, economic, and political power—in a single word, money. "I'm not interested in money," Susie Hopkins taunts her father when he tries to get her to appreciate the enormity of what she will inherit when he dies. "I think money's a bore." "No sane person is interested in money simply as money," her father replies. "But one thing it is not; it is not something any intelligent person can consider a bore."

As the *Reporter*'s review concludes, *The Man in the Gray Flannel Suit* opts for "moral decency" over "success," and this resolution endorses Tom's choosing his family over his career. But just what is it exactly that Tom Rath does at UBC? In the film it's hard to know. In the book, he is a grant and speech writer, hired as Hopkins's personal assistant and specifically charged to work on the tycoon's tentative foray into politics; we can see Tom plying his trade at various points throughout the story. The movie version gives Tom the same assignment but seems more interested in his labor primarily as an occasion for testing his integrity; furthermore, he ultimately resolves his dilemma not in the office, but at home and by way of his wife's moral authority, when Betsy tells him off just for thinking of being dishonest with Hopkins about the speech they are working on. That the film comes up with a blank when it dramatizes Tom's professional life may be less criticism than it is reflection upon his actual relation to the political power of Hopkins's media empire. In the film's first scene, after his friend Bill Hawthorne alerts him to a spot opening up in Public Relations at UBC, Tom replies, "I don't know anything about PR." "Who does?" his friend asks in turn. "But you have a clean shirt. You bathe every day. That's all there is to it."

All there is to it? This job description carries the other-directed performance ethic of the organization man to its extreme conclusion. Hawthorne's remark puts forward the value of packaging over contents, as if a position in Public Relations on Madison Avenue were already indistinguishable from both its task, advertising consumption to the middle class, and its object, mass-produced commodities. As a consequence, in order to succeed at his job Tom simply has to put on his gray flannel suit and look the part—literally so: Tom wears a brown suit in the first scene and changes to gray when he goes for his interview at UBC the next day. Fittingly enough, in its feature on the movie version of *The Man in the Gray Flannel Suit, Life* also depicted Tom in just this other-directed fashion, making him appear not all that different from George Kaplan in *North by Northwest,* as it turns out. With a photograph of Gregory Peck surrounded by the standard signs of his class—"mailbox, martini mixings, required wardrobe and standard commuter's equipment"— the magazine's article on the film begins by noting, "The picture above, which could be an advertisement for a delicious new drink, is really a recipe of the basic ingredients that go into the making of a man in a gray flannel suit— including, in this instance, the man himself" ("Man," *Life* 111). But the man himself here—the body in that gray flannel uniform—simply turns into a uniform figure, the logo of corporate capital, an empty signifier of the consumerism he promotes. Small wonder that, some thirty years later, the telltale gray flannel marker of fifties hegemonic masculinity would itself end up being turned into a consumable item, a men's cologne.

The ambivalence with which *The Man in the Gray Flannel Suit* views Tom Rath as both a man and a suit becomes immediately evident in the opening credits. Each card features the film's signature logo, borrowed from the novel's dust jacket and also used in the film's advertising—the silhouetted figure of Gregory Peck, tall and stiff in his gray flannel suit and fedora—to produce the impression that the title character is a singular person, standing apart from the pack of other, more anonymous gray flannel men. But the credits also multiply the logo, with each successive card stacking a slightly smaller but still identical version of this figure over the previous ones, so that a crowd of gray flannel men, all looking like Gregory Peck, steadily fills up one side of the wide CinemaScope screen. Like all logos, this one individuates a product while standardizing it for mass reproduction, and as Peck's singular image is multiplied on screen as the credits unroll, his own distinctive appearance becomes the very mark of the crowd's anonymity, in contrast to the novel's dust jacket, where the similar figure has no face.

Even before *The Man in the Gray Flannel Suit* properly begins its story, then, the credits have already begun an effort to mediate—through this double gloss of Tom Rath as individualist and conformist, as singular moral hero and representative family man—the ideological pressure which The Man in the Gray Flannel Suit had to bear as the exemplary middle-class domesticated male breadwinner, namely, the task of representing "America (in very personal terms)," as *The Hollywood Reporter* put it. In *The Seven Year Itch,* recall, when

Figure 9.
The lobby card for *The Man in the Gray Flannel Suit* sports the
logo that is repeated in the film's opening credits.

Richard Sherman bemoans his apparent lack of virility, he tells The Girl: "No
pretty girl in her right mind wants me. She wants Gregory Peck." While this
sly reference to the resident leading male star at Twentieth Century-Fox is a
studio in-joke probably anticipating the expensive production of *The Man in
the Gray Flannel Suit* the following year, like all good jokes, it bespeaks a certain truth. As personified by "tall, dark and dignified" Gregory Peck, the
cultural purchase of Tom Rath's exemplary figure on screen did not depend
upon his representing accurately or even coherently the material conditions
under which fifties men actually lived and worked, because all he had to be was,
literally, just an *image* of middle-class masculinity, the normality of which was
instantly conveyed by his gray flannel uniform.

Tom Rath's masculinity crisis in *The Man in the Gray Flannel Suit* therefore
does not arise from his moral paralysis in resisting the conformity that, as his
wife says, would turn him into another one of those "cheap, slippery yes-men."
Rather, it is symptomatic of his alienation, as an "average" middle-class wage
earner, from the professional-managerial class which his gray flannel uniform
represents. In *North by Northwest,* Roger Thornhill successfully learns how to

use the performance ethic of his class to his advantage, but this film's Man in the Gray Flannel Suit takes himself much too seriously to see that ethic for what it is. "I haven't the faintest idea who's honest in there or not," Tom confesses to Betsy when he explains why he is trying to play all the angles. But how can he look for angles when he has trouble reading the performance signs of corporate dealings? Upon learning the terms of the new job at UBC, for example, Tom takes Bill Ogden and Gordon Walker at their word, although we learn afterward that Hopkins's executives have simply set the stage for bargaining and that they expect Tom to ask for more money, which he does but only after Betsy's urging.

Like one of the possessed bodies in *Invasion of the Body Snatchers* (1955)—who display no feeling, as Miles Bennell (Kevin McCarthy) explains, "just the pretense of it"—Tom himself is all surface, masking his emotions to the point where nothing is left but a persona attached to the blank surface of a mass-produced body in a suit.[7] It is therefore all too fitting that his occupation at UBC is to serve as Ralph Hopkins's ghost writer in the latter's bid for political office. Valued as the logo of corporate America, Tom himself does not occupy the powerful position of media manipulation and political control that he represents when he puts on his gray flannel suit. His repudiation of Hopkins's ambition, the source of the latter's money and power, allows Tom to wear the persona of a typical American male, but it is small compensation since that mask of hegemonic masculinity stifles his anger with the assurance that his being one of "those nine-to-five fellows" is a form of personal empowerment.

The Man in the Gray Flannel Suit and *The Seven Year Itch* mirror each other's representation of hegemonic masculinity in crisis. Particularly given Tom's passing comparison of the UBC and the federal government, an analogy then strengthened by the flashback structure, this film too can be seen to recognize, but only through its hero's discontent, the subjection of its ordinary, middle-class Man in the Gray Flannel Suit to corporate power. Whereas *The Seven Year Itch* stages Richard Sherman's crisis in sexual terms, implying that his inability to commit adultery signals the failure of his middle-class life to align male fantasy with social reality, *The Man in the Gray Flannel Suit* dramatizes Tom Rath's subjection in gendered terms, interpreting it as a crisis of conscience that pertains directly to his manhood and proposing that a historical event—World War II—is responsible for his failure of nerve, all so that his hegemonic masculinity can efface the more immediate circumstances motivating his affectless performance as the man who is inseparable from his suit. Lyndon may have warned his readers not to inhibit the breadwinner's innermost nature or "the man in the gray flannel suit will stop being a man," but this film shows that, if you take away the suit, you will have trouble finding the man.

Tough Guys Make the Best Psychopaths

HE'S NO ROMEO

"I'm Tough And Intend to Remain That Way"
Says Hard Guy Humphrey Bogart

Hollywood, Calif. (June 00)—Humphrey Bogart is n-o-t going to become a screen Romeo, contrary to current rumors which seem to have stemmed from his recent and highly romantic marriage to Lauren (The Look) Bacall and his unpolished but ardent love work in such films as "To Have and Have Not," "Casablanca," and "Passage to Marseilles."

Says Mr. Bogart:

"If people have seen me as a romantic and pleasing-to-woman type, I am highly flattered and I shall go right on trying to please them.

"But, there's going to be no basic change in the kind of roles I do.

"I hope to go on playing everything that comes along in the story line—evil, criminal, romantic, sympathetic or what have you—just so long as it's tough. By that I mean that while I may give out with the tender feelings once in a while, I'll always be the toughie, the roughie, the kind of guy who's incapable of being eloquent about it.

"As a matter of fact," concluded Bogart, "I'm incapable of eloquence, on or off the screen. If you don't believe me, ask 'Baby.'" (Warner Bros. Press Release)

When the history of Hollywood is written in some future epoch, the name Humphrey Bogart will undoubtedly appear on several pages of the index—as producer, pundit, and player of such diverse roles as Wall Street banker, treasure seeker and African river boatman.

But the page devoted to "tough guys" will probably abound in Bogart references, for no actor has typified the callous product of the American underworld—prison-bound, in-prison, just-out-of, and between-trips—as thoroughly as has Mr. Humphrey Bogart, late of Phillips Andover Academy. ("Biography")

These two excerpted press releases, one from 1945 and the other from 1955, roughly span the high point of Humphrey Bogart's popularity as a major box-office draw, giving every appearance of recording the continuity of his tough-guy star persona. The adjective "tough" was the central metonymy condensing the star's identity in noncinematic contexts too ("Bogart's a Tough Guy—Even at Chess Board," heralded a news headline in 1952), and it served as his signature in obituaries when he died in January 1957 ("Cancer Kills 'Tough Guy' Bogart").[1] After the actor's death, his tough-guy persona was celebrated even more in the "Bogie" cult that first became apparent with Jean-Luc Godard's reference to the star's value as an icon of masculinity in *Breathless* (1959), flourishing with the successful revival of Bogart's Warner Bros. films in art houses throughout the 1960s. *Play It Again Sam* (1972) then canonized the actor's standing as an icon of romantic masculinity when it invoked Bogart's ghost from *Casablanca* (1942) to personify for the meek, insecure hero (Woody Allen) the male fantasy of impeccable virility—"the toughie, the roughie, the kind of guy who's incapable of being eloquent about it"—structuring the heterosexual masculinity of the average American man. Today, Bogart is popularly remembered for "the purity of his tough-guy persona," which "exude[s] the very qualities that still represent important aspects of American screen masculinity" (Neibaur 72).

What's significant about the two press releases quoted above, in contrast to the romanticization of the star by the later Bogie cult, is that they acknowledge the basis of his masculine persona in an ongoing gender performance. To be sure, the particular films being promoted may be partly responsible for this impression since Bogart plays an anti-heroic role on the occasion of each press release. The one issued in 1945 concludes by mentioning the star's part as a man who strangles his wife in *Conflict,* and the one in 1955 announces his casting as a psychopathic criminal in *The Desperate Hours.* Given these roles, one can readily understand why studio publicity would seek to distance the actor from his villainous characters as a means of preserving his star image, but this effort only calls into question the authenticity of his virile screen presence all the more.

In each press release an allusion to the "real" Bogart (newly married and domesticated in the 1945 piece, hailing from an elite social background in the 1955 one) momentarily falsifies the star's persona, pulling away the mask in order to authenticate his consummate skill as an actor. Far from being "pure" or exuding from some ineffable gender essence, Bogart's virility continually needs to be *performed* in a discursive setting (supplied by the publicity machine as well as the films themselves), and his screen virility is always in danger of being *reformed* there as a psychotic villain, as in the cases of *Conflict* and *The Desperate Hours.* Warner Bros. even went so far as to incorporate the dimension of masquerading that informs the star's persona into the narrative of *Dark Passage* (1947), his third pairing with wife Lauren Bacall. He plays an escaped convict whose plastic surgery midway through the film turns him into "Bogart," that older, more lined, and—paradoxically, since it is meant to disguise his identity in the diegesis—more familiar face that, in finally restoring the character to the body of the actor, recognizes how the tough persona is indeed a mask which functions to authenticate the star's masculinity. It is highly fitting that at one point in its production, *In a Lonely Place* (1950), one of the three Bogart films I analyze in this chapter, was temporarily retitled *Behind the Mask* (Polan, *Lonely* 23).

Of the two press releases, the one from 1945 is more revealing of the historical circumstance pressuring the stability of the star's tough-guy persona. Meant to reassure fans that Bogart will not soften his "hard guy" image and turn into a "screen Romeo" following his highly publicized romance with and marriage to Bacall, this press release represents the domesticated heterosexuality characterizing the actor's private life as an intrusion upon his tough-guy screen characterizations. The press release begins by quoting the actor's own admission that he performs his brand of masculinity to please his audience ("there's going to be no basic change in the kind of roles I do"), and then it disavows the noticeable gap which this quotation has opened between the star and his persona. The quotation from Bogart aligns the performer with his performances ("while I may give out with the tender feelings once in a while, I'll always be the toughie, the roughie, the kind of guy who's incapable of being eloquent about it") in order to prove that the persona is a faithful copy of the original ("I'm incapable of eloquence, on or off the screen"). However, if Bogart's virility is so transparently truthful, why do we need to get proof of it from Bacall ("if you don't believe me, ask 'Baby'")? Simply because the 1945 press release makes the offscreen personality appear a bit *too* eloquent. Bogart's own understanding of his star appeal in the quotation recognizes the theatricality that underlies his persona; he directs his performance of virility for the benefit of a male audience off the screen as well as on it. "You don't have to act around me," Bacall reassures Bogart in *To Have and Have Not* (1944), and this sentiment summarizes their teaming as a star couple. By contrast, his tough-guy characters *do* act around other men, as when Bogart's Sam Spade feigns a fit of anger before Gutman (Sidney Greenstreet) in *The Maltese Falcon* (1941). His performance is so thorough and convincing that when he leaves the hotel room and smiles, as if to tip his mask to the audience, Spade's hand still shakes uncontrollably.

The 1945 press release is consistent with later accounts of the public's reception of Bogart's tough persona. Biographer Joe Hyams reports that in private life Bogart was continually harassed in nightclubs by hecklers trying to provoke him into a fight as a means of performing their own virility. "His usual answer to the stock question—'So you think you're so tough?'—was a tired smile and soft answer. But sometimes his patience would be worn thin and he would react in the way expected of him." Just a few paragraphs later, though,

Hyams also reveals the actor's pleasure in donning his mask of virility, evoking similar scenes in Bogart's films: "Sometimes, in public, Bogie would retreat into his screen image because it was expected of him—and because it was fun" (*Bogie* 112). "You like to play games, don't you?" Bacall asks Bogart in another one of their collaborations, *The Big Sleep* (1946): his "games" differentiate bogus male posing from his own performativity, which successfully allows persona and personality to cohere. "The happy reconciliation between private and public image was heavily exploited in the press," Hyams observes in the conclusion to his biography—and this comment could as easily apply to the moment in *Dark Passage* when the bandages come off, finally revealing the long-delayed sight of Bogart's face—"to the delight of a public that found in the screen shadow the substance of the real man" (172–73).

In this chapter I challenge that "happy reconciliation," not by interrogating the "real man" hidden by or expressed in the actor's mask of virility, but by re-reading Bogart's postwar star persona historically as an indirect measurement of the culture's reconfiguration of hegemonic masculinity through the fifties domestic mystique. Bogart makes for a fitting illustration of this transformation. The strong element of performativity in his persona, which the two publicity releases quoted at the start of this chapter bring out, bases his virility in masquerade even when he registers most normatively, as in his films with Bacall. But roles in three star vehicles made without Bacall—*Dead Reckoning* (1947), *In a Lonely Place,* and *The Desperate Hours*—reveal even more clearly how the ongoing renegotiation of Bogart's persona after World War II charts the transformation of the 1940s film noir tough guy into the fifties psychopath, "a violent, male, sexual criminal" (Freedman 202).

Bogart was not the only middle-aged star whose tough-guy persona was repositioned in this fashion: recall James Cagney's Cody Jarrett, a manic momma's boy, in *White Heat* (1949) or John Wayne's Ethan Edwards, a racial fanatic, in *The Searchers* (1956). As Peter Biskind points out, "Almost every star of the thirties and forties associated with this version of masculinity took the roles with which he was synonymous and transformed them, in the fifties, into neurotics or psychotics" (252). This radical alteration of Bogart's persona may be partly explained by the fact that, like Cagney and Wayne at this time, he was an established star whose choice of roles in the 1950s had to accommodate middle age. Bogart, however, played such roles with a consistency that other actors of his generation did not, and they only added to his stature as a major star after the war, as in his well-received acting turns in *The Treasure of the Sierra Madre* (1948), *The African Queen* (1951), and *The Caine Mutiny* (1954). Nor, with the cracking of his hard-boiled demeanor, did Bogart cease to epitomize unblemished virility in the popular imagination. Rather, Bogart's fifties films demonstrate that his virility itself is what disturbs his characters' relations with women and other men, with his "toughness" functioning not as the epitome of an unimpeachable manliness, but as a mechanism of sexual regulation supporting the authority of postwar hegemonic masculinity.

The Bogart Persona and Film Noir

In her study of masculinity in American movies, Joan Mellen points out the tough-guy mold from which one after another of the leading male stars of the sound era were cast:

> Film after film has insisted that the masculine male is he who acts—and kills—without a moment's thought. To think is to be a sissy, a bumbling eunuch of a man. At worst, the male in American movies has brutalized women, his violence incomplete unless it is reflected in his sexuality. It is as if masculinity would vanish were the male prerogatives of assertiveness and domination over others relinquished. (9)

In Mellen's view, the style through which Bogart in particular advanced this representation of masculinity made him the star who best personified manliness for the 1940s: "Bogart's Sam Spade is supremely masculine because he is his own man" (153). Whether as reluctant wartime patriot (as in *Casablanca*) or postwar cynic (as in his film noir roles), Bogart's star persona romanticizes the familiar qualities of the tough movie hero she describes: independent, competitive, aggressive—and, let me add, potentially homosexual.

In mentioning that last characteristic, I do not mean to suggest that the Bogart persona is not outwardly and emphatically heterosexual. The four films that Bogart made with Lauren Bacall during this period—*To Have and Have Not, The Big Sleep, Dark Passage,* and *Key Largo* (1948)—by and large formed the basis of his postwar screen image. Each successfully integrates his tough-guy masculinity, depicted as volatile and uncontrollable through a crime plot, into the social order by heterosexualizing it through a romance plot featuring Bacall. Offscreen, Bogart and Bacall's well-publicized romance and marriage helped to maintain the heterosexuality of his screen image, even to domesticate his tough persona to a large extent, particularly when the contentment of his married life with "Baby" was contrasted with the drunken public brawling that had characterized his previous marriage to Mayo Methot.[2] However, at the same time that he starred as a romantic lead opposite Bacall, crystallizing his value for Warner Bros. as the male half of a popular heterosexual movie couple (in trailers for their films, the studio advertised them as "That Man Bogart" and "That Woman Bacall"), Bogart also played a maniacal Bluebeard in *Conflict* and *The Two Mrs. Carrolls* (1947), a misogynist war veteran in *Dead Reckoning,* and a greedy, paranoid prospector in *The Treasure of the Sierra Madre.* The title of an interview in 1949, given while the actor was filming *In*

a Lonely Place, summarized the uncomfortable feeling about romancing
women that, remaining central to Bogart's persona as a tough guy, found its
way into the misogyny of his postwar film noir roles when he did not star opposite his wife: "Leading Ladies? Kisses? 'Phooey,' Says Bogie." After quoting
the actor's discomfort with kissing scenes, as well as his disinterest in leading
ladies other than Bacall—because "as a class," he observed, they are so much of
a bother to work with—the interview concludes: "All of which adds up to the
fact that he'd rather work with men" (Sloan).

Always perceived as "a man's man," Bogart's persona did not disguise the
homosociality structuring his performance of masculinity on screen. Strictly
speaking, male homosociality, Eve Sedgwick's invaluable term for describing
the basis of patriarchal masculinity in the bonds between men, is not homosexual, at least not overtly so; rather, it institutes "male heterosexual desire, in
the form of a desire to consolidate partnership with authoritative males in and
through the bodies of females" (*Between* 38). Homosociality has as much to do
with power (*over* women as well as other men) as it does with desire (*for* other
men as well as women), which is why it so readily takes the form of one man's
domination of another, emphasizing independence, competition, and aggression as the hallmark features of virility, and usually going even further to manifest fear of alternate male behavior—such as effeminacy—in homophobic
violence. Drawing on a prewar gender ideology of male performativity, which
George Chauncey identifies with working-class culture (127), film noir uses
displays of violence (physical, sexual, mental) to create a hierarchy of men
outlining homosocial power relations among hegemonic, conservative, and
subordinated masculinities within its diegesis. As weaker men fall to the bottom (often anticipated by their effeminate behavior and subsequent implications of homosexuality, as in *The Maltese Falcon* and *The Big Sleep*), the tough
hero rises to the top, in validation of his brand of masculinity. As Frank Krutnik demonstrates in his study of film noir, what then overrides the hostility
otherwise resulting from this competition for power is a sense shared by all
men in the hierarchical structure that femininity—the dangerous female with
the gun—is the great unsolved mystery. Female agency generates the oppressive sense of fatality that envelops the tough guy's fortunes, diminishing his
control over events and, in many cases, plunging him into an existential angst,
which can be mitigated only by his intimate bonding with other men.

While it has become a widely recognized feature of film noir and of
American male culture generally, this homosocial organization of masculinity,
which characterizes Bogart's postwar films, did not occur in a historical
vacuum but took its currency from the central tension that defined a soldier's
masculinity during wartime: between the military's regulation of men and the
war's deregulation of their sexuality, particularly through the strong homoerotic undercurrent of the army buddy relation. Bogart's tough-guy persona in
his late 1940s films therefore needs to be placed in the context of the Second

World War and demobilization, not to view a transition from wartime patriotism to postwar cynicism, as Mellen depicts it, but to recognize how and why that persona registers cultural apprehensions about the dangers of a militant, aggressive, and latent homosexual masculinity once removed from its wartime setting.

The Buddy System

In their history of American sexuality, John D'Emilio and Estelle B. Freedman conclude, "World War II brought unprecedented opportunities for premarital experience. The war released millions of youth from the social environments that inhibited erotic expression, and threw them into circumstances that opened up new sexual possibilities" (260). Even more disruptive of sexual mores in mainstream culture, as D'Emilio explains in another study, the war "marked a critical turning point in the social expression of homosexuality. It created a substantially new 'erotic situation' that led to a sudden coalescence of an urban gay subculture in the 1940s.... Wartime society freed millions of the young from the setting where heterosexuality was normally encouraged" ("Homosexual" 233–34).[3] Obviously, the number of men who had homosexual experiences during the war for whatever reason (deprivation, boredom, experimentation, or inclination) cannot be exactly documented, but, according to another historian of wartime sexual behavior, the available data does suggest that "the percentage of homosexually inclined servicemen in the armies of World War II was also greater than in the population as a whole" (Costello 104).

Because military thinking believed that "a sexually aggressive man makes the best fighter" (Costello 76), homosexuality seemed, on the surface, to be completely incompatible with army life, connoting just the opposite of aggression: passivity, vulnerability, cowardice, effeminacy—in short, the sissy stereotype that guided military doctors when screening draftees and enlistees at induction centers (Bérubé 19–20). However, given the lack of privacy in military barracks, the "oppressively masculine" atmosphere of the armed forces encouraged, albeit under the cloak of virility, the homoeroticization of soldiers' bodies as an element of the war's "break from the feminine and 'civilizing' influences of civilian life" (Costello 76). Writing about the suspension of "toilet taboos," for instance, one GI remembered: "We soon learned to flaunt our genitals and brag about our toilet mannerisms. Anyone who was modest about these was immediately and forever labeled a homosexual" (qtd. in Costello 76).

Failing to take into account that gay and bisexual men can flaunt and brag about their bodies with the ease of straight men, and perhaps even enjoy the bravado all the more for its spectacle, this assumption followed the official

military line in defining homosexuality as a visible gender inversion, but it
suggests, too, how "virility" took on an important homosexual dimension
while still being recuperated as strict heterosexuality. Homosexuality was
localized as a specific category of deviation (the "sissy") while, at the same time,
diffused throughout the same-sex culture of the military as one of the primary
mechanisms by which men defined their relations to each other, bonded
through their bodies, and, under the circumstances of sexual deprivation and
if the desire was there, even found physical relief, without severely challenging
their sense of normality. As novelist Harold Robbins remembers about his
wartime bisexuality: "I was on a submarine, and if you're on a submarine for
22 days, you want sex. We were either jacking each other off or sucking each
other off. Everybody knew that everybody else was doing it. . . . So we did it,
it was fun, and it was over. I don't know whether any of them were really
homosexual" (Kroll 42–43).

The military voiced an official stand in favor of traditional sexual abstinence
among unmarried servicemen and fidelity for married ones, but it also recognized that men could not be expected to put their sex drives on hold indefi-
nitely. One 1943 army manual, *Psychology for the Fighting Man,* informs
soldiers that "the sex drive is one of the most plastic of human desires, capable
of an almost infinite combination with other needs." While it maintains belief
in the category of "normal men," this manual also recognizes that male sexuality is a continuum: "The strength of the sex drive varies in different men and
at different times in the same man. At one extreme it is apparently absent; at
the other it is an abnormally keen intense compulsion. All normal men feel it
keenly at times" (336). The manual makes an explicit point of *not* condemning
so-called abnormal sexual behavior—fantasy, masturbation, promiscuity, even
homosexual activity—but only as long as soldiers resort to these outlets as a
"substitute" for "a man's preferred form of sexual gratification" (339).

After a three-page listing of the various academic experts and military officials who collaborated upon its contents, the manual claims that its opinions
are not to be construed as "official or reflecting the views of the U.S. Army or
the U.S. Navy or any of the armed or government services at large" (7). Nevertheless, while not reflecting official policy, *Psychology for the Fighting Man*
represents how experts, leaders, and servicemen saw the effect of wartime on
male sexuality. The manual's cautious advice about the likelihood of homosexual encounters in the army's all-male environment is therefore quite striking, given the homophobia which erupted in periodic purges of effeminate
men during the war and which, more perniciously, came to dominate military
policy after the war ended. To start with, the manual acknowledges, not only
that there are homosexuals in the army, but that "[s]ome of these men have
no feelings of inferiority or shame, no mental conflict, over their homosexuality," that "they are content with quietly seeking the satisfaction of their sexual
needs with others of their own kind," and that, despite "their perversion," they

"even become excellent soldiers." According to the manual, court-martial of homosexual soldiers proves necessary only if they force their attentions upon "nor-mal men" (340). In making this concession, it goes on to recognize that army life also produces an extraordinary situation of deprivation which encourages homosexual encounters between normal men as a temporary sexual outlet:

> The man whose homosexuality develops for the first time in a situation where he cannot have normal sexual satisfaction may be only mildly disturbed by what he has done, but it is more likely that he will suffer from mental conflict. He will feel inferior to other men, ashamed and worried for fear he will become a confirmed homosexual and become unable to enjoy normal sexual intercourse when he gets back home. Or he will feel afraid of being found out and punished by dishonorable discharge and a long sentence; or he will suffer strong feelings of guilt. Or he may have all these feelings at once.
>
> So long as he is thus seriously worried and dissatisfied with himself, the chances are that he may be all right again, when he returns to normal conditions of life. But he should put up a strong fight with himself to control his homosexual impulses and find some other outlet for his sex drive as soon as he can. (340–41)

The priority here is not to regulate sexual behavior but to maintain a well-oiled fighting machine. Consequently, the manual emphasizes the mental and not moral danger of a soldier's submitting to "his homosexual impulses." Because, it goes on to point out, "there are no real substitutes for sexual satisfaction" and "no real way to kill the sex need" (341), in guarded language, the manual advises soldiers to give way to their desire if they must—and not to feel *too* guilty about it afterward: excessive preoccupation with guilt for having sex with another man would adversely affect a soldier's performance in battle. By the same token, the manual goes on to comment, feeling *some* guilt afterward guarantees the soldier's normality for the time when he will return home and no longer have to rely upon the company of men for his sexual release. In taking this position, the army manual shows a surprising awareness and, more significantly, toleration of the "deprivation homosexuality" (Costello 106) that military life fostered among men.

As well as giving many men an opportunity they would not otherwise have had to admit and satisfy their homosexual desires and/or to identify with a previously unknown and unsuspected gay subculture within the army, the conditions of war forged intense same-sex bonding for straight men. True, these buddies may not have acted upon the affection they felt for each other nor acknowledged it as sexual desire. Nonetheless, in his history of gays and lesbians in the U.S. military, Allan Bérubé concludes: "Veterans of all kinds describe the love they felt for each other with a passion, romance, and sentimentality that often rivaled gay men's expressions of their love for other men and made gay affections seem less out of place" (186).

In some Army and Navy outfits, commanding officers instituted an official "buddy system" in which they formally organized men into pairs.... A more informal buddy system also operated in combat units in which two men of equal rank or rating chose to pal around because they liked each other.... By encouraging men to pair up, the buddy system gave a respectability to devoted male couples, whether or not they included gay men, that was unusual in civilian life.... Buddy relations easily slipped into romantic and even sexual intimacies between men that they themselves often did not perceive to be "queer." (188)

When interviewed by Studs Terkel, one war widow remembered this kind of buddy intimacy without in any way considering it queer: "There's a closeness that these boys feel with their buddies," she observes, "because they didn't know from one minute to the next whether they were gonna be, you know ...There's a bond there that I think never is broken" (269, ellipsis in original). Widowed in 1944, in 1949 this woman married her late husband's "very best buddy," who was with him when he was killed. (In fact, the husband died in his buddy's arms.) "It was like he came back instead of Kevin," she says of her present husband, who himself continued to mourn his dead buddy and to feel guilty about his death (267–68). Marriage, while consolation for the widow, failed to serve the same purpose for the surviving buddy.

While the intensity of the wartime buddy relationship described by both this woman and her second husband appears to have been a common occurrence of military life during the war, and was, in fact, central to the disciplinary tactics of the army, it was also antagonistic to postwar civilian heterosexuality. In this respect, Kevin's death conveniently foreclosed upon any danger of implicit (or, for all we know, explicit) sexual rivalry on the part of either the buddy or the wife. As *Psychology for the Fighting Man* suggests, too great an intimacy between men posed a serious question about the "normal" masculinity of returning soldiers, and this suspicion supplies a historical context for the ambivalence coloring male friendships in much postwar film noir, particularly when the narrative works to transfer the hero's emotional bond from his buddy to his girl. This goal motivates the triangulation of male desire in *Gilda* (1946), as Johnny Farrell's (Glenn Ford) relation to Ballin Mundson (George Macready) openly competes in homosexual intensity with the heterosexual desire of both men for Gilda (Rita Hayworth). Albeit less problematic than *Gilda*, *The Blue Dahlia* (1946) and *Key Largo* similarly recount a veteran's successful transition from male bonding to heterosexual romance. Bogart's character in the latter film, in fact, pairs off with his dead friend's wife (Bacall) at the end much like the real-life couple whom Terkel interviewed.

Not all films made at this time were as sanguine about the prospects of re-integrating men following their intense experiences of male friendship in war-time. Another Bogart film noir about a returning vet, *Dead Reckoning*, shows the incompatibility of postwar heterosexual civilian life and wartime buddy love. "You're going to fry," Rip Murdock (Bogart) tells Coral Chandler (Lizabeth Scott) at the end of this film. What has Coral done to deserve such rejection, not to say condemnation and punishment? Well, in addition to being a bigamist and shooting her (first and legal) husband, the gangster Martinelli (Morris Carnovsky), and then trying to do the same to Rip, she helped to pin a murder rap on Rip's war buddy, Johnny Preston (William Prince), and even indirectly caused his death. Coral, of course, wants to forgive and forget. "Oh, Rip, Rip," she says, "can't we put this behind us?" Rip, however, remembers Coral's duplicity all too well, his response echoing Bogart's earlier tough-guy role in *The Maltese Falcon:* "When a guy's pal is killed he oughta do something about it." But Coral presses further, now playing what she thinks is her ace in the hole: "Don't you love me?" she asks. "That's the tough part of it, but it will pass," Murdock sneers. "These things do in time. . . . Then there's one other thing: I loved him more."

Does this closure help to explain why, in its review, *The Hollywood Reporter* thought that *Dead Reckoning* may have been, in the long run, "almost too tough for its own good"? With a screenplay concocted out of bits and pieces of Bogart's popular Warner Bros. movies of the period, *Dead Reckoning* pushes his tough-guy persona to the point of unintentional self-parody, which is perhaps all that the *Reporter* reviewer had in mind.[4] But the uneasiness suggested by that remark also indicates how this film troubles the tough-guy masculinity that Bogart personified. In its unabashed plagiarism *Dead Reckoning* exposes the constructedness of his persona, frankly acknowledging that the authenticity of this "man's man" is derived from his performance of virility in other films. A copy of a copy, Rip Murdock much too easily confuses the distinction, central to Bogart's 1940s homosocial persona, between identifying with virility and desiring it, and that is why *Dead Reckoning* is really too tough for its own good.

Dead Reckoning: The Buddy, His Blonde, and Bogart

With its narrative recounting how a war hero returns home to discover that a treacherous woman has betrayed him during his enforced absence, *Dead Reckoning* openly foregrounds the organization of Bogart's tough masculinity out of two disturbing coordinates which his films with Bacall tame through their heterosexual romance narratives. Rip Murdock is overtly misogynistic on one hand ("I forget to tell you," Rip tells Coral, "I don't trust anybody—especially women"), and covertly homosexual on the other ("Let's just say I remembered Johnny," he says in voiceover, "laughing, tough, and lonesome"). By the end of *Dead Reckoning*, Rip proves to be dead-on in his suspicion of Coral, just as a homoerotic memory of Johnny appears to have been the primary motive of his heterosexual desire for her. Rip himself explains when he first meets Coral: "I hated every part of her. I couldn't figure her out yet. I wanted to see her the way Johnny had."

Rip not only comes to view Coral through that male lens but, as he does so,

Figure 10.
The caption on this lobby card for *Dead Reckoning* summarizes the threat of its
femme fatale: "To kiss her . . . or to kill her—he's never quite sure!"

he effaces her sexual difference. He turns her, as Krutnik puts it, into "a replacement for Johnny, his lost buddy," by changing her name from "Coral" to
"Dusty" (Johnny's nickname for her, which Rip appropriates) to "Mike" (Rip's
own name for her)—to the point where, her deceit notwithstanding (or, more
likely, as a means of recovering from it), she finally becomes, in the fantasized
last shot of the film, another one of the paratroopers in his unit parachuting to
death (*Lonely* 172). As it closes with this image proposing, in effect, that the
only good woman is really a cross-dresser, *Dead Reckoning* visualizes the figure
of speech through which Bogart's Sam Spade appreciates the worth of his Girl
Friday, Effie Perine (Lee Patrick): "You're a good man, sister."

   Dead Reckoning reproduces the misogyny of *The Maltese Falcon* right down
to rejecting the *femme fatale* out of loyalty to a dead buddy and recuperating her
dangerous femininity by reimagining it in masculine terms. But *Dead Reckoning* also goes further than that earlier Bogart film in implicating the tough guy's
mistrust of women and his corresponding respect for/rivalry with other tough
men in a homosexual desire for the phallic virility with which he identifies as
the measure of his manhood. Because he narrates in voiceover for the first two-

thirds of the film, Rip's story of a dangerous blonde encourages viewers to interpret his misogyny in relation to his homoerotic bonding with Johnny, the memory of which relieves the threat that the treacherous Coral poses to the tough guy's masculinity. The film's quest-narrative frame then places additional emphasis on the buddy pairing over the heterosexual coupling of the tough guy and the blonde. In contrast to most film noir, the enigma which Rip follows as a means of leading him to "truth" is not prompted by the dangerous female, as in *The Maltese Falcon,* but is instead instigated by a male, the buddy. Prior to the *femme fatale's* appearance in the film, Johnny jumps off the train taking them to Washington, D.C., and Rip goes in pursuit of him. "There were three things I had to find out," Rip recapitulates after getting to the point in his narrative where he has followed Johnny's trail to Gulf City. "How could Johnny possibly be a murderer? Why did he come back here when he was even hotter than the weather? . . . And why, why not another word from him since that first call?"

I think it is because these questions all appear to lead Rip to Coral for their answers (though it is Martinelli who actually supplies them to Rip in the film's climax) that Krutnik reads *Dead Reckoning* as the quintessential film noir working out the "problem" of femininity; its narrative stages the classic psychoanalytic scenario of male disavowal in which the "'tough' controlled masculinity" that Coral disturbs can be restored only through "concerted, sadistically managed repression of the feminine" (181). According to Krutnik, in order to recuperate Rip's endangered masculinity *Dead Reckoning* represents its *femme fatale* as a castrated woman—which amounts to Rip's imagining her as another man ("Mike"). Coral's transformation into "a man" may repress the threat of her femininity, as Krutnik proposes, but, to follow his logic, it also puts masculinity back under the sign of castration. For if the film's ending turns Coral into "a man" just like Rip, shouldn't the principle of similarity by all rights be reversible, meaning that Rip must implicitly recognize himself as a fellow "castrated" woman just like "Mike," this other non-man? Resemblance does not efface so much as confuse sexual difference: Coral indeed poses a problem for Rip, but its name is "masculinity" not "femininity." Femininity is simply the come-on in this film to disguise the ease with which the homosocial regulation of tough masculinity gives way to the homosexual desire that fuels it. "Where have we met?" Coral asks Rip when they first meet at the bar of the Sanctuary Club. "In another guy's dreams," he replies, and one has to stop and wonder: what on earth was he doing *there?*

Coral acts destructively—and incoherently—in *Dead Reckoning's* narrative, leaving a trail of betrayals and dead male bodies behind her, because of what she reveals about the origins of the tough guy's heterosexual desire in the intense and revered homosocial buddy relation of wartime. "What does a girl have to do with you?" she asks Rip at one point. "Turn inside out to make you see?" The answer is, resolutely, yes! Phrased in terms of interior space, as if she were hidden inside a glove or a sheath, Coral's question refers back to Rip's earlier claim that a woman should be, well, like the phallus: "capsule size, about four inches tall," kept in a man's pocket and inflatable to a larger size only when he wants to look at her, "and that way he knows exactly where she is." When discussing Rip's belief that the ideal woman belongs in his pocket, Krutnik explains that Rip refuses to accommodate women, desiring instead to contain them, so as a result they remain forever unfixable and unknowable, in contrast to a man like Johnny (172–73). I agree, but I think this account includes only half the story, omitting the homosociality of Rip's sentiments. After all, in his account of the perfect woman, Rip also elaborates on her function when he goes out on the town with the guys. First, he removes her from his pocket and puts his four-inch doll on the table, where she can "run around the coffee cups while he swaps a few lies with his pals." Then he puts her back, reserving her for "that time of the evening when he wants her full-sized and beautiful." What happens then? "He just waves his hand and there she is—full size." Because of the specificity with which he describes a woman's sexual function here (she appears as the phallus because she is described as being like a penis), Rip's configuring of woman as *his* phallus amounts to a confession, not so much that a female motivates his desire, but that his desire has attributes which he disavows as "feminine" (instability, mystery, lack, destructiveness) in order to repress what he shares with Coral (while she is in his pocket?), namely, sexual attraction to Johnny.

Coral, in short, embodies for Rip the slippage he himself experiences between identification with and desire for Johnny. Turn her "inside out," and what we find is Johnny, her double. Having the same disturbing effect upon the film's narrative, one love object is substitutable for the other. Whereas she triangulates Rip and Johnny's relation during the war (they take their leaves together, Rip tells Coral: "Me with a gal. Him without one. Just a picture of you in his eyes"), afterward memory of the dead buddy triangulates Rip's relation to her, as in his voiceover comment about wanting to see Coral through Johnny's eyes. The buddy and the blonde are equally enigmatic and duplicitous, their instability fittingly represented by the transmutations of their names. Not only is Coral turned into "Dusty," "Mike," and also "Mrs. Martinelli," but Johnny himself uses a pseudonym, allowing him to keep his real identity even from Rip throughout the duration of the war. Like the *femme fatale* of film noir embodied by Coral Chandler, Johnny has a history of heterosexual desire outside Rip's ken, which is why the thriller plot line arises from Rip's investigation of that enigmatic male history, not Coral's.

Dead Reckoning problematizes the usual heterosexual concerns of film noir, even to the point of contradicting its own advertising campaign, which focused on a female's enigma and the threat she poses to the stability of the straight couple. For this film treats Johnny as if *he* were the dangerous *femme fatale*. After all, he is the one who is investigated, demystified, and finally "saved" as Johnny Drake, war hero, with his dubious sexual past erased. Coral herself does not disrupt the homoerotic structuring of Rip's masculinity around this male enigma, but she does give it a heterosexual cover. When he identifies with Johnny's heterosexual desire for Coral as the primary inducement of his own desire for her, which he in turn views through his misogyny, Rip can then articulate as an overt denial ("I don't want to desire a false woman") what is really a covert declaration ("I desire my buddy's desire"). Rip identifies with Johnny's desire so strongly that he boasts he knew his buddy "like my own birthmark." This striking comparison equates Rip's personal knowledge of his best friend with the most intimate inspection of his own body, and it goes further, I think, indirectly to reveal the slippage of his interest from his buddy, to his own body, to his buddy's body—which, not accidentally, gets burned so badly that it is, finally, unrecognizable to everyone *but* Rip.

The ultimate indecipherability of Johnny's body returns our attention to the opening scene between the two men on the train, to the early point in the film when the camera puts Johnny's body on display as an eroticized object for Rip. As the two talk about the future of their friendship, Johnny takes off his shirt to wash up. In response, Rip shifts his position on the seat, his gesture suggesting that he wants to look the other way so as not to stare at his buddy's exposed body. However, the shot/reverse shot editing indicates, from the direction of Rip's eyes, that he *does* continue looking at his friend throughout their conversation. True, we may conclude that Rip watches Johnny intently to scrutinize the latter's secretive handling of his college pin, the one reminder of his real identity; but since Johnny takes the pin from his T-shirt and puts it in his mouth for safekeeping, Rip also has a clear view of his buddy's seminude body as he watches, which the editing emphasizes by cutting back and forth between three-quarter shots of Rip seated and talking, and medium close-ups of the bare-chested Johnny replying. Underscoring the tracking of Rip's gaze here, his language also gives rise to an eruption of homoerotic content. Rip immediately starts talking about their mutual interest in "dames" to heterosexualize their banter; but when he states, with perfect tough-guy cynicism, that all women are the same with their faces washed, what should we make of the fact that, while Rip makes this observation, Johnny is himself washing up? When all is said and done, the *hermeneutic* look (at the pin in Johnny's mouth) naturalizes but also motivates a *homoerotic* look (at Johnny's upper torso), which is why the remains of that pin later turn out to be the only means of identifying his unrecognizable corpse to Rip's complete satisfaction. "It might be Johnny; it might not," he says in voiceover; then he sees the lump of melted gold that has to be the pin, and he is certain.

Only the all-male army, more than repression of the feminine, finally rescues Rip's threatened masculinity at the end of the film. When he reports to General Steele that he has found the missing Johnny Drake, Rip reverts back to his military title (the police now address him as "Captain Murdock") and to military discourse ("Mission all cleared up, sir"). Significantly, Rip does not tell the general what he has actually discovered about Johnny Preston but maintains the latter's cover of "Johnny Drake." Under his real name, Johnny

Preston—a southern college professor and Yale alumnus—embodies fundamental social differences from Rip, a cabby from St. Louis with vague mob
connections. The war may have suppressed their class difference, thereby
fostering their intimacy, but postwar home life reasserts it, threatening the
future of their friendship.[5] In contrast to the home front, army life blurred
existing ethnic and class (but not racial) divisions, producing an homogeneous
all-male society that was in turn regimented through a different form of
homosocial hierarchy, the military and its buddy system, which in this film still
reigns for Rip as the ultimate form of masculine authority.

Outside of the army, Rip and Johnny's friendship could not survive the
social as well as geographic divide that the two men discuss on the train in the
opening scene. When Rip expresses his anxiety about the future under the
cover of talk about "dames," Johnny tries to reassure him: "I think you're a great
guy, too, Rip, if that's what this conversation is about. Even in the USA—this
world." (Incidentally, it is while finishing this speech that Johnny starts to un-
button his shirt prior to stripping for a wash.) However, almost as soon as his
buddy jumps from the train and he starts to track him down, Rip reenters
civilian life and immediately confronts his social difference from Johnny. On
the phone to Johnny's alma mater, Rip does not even know the right words to
use: "Yale? Give me your top man there. Whatever you call him. What college?
Yale, of course. Okay, so it's a university. How would I know? I just a run a fleet
of taxis." Taken as fantasy, the film's closing shot of Coral parachuting to death
as "Mike" allows Rip to collapse social hierarchy and heterogeneity back into
the democratic and homogenous figure of the "troop." Telling the dying Coral
to let go, like one of the paratroopers under his command making a jump, Rip
assures her: "You'll have plenty of company, Mike." Then he adds, with a line
that refers back to his opening conversation with Johnny on the train: "High-
class company."

The fantasy of social amelioration ending the film is appropriate because
Coral functions so emphatically as the overt object of Rip's anger over Johnny's
death. Thus, as well as siphoning off the sexual energy of Rip and Johnny's
buddy relation, Coral serves to distract attention from the social disturbance
their friendship signifies. Variously representing herself or identified by others
as a rich man's widow, a professor's girlfriend, a nightclub star, a carhop from
Texas, a mobster's moll, and finally a survivor of the slums of Detroit, her
feminine masquerade epitomizes the social differences which characterize
postwar America for Rip upon his return. With her indeterminate background, Coral condenses the profound social divisions, narratively manifested
in conventional film noir style as "corruption," characterizing the aptly named
"Gulf City."

But even more so than Coral, it is Rip himself who registers the effects of
postwar social displacement. In that conversation with the switchboard operator at Yale, for instance, Rip enacts what the fifties will prove: that education
socially differentiates among white- and blue-collared men to empower the

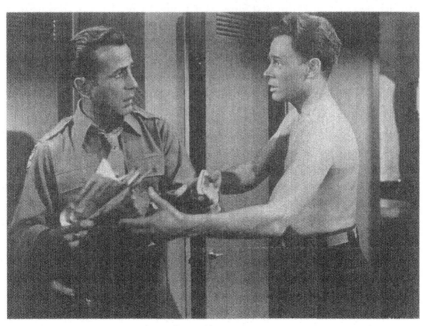

Figures 11a and 11b.
Rip (Humphrey Bogart) and Johnny (William Preston) on the train: first they talk
about "dames" (top), but after Johnny strips for a wash (bottom),
they playfully tussle.

haves against the have-nots. Given the obvious social gulf between Rip and Johnny, the surest way for the film to preserve the intensity of their friendship without ever having to confront its dubious sexual *or* social future in civilian life is to kill off one of the buddies early on. Once the film follows this tactic, however, the dead buddy all too easily turns into an idealized and unattainable figment of desire, which mourning turns inside out as anger, the anger motivating the violence Rip gives and receives during his investigation of Johnny's past. The triangulation of both Rip's desire and anger through Coral then censors the significance of Johnny's social difference from Rip because of her obvious sexual difference from both men.

Unable to continue thriving in postwar home life, the buddy relation in *Dead Reckoning* romanticizes both the war's deregulation of male sexuality and its temporary effacement of social divisions. Returning Rip to the military in its ending, the film makes no effort either to reinstate him in civilian society or to reconfigure his masculinity in a normative heterosexual frame. *Dead Reckoning* thus differs from other noir films of the period, such as *The Blue Dahlia* and *Gilda*, which fabricate closures that require a man's readjustment to the strict heterosexual regime of postwar life. This difference has a lot to do with *Dead Reckoning*'s industrial function for Columbia Pictures as a star vehicle for Bogart, making one of his first films away from Warner Bros. according to his newly renegotiated contract with that studio. With its representation of masculinity shaped to reiterate the actor's star persona, *Dead Reckoning* was clearly designed to give Bogart every opportunity to perform his tough-guy act convincingly, which meant borrowing authentifying moments from his other films. The screenplay written for the star consequently reproduces both the homosocial structure that invests his presence on screen as a "man's man" and the 1940s ideology of aggressive masculinity that gave his toughness its historical purchase. However, when put together, these two elements make the buddy relation more central than usual in Bogart's films of this period, bringing out the homoerotic undercurrent of his virility, the way it is staged, both on screen and off, for an audience of other men. By contrast, without the war setting to justify the homosocial structure of his masquerade as a heterosexual tough guy, his 1950s films draw on the same persona but give his virility a much different ideological currency.

In a Lonely Place: Anger Repression and the Wounds of War

The closure of *Dead Reckoning* anticipates the strain of film noir in the fifties that, with its projection of a conservative masculinity, appears to resist postwar hegemonic masculinity and its containment by the domestic mystique of mainstream American culture. However, while the many action movies regularly produced by the studios throughout the fifties—not only film noir thrillers, police melodramas, and crime capers, but Westerns, historical epics, and war films, too—seem far from committed to domesticity, most of them inevitably validate its importance, if only to show it functioning indirectly as the safety valve for male aggression. Film noir produced in the 1950s thus makes much more out of the perverse heterosexuality motivating aggressive inflections of masculinity, foregrounding the sadism, masochism, and fetishism that 1940s noir for the most part evaded, even in the process of representing it.

For example, in *Laura* (1944) detective Mark McPherson's (Dana Andrews) desire for Laura Hunt (Gene Tierney) originates in his fetishizing of her portrait while he believes she is dead; but the film puts acknowledgment of his perversion in the mouth of effete and snobbish Waldo Lydecker (Clifton Webb), the film's murderer. Waldo notices Mark's growing sexual obsession with the painting of Laura and does not refrain from taunting the cop with an accusation of perversion. Later, Waldo warns Laura of her "one tragic weakness," namely, that she foolishly believes "a lean, strong body is a measure of a man." That Waldo turns out to be obsessed with Laura himself, however, calls his own suspicions about the cop's normality into doubt, and his critique is disavowed all the more because of his own effeminacy and its suggestion of homosexuality as well as psychosis (though Waldo also supplies the film's voiceover, so textual authority here is by no means clear-cut or coherent).

By contrast, *Where the Sidewalk Ends*—a 1950 follow-up from the same studio (Twentieth Century-Fox) with the same director (Otto Preminger) and the same two stars (Andrews and Tierney)—no longer takes the tough guy's normality at face value. More openly displaying the sadism motivating and corrupting the tough phallic cop who thinks with his fists, *Where the Sidewalk Ends* begins with detective Mark Dixon (Andrews) officially reprimanded for using force too readily and too often. With Andrews playing a part much like the one in *Laura* (both detectives are even named Mark), the tough guy's sexual pathology is laid bare. His violence gets out of hand as he accidentally murders a man he is interrogating, giving ample evidence that a cop's muscular body is not the final measure of a man. The object of the rogue cop's uncontrollable violence, moreover, is quite an overdetermined victim: a war veteran with a metal plate in his head *and* the estranged husband of the woman (Tierney) the cop falls in love with. Later, the police arrest her father for the murder, driving the cop to confess his criminality. The trailer for this film well summarizes the dangers of this tough guy's masculinity, his marginality, as well as his means of recuperation (if not complete juridical vindication) through domesticity. "Dana Andrews," the voiceover narration exclaims, "a detective who could kill a man with his fists—and one night he did! Gene Tierney, who brought him love in place of his strange passion for hatred!"

Produced by Bogart's own company, Santana, *In a Lonely Place*, made the same time as *Where the Sidewalk Ends*, follows a similar course in its repudiation of the star's 1940s tough-guy persona. Screenwriter Dixon Steele (Bogart) has failed to adjust to postwar life. He hasn't written a hit movie since before

Figure 12.
Dix Steele (Bogart) under interrogation by the police for
the murder of Mildred Atkinson.

the war, the years following his return home have been chronicled in a police
file recording numerous incidents of drunken brawling with men and brutal-
izing of women, and he is now the prime suspect in the murder of Mildred
Atkinson, a hatcheck girl at the nightclub he frequents. In one vivid scene
midway through the film, Dix nearly kills a young man who berates him for
carelessly sideswiping his car. "This guy asked for it," Dix says afterward to his
companion, Laurel Gray (Gloria Grahame):

> *Dix:* "I've had a hundred fights like this one."
> *Laurel:* And you're proud of it?
> *Dix:* No, but I'm usually in the right.

The film recounts Dix's effort to get his life back together through Laurel's
intervention. His neighbor who provides him with an alibi for the night of the
murder, she, too, tries to bring him "love in place of his strange passion for
hatred." Once they begin an affair, Laurel brings some order to Dix's life,

influencing him to write again—and to do so brilliantly, it appears. However, even though Laurel knows Dix is innocent, his violent, uncontrollable temper finally makes her so fearful that she tries to break off the relationship. "But Dix doesn't act like a normal person," she tells his best friend, agent Mel Lippman (Art Smith). "You don't go around hitting people, smashing cars, torturing your best friend. I'm scared of him. I don't trust him. I'm not even sure he didn't kill Mildred Atkinson."

While Dix's violence frightens Laurel, it is also what attracts the coterie of male friends who surround him. Dependents such as Mel and the alcoholic ex-actor Charlie Waterman (Robert Warwick) validate Dix's aggressive masculinity through their uncritical admiration of his virility. Dix has always been violent, Mel tells Laurel: "It's as much a part of him as the color of his eyes or the shape of his head." Whereas Mel naturalizes Dix's aggressive masculinity through homosocial bonding, the writer's other crony homoeroticizes it. Charlie does not openly desire Dix, but he does rhetorically eroticize him, calling the writer "noble prince," for example, or reciting Sonnet 29, "When in disgrace with fortune and men's eyes," as he heads to Dix's bedroom to put him to bed. This former movie idol, moreover, evokes every stereotype of the hammy Shakespearean actor in order to emphasize his own outmoded theatricality and thereby play up Dix's (and Bogart's) authenticity. In their admiration for Dix, both Charlie and Mel dramatize how Dix Steele's tough masculinity depends upon his subjection of older men like themselves, which is simply the other side of his violent competition with younger men like the ones he brawls with in bars or on the streets. The older men excuse Dix's violence because they have an economic investment—Mel, after all, is his agent and Charlie takes regular handouts from him—in the homosocial power structure that his masculinity underwrites, the film implies, at the expense of masochistic women like Laurel, who has her own history of becoming involved with and running away from brutal, mastering men.

Originally the intention when filming of *In a Lonely Place* began was to have Dix turn out to be Mildred's murderer. This idea was soon dropped, although he still killed Laurel in the end in order "to keep her," as a detailed synopsis of the screenplay puts it (L. Smith). After production got underway, the script was revised yet again so that it became "a film about a man with rage enough to kill, but who does not" (Sklar 234).[6] Even with these significant alterations of its original story line, *In a Lonely Place* retains enough elements of Bogart's offscreen life as a notorious nightclub brawler to give Dix Steele's character resonance as an extension of the star's own tough-guy persona, particularly with respect to the violence he directs against women as well as other men.

One notorious incident involving Bogart in a drunken brawl is particularly important in helping to make the violence of *In a Lonely Place* more legible as some form of commentary upon his 1940s star persona. Just a month or two before filming began, Bogart, who still liked to go out drinking with a buddy or two while Bacall stayed home, was temporarily banned from the El Morocco nightclub in New York City because of an altercation with a young woman. She claimed that the drunken actor had shoved her across the room when she touched the three-foot stuffed pandas he and a pal were sporting around as their "girlfriends." Shades of Rip Murdock's description of the ideal woman? The parallel is not at all far-fetched since, in her autobiography, after Bacall reports the incident, she explains that Bogart never got into any real legal trouble following his various escapades because his "derring-do" was "always innocent"—i.e., a masquerade. In illustration Bacall unknowingly plagiarizes from *Dead Reckoning:* "Bogie had a joke dream—that a woman should be able to fit into a man's pocket. He'd take her out, talk to her, let her stand on the palm of his hand, dance on a table; when she got out of order— back in the pocket. And she could be made life-size when desired" (176).[7] The young woman at El Morocco refused to get back in his pocket, however; instead, she pressed charges, which were subsequently thrown out of court, but not before the story provided the papers with several days' worth of juicy copy.[8]

The panda affair, as it became known in the press, helps to bring out how *In a Lonely Place* dramatizes the problematic position of Bogart's tough-guy masculinity once it lost its necessary homosocial support and had to leave the 1940s nightclub scene—whether El Morocco or, as in this film, Paul's Restaurant or, by implication, the neighborhood bar—exchanging that setting for the domestic environment of postwar married life. Witness what happens when Dix tries to surprise Laurel with breakfast. Unfamiliar with the proper shape of a grapefruit knife, he straightens it with his bare hands, his gesture vividly displaying not just his innocence of domesticity (though it does that, to be sure) but, more ominously, the physical threat to Laurel inherent in his strong grip as well, which the climax of the film brings out when he loses control and *almost* strangles her. Whether or not he turns out to be a murderer, his masculinity is shown to be dangerous to both domestic life and heterosexual coupling.

A source of aggression and, because of the many revisions in the screenplay, a site of unfocused anger lacking a discernible object in the diegesis, Dix's body therefore demands continual surveillance.[9] Although the revised ending of *In a Lonely Place* will not allow his anger to turn into an act of murder, his rage still comes to dominate his possessiveness of Laurel; whenever Dix puts his arm around her it is difficult to tell whether his intention is affection or murder. Like Rip, Dix tries to keep a woman in his pocket, letting Laurel out to dance on the table, so to speak, as when she accompanies him to Paul's Restaurant, where, with all his male cronies in tow, he celebrates their engagement. His unruly behavior lacks the "innocence" which Bacall attributes to Bogart's "joke dream," however, because the character's "derring-do" underscores the violence that tries to compensate for his sense of sexual powerlessness when Laurel, refusing to stay in his pocket, tries to leave him. Even after the official plot vindicates him in the film's final minutes, suspicion about his masculinity still lingers because his violence prevents his redemption via the heterosexual couple, unlike *Where the Sidewalk Ends*, to cite a comparable example. As a consequence, *In a Lonely Place* places the film noir tough guy in the position more commonly occupied by the *femme fatale* (or, as in *Dead Reckoning*, by the beloved buddy). Dix is not only investigated by the law as the prime suspect in the murder, but, it turns out, prior to that killing, he has already been made the object of the police's ongoing surveillance because of his violence, producing their documentation of his street brawls and sexual abuse to suggest that his phallic bravado is less a confirmation of his masculine mastery and more a symptom of his anger at the failure of that masquerade to secure his virility.

In a Lonely Place may ultimately refuse to make him Mildred Atkinson's murderer, but Dix still turns out to be the most credible suspect because, in his anger, he identifies with the emotions of her killing so intensely. During one memorable sequence, Brub Nicolai (Frank Lovejoy)—a war buddy from Dix's old army unit who is now one of the detectives investigating the Atkinson murder—invites the writer to his house for some supper and surveillance.

Figure 13.
When Dix puts his arm around Laurel (Gloria Grahame), it is difficult
to tell whether his intention is affection or murder.

With Brub's encouragement, Dix uses his skill as a screen fabulist to dramatize how the murder was probably committed. The film accounts for Dix's deductions by referring specifically to his former experiences as a GI trained to kill, thereby setting his own violent behavior in the present against the historical context of the war. "First you have to have enough imagination to solve the crime," Dix remarks as he sets the stage with his two dinner hosts, Brub and the latter's wife, Sylvia (Jeff Donnell), taking the parts of Mildred Atkinson and her unknown assailant. Dix sits opposite them, his face lit from above so that it appears to glow from excitement, and the editing cuts back and forth between him speaking and his two friends acting out what he narrates: "You put your right arm around her neck. You get to a lonely place in the road and you begin to squeeze. You're an ex-GI. You know judo. You know how to kill a person without using your hands. You're driving the car and you're strangling her. You don't see her bulging eyes or protruding tongue. Go ahead, Brub, squeeze harder. . . . It's wonderful to feel the throat crush under your arm." The writer's excitement in imagining the murder is contagious. Brub acts out the killer's part so well that his wife has to stop him from hurting *her*. Once Dix leaves, Sylvia remarks to her husband: "He's a sick man, Brub. . . . There's something wrong with him." Brub, however, disagrees: "He's always been like that. He's an exciting guy." After arguing, Sylvia finally concedes, "Well, he's exciting because he isn't quite normal." Brub still goes to his buddy's defense, trying to attribute his abnormality to his superiority, but Sylvia admits that she likes her husband just the way he is: "attractive and average."

With both his first and last names obviously meant to pun on his phallic masculinity, Dix Steele is clearly a menace to the health of the heterosexual couple not only because of his violence, which tears apart his relation to Laurel, but also because of his influence on "attractive and average" men like Brub. Their admiration may be appropriate for the bonding of buddies in wartime, but it is clearly dangerous to their wives when revived in a living room. In contrast to *Dead Reckoning, In a Lonely Place*, made just three years later, already shows how attitudes toward the expression of male anger had shifted considerably during the postwar years. Prior to this time (that is, from the 1860s to the start of WWII) treatment of anger in middle-class American culture generally followed a pattern of sexual differentiation, with girls trained to repress their anger in the interest of preserving the quiet temperament of home life, and boys encouraged to channel theirs outside of the home, first in competitive sports as youths and then in business as breadwinners. After the 1940s, however, "anger now had no good purpose," and psychologists advocated the repression of anger for men as well as women (Stearns 87).

In illustration, consider that, before World War II, a typical coming-of-age present for boys was "a growing-up gift of boxing gloves." Boxing was recommended by experts "as a perfect means of training adolescent males in anger control for it channeled the emotion away from unwarranted targets without quelling it" (Stearns 84). From the Victorian period through the onset of the

Second World War, the so-called manly art of boxing, initially begun in city street life among working-class men to compensate for the undermining of their masculinity by hard daily labor in factories, began to epitomize the required channeling of male anger into sanctioned forms of physical aggression and competition for middle-class men, too: "Toughness, ferocity, prowess, honor, these became the touchstone of maleness, and boxing along with other sports upheld this alternative definition of manhood. The *manly* art defined masculinity not by how responsible or upright an individual was but by his sensitivity to insult, his coolness in the face of danger, and his ability to give and take punishment" (Gorn 141). It was through such socially welcomed activities for young men boxing, in fact, that, by the end of the nineteenth century, "the old bourgeois meaning of 'manly'—to be adult, responsible, mature, self-possessed, independent, not childlike—was transformed into a negation of all that was soft, feminine, or sentimental. Being manly now meant being not womanly" (193).

The postwar ideology of anger repression, however, devalued boxing's ritualized enactment of a healthy, competitive, and unfeminine masculinity. A number of noir boxing films made after the war, such as *Body and Soul* (1947), *The Set-Up* (1949), and *Champion* (1949), depict the sport's corruption, using this setting as an occasion for interrogating the morality, not to say the efficacy, of boxing as an institutionalization of virility. In much the same vein, when *From Here to Eternity* (1953) endorses a conservative masculinity whose integrity can be defended against the domesticating influence of women only by its location in the enlisted man's army, the film embeds boxing within the rituals of prewar military life as the central outlet for male-male competition. As part of its repudiation of domestic ideology, *From Here to Eternity* uses boxing as a moral yardstick to differentiate Prewitt (Montgomery Clift), the good soldier and expert boxer, whose respect for the manly art and its risks causes him to refuse to fight for ignoble motives, from those officers in "G" Company whose relation to the sport has been corrupted by their ambition.

Promoted by the social science experts as a necessary condition of normal men, anger repression was certainly consistent with the domestic mystique of fifties hegemonic masculinity, but it was perhaps even more directly responsive to the war's promotion of male aggression as the basis of good soldiering. The war's ideology of militant masculinity not only challenged the traditional articulation of "manliness" through anger channeling, but, more disturbingly, it also opened a gap between the representation of male valor in combat and the actual conditions of men in battle. Movie characters like Rip Murdock and Johnny Drake at the start of *Dead Reckoning*, recovering from war wounds and awaiting medals of commendation for their bravery, reproduced the official view of heroism authorized by the military and celebrated by the various media as well as government propaganda. Actual accounts of the war, however, differed from the movies' representation of American heroism, and Dix Steele's brutality in civilian life signifies this difference and the ambivalence about male aggression that it produced for representations of virility after the war ended.

Whether venerated or mocked, heroism in battle was viewed, to start with, as a masquerade. "While most soldiers would and often did risk their lives to protect their buddies," Bérubé reports, "they shunned heroics and often used the term *hero* as an insult rather than a compliment. *Hero* described the undependable man who displayed a foolhardy bravado that could get him killed or endanger the lives of his buddies" (177). Similarly, in his articles for *Life* on one of the marines' campaigns at Guadalcanal, the novelist John Hersey observed that courage is "largely the desire to show other men that you have it" (78). As the writer illustrated when describing the inspiring self-control of a "terrified" marine captain, courage in battle amounted to exhibiting "as cool a performance as you can imagine" (79).

The performativity of heroism in battle, however, in no way mitigated or excused the violence of its setting. Looking back on his comment about courage, in his preface Hersey disclaims its performative value, describing it instead as a range of responses from "pure self-sacrifice for the sake of others to the release of a deep and gross bloodlust," but he still admits that the pressure to perform for a watchful audience, "to show your mettle to your friends," would have been especially strong "in a proud corps like the Marines" (xxiv–xxv). His account of the war, both when experiencing it firsthand and then when remembering it nearly thirty years later, means to document the fundamental bravery, stoicism, and dignity of American soldiers in the face of the war's horrors. Yet what Hersey described in 1943 often produces a more disturbing impression, since he gives evidence of men morally as well as physically and psychologically brutalized by this war, particularly given the undisguised racism that drove American fighting in the Pacific. This war may have been remembered afterward as a great adventure, a premature climax to a man's life, but it severely undermined conventional notions of masculinity, not only by revealing the performativity of courage, but by collapsing, in the barbarism of ordinary soldiers on both sides of the fighting, the line separating bravery from brutality as well.

With combat devalued as the consummate test of heroism, a number of films produced immediately after the war, as Kaja Silverman points out, "attest to a radical loss of belief in the conventional premises of masculinity" (51). She defines "conventional masculinity" in psychoanalytic terms as the denial of castration or symbolic lack upon which male subjectivity is founded, as achieved primarily through the safeguard illusion of a whole and inviolate male anatomy. This "dominant fiction" allows the male ego to function as a kind of armor, "predicated upon the illusion of coherence and control" (62). A hard male body—or its symbolic externalization in clothing, as in breastplate or a football uniform—reinforces that dominant fiction because "only through the mediation of images of an unimpaired masculinity" (42) can the body appear perfectly self-contained, whole and unified, with no openings or gaps, no orifices to make it vulnerable to penetration. In her accounts of sexual difference in various tribal myths, anthropologist Françoise Héritier-Augé goes so far as to propose that control of blood as a means of maintaining the illusion of bodily wholeness may well be the key to male domination of the female in its variety of symbolic guises (and, I might quickly add, to heterosexual men's homophobic panic over anal penetration): "What man values in man, then, is no doubt his ability to bleed, to risk his life, to take that of others, by his own free will," contrasting to a woman, who "sees her blood flowing from her body" at periodic intervals to suggest her inability to control bleeding (298).

Needless to say, wartime makes it extremely difficult to maintain the credibility of this dominant fiction. As Silverman puts it, war makes "the impairment of anatomical masculinity" an issue of "*psychic* disintegration" (62), and the correlation works in both directions. In his articles for *Life*, Hersey reported that the group of men he was following were, after one horrendous three-day battle, "wounded in a dreadful way. They had no open wounds; they shed no blood; they seemed merely to have been attacked by some mysterious germ of war that made them groan, hold their sides, limp and stagger. They were shock and blast victims" (85–86). But as well as assaulting the psyche, the war created conditions in which the unified, seamless, and mastering bodies of men were punctured and mutilated, in a word, bloody, or as Hersey describes one "handsome" blond boy—with a "caved-in chest" and a leg "bruised almost beyond use"—"a mess" (88). The war may therefore have glamorized the hard, impenetrable body of the warrior (as in the iconic use of statues to celebrate—during and also after WWII—the marines' taking of Iwo Jima in February 1945)[10] but it also magnified the male body's impairment. Littering the battleground with the devastating sight of broken, penetrated, and bleeding male bodies, the war resulted in what Silverman calls "a historical trauma": an event which brings large groups of men into "such an intimate relation with lack that they are at least for the moment unable to sustain an imaginary relation with the phallus," causing, as far as the entire culture was concerned, a profound crisis of disbelief in the dominant fiction of male coherence and impenetrability (55). And one does not need recourse to psychoanalysis to find ample evidence of what Silverman is theorizing. Both Lawrence Alloway in *Violent America* and Dana Polan in *Power and Paranoia* take note of the increased violence that occurs in postwar Hollywood cinema, "a kind of cataloging of all the wounds that can be inflicted on bodies" (Polan 213), which each relates to the war's machinery of death and mutilation as it affected the popular imagination.

Given the logic with which, according to the manly art of physical and professional competition, "manliness" had come to mean the antithesis of "womanliness" for middle-class men before the war, it's no wonder that, when World War II appeared to negate the traditional method of validating masculinity through trial by combat and instead gave graphic illustration of the male body's inherent capacity for penetration and impairment, the war's impact was perceived as "a historical trauma" and represented, as Silverman shows with her analysis of *The Best Years of Our Lives* (1946) as well as several other films, a symbolic castration. With anger ceasing to differentiate masculinity from femininity, as had been the case before the war, the fifties domestic mystique easily gave rise to the widespread anxiety circulated by the popular press that hegemonic masculinity was tantamount to a feminizing of men because it went against the grain of a male's "inborn" nature. But more to my point here, when displaced from the official arenas of man-to-man competition like boxing, the aggression formerly regulated through anger channeling and given freer reign in the theaters of war also exposed the cultural production of virility as a gender performance, one built upon homosocial bonding and its grounding in homosexual desire, as I argued about World War II's institutionalization of the buddy relation. In *Dead Reckoning,* the intense bond between Rip and Johnny brings to this film traditional characteristics of masculinity that had formerly vindicated the virility of a "man's man" in working-class culture and had been epitomized, in a nonmilitary setting, by the manly art of boxing: camaraderie, loyalty, courage, honor, integrity. Consequently, if Rip embodies, as his name implies, some sort of tear in the dominant fiction of unimpaired masculinity that Silverman describes, that crisis in the phallic organization of his virility is made evident in the relative ease with which the homosocial structure of his manly façade slides into homosexual desire.

By contrast, in *Lonely Place,* the homosocial structure of Dix's virility is represented much more diffusely, manifesting itself in his violence and misogyny, all recorded in his police record, and set in opposition to the "attractive and average" masculinity personified by his ex-war buddy, Brub, whose stolid demeanor is obviously regulated by an ideology of anger repression. Though many of the same acting mannerisms remain, the shift in tone and temperament from Bogart's quintessential performance as street-smart Sam Spade in *The Maltese Falcon* to street-brawler Dix Steele in *Lonely Place* shows how quickly (just ten years) this revaluation of tough masculinity took hold, at least within the contours of a popular actor's persona. It suggests, moreover, how thoroughly middle-class America had reconceived its standard of hegemonic masculinity following the war, and, as importantly, how the homoerotic undercurrent of Bogart's 1940s tough-guy mask, which he still puts on to perform his virility for the appreciation of other men like Mel, Charlie, and Brub in *Lonely Place,* had been reinterpreted as a symptomatic eruption of male psychopathology: a kind of war wound but without the war to account for it.

The Desperate Hours: The Tough Guy as Psychopath

The production of violent action movies of all sorts during or immediately after another war in Korea helps to account for the ongoing prominence of the movie tough guy, particularly during the first half of the 1950s. With the cold war warming into military action, an aggressive masculinity still had to retain a certain ideological hold on the culture. Cold war movies warn about encroachment and invasion under many guises and in different genres, always reiterating the values of political and sexual containment, and often doing so by counterpointing the breadwinner to a solitary, undomesticated, mysterious male figure who comes to his rescue but is, ultimately, unassimilated because of his toughness. A Western such as *Shane* (1953) works toward this end, finally valuing the homesteader (Van Heflin) as the norm over the gunfighter (Alan Ladd), just as a film noir such as *Panic in the Streets* (1950) upholds the hegemonic masculinity of the married doctor (Richard Widmark) over the more conservative inflection of the widowed policeman (Paul Douglas). In this latter film, the hierarchical relation of hegemonic and conservative masculinities is ultimately what allows the two men to work together in effectively containing foreign Otherness, here troped as a contagious disease carried into the United States by an illegal alien from Eastern Europe. "What are you getting so tough about?" the doctor asks the cop when the latter growls about being sent to investigate a barking dog in the closing moment of the film; and the cop replies, in acknowledgment of his new colleague's authority, "I don't know."

The 1950s career of tough-guy Glenn Ford, in this regard, makes for an illuminating counterpoint to Bogart's. *The Big Heat*, a Columbia programmer that played the top half of double bills in 1953, best typifies Ford's early film noir roles, which initially made his reputation. For the first half hour or so of *The Big Heat*, police detective Dave Bannion (Ford) is successfully domesticated according to all the codes of fifties togetherness. However, organized crime invades the Bannions' ranch house when a bomb planted in the family car goes off and kills wife Katie (Jocelyn Brando), instead of Dave, the intended victim. Following his wife's funeral, Dave quits the force and goes on "a hate binge," which the film justifies in the name of the violated middle-class home. Significantly, though, what most threatens the sanctity of "home" in *The Big Heat* is not the mob but Dave's own masculinity, which causes his hegemonic persona as the family breadwinner to implode. In one striking scene of family life, Dave returns home from work to find his young daughter, Joyce, building a house of blocks. He remarks, "That's the most beautiful castle in the world," but she corrects him: "It's a police station, daddy, just like yours." Agreeing to help Joyce put the roof on her toy building, Dave resists his wife's questions about his irritable mood but finally admits that, in snapping at Katie, he's letting off steam gathering from his frustration over a case. To make up for his show of temper, he starts to tell his wife about the case disturbing him, while turning to help Joyce with her building. One touch from Dave, and the toy police station topples over, leaving Joyce in tears at the damage caused by her father's hand. As if to underline the point that home life requires the repression of Dave's violent temper but also has great trouble doing so, after the toy building collapses, the phone rings and Katie gets a threatening anonymous phone call, which sends her husband over to confront the mob boss personally, starting the chain of events that leads to the bombing of the Bannion car.

When Dave goes out of control after his wife's death, *The Big Heat* tries extremely hard to motivate his uncompromising anger while at the same time disavowing his capacity for violence so that it can appear quite alien to his masculinity. In order to keep Dave's moral honor intact, B-girl Debby Marsh (Gloria Grahame), who has her own score to settle with the mob, does what Dave cannot do, as she herself explicitly states, without his becoming no different than gangster Vince Stone (Lee Marvin), her sadistic lover: murder Bertha Duncan (Jeanette Nolan), who holds in trust the crucial document that will bring the mob's infiltration of the police department to light and break its hold on the city. Debby may distinguish the lawman from the psychopath but, as importantly, she also highlights their comparability. While, in his brutality and sadism (as when he splashes scalding coffee on Debby's face), Stone comes off as the moral opposite of Bannion, the masculinity of *both* men still relies upon their exploitation of women, whether this occurs in a bar or a suburban home. Stone tortures and mutilates women, and Dave then goes to their rescue, though in every important case (Lucy Chapman, Debby Marsh, Bertha Duncan, even his wife), he not only fails to save them but is the one who marked them for death in the first place. Through the doubling of cop and criminal, family man and sadist, *The Big Heat* achieves the expulsion of the feminine from Dave's life in a way that allows him to disown the misogyny on which his "tough" masculinity, like Vince Stone's, is founded.

In its violence and misogyny, *The Big Heat* was not an unusual film for Glenn Ford to make in the early fifties. During the shooting it was reported in a Los Angeles paper that "[he] is turning down all scripts in which women crack the whip and make him grovel in their dust." The actor explained in an interview: "One of the things I found out in making pictures outside of Hollywood is that my fans don't want to see me dominated by women. They might take it in other men, but they resent it when it happens to me."[11] Ford made another film for Columbia a year later, aptly titled *The Violent Men* (1954), which cast him in a similar vigilante role as Captain John Parrish, a tough veteran, injured and back from the war—the Civil War, in this instance—who breaks his engagement when he agrees to put on a gun to defend his property and that of other homeowners ("nesters," they are called) against the efforts of the local cattle baron to incorporate the entire territory within his own empire. In fighting Wilkerson (Edward G. Robinson), Parrish uses the scorched-earth tactics he learned as a Yankee soldier, much to his nemesis's admiration. "He let his whole ranch go up in smoke simply to start an ambush," Wilkerson says. "There's a true cold-blooded devil. I didn't know he had that much iron in him."

By mid-decade, however, Ford's persona had noticeably minimized his purity as an iron man. In *Blackboard Jungle* (1955), meek, soft-spoken Rick Dadier (Ford) is a Korean vet trying to make a go of his first teaching job in an unruly high school. After students assault him in a back alley, Dadier—or "Daddy-O," as his students call him—swears: "I may be beaten up, but I'm not beaten. There's a big difference. I'm not beaten. And I'm not quitting." Rather than burn down the school to fight his enemies, Dadier uses the techniques of the advertising man (subtle manipulation of representation rather than brutal imposition of force), regulating his delinquent students by getting them interested in a cartoon, "Jack and the Beanstalk," which stages for them the ideological power of narrative (Biskind 212–13). On the home front, Daddy-O achieves the same end. After his wife (Anne Francis) vindicates his patriarchal position in the classroom by giving birth to their son, she confesses that, in her anxieties about his job and his fidelity, she was acting just like one of "the bad kids" in his class, acknowledging that she too needs his supervision and instruction.

Blackboard Jungle marked an important transition in Ford's career. Despite his success in noir thrillers and Westerns, the actor did not achieve bona fide movie stardom until he moved from Columbia to Metro-Goldwyn-Mayer (he was one of the few leading men who, during this period, sought nonexclusive contract status with a major studio) and considerably modified his tough-guy persona more along the lines of Rick Dadier's character. MGM followed *Jungle* with films in a similar key of anguished hegemonic masculinity, such as *Trial* (1955) and *Ransom* (1956). By the end of the decade, when Ford had risen to the top of box-office polls as one of the industry's most popular male stars, he had further turned his tough screen image inside out through a comic style that allowed his sincerity and ordinariness, rather than his clenched fist or iron will, to subvert oppressive and outmoded forms of male authority. In these films, Ford's subversion of the tough and aggressive masculinity he himself had once exemplified (as in *The Big Heat*) often takes place within a military setting, usually to his own bewilderment and always to his credit, as in his MGM comedies *The Teahouse of the August Moon* (1956), *Don't Go Near the Water* (1957), *Imitation General* (1958), and *It Started with a Kiss* (1959). To be sure, at the same time Ford continued to star in action films for Columbia such as *3:10 to Yuma* (1957) and *Cowboy* (1958); but as Michael Wood recalls, this is still an actor who "contributes great washes of torment and strangled repression to any movie he is in" (84). In short, the pretty young tough who slapped Rita Hayworth around in *Gilda,* and then again (albeit with a bit less box-office success) in *Affair in Trinidad* (1952), had to play *The Sheepman* (1958), defending his right to domesticate cattle country with fencing, in order to become a big fifties star in his own right.

In contrast to Ford, although the cultural position of his star persona shifted as considerably, Bogart remained firmly identified with his tough-guy roles of the 1940s, as publicity for *The Desperate Hours* reminded audiences. As he stated in the 1945 press release quoted earlier, he was willing to take on any sort of role, "just as long as it's tough," and (with the exception of 1954's *Sabrina*, in which Bogart uncomfortably played a part that director Billy Wilder had planned for Cary Grant), this intention was reflected in the films he made once he became completely independent of his Warner Bros. contract. However, Bogart's determination to play the escaped convict in *The Desperate Hours* (he tried to purchase rights to the property himself before being outbid by Paramount), also shows his recognition of the revised status of his tough-guy persona in the decade after the war. For his violent character in this 1955 film, while appearing to draw upon the star's previous roles as a gangster, particularly the one that made him famous in *The Petrified Forest* (1936), now illuminates what *In a Lonely Place* had only implied five years earlier: the extent to which a discourse of psychopathology had come to fully contain the anger and violence of his tough masculinity.[12]

The Desperate Hours is a home-invasion narrative which operates according to the same ideological agenda governing similar treatments of this plot situation in cold war films of all sorts. Three escaped convicts led by Glenn Griffin (Bogart) invade an ordinary-looking house in a quiet residential neighborhood of Indianapolis and hold the family living there hostage. The convicts do not invade this house randomly; rather, sighting a child's bicycle on the front lawn, Griffin takes advantage of the family's inherent vulnerability. "Why here?" the middle-class father wants to know. "Why *my* house?" The escaped convict opines rather matter-of-factly: "People with kids don't take chances." The effectiveness of the home-invasion story line in *The Desperate Hours* arises, first, from the way that the hostage situation plays out *inside* this particular middle-class house more generalized fears about what dangers to the coherence and continuity of "normal" family life lay *outside* every American home; and second, from the way that the hardened criminal's personification of those dangers, positioned in opposition to the norm of the homeowner's hegemonic masculinity, externalizes them as psychological deviancy.

The narrative logic of the popular fifties invasion narrative—whether in Westerns, science-fiction, or thrillers such as *The Desperate Hours*—was motivated by a domestic ideology which gave special privilege to a masculinity securely positioned within the home as the one guarantee of family security. What does the younger generation want? *Time* asked in 1951. Inspired by "an American tradition older than its parents," the magazine concluded, this generation of people aged 18 to 28 "wants to marry, have children, found homes, and if necessary, defend them" ("Younger" 48). In *The Desperate Hours*, when the convicts first take his family hostage, the middle-aged father, Dan Hilliard (Fredric March), appears emasculated, unable to defend his home against this invasion, especially as personified by the menacing figure of Glenn Griffin. "I

Figure 14.
Griffin (Bogart) and Hilliard (Fredric March) battle over
the body of young Ralph.

lost my temper," Hilliard confesses early on, after unsuccessfully resorting to physical violence when his young son, Ralph (Richard Eyre), is threatened. "I can't do that again," he swears.

> *Ralph:* You're afraid, aren't you.
> *Hilliard:* Yes, son. I'm afraid and I'm not ashamed to admit it. Sometimes it's better to be afraid.

As the exemplar of fifties hegemonic masculinity, the breadwinner in *The Desperate Hours* has to learn to turn the other cheek, knowing that brains rather than brawn will be his only deliverance. "Clickety, clickety, click," Griffin keeps warning Hilliard, often with a wave of the gun, whenever the wheels in the latter's head appear to be turning too fast for the convict's comfort.

Structurally, *The Desperate Hours* builds its thematic tensions from a schematic opposition between the two middle-aged men, both played by stars of long-standing popularity. One is brutish and daring, and the other gentle and cautious; one uses force, the other intelligence. At moments, the film even acknowledges the class politics underlying this opposition. Griffin's violence is socially motivated, his anger directed at the middle-class establishment which has disempowered him and his younger brother, Hal (Dewey Martin). When Hilliard tells his wife, Ellie (Martha Scott), not to cook for the convict, an infuriated Griffin screams back at him: "Listen, Hilliard, you ain't calling the tune! I got my guts full of you shiney-shoes, down-your-nose wise guys with white handkerchiefs in their pockets." Pulling the handkerchief out of the breast pocket of Hilliard's suit jacket, Griffin drops it to the floor and stomps his feet on it, warning: "Next time I'll wipe them on you!"

According to Robert Sklar, in its polarizing of Griffin and Hilliard, *The Desperate Hours* moves "beyond black-and-white dichotomies" through its "comparison of the two men as educators and authority figures—the father to his wife and children, the criminal to his confederates, one of whom is his younger brother" (249). However, while the film appears to be staging a battle between violent (and conservative) and gentle (and hegemonic) masculinities, the latter's victory has already been decided in advance, so it's really no contest. At one point, from his hidden vantage point behind the drapes of the Hilliard living room, Hal Griffin watches a group of teens piling into a convertible outside, a scene which underscores his alienation from normal life. "Yeah, you taught me everything," Hal later accuses his older brother, "'cept how to live in a house like this." Glenn Griffin remains mystified by his brother's growing respect for "*Mister* Hilliard," unable to understand why Hal persists in addressing their hostage so formally when the latter and his class have never shown any respect to their kind. The attraction of middle-class life thus drives a wedge between the two brothers, rupturing the only relation that moves the older man to show any affect other than anger.

The strong bond between the two brothers also allows for a glimpse of the familiar homosocial structuring of Bogart's persona through a buddy relation, although the film censors whatever homoerotic value their affection for each other may generate by making the two men siblings. Nevertheless, Griffin's strong feelings for his brother are clearly mediated through the delight he takes in Hal's heterosexuality: "You oughta see him dance," Griffin boasts to Hilliard's daughter, Cindy (Mary Murphy). "He has all the dames groggy." Griffin consequently believes that Hal is "mixed up" only because Hilliard's daughter sexually excites him. "I know what's eating you, kid," he reassures his brother. "I'll tell you what, we'll take the girl along, just for you." For his part, Hilliard recognizes that he can turn the younger man's sexual interest in Cindy to his own advantage, in effect making Hal a point of rivalry between the two older men as they vie for control of the house.

Both Hal's attraction to the middle-class life of the Hilliards and Griffin's identification with his brother's sexuality help to coarsen the convict's character so that he appears to equate power solely with physical force. What Glenn

Griffin does not understand, because he keeps falling back on a tough-guy working-class mentality, is that Hilliard intimidates Hal precisely because the superiority of the middle-class father's social position manifests itself in less tangible form than a clenched fist or cocked trigger. Indeed, if Hal's encounter with the Hilliards accounts for the ambivalence he comes to feel about his brother's motives for staying on in the house, causing him to break the sibling bond and go off on his own, loyalty to his brother, it turns out, is also what causes his death when he tries to warn Glenn that the police are closing in, only to be discovered by a cop himself. Shooting wildly in panic, Hal is shot in turn and, when he flees, is run over by a truck, information which Hilliard later uses to hurt Griffin in their final showdown.

Another plot movement validating Hilliard's masculinity over Griffin's involves the former's own son. "Don't let them take me," young Ralph cries out in his sleep. "I won't let them take you or anyone," his father tries to reassure him. "I'll stop them." Then Ralph asks the deflating question: "How are you going to stop them?" While Ralph believes that his father is too frightened to act, the boy's own gestures at movie-style heroism (he climbs out of his bed-room window onto the garage roof and then drops to the ground, only to be captured by Griffin) end up spoiling his father's momentary victory over the convicts midway through the film, when he locks all three out of the house. Having disobeyed his father, Ralph subjects the family to further victimization since Hilliard has to surrender the house to save his son from the convicts outside. When the film later repeats that same dilemma in another showdown over Ralph's body, the middle-class patriarch now demands of his young son the same kind of absolute faith which God demanded of Abraham when ordering him to sacrifice Isaac. Griffin holds a gun to Ralph's head, and only Hilliard knows the weapon is not loaded. He asks his son, "Will you do exactly as I tell you, Ralph?" and then orders the boy to run to safety, despite Griffin's threat to shoot him in the head if he should make a move. Placing complete trust in his father's command, even if that means to go against all reason since the boy can feel the barrel of the gun pressing into his skull, Ralph obeys.

While *The Desperate Hours* opposes the masculinities of Griffin and Hilliard in this manner, the domesticated breadwinner also has to recognize his likeness to the brutish convict. Griffin, in other words, shows Hilliard what the latter himself must repress in order to keep the domestic space safe and secure for his family: his own anger and the violence erupting from it. The difference between the two men thus results from Hilliard's restraint in contrast to Griffin's lack of self-control. "I know exactly how you feel," the breadwinner shouts at the convict, referring to the latter's rage. "I have the same thing in me. I want to kill you." Hearing this, Griffin turns to Ellie Hilliard and comments, "Lady, you didn't know what a tough old bird you married, did you?" At the end, Griffin—now unarmed through a trick of Hilliard's and trapped in the house alone with him while the police wait outside—tries to goad his former captive into shooting him, but Hilliard will not do it. "You ain't got it in you," Griffin taunts. Hilliard claims that he *can* pull the trigger—"I got it in me; you put it there"—but he refuses to do so, resorting instead to a much more potent threat: "Get out of my house!"[13] With the tables turned, Hilliard's moral authority as a domesticated man revitalizes his masculinity in direct proportion to its emasculation of Griffin. Pushing the convict downstairs, Hilliard shoves him outside of the house, where the police take care of the disarmed convict with *their* guns.

Sklar describes Bogart's character in *The Desperate Hours* as "probably the most brutal role of his career," one which contrasts to his earlier criminal roles in the 1930s at Warners, because "there is little effort to situate Griffin's criminality in a social context—he is an antisocial deviant whose resentment of the bourgeois father is a sign only of his personal weakness and envy, not of any failures of the social order" (249). The press release for *The Desperate Hours* similarly accepts as a given that "the callow product of the American underworld," an inflection of his tough-guy persona which Bogart still "typified," had now turned into "the most viciously intelligent criminal ever put to film" ("Biography"). But this does not mean as a consequence that Glenn Griffin lacks social context of any sort. Whereas Dan Hilliard, the establishment figure, wins the field in the end by successfully repressing his anger as proof of his civility (and as moral evidence of his social right, as a member of the middle class, to the property which the convict invades), the social deviancy exhibited by Glenn Griffin links him to the frightening cultural figure of the amoral, uncontrollable, and sadistic juvenile delinquent. In fact, in the original Broadway play, the part of Griffin was played by a rising young star, Paul Newman, not a middle-aged actor like Bogart.

Truth to tell, in 1955 age (and cancer) would appear to have withered Bogart to the point where his persona and the violence it generated on screen must have seemed eons apart from the more youthful actors who played delinquents on screen, like James Dean in *Rebel without a Cause* or, more disturbingly, Vic Morrow in *Blackboard Jungle*, two popular movies about teenage delinquency produced the same year as *The Desperate Hours*. While in a later chapter I will be taking up the figure of the young rebel again, for now I want to stress the delinquency which the youthful and aging criminals have in common. At the time, the similarity of Bogart's character in *The Desperate Hours* and the teen criminals of numerous juvenile delinquent films did not go entirely without notice. Writing in *Shenandoah* in 1960, Martin Dworkin began an analysis of violence in American cinema with this observation: "*The Desperate Hours* and *Teen Age Crime Wave* are major versions of a recurring melodrama, in which a family or community—here the former—is imprisoned, or besieged by criminals" (39). In drawing this comparison, Dworkin sensed how the older antisocial figure of Glenn Griffin shares with Hollywood's juvenile delinquents the same cultural intertext for violent disregard of family and property, and that is the discourse of the psychopath, which acquired special currency in the fifties as an accounting of antisocial male behavior.

In his thorough history of delinquency in the fifties, James Gilbert points out that public concern with the severity of juvenile crime at that time exaggerated its danger, at least if one keeps in mind the statistics collected during the period, particularly in comparison to the following decade, when Children's Court cases significantly increased, while public agitation lessened. "Juvenile delinquency was thus a word that contained a large measure of sub-surface meaning," Gilbert concludes (70–71). "What it often represented was a vaguely formulated but gnawing sense of social disintegration—symbolized in the misbehavior of youth. . . . The point is that a large portion of the public thought there was a delinquency crime wave, and they clamored to understand how and why this was happening" (77).

Trying to explain this perceived crime wave, popular accounts of the juvenile delinquent characterized him with much the same rhetoric of deviant personality that, forty years later, Sklar uses in his description of Griffin. *Newsweek,* for instance, pictured gangs of male youths turning every major city into "'juvenile jungles' where prudent men walk cautiously after nightfall" ("Why" 26). "Here occur most of the serious crimes of murder, rape, robbery, theft, and vandalism—and for them, the sociologists blame what they term another major flaw in American society today: The breakdown of authority" (28). Repeating the conclusions of social science experts, the magazine attrib-uted the delinquent's violence to the misunderstood lessons of World War II, when, in the words of one anonymous sociologist (who was actually para-phrasing the postwar advertising slogan of the movie industry), "Violence was bigger and better than ever," and young men, who had experienced the war only secondhand, "accepted the premise that total violence could be a solution to world problems. The delinquents turned to total violence to solve their own problems" (26).

Time likewise wondered if these young criminals were "rebels or psycho-paths." In search of an answer the magazine quoted psychologist Robert Linder, who had coined the signature phrase "rebel without a cause" in 1944 as a means of describing the juvenile delinquent's psychopathic behavior.

An anxious and concerned public, Linder says, has received from the "experts" only absurd theories and warmed-over nostrums: "Throw away the comic books," "Close down the TV stations," "Return to breastfeeding," and "Get tough with them." But, he adds, "really to understand what is happening to youth requires psychological knowledge. Both the basic tendencies of modern youth—to 'act out' and to drift into herds—are symptomatic of a psychiatric condition, worldwide in scope, related directly to the social and political temper of our times. There is only one mental aberration in which these two symptoms coexist: in the psychopathic personality, essentially antisocial, conscienceless, inclined to violence in behavior, and liable to

Figure 15.
The showdown between Rick Dadier (Glenn Ford) and
Artie West (Vic Morrow) in *Blackboard Jungle.*

loss of identity in the group, gang, mob or herd. The psychopath is a rebel without a cause—hence in a chronic state of mutiny. He strives solely for the satisfaction of his moment-to-moment desires. Raw need is all that drives him. . . .

The youth of the world today is touched with madness, literally sick with an aberrant condition of mind formerly confined to a few distressed souls but now epidemic over the earth. ("Rebels" 64, ellipsis in original)

In their violent antisocial behavior, both glassy-eyed, thumb-sucking Artie West (Vic Morrow) in *Blackboard Jungle,* the quintessential fifties teen-crime movie, and Bogart's Glenn Griffin in *The Desperate Hours,* the quintessential fifties family-hostage movie, display on screen the same "psychopathic personality" described by Linder in *Time;* in its defiance of authority, this deviant personality type appears to justify the need for social control of male aggression. *Blackboard Jungle* ends with a showdown between West and schoolteacher Rick Dadier that, in demonstrating the moral weakness of the tough young hoodlum, is similar to the climax of *The Desperate Hours.* "You're the leader! You're the tough guy!" Dadier shouts sarcastically after disarming West and slamming him against the blackboard. "You're not so tough without a knife, are you?"

While *Blackboard Jungle* and *The Desperate Hours* primarily dramatize the psychopathic criminal's destruction of private property, the violence in both films has a decided sexual edge that cannot be ignored. The teens' beatings of two male teachers and their destruction of physical property may be what linger in a viewer's memory, but the first act of delinquency shown in *Blackboard Jungle* is an attempted rape of a female teacher by a student, Joe Murray, which Dadier stops. The reign of teenage terrorism that follows includes psychological harassment of Dadier's wife as well as the rumble in an alley, and it appears to be the effort of West and his gang to avenge the teacher's role in sending Murray first to the hospital and then to reform school. *The Desperate Hours* is not without its threat of sexual menace either. One way that the convicts terrorize the Hilliards is with their ability, at any given moment, to molest the two women in the house, the daughter Cindy especially. "It don't hurt to look," Griffin tells her father through clenched teeth when the latter starts to object to Hal's obvious interest in Cindy, though clearly the implication is that looking *can* lead to something much more dangerous, as Griffin confirms when he offers Hal to take the girl along "just for you."

In both films, the underlying threat of sexual violence is symptomatic of the criminal's uncontrollable aggression and inarticulate anger. This is not surprising because the psychopathic criminal type epitomized by both Griffin and West was the discursive product of the increasing number of sex-crime laws passed after the war, most notably during the years 1949 to 1955, which Estelle B. Freedman describes as one of the two periods of modern sex-crime panic (the other was right before the war, 1937–1940) (205). In *The Seven Year Itch* (1955), recall, Richard Sherman's campaign for Dr. Brubaker's pseudo-Kinsey report—retitled "Of Sex and Violence" and with cover art depicting a psychopath terrorizing a young woman—directly alludes to the postwar sex-crime panic. For that matter, so do the circumstances implicating Dix Steele in Mildred Atkinson's murder. Enacted primarily at the state level, the new sex-crime laws, rather than targeting specific acts, worked instead to name a specific criminal personality type, "a kind of personality, or an identity, that could be discovered only by trained psychiatrists" (Freedman 209)—although, presumably, his visage was also instantly identifiable to everyone on the covers of paperback books and in movies such as *Blackboard Jungle* and *The Desperate Hours.* "This new image of aggressive male sexual deviance that emerged from the psychiatric and political responses to sex crimes" was, Freedman explains, complicit in the "establishment of legal and psychiatric mechanisms that were then used to regulate much less serious, but socially disturbing, behaviors" (200).

Freedman's language suggests right away how the fifties psychopathic personality served the same function that, in *Discipline and Punish,* Michel Foucault attributes to "the delinquent" generally, namely, that of disseminating the "penitentiary technique" of social regulation throughout a culture.

"The delinquent," Foucault explains, just as Freedman points out about the psychopath, "is to be distinguished from the offender by the fact that it is not so much his act as his life that is relevant in characterizing him" (251). The invention of delinquency is likewise a construction of psychiatric and legal discourses working in collaboration; it functions to license and make visible some illegalities and to exclude and make invisible certain others. In this way, the delinquent "represents a diversion of illegality for the illicit circuits of profit and power of the dominant class" (280). So, too, with the fifties psychopath. For example, because of this figure's function in mapping the boundaries of deviancy for the middle-class breadwinner, the men institutionalized as mental cases for committing sex crimes, as opposed to those incarcerated as convicted felons, tended to be white. The courts repeatedly differentiated "mental illness" from "willful violence" according to an offender's race (Freedman 209).

In its own ambiguous treatment of race, *Blackboard Jungle* shows how the white psychopathic criminal functioned to make delinquency appear as a symptom of male psychology rather than an effect of the racial or class divisions characterizing U.S. society during this period. The film initially appears to be representing the problem of juvenile delinquency as a racial issue. Dadier makes Gregory Miller (Sidney Poitier) the primary target of his suspicions as well as the object of his manipulations. However, after a heated confrontation between white teacher and black student about the former's racism, which allows the film at once to recognize and deny the place of race in its representation of both delinquency and authority, *Blackboard Jungle* then shifts gears, ignoring the ethnic and working-class composition of the student body to blame all the disturbances in Dadier's classroom on the pathology of the psychologically disturbed white teenager, Artie West.

The Desperate Hours similarly skirts its allusions to social conflict, obscuring the original object of the convict's rage and suggesting what the psychopath meant to regulate in working-class masculinity for the middle class. Griffin's original motive for remaining in Indianapolis after the breakout is vengeance. During a gun battle with police four years before, we learn almost as soon as the film opens, Griffin deliberately shot a policeman and then surrendered; angered by the pointless murder, detective Jesse Barnes (Arthur Kennedy) broke Griffin's jaw. Despite this careful exposition, the expected showdown between an equally violent criminal and lawman never comes to pass (as it did in numerous Westerns of the period), even though Griffin frequently strokes the scar on his jaw to remember why he does not want to leave the city. Instead, the film concentrates on the violation of the middle-class home's sanctity as a privileged domestic space, so the stakes raised by Griffin's anger end up getting more ideologically transparent and straightforward. "The idiot," Barnes exclaims, when he reads an anonymous note sent by Hilliard, warning the cops away in an effort to protect his family. "Doesn't he know you can't play fair with savages like that?"

Whether written about in the news or dramatized in the movies, and whether young (as in *Blackboard Jungle*) or old (as in *The Desperate Hours*), the white male psychopath, directing his uncontrollable violence against property of all forms (homes and public buildings, personal possessions, wives and children), could then be explained away, not as a symptom of social injustices, but as a "savage." The history of the term "psychopath" in classifying male criminal behavior further illuminates how it served as such an instrument of social control. "From the origin of the concept," Freedman comments, "the psychopath had been perceived as a drifter, an unemployed man who lived beyond the boundaries of familial and social controls" (204). The term "psychopath," in fact, was originally synonymous with "delinquent," since it meant to designate "habitual criminals who had normal mentality but exhibited abnormal social behavior" (202). While originally used to classify *women* as a means of controlling prostitution, the term's more exclusive reference to *men* as drifters and delinquents began in the 1930s, when interest in the relation between abnormal sexuality and male criminality coincided with a period of record unemployment that robbed many men of their breadwinner status and disrupted the stable patterns of family life. During the World War II years, concern about the sexual pathology of men abated, at least as far as press coverage was concerned, because of the obvious connection between an ideology promoting male aggression and a lack of outward official concern for violent sexual crimes; and it then reemerged in the 1950s as part of the "modern concern about controlling male violence" following the war (200).

The sex-crime panic of the fifties was more a response to public apprehension over certain antisocial male behaviors than a show of concern for the danger which the sexual aggression of disenfranchised men may have actually posed to defenseless women and children. The psychopath became a specific and highly charged target of legal regulation as a means of specifically addressing problems related to postwar hegemonic masculinity: first, as a means of repealing, in the interests of normalization, the official valorization of hypermasculine aggression which had occurred during the war; second, as an articulation of anxieties about the violence of returning veterans; and third, as a representation of abnormality working to enforce heterosexual conformity for men as well as women. Responses to the pyschopath thus "heighten[ed] the importance of sexuality as a component of modern identity" following the war (215–16). In categorizing deviant masculinity, however, the psychopath had a wide-ranging repressive purpose which measured and, in this way, tightly controlled the liberating effect that Freedman tries to attribute to it.[14] The discourse of psychopathology gave the military its legal mechanism for purging gays and lesbians from the army during the war, for example, and then provided its rationale for officially excluding them from service afterward. No longer declaring that homosexuals were unfit for military duty because of their "effeminacy," the new psychiatric profile defined homosexuality as a pathology, projecting onto gay men all the sexual aggression which the war's ideology of virility had fostered and which the postwar culture now needed to disavow. This is why, as Freedman notes, in popular usage the term "psychopath" became interchangeable with "sex criminal," "pervert," and "homosexual," raising "the question of whether *psychopath* served in part as a code for *homosexual* at a time of heightened public consciousness of homosexuality" (213).[15]

Because both the figure of the psychopath and the psychological discourse explaining him played such an important role in regulating male sexuality after the war, it is hardly adequate, I think, to categorize Hollywood's representation of psychopathic characters—whether in Bogart's films, teen-crime movies, or thrillers adapted from or imitating the immensely popular Mike Hammer novels by Mickey Spillane—as "the return of the repressed." Yet this is what historian Warren Susman claims: "in the 1950s Americans discovered violence," which was "suddenly defined as a major problem that society needed to solve" (24). At the same time, he goes on, "one of the extraordinary features of the period was the celebration of the psychopathic as heroic" (27). Looking to mass culture for the collective unconscious of the more repressed official culture, Susman finds in the era's representations of perverse masculinity a "vision of man as alienated, anxious, psychopathic, and outside social bonds," which he interprets as a form of libidinal resistance ("an inner rebellion") to the dominant, ameliorating ideology of the period (30). His argument, however, vastly oversimplifies the regulating function which the psychotic movie tough guy increasingly came to serve for fifties culture in redefining aggressive masculinity through a discourse of psychopathology that equated it with abnormality.

Far from resisting the repression of male aggression, or allowing it to "return," as Susman believes, as if it were the unconscious of the culture, the movie tough guy served as a mechanism for monitoring that repression in representation. Bogart's postwar career documents how the cultural cachet of the 1950s tough guy clearly differed from that of his 1940s counterpart, and the alteration of that representation of masculinity, once a staple of Hollywood films, was not limited to this star alone. In Mike Hammer's most powerful film incarnation, *Kiss Me Deadly* (1955), the 1940s film noir detective personified by Bogart in *The Maltese Falcon* has been noticeably downgraded to a "bedroom dick," specializing in divorce cases and playing both sides against the middle, just as the black bird ("the stuff that dreams are made of," Spade observes) has been transmuted into "the great whatsit," the mysterious object that everyone in the film seeks, and that Hammer (Ralph Meeker) wants a share of. Unlike Spade (or any of Bogart's characters in his 1940s films, including *Dead Reckoning*), Hammer is no match for his antagonists on either side of the law. For all his cynicism and brutality, he is unable to prevent his best friend from being killed and his girlfriend from being kidnapped, and he is completely taken in by this film's dangerous blonde with a gun. Nor is his tough veneer a guarantee, as it is for Spade, that Hammer can solve the mystery he investigates, since, even when he has the literal "key" in his possession, he still cannot comprehend the enormity of the prized object he seeks: a nuclear device. After learning from a federal agent the identity of the "great whatsit" and what it means, Hammer can only mutter, much like the tough cop at the end of *Panic in the Streets,* "I didn't know."

As the Bogie cult of the 1960s and 1970s bears witness to, the Hollywood tough guy retained a supposed "timeless" appeal as the touchstone of American virility, but only in retrospect. In actual historical fact, postwar America viewed the tough movie hero's virility with decided ambivalence. A nostalgic memory of Bogart's postwar films thus has to forget how closely the fortunes of his star persona followed the course through which, as a legal and clinical category, the psychopath helped to regulate heterosexual conformity for men in the fifties. The homosocial organization of Bogart's persona, motivated by the problematic homoerotics of the wartime buddy relation in *Dead Reckoning,* is made a symptom of male sexual dysfunction in *In a Lonely Place* and then pathologized as the deviant psychology of a criminal type in *The Desperate Hours.* Neither the movie tough guy epitomized by Bogart nor his violence disappeared from fifties films by any means; but when recast through the powerful intersection of discourses about male anger and psychopathology, the ungovernable masculinity he represented, with its origins in a working-class gender ideology of male performativity, was effectively expelled from the domestic space claimed by hegemonic masculinity as "America."

4

The Body in the Blockbuster

With its announcement of "The Greatest Event in Motion Picture History!" the poster for Cecil B. DeMille's *The Ten Commandments* (1956), reproduced as figure 16, aptly summarizes the appeal of the blockbuster motion picture as it has come to epitomize Hollywood product made during the fifties. Big, long, and expensive spectaculars like *The Ten Commandments* were not a new development in the history of Hollywood by any means; like several of the period's other big biblicals, *The Ten Commandments* was itself a remake of a silent version made by DeMille in the 1920s. But a practice in which studios turned out a number of blockbusters each year was a distinct postwar phenomenon. Perceived as that rare big film which, in its wide appeal, could overcome a shrinking and increasingly fragmented audience for motion pictures, the fifties blockbuster was the Cadillac of movies, sold explicitly as a special event: "a film for people who don't go to the pictures" (Houston and Giller 69).

During this period no film epitomized the gigantism of the fifties blockbuster better than *The Ten Commandments*, with its all-star cast, thousands of extras (including the Egyptian army), foreign locations, budget escalations, Academy Award winning special effects, and a final running time of three hours, 39 minutes. This film's enormous popularity was unmatched even by the other big successful films of this period, to the point where its continuous exhibition during the second half of the decade gave it the aura of a major cultural event in its own right, experienced by the entire nation and transcending the circumstances of ordinary moviegoing. First released in New York and Los Angeles on a roadshow basis in November 1956, with additional exclusive runs opening afterward in staggered fashion across the country, after just five months it had already become clear to the industry that "[t]his unprecedented boxoffice achievement answers the big question of whether a picture costing $13,500,000 can pay off its cost, and makes the prediction of a $100,000,000 world gross for the DeMille epic a distinct possibility. . . . New fabulous statistics and new precedents are being piled up by the DeMille production as it

Figure 16.
The poster art for *The Ten Commandments* condenses its epic story into the visual
difference between hoary Charlton Heston and bare-chested Yul Brynner.

steam-rollers along" ("All-Time"). Officially noting the first anniversary of the film's opening in New York City, when *The Ten Commandments* had "[been] seen by more than 22 million moviegoers," *Time* merely had to repeat the obvious: "After some 40 years of moviemaking, DeMille's skilled old hand once again blends, to the public's obvious liking, an unbeatable mixture of color, bigness, heroics, sex and oldtime religion" ("In"). By August 1959, when DeMille's epic had been in continuous release for nearly three full years, *The Ten Commandments* had been seen by an estimated 98.5 million people (DeMille 414n).

Given its indisputable blockbuster status, doesn't the poster for *The Ten Commandments* seem a bit subdued? Where is the sin and sex one expects to find in a Hollywood biblical epic, especially one made by DeMille? Religious spectacles have always been read as "the best excuse for sex on an orgiastic scale" (Schumach 161), and DeMille himself was known to have made his career out of "[s]in and sanctimony"—movies which, based on episodes in the Bible or early Christian history, could get away with more sensationalism than usual under Production Code restrictions "so long as the sinners were punished in the final reel by an avenging God" (Gardner 80). In fact, when the Catholic Legion of Decency condemned Elia Kazan's film of Tennessee Williams's *Baby Doll* (1956), opponents of the Church's censorship were quick to shout "hypocrisy," naming as evidence *The Ten Commandments*, a film that, while much "sexier" than *Baby Doll*, had just been loudly applauded by the clergy for being wholesome family entertainment.[1]

The poster for *The Ten Commandments* promises none of that sexiness; nor does it follow the custom of the day in advertising big-screen spectacle. Instead, this poster condenses the film's blockbuster subject matter—the departure of the Hebrews from Egypt as described in *Exodus*—into a simple visual difference between hoary Charlton Heston (who plays Moses) and bare-chested Yul Brynner (who plays Rameses). Fully if simply clothed and thickly bearded so as to resemble Michaelangelo's famous sculpture of the prophet, the white-haired Heston contextualizes the film's title, representing the authority of the Judeo-Christian law that holds Western civilization together in a continuous tradition. The more exotically underdressed Brynner, by contrast, his shaved body adorned with ornate gold jewelry, represents pagan idolatry, racial Otherness, and imperial tyranny. The poster therefore promotes, not the "sin and sanctimony" expected of a biblical epic, but ideologically loaded antinomies organized by the pairing of these two male stars: modern v. ancient civilizations, monotheistic v. pagan religions, free v. slave states, and, most important of all, Western v. Oriental masculinities.

The poster for *The Ten Commandments* follows the logic by which the film itself reproduces the central binarism of cold war ideology: the opposition of American and alien. More overtly than any of the other biblicals of this period, *The Ten Commandments* was marketed to—and perceived by—its audience as an active agent of God in the battle against communist devils. *The Holly-wood Reporter* remarked about the film in 1958: "The DeMille classic, of course, still is barred in the Soviet Union, Red China and all countries held captive behind the Iron Curtain. It will never be shown—without distortion—in a communist country, for that ideology denies God and preaches deceit and ill-will toward all men and nations not held in bondage to the Kremlin" ("Pakistan"). Befitting the film's status as a political weapon in the box-office war against communism outside of the United States, the *Reporter* even kept tally of the outcome through headlines such as "'Commandments' Tops Com-mie Pic's B.O. Record in Singapore." *The Ten Commandments* achieved this kind of extracinematic stature because its historical timeliness in 1956 made it seem significantly different from other films that shared its "us versus them" mentality, and, even more strikingly, because it explicitly extended cold war thinking to the representation of masculinity, visualizing in the bodies of its two male stars that racial opposition which Heston and Brynner represent so vividly in the film's poster.

The Biblical Cycle and the Fifties Religion Boom

The blockbuster mentality of the fifties was responsible for a number of different types of big productions, from Cinerama travelogues (*This Is Cine-rama*, 1952, and its successors), to Todd-AO roadshow presentations (*Around the World in Eighty Days*, 1956), to historical epics (*The Bridge on the River Kwai*, 1958). But it is perhaps best remembered now for the cycle of big-budget religious spectacles spanning the decade, films set either in the Bible lands or in imperial Rome.[2] In addition to *The Ten Commandments* there were *Samson and Delilah* (1949), *David and Bathsheba* (1951), *Quo Vadis* (1951), *The Robe* (1953), *Demetrius and the Gladiators* (1954), *The Egyptian* (1954), *The Silver Chalice* (1954), *Land of the Pharaohs* (1955), and *The Prodigal* (1955). By the time *The Ten Commandments* was released in 1956, the biblical cycle had temporarily passed its peak; aside from the DeMille picture, no other big-budget biblical films were released for three more years (though historical epics set in more recent times were still very much in vogue). The thundering success of *The Ten Commandments* gave new life to the biblical cycle, inspiring the release of a half dozen more high-profiled films—*The Big Fisherman, Solomon and Sheba*, and *Ben-Hur* in 1959, and *Esther and the King, The Story of Ruth*, and *Spartacus* in 1960. The prodigious box-office returns of *The Ten Com-mandments* and *Ben-Hur* then pushed the cycle into its self-destructive period during the 1960s, when the size and scale of films such as *Cleopatra* (1963) and *The Greatest Story Ever Told* (1965) financially overwhelmed the companies producing them.

These epics were made by well-respected directors (William Wyler, King

Vidor, Michael Curtiz, and Howard Hawks, as well as DeMille), just as they featured name stars (not only Brynner and Heston but also Victor Mature, Howard Keel, Susan Hayward, Lana Turner, Kirk Douglas), served to introduce new contract players (Edmund Purdom, Paul Newman, Joan Collins, Richard Egan), and even supported a kind of unofficial stock company of British actors (Richard Burton, Jean Simmons, Peter Ustinov, Stephen Boyd). The popularity of biblicals during the fifties, in fact, gives quite an ironic twist of film history to Billy Wilder's satire of Hollywood in *Sunset Blvd.* (1950), where former silent screen star Norma Desmond (Gloria Swanson) hopes to revive her career by acting in the story of Salome, a religious spectacle to be directed by DeMille himself (shown in the film hard at work on the actual set of *Samson and Delilah*). While everyone else in *Sunset Blvd.*, DeMille included, dismisses Norma's project, historically speaking it turns out that she was quite right in predicting the next big trend to hit Hollywood, much more so than Wilder and company probably imagined. Fittingly enough, *Salome* itself became a lavish Hollywood picture in 1953, a Columbia vehicle for Rita Hayworth, jump-starting her career after her divorce from Ali Kahn.

One explanation usually advanced for the biblical cycle's popularity with the studios as well as audiences has been a technological one: the deployment of CinemaScope and other widescreen processes to lure audiences back to downtown movie palaces. The studios emphasized the increased size and scale of these films as a means of differentiating their product from competing leisure industries, not only television but also professional sports and amusement parks, legitimate theater and nightclubs, and the new developments in the recording industry, such as long-playing albums and high-fidelity equipment. To borrow a phrase of the State Department at that time, a biblical in widescreen, with its potential for impressing audiences with oversized spectacle, gave customers more bang for their buck. However, with the successes of *Samson and Delilah, David and Bathsheba,* and *Quo Vadis,* the biblical film was in place and ready to take off as a cycle even *before* Fox launched CinemaScope with its production of *The Robe* in 1953. Technology was therefore not the only reason for the cycle's renewed currency in the marketplace.

A more important source of the biblical cycle is the so-called "religion boom" of the period, which had its roots in the postwar repositioning of the United States as the leading global power, its hegemony initially dependent upon and then, as other nations acquired it, jeopardized by the atomic bomb. Fifties movies, like fifties culture generally, tended to assume that, as far as cold warfare was concerned, Americanism and Christianity were synonymous, particularly in representations of American global hegemony, and the postwar biblical gave this important ideological equation an apparent historical ground. In their various stories of a persecuted group (usually early Christians) oppressed by an imperial state (frequently Rome), the biblicals offered ready-made parallels between the foundation of religious freedom in ancient times and the origins of the American nation in its own revolution against a tyrannical empire. Romans in these films are usually portrayed by British actors (M. Wood 183–84), a convention that makes itself present even in *The Ten Commandments* with the casting of Sir Cedric Hardwicke as the elder pharaoh, Sethi. As well as invoking America's birthright, this casting convention implies, through the historical narrative of Rome's displacement by Christianity, the passing of one world power—Britain—and the moment in the sun of another—America—particularly in the Bible lands of the Middle East, which Britain had governed in the nineteenth and early twentieth centuries much as Rome had once done.

Its Hebraic narrative notwithstanding, *The Ten Commandments* was marketed to audiences of all faiths as another Bible story paralleling the epic narrative of America's own nationhood under God. "[I]n leading the exodus," Marc Vernet comments, "Moses saves the Church by founding Israel, just as the pilgrim fathers saved the Puritan faith by founding the United States. . . . England is to the Puritans what Egypt was to the Jews, and what Rome was to Christians. Egypt stands for monarchy, Israel stands for the republic" (69). This homology colors the film's closure, when the Hebrews finally reach the Promised Land after forty years of wandering in the desert. Moses, about to join God on Mount Sinai, turns back to his followers and shouts from on high: "Proclaim liberty throughout all the land unto all the inhabitants thereof." It's no wonder that, in describing the film's closing moment, when Moses raises his hand to wave his final good-bye to Joshua (John Derek) and Sephora (Yvonne De Carlo), Michael Wood has the impression that the prophet "looks just like the Statue of Liberty seen across New York Bay" (187). For with this closing shot, *The Ten Commandments* follows the same kind of assimilationist thinking that led Temple Israel, a leading synagogue of Jewish Hollywood, to pair images of Moses and the Statue of Liberty in the masthead for its temple bulletin (Gabler 307). The logo well summarizes how the studios framed the politics—and the history—of their biblical epics so as to represent Bible narratives of all sorts as patriotic allegories about the struggle for democratic freedom against the cold war backdrop.

Whether finding its source in the Old or New Testament, the biblical epic's implicit identification of American interests with Christianity gave apparent truth to the widely held nationalistic assumption that whatever the United States did "had the endorsement of the Almighty, the Divine Seal of Approval" (Biskind 115). It was in the fifties, recall, that Congress added the phrase "under God" to the Pledge of Allegiance and placed the slogan "In God We Trust" on U.S. currency (Oakley 321). Asked in a survey if they were an active member of a religious group, seventy-three percent of the population answered "yes" (Miller and Nowak 85). "The insecurity brought on by hydrogen bombs and atomic spies made the churches seem the mainstay of traditional values. . . . Religious organizations played down doctrinal differences and stressed common moral values and religion in general" (92–93). With religiosity among Americans at an all-time high, church attendance on Sunday, like synagogue attendance on Saturday, became tantamount to a declaration of patriotism on the part of Americans everywhere, especially in suburban communities across the land. If the nation's churches had discovered how to fill a house every weekend, Hollywood, having apparently lost the knack, followed their lead. As *Time* put it, when announcing the premiere of *The Ten Commandments* in New York City, "The religious movie epic—along with the 'religioso' pop tune and the Biblical bestseller—is more than ever a part of the U.S. scene" ("Mount").

While all the studios responded to the religion boom when merchandising their biblicals, no producer did it more piously or masterfully than DeMille when it came to promoting *The Ten Commandments*. To start with, his studio offered religious leaders regular access to the set during production in Hollywood so that they could watch DeMille at work bringing Moses to life. Before the premiere, Paramount then screened a rough cut for "[o]utstanding religious leaders of three faiths—Protestant, Catholic, and Jewish," soliciting their responses so that advertisements and news releases could quote "their highest praise" in the manner customarily reserved for film critics (Paramount press release). On the Sunday prior to the film's world premiere, the customary full-page advertisement in the *New York Times* displayed these quotes along with the same photographs of bearded Heston and bare-chested Brynner prepared for the poster.

As part of the hoopla preceding the New York opening, moreover, DeMille himself asked an audience of religious leaders at a benefit luncheon in his honor "to use this picture, as I hope and pray that God himself will use it, for the good of the World." Afterward, he solemnly announced that his own profits from *The Ten Commandments* would be turned over to a foundation in his name devoted to "charitable, religious, and educational purposes" ("Mount"). The result of this hard sell to the clergy, as Anglican writer Malcolm Boyd remembered in 1958, was to give God's license to *The Ten Commandments:* "It became a kind of heresy, for a crucial period of several weeks around the release date, to speak against the picture" (60). Looking back on the aggressive publicity campaign designed for this "most costly, most spectacular 'religious' entertainment of all time" (79), Boyd complained that the hoopla, which "crossed over from Hollywood publicity into religious promotion" (61), blinded everyone, even the clergy, to the film's spiritual crudeness. In particular, Boyd criticized the literalism of DeMille's gaudy spectacle in *The Ten Commandments*, arguing that the film's efforts at "realism," achieved through its costly special effects, considerably reduced the spirituality of events such as the Burning Bush and Pillar of Fire (61). "The 'God' of the movie is a technological creation of man," Boyd concluded, "cut down to the size of mechanical miracles" (78).

Boyd's criticism of the film's marketing as an ersatz religious event is well observed, but he also missed what the technology of a biblical epic like *The Ten Commandments* seeks to evoke through its religious spectacle, particularly when it comes to presenting the genre's signature scenes, what Wood calls "the great crash" (178): when Rome burns, Gaza crumbles, or the earth opens up to swallow the unfaithful for worshiping the Golden Calf. Using expensive movie technology to engage in what can only be termed conspicuous destruction, these big blockbuster films yoke suburban religious conformity to the Sturm und Drang of Bible-thumbing revivalism, itself a burgeoning postwar business of blockbuster proportions. Two days after President Truman's announcement of the first Soviet atomic test (on September 23, 1949), Billy Graham held his first tent revival in Los Angeles (on September 25, 1949). The timing could not have been more opportune for the revivalist movement:

> For centuries, evangelists had evoked images of sudden death and hellfire to frighten their listeners into repentance. Graham now had available the most potent scare tactic of all: atomic war. If he dwelt less on the terrors of hell than his predecessors, it was perhaps because it now seemed superfluous. (Boyer 239)

Nor was it just coincidence that *Samson and Delilah* and *Quo Vadis* both became big box-office hits without the extra lure of widescreen, reviving the public's interest in biblical pictures shortly after the so-called traumatic events of 1949:

> August, the concession of China to the Communists; September, the announcement of the Soviet atom bomb; August and September and the months before and after, explosive questions raised by the [Alger] Hiss case—1949 was a year of shocks, shocks with enormous catalytic force. (Goldman 112)

Or that the great first wave of biblical pictures shot in CinemaScope in the wake of *The Robe*'s big success occurred between 1954 and 1955, "the period when it became clear that both the United States and the Soviet Union had an effective H-bomb and that both were far along in the development of intercontinental missiles" (263).

Placed in its historical context of cold war nuclear politics, the expensive fifties biblical epic turns out to have had much in common with another genre popular during this period—those low budget, black-and-white science-fiction monster films that Hollywood also began turning out on a regular basis at the same time. True, the science-fiction films used a premise either of alien invasion or atomic mutation as their primary means of narrativizing "the most potent scare tactic of all: atomic war," whereas the biblical epics drew upon ancient history for miraculous accounts of apocalyptic destruction that likewise evoked the "sudden death and hellfire" of atomic warfare—a sea parted by the hand of God, a generation of men wiped out by the Angel of Death. But while a religious setting may have made the more lavishly produced biblical epics seem safer, historically as well as geographically far removed from con-temporary anxieties more openly depicted in the science-fiction films, the revivalist movement and its fire-and-brimstone rhetoric surely helped to make the biblicals' own setting in cold war anxieties just as visible.

U.S. and "Them": Free State/Slave State

The comparison between the two genres is worth pursuing for a moment. Along with their generic cousins (the equally popular alien-invasion films), the atomic-monster films of this period have long been read as transparent parables of cold war containment.[3] Usually the unhappy indirect result of A-bomb testing, the monsters of these films bring to life the fear of invasion by taking literally and putting on screen some of the most commonplace tropes used to picture subversion of U.S. society by an enemy force. For example, in his testimony before HUAC in 1947, Jack Warner compared American communists to "ideological termites [who] have burrowed their way into American industries, organizations, and societies. Wherever they may be, I say, let us dig them out and get rid of them."[4] Not only did Warner simply update what had been a commonplace representation of Nazi Germany's occupation of Europe, but he also invoked the allegorical frame of reference that would repeatedly be put forward by the atomic-monster films of the fifties.

In Warner Bros.' own *Them!* (1954), to take one of the best films from this cycle, giant carnivorous ants—mutations resulting from atomic bomb testing in 1945—evoke the haunting fear of an all-out nuclear strike by a sinister, in-human, and well-organized enemy nation. The ants announce their presence in the New Mexico desert with a clickety sound similar to a Geiger counter when it discovers radioactivity, and they emit a shrill whine that resembles an air-raid siren (Sobchack, *Screening* 218–19). Eventually, two giant queens escape with a pair of drone consorts from the containment of their under-ground nest before they can be annihilated with the rest of their colony, and one surviving queen, after mating in the air, ultimately establishes a new colony in the Los Angeles sewer system. These giant mutant ants play upon cold war anxiety because they endanger national security, creating a political situation which calls for authoritative leadership and, ultimately, because all other measures fail, limited military action. Invariably the army has to be called in to provide scientists, the local police, *and* the FBI with the firepower needed to destroy the giant ant colony.

Like other films of its genre, *Them!* uses the atomic-mutant premise to worry about "the preservation of social order" (Sobchack, *Screening* 45). As Dr. Medford (Edmund Gwynn), the scientist in *Them!*, ponders the future of humankind if the giant ants are not destroyed, he observes: "We may be witnesses to a biblical prophecy come true. 'And there shall be destruction and darkness come of the Creation, and the beast shall reign over the earth.'" The doctor's remark suggests the ease with which "biblical prophecy" and the bomb had become knotted together in the popular imagination, in large part as a way of disavowing the United States' own reign of destruction and darkness begun in the ashes of Hiroshima. But *Them!* does not mean to raise doubts about the achievements of science in unleashing the bomb any more than the postwar biblicals mean to question the existence of God in the wake of Auschwitz. Rather than evoke intellectual or moral interrogation by its audience, *Them!* takes pains to differentiate one social order, that of the ants, from another, that of the human community which the monsters threaten. To a room full of unconvinced government and military officials, Dr. Medford shows a movie about ant life and then explains the danger which this mutation of the species poses to the human race: "Ants are the only creatures on Earth other than man who make war. They campaign, they are chronic aggressors, and they make slave laborers of the captives they don't kill. . . . Even the most minute of them have an instinct and talent for industry, social organization and savagery that makes man look feeble by comparison." "In 1954, when *Them!* was made," Peter Biskind comments with reference to Dr. Medford's speech, "those humans that Americans regarded as antlike, which is to say, behaved like a mass, loved war, and made slaves, were, of course, Communists" (132).

The ideological thinking behind *Them!*, which has become a truism about the fifties sci-fi cycle itself by now, operates much the same way in the period's biblical epics. What I find most striking about Dr. Medford's description of the militant ant society in *Them!*, in fact, is that it imports so easily—indeed, so literally—to DeMille's version of ancient Egypt in *The Ten Commandments*. The ant colony's "instinct and talent for industry, social organization and savagery" evokes instant comparison to the slave labor, monumental architecture, and military ambition of imperial Egypt. Ancient Egyptians and giant ants alike make their civilizations known through the mounds they tirelessly build in the desert. This comparison fits *too* closely simply to be an accident of metaphor. Not only do DeMille's long shots reduce the cast of thousands to the size of insects, dwarfed by the height of the pylons, obelisks, pyramids, and sphinxes standing high against the barren desert landscapes, but here too we find a militaristic culture with a society as rigidly stratified as an ant colony is around labor—and one with a royal genealogy similarly organized around the body of a queen, the "throne princess" Nefretiri (Anne Baxter).

Actually, DeMille overdetermines ancient Egypt with so many references to Otherness that it is impossible not to view it as the antithesis of America. For all the painstaking research into the customs and costumes recorded by Henry Noerdlinger in his scholarly monograph that was published as part of the film's promotion, the mise-en-scène of Egypt in *The Ten Commandments* evokes ready-made parallels to Stalin's Soviet Union, Hitler's Nazi Germany,

Figure 17.
DeMille's longshots reduce the Egyptian army to the size of ants.

even Native American culture of the southwest United States and Mexico.[5] For instance, the monolithic architecture of Per-Rameses recalls Albert Speer's monuments to the Third Reich, an allusion made all the more pronounced by the blond Aryan-looking muscle men who appear now and then in the margins of the camera frame as attendants to Pharaoh and Nefretiri. Furthermore, the slave camps evoke the concentration camps with more historical precision than one might suspect: just as the Hebrews toil under the whip to turn straw into bricks for Pharaoh, so did Jews supply slave labor for a fuel plant adjacent to the Auschwitz concentration camp, where they turned coal into synthetic oil for Hitler (Yergin 345).

To ensure that Egypt stands for the political opposite of "America" in every conceivable way, before the film begins DeMille himself appears in a prologue and interprets his motion picture through the opposition of free and slave nations. "We have an unusual subject," he solemnly announces. "The story of the birth of freedom. The Story of Moses. . . . The theme of this picture is whether men are to be ruled by God's law or whether they are to be ruled by the whims of a dictator like Rameses. Are men the property of the state—or are they free souls under God? This same battle continues throughout the world today." An obvious reference to cold war politics, these remarks were not limited to the text of the film but were repeated almost verbatim in the trailer, the souvenir program, news releases and promotional pamphlets, even reviews, leading *The Boston Herald* to remark: "Cecil B. DeMille is to motion pictures what Winston Churchill is to statesmanship" (qtd. in souvenir program).

While today the thought of comparing Cecil B. DeMille to Churchill is all too laughable, it would be a mistake to underestimate the considerable power of the free state/slave state binary opposition that the director invokes in his prologue to *The Ten Commandments*. In the first of the 1960 televised presidential debates, John F. Kennedy began his introductory statement, ostensibly on the subject of domestic affairs, by representing the world scene in almost the exact terms that DeMille had used four years earlier: "In the election of 1860 Abraham Lincoln said the question was whether this nation could exist half slave or half free. In the election of 1960, and with the world around us, the question is whether the world will exist half slave or half free, whether it will move in the direction of freedom, in the direction of the road that we are taking, or whether it will move in the direction of slavery" ("As").

Both speeches condense the problems which cold war ideology posed to representations of the American nation, and these ideological difficulties inform the historical timeliness of *The Ten Commandments* in its production, its reception, and its narrative. DeMille and Kennedy each cast their address in a rhetoric that allows for no reconciliation of opposites, no half measures. The mutually exclusive pairing of free state/slave state leaves no space for a third term to enter, and consequently disrupt, the binary formulation. The historical existence of a "third world"—a concept coined by Nasser of Egypt, Tito of Yugoslavia, and Nehru of India in the 1950s to articulate the relation of postcolonial nations to the postwar political order—directly challenged that binarism because it raised the symbolic ante beyond the simple choice of freedom or slavery. But perhaps even more disturbing to the ideological boundaries of cold war representations of "America," that frequently evoked dualism of freedom and slavery, so central to 1950s political rhetoric, also exposed the contradiction inhering within both the United States' own domestic operation as a modern national-security state and the traditional imbrication of masculinity in the nationalistic myth of rugged American male individualism.

According to Michael Rogin, while the cherished notion of the free man's "heroic, individual achievements" has always been an essential component of American nationalism, perpetuating the myth of the self-made man, "the free man's dependence on the state, which lies at the center of cold war ideology, goes back to the origins of America." As a consequence, Rogin concludes, "The free man and the military state are not two alternative poles in American ideology, nor are they merely a recent symbiosis. Their marriage goes back to

Figure 18.
In *Them!*, "us" turns out to look just like "them" when the humans don gas masks
to inspect their handiwork in the nest of the giant ants.

the beginning" (239–40). Representing the free state as the guarantee of the
free individual, cold war ideology put extreme pressure on this so-called
marriage of the free man and the military state because it pulled loose the veil
of romance concealing the real political relationship of those two partners.
The postwar "free man" had to depend upon the state to preserve his independence in the face of the communist threat, thereby calling into question the
myth of rugged, rebellious, and masculine American individuality, particularly
when viewed against the shrunken expanse of the nations' manifest destiny on
the continent. The free state itself could guarantee freedom for every individual, man or woman, only by adapting the same methods as the slave state—
bureaucracy, militarism, surveillance—all too closely resembling the demonic
Other it meant to overcome. *Them!*, seemingly the perfect example of a Hollywood narrative effortlessly maintaining cold war binary logic, offers a vivid if
probably unknowing glimpse of "us" turning into "them": when the humans
don gas masks in order to inspect their handiwork in the ant nest, they look
remarkably like the bug-eyed monsters they have just destroyed. The image is

fittingly ironic because the resemblance of ants and humans is, as Dr. Medford's comments indicate, the implicit logic of the ideology that constructed their difference in the first place.

Hebrew or Egyptian, Is He Still Moses?

Taken together, the two binary formulations of cold war representations (e.g., free man versus the state, free state versus the slave state) always threatened to collapse into each other in moments of ideological incoherence. One important function of fifties movies as cold war cultural texts was to mask the contradiction motivating that double division in the very act of representing it, and *The Ten Commandments* is no exception. In order to set up the free state/ slave state binary which DeMille introduces in the prologue, the film needs to keep juxtaposing Egyptian and Hebrew cultures. There has to be an absolute difference between the two so that Moses' birthright and not his upbringing will determine his individualistic character. From the beginning of the film, when the warrior prince Moses returns to Egypt in triumph after securing his nation's imperialist ambitions in neighboring Ethiopia, we are asked to believe in the independent nature of this impressive and charismatic male figure, who is a "self-made" man in the sense that God has, we already know, fashioned him for His purpose, meaning that Moses transcends his adopted culture and its influences. "What change is there in me?" Moses asks his two mothers after he learns the truth about his birth. "Egyptian or Hebrew, I am still Moses. These are the same hands, the same arms, the same face that were mine a moment ago."

According to the film, he is still the same Moses after he learns of his Hebrew origin, but only in the sense that he has *always* been a Hebrew in spirit. Moses' humanity when it comes to the Hebrew slaves, in contrast to Rameses' cruel disregard for human life, signifies his innate difference from Egypt, which amounts to his secret identity as a Hebrew. Moses and his kind (i.e., the nation of Israel, old and new) stand for sincerity, honesty, and compassion, while Rameses and his kind (i.e., the nation of Egypt, ancient and postcolonial) stand for just the opposite values. When Rameses works with the Hebrew informer Dathan (Edward G. Robinson) to ferret out the identity of the Deliverer, their secret collaboration has the important result of expelling Moses from Egypt so as to distance the heroic male and his masculine authority from any further association with that slave nation and its militarism, its imperialism, and, as Rameses and Dathan show, its surveillance.

The casting of primarily non-Jewish American actors in the parts of the leading Hebrew characters further makes the Egyptian-Hebrew polarity stand out to the film's audience. The only Jew among the leads is Edward G. Robinson in the role of the villainous Dathan. Robinson's Jewishness was a central element in his postwar public persona, so it would not have gone unnoticed by the moviegoing public when they watched him play an informer who keeps selling out the Hebrews to the Egyptians. In fact, on the page before the big ad in the Sunday *New York Times* on November 4, 1956—the one trumpeting the premiere of *The Ten Commandments* at the end of the week with glowing praises from clergymen of various religious affiliations—there appeared one announcing Robinson's participation in the Chanukah Festival for Israel at Madison Square Garden during the first week of December. The placement of this ad near that for *The Ten Commandments* was no doubt coincidental, as was Robinson's involvement (he was starring on Broadway at the time), but its timing surely helped to promote awareness of the actor's Jewishness at the moment of the film's big opening. Furthermore, given Robinson's history of leftist politics, his playing the key role of the informer alludes to the HUAC hearings and supplies additional ground for Alan Nadel's claim that, through its casting, the film means to imply that "the 'free world' is safe because the true Jews are Christians and subversives are false Jews" (114). Not only had Robinson been baited by HUAC in 1947, but the actor's desire to be "cleared" in order to get film work had partially prepared the way for the committee's return to Hollywood in 1950 (Ceplair and Englund 365). Robinson's political persona as a *compromised* activist colors his ethnicity as a Jew with the deep suspicion of Red subversion, which the film fully exploits in its characterization of Dathan as the one Hebrew who conspires against the slaves' freedom by disclosing the name of their Deliverer to Rameses.

Although the film's opposition of Egypt and Israel seems straightforward enough through its numerous textual and intertextual cues, the ideological incoherence implicit in cold war representations of the "free" national-security state makes itself immediately evident as soon as *The Ten Commandments* goes on to represent ancient Egypt as America's Other, too. Nadel contends that DeMille's Egypt bears the marks of colonial discourse, which is to make the Other the same: "The ancient Egypt of *The Ten Commandments* thus strikingly resembles America after World War II." It, too, is a nation "undergoing massive expansion by an increase in construction," but is "[l]ess like a nation than a corporation. . . . a construction company that builds pyramids," suggesting the close ties between government and big business that characterized postwar America (97). Nadel's claim about Egypt's resemblance to Eisenhower's America, however, is not exactly borne out by the film's diegesis. For instance, however much Nadel tries to portray it as a three-class corporate society (with the pharaoh's court as upper management, the master builders as middle management, and the Hebrew slaves as working class), the Egypt of DeMille's film is still a master/slave economy governed by a semi-divine, authoritarian figure: slavery constitutes a pharaoh's wealth and produces the monuments to the splendor of his reign. While a citizen of Egypt, Moses himself pivots across this binary, figuring first as "master," the prince in charge of building the new treasure city of Per-Rameses to honor Sethi's imperial achievements and store his booty, later as "slave," the anonymous Hebrew caked in mud and then brought to the court in chains in shame on the day of Sethi's Jubilee. Significantly, only *after* he leaves Egypt does Moses give any appearance at all of being a proper capitalist; he organizes a cartel among the sheep herders of Midian, selling the shearing of the entire tribe to one purchaser for a single price. As the sheiks meet in Jethro's tent to celebrate their profit, one of them remarks happily: "Never before, our brothers, has our wool brought so rich a payment."[6]

What I believe Nadel actually senses—which is why he insists upon the comparison of Egypt and America with so much dogged if erring conviction—is the ideological incoherence symptomatic of cold war representations generally. When Egypt most seems to resemble cold war America it does so not because its fictive world mirrors the United States' own capitalistic society, as Nadel tries to prove, but because of the imperialism, militarism, and surveillance that sustain the power of the Egyptian monarchy. This resemblance collapses the difference between what the United States signifies as a free state and what the idea of "Egypt" is supposed to represent as the opposite of the United States. Here *The Ten Commandments* does betray its own colonizing spirit as a capitalist enterprise: it makes a modern Third World nation, Nasser's Egypt, the site for articulating the difference between First and Second Worlds. However, "Egypt" readily troubles *The Ten Commandments'* system of binarized differences because it also introduces into the film a field of historical connotations, both ancient and contemporary, which exceed the free state/ slave state opposition.

Egypt versus Israel: "The Coincidence was Profound"

Because Paramount's promotion of *The Ten Commandments* emphasized how DeMille trumped history itself in his recreation of the past on so grand and extravagant a scale, the actual production of this blockbuster film consequently appeared to have taken place without an apparent history of its own.[7] Thus when *Life* somewhat smugly noted in its cover story on the location shoot that "Egypt becomes a set for 'The Ten Commandments'" ("DeMille Directs" 143), the magazine's colonizing rhetoric simply followed the studio's own example in erasing the historical conditions of the film's production in the Middle East.

This does not mean, of course, that *The Ten Commandments* could actually distance itself from contemporary history; nor could publicity for the film prevent events in the Middle East from influencing the context of its reception. To start with, DeMille's negotiations to film on location in Egypt bore the signs of that new nation's own political struggles. He began planning to shoot the big set pieces—the long shots of Per-Rameses, Moses on Mount Sinai, the Exodus, Pharaoh's charioteers chasing after the departing Hebrews, the Red Sea—on their actual locations while King Farouk was on the throne but ended up dealing with President General Mohammed Naguib in 1953 because a military coup had deposed the king the previous year. Then, by the time he showed up in early October 1954 to begin two months of filming with Charlton Heston, Colonel Gamal Abdel Nasser had eased his colleague Naguib out of power.[8] Following the location shoot in Egypt (which Nasser allowed because Egypt, not having oil to sell, needed the cash), production at Paramount Studios in Hollywood continued until mid-August 1955. The film then went into postproduction at about the time that Nasser began purchasing arms from the Soviet bloc, initiating the chain of events that resulted in the United States' cancellation of funds for the Aswan Dam project on July 19, 1956, and Nasser's retaliation on July 26 with Egypt's nationalization of the Suez Canal. The canal was the primary means of transporting petroleum from the Persian Gulf to Europe; DeMille's epic about Egypt's enslavement of the Israelites was thus awaiting its immediate first-run release during the period when Nasser's pan-Arab nationalism movement, a key feature of his leadership throughout the fifties, most directly threatened the sovereignty of the big oil companies of the United States, Britain, and France.[9]

The Suez crisis was the second time after the Second World War that a Middle Eastern nation preempted Western control of oil. Iran had nationalized Anglo-Iranian Oil in May 1951, and that crisis was not resolved until the CIA helped the Shah return from exile in the summer of 1953.[10] During the Suez crisis, the nation causing trouble for the West was not an oil-producing country but a vocal proponent and gathering point of Arab unity, a factor which made Nasser's ambitions seem even more dangerous to the balance of power in the Middle East. In 1955, Americans reading about *The Ten Commandments* in *Life* would have been hard pressed *not* to view the sight on the magazine's cover of DeMille turning Egypt into a movie set against the implied backdrop of Nasser's pan-Arabic nationalism, with its "dreams of modernizing Egypt, unifying all Arab states under Egyptian rule, and destroying the state of Israel" (Oakley 222).[11] Indeed, in 1953 when associate producer Henry Wilcoxon announced DeMille's intention to make the film, he placed the project specifically in the political context of Middle East tensions resulting from the establishment of Israel: "What western statesmen have thus far failed to do, in their efforts to quiet the Middle East, Hollywood will make a strong bid to accomplish through the persuasive subtleties of celluloid" ("'10 Commandments' As Pic").

While *The Ten Commandments'* entanglement in Middle East politics was unavoidable from the start of its production in Egypt, the acceleration of events in that region right before the film's opening then made it absolutely impossible not to see the film in the glowing light of contemporary history. The world premiere of *The Ten Commandments* in New York City on November 8, 1956, came fast on the heels of what one journalist has called "the week of truth" (Attwood, *Twilight* 176–77): when the Soviets put down Hungarian resistance almost at the same moment that Britain, France, and Israel invaded Egypt in response to Nasser's takeover of the Suez Canal, with Israel consolidating its control over the Sinai and Gaza strip just three days before *The Ten Commandments* opened. It has been argued that this particular week was a milestone of sorts for the cold war era, as events in Eastern Europe and the Middle East escalated to reveal just how far the United States and the Soviet Union would go in the wake of Korea. Hungary showed, on one hand, the Soviets' ruthless determination to maintain the status of their buffer states at all costs and, on the other, the Western bloc's reluctance or inability to stand up for Eastern Europe; while Egypt confirmed the effective end of British and French hegemony in the Middle East, the final curtain pulled down all the more abruptly by the United States' vociferous refusal to support its closest allies out of a desire "not [to] appear associated, even indirectly, with sponsoring what seemed a return to the era of colonial domination" (Yergin 484).

Given the contextualization of *The Ten Commandments* in Israeli-Egypt relations both at the level of the film's narrative and its production, events occurring at the end of October 1956 created a circumstantial setting for the film which Hollywood publicists dream about but can never finagle to bring about on their own. In his review for the *New York Times* Bosley Crowther began by noting: "Against the raw news of modern conflict between Egypt and Israel—a conflict that has its preamble in the book of Exodus—Cecil B. DeMille's 'The Ten Commandments' was given its world premiere last night at the Criterion theatre, and the coincidence was profound" (35). Likewise, the issue of *Life*, with its glowing review of the film, also featured prominent coverage of the Suez crisis, including maps illustrating the Israeli invasion and an editorial announcing "the new mandate for moral leadership" that Britain's "tragic blunder" had thrust upon American shoulders ("Edens"). Throughout this period, Israel—a nation not even a decade old at this point—loomed large in the American imagination, appearing always as an implicit referent of the Egyptian/Hebrew conflicts portrayed by *The Ten Commandments*, with the biblical Exodus itself supplying the "preamble," as Crowther pointed out, for modern history in the Middle East.

Today, over forty years after the release of *The Ten Commandments*, it is still difficult not to view this film's historical relation to the Middle East through an American identification with Israel—a mythic "Israel," to be sure, but one which served to project the United States' own political and religious interests onto that new nation's Zionism and Jewishness as well as its fight for life with the surrounding Arab nations. Nadel, in fact, sees DeMille's blockbuster epic participating, as it were, in U.S. foreign policy: "In the context of geopolitical conflicts of 1956, *The Ten Commandments* thus reclaims the Middle East not as a Jewish homeland but as part of the Judeo-Christian tradition, that is, the American sphere of influence. . . . [contributing] to America's global economic policy by claiming the site of oil in the name of God" (115).

The Ten Commandments helped to circulate this mythic representation of the Middle East at a crucial historical moment: when Eisenhower forced his allies, Israel included, not only to withdraw from Egypt but to pay for their actions as well through economic sanctions. The effectiveness of *The Ten Commandments* in doing the ideological work that Nadel attributes to it must therefore be placed in the historical perspective of Eisenhower's actual indecision and inaction, about which Western allies and even Nasser himself complained. Put most plainly, the prime motive of Eisenhower's administration was "not to 'get the Arabs sore at all of us,' because they might embargo oil shipments from the entire Middle East" (Yergin 491). As Hungary demonstrated, the special interests of ethnic groups made good press in America and were often the occasion for the State Department's taking a strong rhetorical stand against the Soviets, but they actually held little sway over U.S. foreign policy. Despite its importance to American Jews following the war, Israel was no exception. After all, neither Israel nor Egypt have any oil to claim in *anyone's* name. The United States' "special relationship" with Israel, long taken for granted as the cornerstone of its Middle East policy, was in fact "not a sudden, dramatic development that would have triggered an explosion of Arab anger, but a slow, incremental process nearly two decades in the making" (McCormick 11–12). The entire Middle East was essentially up for grabs after WWII because Britain could no longer afford to finance its hegemony there or resist Arab nationalism. Postwar guilt over the Holocaust weighed heavily on the shoulders of U.S. foreign policy, to be sure; the United States immediately recognized the independence of Israel, but then so did the Soviet Union. Oil, however, made more tangible claims on national policy. As the Suez crisis showed, if Congress always kept glancing at the Jewish vote at home, the State Department's decisions about the Middle East were made with an eye open even wider to on-site Arab reaction.

When *The Ten Commandments* uses its biblical narrative to rationalize the United States' relatively new economic investment in the Middle East, it does so in such a way as to obscure the much more confused and conflicted political relations of the United States at the time both to Israel and to Egypt. And such obfuscation is only the beginning of the ideological work which the DeMille epic performs as a cold war blockbuster text. When Moses waves good-bye in the film's last shot, he does not resemble the Statue of Liberty so much as take *her* place as the symbolic guarantee of American freedom. This replacement of Lady Liberty by the Mosaic Male is historically resonant of the masculinity crisis that preoccupied American culture during this period: it puts forward within the historical setting of cold war global politics the claims of a conservative masculinity, identified with the state itself, which had been subordinated to the cultural hegemony of the domesticated breadwinner after the Second World War.

Indeed, though Nadel does not mention this, perhaps the strongest and most unexpected resemblance between Egypt and 1950s America occurs because of a point in fact having to do with the royal succession, which in ancient Egypt passed through the female rather than the male. Implicitly calling into question the patrilineal basis of inheritance, one of the touch-stones of masculinity in modern Western cultures, Sethi's reluctance to name Rameses as his successor calls to mind Eisenhower's much publicized indecision about retaining Richard Nixon as his running mate for the 1956 election. Any resemblance between these two indecisive leaders was by no means part of a consciously constructed parallel on the part of DeMille and his four screenwriters—after all, the film began production midway through Eisenhower's first administration—but is another of those "profound" coincidences of history that helped to increase the timeliness of *The Ten Commandments* for the public. Particularly when set in the context of ancient Egypt's matrilineal state, the coincidence serves as a key marker of the film's conservative response to the gender crisis characterizing the hegemonic masculinity of this period, which amounts to replacing Sethi's weakened patriarchal figure with Moses, who confidently hands over *his* leadership of Israel to Joshua before ascending Mount Sinai to rejoin his spiritual Father. Thus the final shot of the stern, uncompromising patriarch means to restore virility to a nation whose leadership, perceived in a disturbing state of inaction and vacillation (over Nixon, over Israel) was feared to be its fundamental political weakness.

Whose Son Is He, Anyway?

In any number of ways, then, the ancient Egypt of *The Ten Commandments* turns out to be a great symbolic instability, a historical *and* historicized setting where crucial binary categories of cold war ideology like Hebrew/Egyptian, master/slave, and us/them are set up but also crossed. Cold war films generally resolve the ideological incoherence resulting from such inevitable slippage of binary categories by displacing the political (the realm of the state and the site where the crisis of meaning occurs) onto the personal (the realm of the domestic and the site where the crisis can be more easily contained). This tactic, as I observed in chapter 1, has the effect of introducing "femininity" into the ideological formulation as a mediating term, thereby recasting questions of the state's identity into ones about the constitution of masculinity. This is not simply a matter of polarizing masculinity against a feminine Other, but of shifting anxiety about the state's political control onto concern about excessive feminine influence over domestic life.

According to the narrative manufactured for *The Ten Commandments*, feminine influence is a problem in Egypt precisely because the successful continuity of its royal government muddies the waters when it comes to either politics or domesticity. Moses' two mothers each pull him toward an opposing culture, and this conflict has the effect of challenging his masculinity: "I love you, my mother," he tells Bithiah (Nina Foch) after he learns of his true identity. "But am I your son?" Significantly, Moses continues to think of Bithiah as his mother even after the revelation of his secret origin, while *his* identity as a son (hers, Egypt's) is permanently altered, with wide-ranging political consequences.

In general, the film's Egyptian women (Bithiah, Nefretiri) threaten the security of the men in power because they act impulsively, putting their feelings over the good of the state, dramatizing the perils of feminine influence when it comes to governance. "Do you think I care *whose* son he is?" Nefretiri snarls to the slave Memnet (Judith Anderson), when the latter reveals the long-kept secret of Moses' birth. Later, when he returns from exile to demand that Rameses let his people go, Nefretiri is still willing to betray her husband and sell out the state by meeting Moses in secret. By contrast, the Hebrew women all eagerly sacrifice themselves for the good of men and the patriarchal Hebrew nation. Whereas the Egyptian Bithiah is punished with banishment from court once her brother Sethi learns of her deception, the Hebrew Yoshabel (Martha Scott) gets to relish in the mother's ultimate reward for her part in the lie. Reunited with her son, Yoshabel proudly boasts: "Blessed am I among all mothers in the land for mine eyes have beheld the Deliverer!" With that blessing on her head, Yoshabel's own life itself seems not to count for much more than that little bit of *mazel tov*, since the film then lets her die offscreen, conveying the information to Moses through dialogue after the fact. In similar fashion, Lilia (Debra Paget) gives herself to Dathan in order to save Joshua's life, accepting humiliation and exile from her people as the price of her prostitution; later, this daughter of Israel is made into a literal object of sacrifice during the worship of the Golden Calf.

Politically speaking, however, the difference between Egyptian and Hebrew women goes way beyond their being either selfish and actively desiring, or selfless and passively desired. From Nefretiri's point of view, which is that of Egyptian law as well as her own sexual desire, Moses' paternity actually does matter for very little when it comes to the royal succession. Egypt, this is also to say, is a "feminized" state in contrast to the federation of patriarchal Hebrew tribes, because its customs undermine the organization of manhood through primogenitary succession, the bedrock of patriarchy in law as well as in Western male psychology.

Thus the factor in *The Ten Commandments* which most raises anxieties about the boundaries and autonomy of both the state and masculinity is the precarious position in which sons find themselves in ancient Egypt. The film's narrative begins with the first Rameses ordering the slaying of Hebrew male infants, and it reaches its climax, the Exodus, only after the second Rameses unknowingly inspires (through the mediation of Nefretiri) the tenth plague, resulting in the slaying of Egypt's first-born. And as I have already indicated, Sethi, the Pharaoh who favors Moses as his successor, himself shows the same disregard for *his* son that the throne princess voices. "I am the son of your body," Rameses reminds his father. While this fact alone would be enough of a guarantee of royal succession in any Western monarchy, it matters not a fig in ancient Egypt. Rameses persists: "Who else can be your heir?" To put his cocky, ambitious son in his uncertain place as the mere biological issue of Pharaoh, Sethi reminds him: "The man best able to rule Egypt shall follow me. I owe that to my fathers. Not to my sons." In making this declaration, Sethi conveniently forgets his own debt to all the past queens of Egypt, including his absent wife, since she was the one who brought him the throne upon their marriage. Much to Rameses' dismay and Sethi's amusement, succession within an Egyptian dynasty did not issue through the male body. Rather, succession was achieved through marriage to the designated future queen (the throne princess, most likely a sister or a cousin), whose own bloodline confirmed the divinity of a new pharaoh, whoever he was, just as her own eventual ascent to the throne as his consort legitimized his reign.

Sethi's erasure of his own wife's role in acquiring the throne for him summarizes the film's ambivalence about how even to represent Egyptian succession. For at the same time that it acknowledges this important fact about ancient Egypt, *The Ten Commandments* can interpret the throne princess and the matrilineal succession she embodies only through phallocentric eyes. Locating Nefretiri's political power solely in terms of female sexuality, so that her ambition can be viewed more crudely as an expression of desire for Moses, the film makes her the victor's reward, handed over from father to son to define generational continuity as a homosocial exchange. *The Ten Commandments* consequently appears best able to respond to Nefretiri's political presence in the court of Sethi by representing her as a screen vamp in the Theda Bara tradition. Rather than acting as an arbiter of succession in her own right (as Gene Tierney's character Baketamon tries to do in *The Egyptian*, for example), Nefretiri has to keep charming Moses into striving for the throne as their only way to marry. Not a man to be accused of insincerity, Moses claims he acts "for love of Sethi, not for the throne of Egypt." "But *I* am Egypt," Nefretiri reminds him, and quite rightly so. The throne princess's function in guaranteeing royal succession in Egypt "through the female line" (DeMille 413) disrupts the patriarchal structure of masculinity which the principle of primogeniture supports. Nefretiri's prominence in the film, while mediated by all the stereotypes of the Hollywood *femme fatale*, lays down perhaps the most central condition of ancient Egypt's political difference from the Hebrews (and fifties America), particularly in contrast to the heavy patriarchal encoding of both the twelve tribes and the elder Moses, which determines the masochist character of the Hebrew women.

As *The Ten Commandments* illustrates, cold war films displace onto femininity the ideological incoherence produced by the collapse of difference between the free state and the slave state, so they end up addressing a secondary set of anxieties about the collapse of the patriarchal support of traditional masculinity. In turn, these anxieties use the feminine to conceal any criticism of the work of patriarchal men in modern America, namely corporate capitalism and its creation of a faceless, standardized mass culture through advertising. "[Cold war] films suggest ... that the menace of alien invasion lay not so much in the power of a foreign state as in the obliteration of paternal inheritance and the triumph of mass society" (Rogin 245–46). Rogin specifically addresses his comments here to the atomic-monster and invasion narratives of science fiction, where mass reproduction is literally made the ultimate threat to American society. The giant queen ants in *Them!*, for instance, breed indiscriminately and without regard for the males who fertilize their eggs. "The ants are bad mothers who breed in storm drains instead of the home. But breeding itself is the problem. ... The creatures they create are interchangeable parts, members of a mass society. Freed of the name of the father and of the mother's singular love, these creatures lack the stamp of individuality" (265).

Rogin does not mention the era's biblicals, but the same suspicion of mass culture occurs in *The Ten Commandments* during the Golden Calf sequence. The collective hysteria resulting from their fear of being abandoned by Moses reduces the Hebrews to "children," as DeMille's voiceover narration describes them—children being led down the garden path of damnation, significantly enough, by Dathan, the man whom the Egyptians say will sell his own mother for a price. Without Moses to guide them, the anxious Hebrews fail to recognize Dathan's danger as a subversive, presumably because he is a fellow Israelite. They then achieve the ultimate confusion of Egypt and Israel, persuading Moses' own brother Aaron to fabricate a Golden Calf for them to worship. During this sequence, the errant Hebrews not only reject the God of Abraham and repudiate the prophet who has delivered them from slavery, but they become indistinguishable from each other as well: none of the hundreds of extras can be told apart during the drunken, riotous orgy that follows. In other words, without a strong national leader to guide them, when the Hebrews forsake mass production (their labor under slavery) for mass consumption (their pleasure once liberated), they degenerate into a lawless mob and are consequently made vulnerable to the manipulation of a subversive like Dathan.

The two stone tablets which Moses brings down with him from Sinai restore the crucial ground of the Hebrews' difference from the Egyptians, which is based in the former's future observance of a patriarchal law "written," so Moses utters in awe as he watches, "with the finger of God." Publicity for the film represented the commandments inscribed on those tablets as lawfulness itself, or more accurately, as the legal foundation of the modern (and implicitly Christian) national-security state's authority to govern its citizens. "The Ten Commandments are not the laws," the souvenir program states in its introduction, echoing DeMille's own comments elsewhere, "They are THE LAW." In order to achieve this degree of universality, the film has to purge "THE LAW" of its origin in Orthodox Jewishness, omitting specific mention of Mosaic law's complex regulation of all aspects of Hebrew life as recorded in the Old Testament after the Exodus story (Babington and Evans, *Biblical* 35). With its historical and cultural specificity conveniently obscured, "THE LAW" can then function as the principal abstraction of patriarchal male subjectivity. "I will put My laws into their hearts and in their minds will I write them . . ." the voice of Yahweh instructs Moses: "I am that I am. Say 'I am' has sent me." While Moses believes that he does not change when he learns his true identity in Goshen, he does become altered once he sees the Burning Bush and climbs Mount Sinai. More precisely, he becomes divided, subject to the discourse of the Almighty and positioned squarely in relation to "THE LAW" of the Father. Every utterance of "I am" refers, literally in this context but also, one can assume, symbolically in a psychoanalytic sense too, not to Moses himself but to an Other.

The voice recorded to speak God's word on Mount Sinai in this scene—though not in the later one when Moses receives the Commandments—is Heston's own, played at a different timbre and slower speed than normal, which means that the film uses the actor's audible disembodiment from his own voice at this point to signify the divided subjectivity required of Moses before the word of God. In this same sense, Yahweh ("I am") inscribes "THE LAW" of His presence on Moses' body, notably in the prophet's whitened hair (which Sephora comments upon when he returns from Mount Sinai), this divine action reversing the earlier proclamation of Sethi, who has had Moses' name removed—erased as a text—from every pylon and obelisk. Moses then becomes so fully realized an effect of Yahweh's patriarchy, the perfect subject of "I am," that he cedes all human will, all sexual desire, to "THE LAW." Subsequently, when Nefretiri begs him to interfere with God's intention of slaying the Egyptian firstborn, Moses has to refuse: "By myself I am nothing. It is the power of God which uses me to work his will." In another scene, she tries to seduce Moses into leaving Egypt with her, but he spurns her invitation: "The Moses who loved you was another man." When she declares, "I do not believe that only the thunder of a mountain stirs your heart as you stir mine," he responds by informing her that, having stood in God's presence, he now transcends mere physical desire. With this kind of admission, it's no wonder Sephora abruptly leaves Goshen as soon as the first opportunity comes her way! "He has forgotten both of us," she tells Nefretiri. "You lost him when he went to seek his God. I lost him when he found his God."

Fittingly enough for a motion picture which, in the purported motto of ancient Egypt, makes writing equivalent to action ("so it is written, so it shall be done"), the Mosaic body itself becomes text; and as "THE LAW" of the Heavenly Father ("I am") inscribes itself on this divided corpus, Moses can then return to Egypt to perform what the film represents as a divinely sanctioned form of patriarchal masculinity. Once Moses is made subject of "I am," that is also to say, his own body becomes the primary site of libidinal repression, establishing another contrast to the narcissistic excess signified by Rameses' royal body in the second half of the film.

Moses and Rameses

As its poster art intimates, *The Ten Commandments* condenses the binary logic of cold war thinking on the surface of the male body, setting up a governing opposition between Moses and Rameses, between the Americanized Hebrew prophet and the demonized Egyptian dictator, which extends to the film's treatment of the two male costars, Charlton Heston and Yul Brynner. What the poster art for *The Ten Commandments* reproduces, first of all, is the manner in which the film, through its diacritical marking of Moses and Rameses, registers the binary logic of a cold war narrative at the site of the male body; and second, how the film supports that overarching system of symbolic representation with an aesthetic of male spectacle that brings this ideological operation to the foreground.

In his commentary on *The Ten Commandments*, Marc Vernet isolates one scene in particular which makes vivid use of the stars' opposition on film:

> Ramses [*sic*] decides on the expulsion of Moses from Egypt and leads him to the brink of the desert. DeMille films the scene in shot/reverse shot: Ramses is in brilliant armor, in his chariot, with the edge of the desert and a distant rising pyramid for a background. Moses, in his robe, staff in hand, is on foot with the immense desert stretching out in the background. The result is parallelism and opposition since DeMille cannot resist contrasting the men aesthetically: Ramses-Brynner receives complex studio lighting and stands before a back-projection, while Moses-Heston is in real exterior with a purity and simplicity of colors and sunlight. Nature versus artifice, simplicity versus pride, truth versus trickery, movement versus stasis. (67)

According to Vernet, both the Western and *The Ten Commandments* organize the myth of the pastoral republic (nineteenth-century America, ancient and modern Israel) by arranging binaries of the sort he analyzes in this passage to give specific meaning to the frontier, which in both cases is the desert.

Vernet wants to show how *The Ten Commandments* resembles the Western in its underlying binary structure (i.e., "nature versus artifice," etc.), but what actually motivates his observation is a network of visual codes through which Heston and Brynner signify the antinomies central to cold war ideology by virtue of the stars' being rendered as male bodies that are textually marked (in this scene, through the material, detail, and color of their costuming), techno-logically positioned (here, through artificially differentiated backdrops), and discursively mediated (through the antithesis of nature/culture that Heston's appearance in a location shot, when set in contrast to the studio-bound Brynner, evokes for Vernet). While an important turning point in the narra-tive, the scene of Moses' exile is not, as Vernet's rhetoric implies, a privileged moment of meaning in the film. On the contrary, the bodies of the two stars visualize the difference between Hebrew and Egyptian cultures throughout *The Ten Commandments*.

Color, for example, plays a major role in establishing a ground of contrast between the stars' bodies. Noerdlinger reports that the bright sunlight of location shooting in the Egyptian desert required highly saturated, vividly contrasting colors in order to keep the human figure from blending into the background (130). But even in its studio-produced scenes, *The Ten Command-ments* has a Technicolor brilliance that calls to mind MGM musicals of the 1940s and early 1950s. The cinematography repeatedly juxtaposes bright coral reds to deep turquoise blues, beginning with the moment when Bithiah casts aside the predominantly red Levite cloth covering the abandoned baby Moses and wraps him instead in a blue blanket. From this point on, a red/blue contrast calls visual attention to Moses in relation to Rameses so long as the former is a member of the Egyptian court. If red dominates Moses' costume in a given scene, then blue dominates Rameses, or vice versa, as is sometimes the case. Even variations of this code—for example, Rameses wears a costume combining both colors when he rides up in his chariot following Moses' rescue of his Hebrew mother Yoshabel, and the mise-en-scène of Nefretiri's private chambers when Moses learns of his birth reproduces the coral/turquoise contrast to surround him with the two colors—refer back to that chromatic design to indicate Moses' innate difference from Egypt.

With Moses' return from exile, the film then differentiates the two male stars according to the presence or absence of bright color on their bodies. Moses goes back to Egypt to demand freedom for his people, and Rameses' costume alone now contains what had been the chromatic contrast between the two men in earlier scenes. In visual opposition to the prophet's shapeless Levite cloak, which registers on screen as a dull reddish covering (it is actually a red, white, and black striped material), the pharaoh's costume is a brilliant rainbow, featuring a bright red headdress adorned with gold cobra, a blue pinstriped cape, and red embroidered kilt. This secondary diacritical scheme picks up the earlier contrast between the well-lit, spacious, and luxuriously appointed palace of Egypt on the one hand, and the dark, cramped, and spare hovels of Goshen on the other. Whereas Rameses' spectacular costuming incorporates the brightly colored mise-en-scène of ancient Egypt, the drab Levite robe sets Moses apart as an index of his moral alienation from that pagan land. Rameses' costume, moreover, makes the pharaoh a site of vibrant color that, visually speaking, not only bears the same value as the setting, but also has the same chromatic brilliance and intensity as the visualization of the plagues, as when the blue sky over the palace is furled with green prior to the hailstorm, or when the Nile turns the vivid red color of blood. Color has the effect of equating Rameses' body with Egypt to the point where, in this respect, he too can rightfully say, "*I* am Egypt." Within a mise-en-scène that puts primary colors forward so insistently and intensely, the contrasting dullness of Moses in the second half of the film registers the prophet's body in turn as a blank or an absence, a site of visual repression consistent with his symbolic position as the sign of "I am."

In addition to color, camera setups give a decided prominence to the stars' bodies. DeMille's style of camerawork has the intent of reproducing melodramatic and painterly tableaus (the compositional logic of most of his establishing master shots), within which he places the actors' bodies in physical support of each other or in spatial conflict; these relations are indicated either within a single shot or through shot/reverse shot editing. Throughout the nearly four-hour running time of *The Ten Commandments*, and in contrast to other epics of the period, DeMille seldom uses tight close-ups of his stars (there are only two or three medium close-ups of Heston, for instance, in the entire film), but instead films them in medium or three-quarter shots. The director's avoidance of close-ups keeps attention riveted upon the bodies of the actors; cuts to medium shots then sustain that perspective by featuring the torso as part of the (relatively) more intimate and individuated view of a particular performer.

The very first views of Moses and Rameses immediately set up their opposition as bodies in a way that further differentiates Heston and Brynner from their female costars, who are neither as elaborately or scantily costumed nor as openly juxtaposed on purely visual terms. A dissolve from Bithiah—holding up the young babe found in the bulrushes and reciting his new name ("Moses, Moses!")—to a cheering crowd shouting his name ("Moses, Moses!"), as the now grown prince returns to Egypt in celebration following his triumph over Ethiopia, is followed by another dissolve, this time across space to Rameses jealously eyeing his rival's reception in the streets below. This second dissolve momentarily holds the two men together in a double three-quarter shot, and this overlapping image displays but also contains their opposition, which at this point is legible only at the level of the stars' bodies. Whereas Moses/Heston's body is encased in the type of military uniform that conventionally marks a hard phallic masculinity, the absence of such vestments on Rameses/Brynner foregrounds the latter's partial nudity. His bare muscular chest is outlined all

Figure 19.
The rival princes stand before Pharaoh and the two stars are
placed within the same shot for the first time.

the more by the metal jewelry he wears (broad collar, arm bands, bracelets), which frames his naked chest so that penetrable flesh, in contrast to Moses' impenetrable armor, serves as the focal point of Rameses' body. Figure 19 refers to the end of this sequence, when, with the two princes standing before Sethi to receive Pharaoh's orders, the film places the two men and the visual terms of their difference within the same shot for the first time.

Brynner's body, its hairlessness given indirect emphasis by that thick, jet black "prince's braid" sprouting incongruously from a bald pate, connotes his racial difference from Heston's Moses, whose own braid, it turns out, is concealed by his helmet. The prominence given to race in *The Ten Commandments* is uncharacteristic of fifties biblicals since, for the reasons I suggested earlier, British actors usually play Romans opposite American Christians or freedom fighters, thereby maintaining an Anglo-American profile for the ancient world and allowing for the safe inclusion of an exotic muscular black gladiator every now and then, as in *Demetrius and the Gladiators* and *Spartacus*. Truth to tell, given the presence of Anne Baxter and Sir Cedric Hardwicke in the royal court of Egypt, without Brynner in the cast race would probably not have intruded upon *The Ten Commandments* any more overtly than it does in those films. But Brynner *is* in this film, and DeMille's visual treatment of the actor, especially when set in contrast to that of Heston, has the significant effect of aligning Rameses to the West's representation of the East as a site of colonial domination. The conquered Ethiopians appear with Moses at this early point in the film, in fact, precisely to ensure that the racial Otherness of "Egypt" *not* be read as African—which would be to interpret it more dangerously as a "black" civilization—but as Asian, which makes the royal court of ancient Egypt as "Oriental" as, say, that of nineteenth-century Siam, or even that of Japan as demonized by the United Stares during World War II.

Yul Brynner: Baldness Brings Its Own Rewards

The introduction of Moses and Rameses immediately establishes how, through their concealed or exposed bodies, Heston and Brynner objectify the American/alien opposition which ideologically governs the film's attitudes toward "Hebrew" and "Egyptian," and, through the Orientalist intertext evoked by Brynner's physical appearance, goes on to allude to the United States' conflicted position in the Middle East. As played out through the two stars this diacritical pairing has the ultimate effect of repudiating Rameses'/Brynner's masculinity for its Otherness in being Asian, which the film portrays in the gendered terms of bodily spectacle. But despite the feminizing implications of his spectacularity, *The Ten Commandments* never loses sight of Brynner's maleness. His visual difference from Heston does not mean to question Rameses' virility, as we might assume follows from the film's overt inscription of Brynner as an Oriental. On the contrary, the actor's muscularity is highly exaggerated whenever the camera focuses on him bare-chested. As Brynner holds in his stomach and pushes out his pectorals, his self-conscious posing belies any inferences that Rameses' body might be an effeminate or emasculated one—even though the display of bejeweled, bare flesh renders Brynner himself at once erotic (as an exhibitionist) and exotic (as an Oriental)—encouraging us to reassess what "virility" means when played out on the body of such an "alien" male.

The combination of sexuality and spectacle which underlies Brynner's screen presence was, in fact, the important meaning of the actor's early star persona, and DeMille's film makes full use of it. In 1956, as well as appearing as Rameses, Brynner repeated his stage role as the King of Siam in *The King and I* (for which he won an Oscar) and played a Russian general opposite Ingrid Bergman in *Anastasia* (which opened about a month after *The Ten Commandments* began its hardticket runs). All three roles exploited the erotic and exotic connotations of what the media, at this same time, celebrated as the actor's distinguishing characteristics as a new Hollywood star, namely, his baldness and his obscure ethnic origins, both of which were manufactured. Brynner was not actually as bald as he appeared, and his background was not as mixed or enigmatic as he encouraged journalists to think. According to son Rock Brynner (11) and biographer Jhan Robbins (2), the actor was born in Vladivostok, Russia. Feature stories about him in newspapers and fan magazines nonetheless attributed his erotic appeal to his baldness, just as they linked his exotic aura to a mysterious hybrid nationality.

Army Archerd, for instance, represented Brynner throwing the entire star system out of whack because of his shaved head. "Everyone knew that Yul Brynner was an actor of tremendous talent," the reporter wrote in *Photoplay,* "but they never dreamed that a baldheaded man—any baldheaded man— could have and even exude sex appeal." Seeking an answer to this enigma, Archerd quoted one friend, "an intelligent, well-paid studio employee," on Brynner's unique appeal to viewers: "Our friend paused and thought for a minute, and finally summed it up with: 'Yul's appeal to the feminine world is— let's face it—S-E-X. Ask any girl what she thinks of him, and it comes out something like "grrr." One thing you can be sure it is *not,* and that is maternal!'" Archerd finally finds a proper trope for conveying Brynner's impression of intense and aggressive male sexuality ("Those eyes of his seem to pierce you," he also quotes his friend saying) in the metaphor of a predatory animal: Archerd wonders if, with a full head of hair, Brynner would "still look like a panther." As tellingly, in his effort to describe Brynner's "animal magnetism," Archerd implies that some sort of bisexual attraction underlies it. After relating an anecdote about Jerry Lewis's first jovial meeting with Brynner at the Paramount commissary, Archerd mentions in passing that afterward the comedian was "keeping one eye on Brynner throughout his entire lunch" (109).

Actually, Archerd himself can make sense of the actor's bald pate only by picturing it as a kind of phallus. Noting that, in contrast to Brynner, "the top favorites over the years" have "all been handsome, and they've all sported a fair head of hair," Archerd begins by equating baldness with the stereotypical implication of emasculation: "And the ones who weren't so well endowed, or whose locks began to thin come forty, all hied themselves nervously to the toupee artists" (109).[12] The enigma of Brynner's virile screen presence thus arises from its apparent contradiction as a representation of male sexuality. The star makes absolutely no pretense about his lack of endowment in one symbolic sense, only to convince viewers of his well-endowment in another, much more potent sexual sense: the excessive, unregulated physicality of his entire body.

As a consequence of the attention which his body—starting with his bald head—appeared to demand from female and male viewers alike, Brynner's star persona encouraged a visual treatment similar to that traditionally bestowed upon female stars. No wonder that Rock Brynner, summarizing his father's impact upon audiences following the successes of *The Ten Command-*

Figures 20a and 20b.
The erotic and exotic spectacle of Yul Brynner in publicity stills from *The Ten Commandments* (left) and *The King and I* (right).

ments, The King and I, and *Anastasia,* compares him to the most spectacularized female star of the decade: "Yul Brynner was now an established sex symbol, the masculine counterpart to Marilyn Monroe" (101). Figures 20a and 20b, comparing a publicity still for *The Ten Commandments* (left) and one for *The King and I* (above), shows the aptness of this comparison. Each photograph poses Brynner to draw a viewer's eye immediately to the star's bare chest in a manner recalling pinup imagery of Monroe. Shaved for his movie roles, Brynner's entire body, when denuded of its hair, is made to serve as a metonymy of his bald head. In this way his baldness supplied journalists like Army Archerd with a polite cover for writing about his body in explicitly sexual terms, just as it provided the excuse on screen for gazing at his entire body in that same openly sexual way.

Brynner's baldness obviously gave him a look that jarred with American notions about the relation between a full head of hair and virility, and his mythical Eurasian heritage then ensured that his unorthodox physical appearance connoted not the intellectualism of the American egghead, but the exoticism of the foreigner. "Was he a Russian?" asked one of DeMille's writers. "A Tartar prince? A gypsy? A Manchurian acrobat?" (Lasky 304). The press paid acute attention to the star's mysterious origins. Archerd, for instance, reports: "His birthplace is the Russian area of Sakhalin, an island in the northern chain of Japan. His father, though Swiss, was of Mongolian descent. And his mother was a dark-eyed Romany gypsy beauty" (109). Such stories circulated a fictive persona of mongrel ethnicity, the indeterminacy of which connoted Brynner's Otherness as a non-American male:

> "There's no Russian blood in my veins," says Brynner, "but I am part Mongolian and that's a common strain in the USSR. And I do speak Russian.
> "Because of that I'm often mistaken for a Russian. . . . The Russians think I'm Russian. Orientals consider me their own. Parisians think of me as a native because I was brought up there. At one time I was a Swiss citizen." (Scott, "Yul")

Shrouded not so much in mystery as in heterogeneity, Brynner's origins were ambiguous enough to make him convincing as an Orientalized Asian (in *The King and I* and *The Ten Commandments*) or Russian (in *Anastasia* and later *The Brothers Karamazov*, 1958, and *The Journey*, 1959). His star persona consequently made his ethnically ambiguous body legible in a way that supplied the semblance of visual authenticity to DeMille's symbolic equation of ancient Egypt and the Soviet empire in Europe and Asia.

When Brynner first appeared on screen in 1956, he was extremely explosive as a male "S-E-X" star, and his foreignness helped to regulate the blatant sexuality exuding from his body. What we now might call the camp style of Brynner's performance in DeMille's film (in the star's deliverance of his lines; the suggestive positioning of his relaxed body in relation to Heston's stiffer one; his manipulation of props, like his horsewhip, against his body) served only to accentuate the transgressive edge of his screen presence at the time. Needless to say, Hollywood quickly recuperated this uncommon star persona, and Brynner went on to play more Westernized heroic parts. As his popularity soared following *The King and I* and *The Ten Commandments*, with toupee firmly in place he played Jean Lafitte for DeMille in a remake of *The Buccaneer* (1958); starred in, of all things, an utterly bizarre adaptation of *The Sound and the Fury* (1959); and returned to a biblical setting as the replacement for Tyrone

Power in *Solomon and Sheba* (1959). It is therefore important to recall the initial impact of the star's performative masculinity on screen. When *The Ten Commandments* makes a blatant spectacle out of Brynner, it fully exploits what the actor's shaved body originally signified about his erotic and exotic male star image, though to be sure, the film works just as hard to regulate the implications of ungovernable male sexuality connoted by that star persona, primarily by representing Brynner's spectacular male body as a decidedly alien one, the pharaoh Rameses, in opposition to Charlton Heston's all-American Moses.

Charlton Heston: But Size Counts Even More

If baldness was the primary metonymy of Brynner's star persona, then bigness served a similar function for Heston's. As Donald Spoto puts it, "Heston's large form is magnified more, indeed, on the big screen—extended, actually, into some realm of the pure form of man of power" (*Camerado* 214). From the very beginning of the actor's career, there was no getting around his body. When describing Heston, one relatively early interview called attention to his size ("6 feet 2 inches tall") and alluded to his body's sexual power ("He sleeps raw in 7-feet-by-7-feet beds made to order") (Skolsky, "Hollywood" 1955). In another account from the 1950s, Heston is *so* big and brawny that he even begins to parody the physical stereotype of the American jock. "A giant in physique Heston is as impressive offscreen as he is in such epic roles as Moses and Ben Hur," writes a reporter for UPI. "He ordered a large mound of chopped raw steak, his favorite dish, and polished it off quickly." The point in such descriptions is always that Heston's considerable virility, raw meat and all, is an effect of nature. He himself was said to remark: "You've got to keep in good shape if millions of people are going to see you there on the big screen where every defect is magnified. . . . I do a lot of bending exercises and calisthenics but no muscle-building. I'm massive enough as it is" (Musel).

While the first part of *The Ten Commandments* puts Heston's massive body on display, a point I shall return to, the second part conceals it. Once Moses obeys the word of God, his hair turns white and, as a site of erotic spectacle, Heston's body becomes increasingly diminished in visual opposition to Rameses'/Brynner's. As unlikely to feel sexual desire as to experience *any* sort of hunger whatsoever, Moses in the film's second half is now, as Babington and Evans put it, "so far beyond human love that his face doesn't flicker even in minimal response" (*Biblical* 51). "Heston," these writers also comment, conflating the actor with that portrait of Moses, "exemplifies the man who has conquered himself" (229).

The characteristics of sexual repression and moral forthrightness, which inform Heston's physical presence on screen in the latter half of *The Ten Commandments*, helped to crystallize what would become the primary value of his epic star persona. Babington and Evans read in the actor's physiognomy—his eagle profile, chiseled jaw, perfect teeth, broad shoulders—"signs less of sexual readiness than the patriarch's eagerness to respond to honour and duty" (*Biblical* 229). Most critics write about Heston in similar terms, first referring to his big body as a means of accounting for the star's special relation to the Hollywood epic, then concluding that he is the genre's one "true" hero (Richards 50) or its "mise-en-scène" (Mourlet 234), its "objective correlative" (McArthur 142) or the sum total of its effects, as "firm as Moses' rock" (Spoto, *Camerado* 213), comparable to a commemorative "statue" or even a "pyramid" (Malone 109). At the same time that they appreciate what his massive build connotes *as* a body, all these evocations of Heston's "epic presence" (Bruce Crowther) go on to represent him signifying something *other* than his body. It is only through the star's ability to transcend his massive, implicitly sexualized, and even animalistic body (he sleeps in the raw, remember, just as he eats his meat raw) that he can then represent something else entirely (i.e., a genre, a setting, a monument). To be sure, Heston's star-making epic roles invariably subject him to physical punishment or suffering, purging his body of its passions as the prelude to spiritual transcendence, whether this amounts to union with God the Father, as in *The Ten Commandments*, or with God the Son, as in *Ben-Hur*. His "epic presence" thus marks the apparent subordination of his big body to a much greater ideological force: a national narrative.

Referring to Heston's epic *presence*, though, results in something of a mis-nomer. The phrase obscures the troubling relation which the actor poses to his body as a force of masculinity that must be celebrated for its physicality all the while being drained of it. Consequently, while Heston himself projects a rather complicated relation to his own big body on screen in *The Ten Com-mandments*, as far as his star persona goes it usually was and continues to be interpreted as if it were relatively straightforward and unproblematic. Heston's close identification with the epic genre solidified his emerging star image as a patriarchal male as soon as the actor publicly internalized DeMille's Moses into his own offscreen persona to supply the needed extratextual support of his film roles. In late summer 1959, for example, as *The Ten Commandments* finished its last drive-in runs and *Ben-Hur* was being readied for Thanksgiving premieres in select cities, Heston recorded the Five Books of Moses, all in the King James version, for Vanguard Records. More than just a project to sustain his association with the biblicals, his act of recording the Mosaic texts—inspired, the actor said, by his actually setting foot on Mount Sinai during the location filming of *The Ten Commandments* nearly five years before—was itself articulated in much the same way that DeMille's film represented Moses' body as the site through which "I am" signified His monotheistic divinity and as a consequence allowed Moses to transcend his own body. "Curiously," it was reported at the time, "Heston finds that the better his physical condition the more resonant his voice, easily one of the best in films" (Musel). But why should that fact be a surprise? Heston produces his epic presence through his "massive" well-built, well-conditioned body, the significance of which is then displaced onto his "resonant" disembodied voice on a record, in effect reproducing what happens to Moses when he approaches the Burning Bush in DeMille's film and transcends his own body to become the sign of a pure reflexive absence. "I am that I am," the disembodied voice—actually Heston's own, remember—tells Moses on Mount Sinai. "Say 'I am' has sent me." Whether Heston's physical transparency as an epic presence ends up signifying "THE LAW" (as in the DeMille film) or the epic itself (as in the Heston criticism), the effect on his star persona is the same.

Given his big size, effacement of Heston's physical presence on film was no easy task by any means; and while *The Ten Commandments* ultimately subjects Moses/Heston to the law of "I am," the film also has trouble ignoring the star's body altogether. The VistaVision camera process used to photograph the film encouraged a vertical perspective of the human body to start with. More properly achieving a *big* screen effect than a *wide* one like CinemaScope, VistaVision sacrificed extreme width in the interest of achieving greater height, depth, and resolution, so it flattered compositions of the sort DeMille favors in *The Ten Commandments*, which, in contrast to the reclining actors featured in CinemaScope films, stress vertical lines. For example, whereas Victor Mature enters *The Robe* as an escaped slave whose body fills the screen horizontally when he sprawls forward on the city street after being chased by Roman soldiers, Heston first appears in *The Ten Commandments* standing straight and tall in his chariot, the impressive sight of his erect body enhanced by the pronounced vertical axis of the VistaVision screen.

Other scenes in Egypt produce the same visual emphasis on Heston's height. The composition calls attention not just to the straight line of the actor's massive body, but to his spatial command over other, more visibly diminutive bodies as well because of his size: over Moses' soldiers (when Heston/Moses enters the throne room following the conquest of Ethiopia, he appears to be at least a head taller than everyone else); over his future lieutenant and successor (when Moses does not condemn Joshua to death for striking an Egyptian or, later, when he murders the Master Builder to rescue Joshua, Heston is shown to be taller than John Derek, so that the hierarchy among Hebrew heroes is never a question); over his two mothers (when Moses enters the cramped hut of Yoshabel to confront her and Bithiah, Heston fills up the space and looms over them, physically inducing the women to speak the truth); over the Hebrew slaves (even when he crouches in the mud, Heston still stands out among the other anonymous bodies, so much so that Nefretiri can order the mud-caked Moses sent to her quarters by using the excuse that she needs another oarsman for her barge, "a strong slave"); over his guards (brought to the throne room in chains, Heston still towers over the men leading him in, to indicate the awesome physical power which his rival has had to contain in

Figure 21.
When Moses enters the throne room, Heston's height
indicates his superiority.

entrapping the Deliverer). Heston, in short, is photographed so that Moses appears, literally as well as figuratively, to be head and shoulders above the pack, an effect predicting the prophet's later position at the foot of Mount Sinai when he stands ready to hurl the stone tablets at the errant Hebrews worshiping the Golden Calf.

Clearly, as used in *The Ten Commandments*, the vertical aesthetic of Vista-Vision is more than simply an accidental effect of a specific technology (i.e., Paramount's new screen process as opposed to Fox's). By repeatedly placing Heston's tall body in the foreground, the camera process brings out the actor's physical connotations of moral and racial superiority as embodied in his height. All the critics of Heston notwithstanding, it was ultimately the actor's height more than anything else which forged his close identification with the epic genre that made him a star, in much the same way that height signified John Wayne's affinity with the Western. So when *The Ten Commandments* seems to function just like a big Hollywood Western of the period, as Vernet suggests for other reasons, the resemblance arises in large part from the visual prominence of the epic genre's own version of the tall man, Charlton Heston.

"The motif of height in the Western contains complicated meanings," Virginia Wright Wexman comments, "for in addition to moral uprightness it also symbolizes the nostalgia for a vigilante society in which some benefit at the expense of others" (92). Even more importantly, she continues, "the bodies of cowboy stars like Wayne, despite their notable size, do not function primarily in terms of gender-related phallic symbology. In these films height connotes racial rather than gender privilege: what is significant is that the Anglo-identified hero towers over racial others who are thereby marked as moral inferiors" (94). Wexman's observation about the Western hero applies equally well to Heston in *The Ten Commandments*. Here, too, the size of Heston's "massive" body implies Moses' moral stature, which in its turn indicates the racial superiority legitimating his authority as the Man of Law for all faiths, Christian and non-Christian. Even though race may not appear to be made an explicit issue of Heston's physical appearance in the way it is for his costar, the more overt visualization of Brynner as Oriental has the corresponding effect of underscoring Heston's own WASP American identity—beginning with those physical characteristics of body size, facial features, and coloring that critics have routinely celebrated as the features determining Heston's epic presence on screen.

DeMille's film conflates race and gender at the site of the male body, Heston's as well as Brynner's. When contemporary reviewers of *The Ten Commandments* complained at length about DeMille's invention of a sexual triangle to fill in the missing years of Moses' life, they missed the point of the film's resorting to a banal Hollywood formula. The rivalry of Moses and Rameses for the hand of Nefretiri—herself no more than the officially sanctioned object over which the two men vie as they more indirectly compete for the love of the father, Sethi—makes their racial difference a by-product of the phallic regime which supports Moses' conservative masculinity and grants authority to "THE LAW" which he ultimately comes to represent through the visual and psychological repression of his white body. In this way, *The Ten Commandments* encodes racial difference through gender, just as it encodes sexual difference through race; and since both codes foreground the sight of Heston's body alongside Brynner's, the film then attempts to mask the white star's relation to its ideological work by ultimately effacing the value of Moses' body altogether.

Body Doubles

Actually, the film's introduction of Heston and Brynner gives a false impression of differentiating the stars simply according to Rameses' seminudity, which eroticizes the Egyptian prince as spectacle in contrast to Moses, whose military uniform covers his body with a display of phallic overprotection that

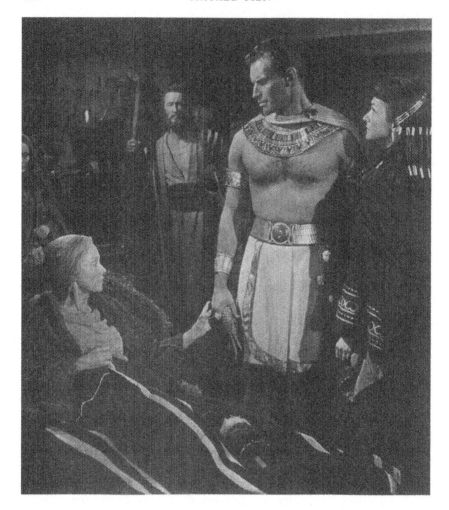

Figure 22.
When Moses confronts his two mothers, Heston's body dominates the cramped
space of Yoshabel's hut, focusing attention on his bare chest.

also accentuates his muscularity, but only indirectly. Moses/Heston himself
also appears bare-chested at several key points in the first part of the film,
although (probably to continue their diacritical marking in the text but also so
as not to homoeroticize their interaction) never at the same time as Rameses/
Brynner. For instance, while Rameses is bare-chested in one scene taking place
in the court, where he taunts Nefretiri with the power dynamics that will play
out in their eventual marriage, in the next scene, when he follows his father to

Goshen where Moses is working bare-chested, the Egyptian appears fully clothed. To be sure, Rameses' skimpy costumes tend to underscore his indolence, while Moses strips to work (first to supervise the labor of the slaves and then to work in the brick pits himself), following Hollywood convention for showing off male beefcake. Even so, such displays of Heston's massive body exceed their apparent narrative motivation. When he pays his visit to Goshen in search of his birthright, the scene in Yoshabel's house visually centers around the sight of Heston's massive, hairy chest to the point where the star is as fully fetishized by DeMille's camera as Brynner is in his seminude scenes. Sethi is perfectly right when he refers to the two princes as crowing roosters. Both men huff and puff and blow out their chests to signify their virility, with Brynner taking a much more self-mocking stance toward his body's posturing than Heston.

Closer inspection of the scanty costumes worn by Heston and Brynner in the first half of the film also reveals that male body *hair*, a secondary gender trait, functions even more strikingly than nudity or body size as the primary signifier of their racial difference as men. The film subjects Heston to a state of undress comparable to Brynner's in order to place their chests in visual juxtaposition: one man has hair while the other one is bare as a means of inscribing racial difference on the body and—in the same visual gesture—of eroticizing that difference by subjecting it to a system of phallic privilege and discrimination. All the Egyptians of the upper ranks (politicians, military leaders, and the priesthood) have shaved bodies, visually reinforcing Egypt's association with Hollywood's traditional representation of Asian and Native American peoples, whereas, beginning with Moses, the Hebrews are all hirsute, even Dathan. Body hair, in this sense, connotes the Hebrews' naturalness in contrast to Egyptian artifice. The absence of body hair is what symbolically subordinates the Egyptians to the Hebrews, while at the same time, in serving as the signifier of this difference, the presence of body hair naturalizes the opposition so that it appears inevitable and not arbitrary—even though the lack of body hair on the Egyptians is in fact the result of contrivance, requiring some form of depilatory.

This visual code also means that, to the discerning viewer, Moses reveals his real Hebrew identity every time he takes off his tunic in Egypt and displays his hairy chest. By the same token, what this code leads that discerning viewer to look at *is* Heston's hairy chest, which makes him an object of a highly eroticized form of male spectacle, as when Rameses has Moses brought into the court in a loincloth and chains. In order to disavow the male masochism connoted by such punishing treatment, the film then displaces the sign "hair" onto another part of Heston's body, his face. Moses ceases to shave once he accepts his Hebrew identity and enters the brick pits, and from this point on his beard becomes thicker, longer, and eventually whiter, signifying his status as the patriarch through the repression of his body and redirecting the site of his authority from his chest (while in Egypt) to his voice (following his communion with the Burning Bush), achieving the effect of self-division I have already analyzed. Peter Biskind notes that "facial hair in the fifties was about as popular as bad breath," with a clean-shaven face often distinguishing the hero from the villain, particularly in cold war movies (127). *The Ten Commandments* reverses this coding of body hair, however, so that the hero is hairy and the villain is not, as a means of visually connoting both the film's historical setting in ancient times and Moses' patriarchal authority. Not only is Moses a head taller than Joshua, for example, but, once he accepts his Hebrew identity, he also becomes progressively more bearded; and this beard visualizes his embodiment of conservative masculinity, implicitly differentiating Moses the patriarch from the hegemonic men of contemporary times who shaved their faces clean every day before putting on their gray flannel suits.

Nevertheless, for all of DeMille's elaborate efforts in *The Ten Commandments* to differentiate his two stars—from their costumes when they are dressed, to their body hair when they are not—the visual attention to their bodies ends up reproducing that unexpected yet inevitable doubling of American and alien that is the inevitable outcome of cold war representation. Conflation of the symbolic difference between Heston and Brynner occurs almost as soon as the film begins, when Moses and Rameses stand before Pharaoh to epitomize their opposition as rivals for the throne in purely visual terms. Significantly, the publicity still reproducing this moment (see figure 19 again) makes the stars' visual opposition more stable than it is on film. In the photograph, Heston, slightly taller than Brynner, looks up and away, concealing his body with his arm as well as his uniform, while Brynner bares his chest and looks straight at the camera in a daring acknowledgment of its gaze. What the publicity still effaces is the film's own disturbance of binary differences within its visual field. For in the film itself, as Moses and Rameses address Sethi, each man also looks intently at his homosocial rival while the other speaks. This particular scene, marked by their gazing at each other's body, records their mutual recognition of the other's visibility, suggesting almost as soon as the film opens how each star functions not in opposition, but as each other's body double. Their visual doubling is inevitable. While *The Ten Commandments* inscribes the opposition of American and alien upon the bodies of Heston/ Moses and Brynner/Rameses as its most striking containment of political and racial Otherness, the "massive" body of the "American" all too easily collapses into that of the exotic "alien" because they are *equally* crucial in providing visual support of the film's reproduction of cold war binaries.

The Ten Commandments has the obvious aim of promoting a renewal of conservative masculinity, to be sure, but the erotic spectacle of Charlton Heston in the first half casts over the entire blockbuster film the tall shadow of the star's implicit resemblance to his partner in spectacle, Yul Brynner. Because Heston's body is so crucial to the visual economy of the film's overarching symbolic structure, *The Ten Commandments* cannot efface it totally; if nowhere else, the significance of the star's physical presence as a body keeps resurfacing in his very own name, which, fittingly if accidentally enough, turns out to be the expansion of his on-screen value as the man of epic spectacle: "*chest.*"[13] The marking of Charlton Heston and Yul Brynner in antithetical terms restores the effaced Mosaic body to visual representation, thereby foregrounding the constitution of its political meaning. As importantly, within that highly charged ideological system of representation, their opposition has the crucial effect of highlighting the performative value of *both* stars as male bodies, and quite spectacular ones at that.

The Age of the Chest

> "Whatever does she see in *him?*" is a common female crack about another girl's
> beau or husband. Or about her movie hero. Marilyn Monroe appeals to almost all
> men, but there is no male movie star who universally sends the girls. Some like them
> tough, some like them tender. Some like them wistful and in need of a mother while
> some others like them as protective as a father. Rippling muscles and a bare chest
> give some women shivers of delight while still others feel that Hathaway has done
> more for men than nature. A dimple in the chin is deliciously sexy to dimple doters
> while other women want to fill it up with putty. Feats of strength and prowess make
> certain women feel all weak and swoony though some want to say, "Come off it, you
> big baboon!" ("Stronger" 93)

This opening paragraph of *Life* magazine's pictorial survey of popular male
movie stars in 1954 is significant for a number of reasons. In stating that
"almost all men" see the same thing in Monroe, the article assumes that masculine desire is universal and uncomplicated; but in going on to comment that,
in contrast, "there is no male star who universally sends the girls," *Life* acknowledges that women go to films to look at men too and, what's more, that
the male image, no less a marketable commodity than the female, is marked
to be looked at in multiple and contradictory ways. As the article reads them,
some stars like Burt Lancaster are tough, with an "unshaved brute force" (93),
while others like Robert Francis are tender, with an "innocent clean-shaven
face" (94).[1]

More importantly, the commentary accompanying the photographs goes
on to suggest that a star's power as an actor in a narrative is deeply implicated
in his sexual value on screen. The description of Rock Hudson in this respect
is quite telling: "In pictures he rides horses and fights off attacking armies and
has the physique for this work, being 6 feet 4 inches tall." After offering this
very conventional picture of masculinity in action, the article then goes on to
point out a much more spectacular dimension of Hudson's star image:
"Students of fan appeal are undecided whether Hudson's lies primarily in his

'basic honesty' or his bare chest" (96). Clearly, this "Hollywood album of male appeal," as the magazine's cover called it, appreciates that it is the sight of these men on screen which provides the source of their tremendous appeal to viewers.

In recalling *Life*'s representation of the fifties male star as an object of spectacle, I do not mean to imply that the article somehow breaks free of the culture's heterosexual, phallocentric bias, because it does not. Even while calling attention to the erotic status of male stars in Hollywood cinema, *Life*'s coverage of their fan appeal still retains a presumption of male dominance throughout—in the active poses of the stars in the photographs, as well as through the accompanying text's engendering of who is looking at these exemplars of the "stronger sex": either teen-age girls infatuated with star idols or "their older sisters" seeking husbands modeled on a star's masculine image (94). The article does not comment on the possible attractiveness of these stars as ego-ideals or libidinal objects for *male* viewers, who surely contributed to these stars' box-office "muscle." In 1954 silence on this point was not surprising because of what the spectacle of male stars would imply for straight as well as gay men about the objectification, narcissism, and homoeroticism underlying the cinema's solicitation of their look at another man. Nevertheless, the *Life* article's attention to the spectacular value of male actors—shaved or not, their faces *are* meant to be looked at—shows how the fifties star system broke with the traditional differentiation of the look according to gender.

Taking the attraction of male stars at face value, quite literally so in the descriptions of Lancaster and Francis, the *Life* article poses a historical problem for the central assumption of much academic film criticism, which, until recently, has pretty much concentrated on the female and not the male body as the given stake of cinematic representation and spectatorial pleasure. "In their traditional exhibitionist role," Laura Mulvey states in her well-known and much-reprinted essay, "women are simultaneously looked at and displayed, with their appearance coded for strong visual and erotic impact so that they can be said to connote *to-be-looked-at-ness*" (19). As an explicit contrast to the female star's basis in spectacle, Mulvey continues, "[a] male movie star's glamorous characteristics are thus not those of the erotic object of the gaze, but those of the more perfect, more complete, more powerful ideal ego" (20).

Although Mulvey's theoretical model has been rightfully challenged for its unilateral assumptions, particularly when applied to non-Hollywood product, anyone seriously interested in film is still indebted to her analysis. Nevertheless, it is a mistake to conclude from the important feminist critique her essay inspired that, even in the studio era, "[t]raditionally male stars did not necessarily (or even primarily) derive their 'glamour' from their looks or their sexuality but from the power they were able to wield within the filmic world in which they functioned" (Kaplan 28). The studios routinely made it their business to sell the imagery of male stars both on screen and off as a major part of the film product, holding out to the spectator, female or male, an opportunity to take pleasure in looking at men. *Movieland,* for instance, referred to Kirk Douglas as "the man who's been a Hollywood favorite since he bared his chest in 'Champion'" ("Hollywood's" 49). This 1949 boxing film clearly exceeds whatever narrative motivation the sport setting supplies for putting the actor's physique on display. The film, in fact, is unwavering in its consciousness of Douglas's contradictory status as both action hero and sex object. At several points the camera catches Midge Kelly (Douglas) in a sparring pose for a brief instant to show off his bare chest and biceps right before he enters the ring to fight. In the diegesis itself, the wife of Kelly's promoter sculpts the boxer in a pose which similarly shows off his body. For that matter, when Kelly defiantly claims that he's not a tramp, even though his protestation refers to his tran- sient state when the story opens, given the embarrassment as well as pleasure he finds in the eroticization of his body by his female fans, which he exploits to get ahead in the fight business, his defensiveness has a shaming sexual im- plication as well.

This disturbing implication of transgressing proper gender roles extended to Douglas's position as a rising star since the actor felt that in order to get the part in *Champion* he had to resort to behaving like a tramp himself. Douglas recalls in his autobiography that he suffered the indignity of doing just "what the starlets do. I took off my jacket and shirt, bared my chest and flexed my muscles. . . . I was probably the only *man* in Hollywood who's had to strip to get a part" (129). After the film's premiere, he reports, "The women ogled me, as if they were looking right through my clothes" (143). In fact, though, Douglas's experience as a male sex object seems to have been the rule, however much he retrospectively tries to pass himself off as the one "manly" exception. As *Photoplay* noticed when reporting on Tab Hunter's having to bare his chest during his first interview for a leading film role, "the newcomer joined the long list of movie heroes who've made good by giving away the shirt off their backs" ("Meet" 41). Indeed, "so crazy a place is Hollywood," the magazine com- mented in a piece on Richard Egan, "that nobody discovered him until he took off his shirt [in *Demetrius and the Gladiators,* 1954]" (Waterbury, "He" 121).

The value of male stars as narrative agents in fifties films was not just am- plified but often exceeded by the sight of their chests. Fan magazines like *Photoplay* and *Movieland* regularly featured beefcake spreads showing off the well-developed bodies of male stars, even including their physical measure- ments (height, weight, chest, waist), just as they did for female stars. "Let us face it," *Movieland* commented in 1954:

> Hollywood without pretty pin-ups and handsome he-men is like hamburger with- out ketchup—or mustard—as you prefer! The body beautiful is one thing most of Hollywood's most successful personalities have in common—and needless to say, the moviegoer is most thankful for that fact. . . . So there you have it—eight pages meant to be looked at . . . and looked at . . . and looked at once again. Happy looking! ("Hollywood's" 48, ellipsis in original)

Such displays of the body, male as well as female, were, as the magazine frankly acknowledges, "meant to be looked at . . . and looked at . . . and looked at once again," so they give quite a different spin to the stereotype of the strong, silent, invisible hero of Hollywood cinema differentiated from his leading lady because of her "to-be-looked-at-ness." In *Photoplay*'s words, "These Hollywood men of muscle don't have to say a word—their figures speak for themselves!" ("Meet" 40–41). Writing in *Playboy* in 1958, humorist Richard Armour even suggested that the fifties be known as "The Age of the Chest, for the upper part of the *male* torso has begun to catch on. . . . A man may not be tersely described as 44–32–34, but his chest may do more for him, on the beach or in Hollywood, than merely serving as the outside of his lungs" (57, 65).

Much more so than either a sports film or a biblical epic, where one could expect to find sufficient excuse for showing off a star's chest, *Picnic* (1955) is an especially revealing (in all senses of the word) example of Hollywood's investment in the spectacle of the male body during this period. As its advertising campaign alerted audiences, the film is organized, in both its cinematic address and its narrative, around the body of its male star, William Holden—whose face, not too coincidentally, was on the cover of that *Life* issue promoting its "Hollywood Album of Male Appeal." What particularly interests me about this film is the highly contradictory marking of its star as an erotic spectacle. On one hand, the narrative of *Picnic* conforms to the familiar practice of classic Hollywood cinema, jeopardizing the masculinity of the Holden character only to restore it at the end. On the other hand, the film repeatedly makes a point of visually foregrounding Holden's seminude body as the object of numerous female and male gazes in the diegesis as well as the cinema auditorium, and such unabashed erotic attention to the body of a major male movie star prevents the film's closure from easily serving as an affirmation of masculinity in the traditional terms one associates with Hollywood cinema. If I may borrow the significant phrasing of *Life*'s description of Rock Hudson's ambiguous appeal, *Picnic* exploits the sight of Holden's "bare chest" as the sign authenticating his virility; but then, as a Hollywood product, the film also tries to minimize that disturbing male spectacle through Holden's star persona, which exemplifies the "basic honesty" of the American male, though not without a high degree of contradiction itself.

Meant to Be Looked At

While William Holden may not be remembered as an icon of fifties male beefcake like Kirk Douglas or Tab Hunter, one shouldn't underestimate his popularity as a male sex star. Holden ranked near the top of exhibition polls during the decade, and he was number one at the time *Picnic* was released: ranking first in the *Motion Picture Herald* poll in 1956, and acclaimed *Photoplay*'s male star of the year in 1955 and 1956. Given his popularity then, it made perfect sense for *Life* to promote its story about sexy male movie stars with Holden's face on the cover. After all, he was the very first movie star that Lucy Ricardo saw upon arriving in Hollywood in 1955, when she stared at his "dreamy" face from her booth at the Brown Derby. Lucy's encounter with Holden plays upon his spectacular value as a male movie star. "What's the harm?" she asks, when she persists in looking at him. "They're movie stars. They're used to being stared at." When a waiter offers to move the star to another booth, Holden refuses, observing: "You know, they say when they stop looking, that's the time to worry."

In confirmation of his value as an erotic movie star at this time, the actor's bare-chested body was prominently used in advertising some of his most successful films, *Love Is a Many Splendored Thing* (1955) and *The Bridge on the River Kwai* (1957), as well as *Picnic*. His success as a leading man some fifteen years after his debut as a boxer in *Golden Boy* (1939) led Sidney Skolsky to mutter ironically in his column several months after the opening of *Picnic*, "I recall Bill Holden a few years back: producers said he'd be big if he had sex appeal. Bill must have bought it somewhere" ("That's Hollywood"). Actually, while winning the Oscar for *Stalag 17* (1953) surely helped his career, Holden didn't project his winning sex appeal until he took off his shirt and let his fans look at his body once again.[2]

Prominently featuring its two leads as sexual bodies—Kim Novak costars with Holden, and their most famous moment together occurs when they perform an erotically charged dance to a version of "Moonglow" overscored with the film's sultry theme music by George Duning—*Picnic* was not a cheap exploitation movie by any means but a prestige production of Columbia Pictures. It opened in Beverly Hills to qualify for Academy Award consideration in late December 1955 (it was nominated for six, including Picture and Direction, and it won two) and then premiered officially at Radio City Music Hall the following February. Adapted from William Inge's Pulitzer Prize–winning play and directed by Joshua Logan, who had also done the play, the film begins with the arrival of Hal (Holden) in a small Kansas town on Labor Day, and then shows how he disrupts the quiet desperation of a group of un-attached women: Flo Owens (Betty Field); her older daughter, Madge (Kim Novak); her younger daughter, Milly (Susan Strasberg); her boarder, Rose-mary Sidney, a self-described old-maid schoolteacher (Rosalind Russell); and her neighbor, Mrs. Potts (Verna Felton). As in the play, the narrative of the film works to replace the attraction of class and status—represented both by Flo's eagerness to have Madge marry the wealthy Alan Benson (Cliff Robert-son) and Hal's need, as he says, to "get someplace in this world"—with the "liberating" sexual desire signified in the lead characters' reciprocal looks and in the camera's gaze at the stars portraying them.

While *Picnic* was the breakthrough film for Novak, even more provocative is its visual as well as narrative reliance on the spectacle of Holden's body.

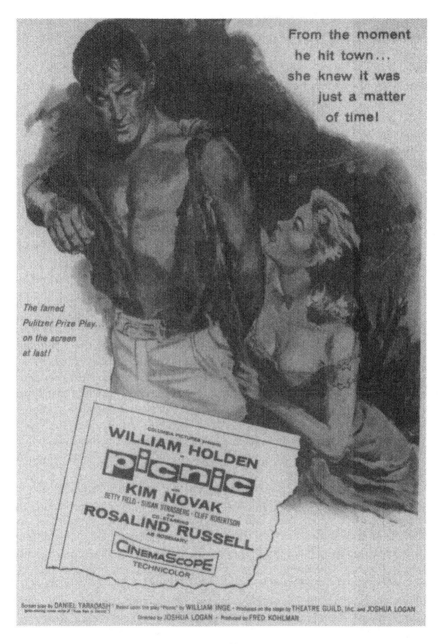

Figure 23.
The advertisement for *Picnic* does not disguise the importance of
William Holden's body in selling the film.

Indeed, the impression persists that Logan uses any excuse to get Holden to take off his shirt: the star appears bare-chested during the opening credits, when he is washing in a stream; during the first extended scene in the yard, when he is burning trash for Mrs. Potts and meets the other women; during the afternoon, when he goes swimming with his friend Alan and the two Owens daughters; during the last part of the picnic, when, after he dances with Madge to "Moonglow," Rosemary verbally and physically attacks him, ripping open his shirt; and finally during his love scene with Madge. All of this amounts to quite a lot of bare skin for an actor who wasn't working for DeMille or playing Tarzan.

Holden's shirtlessness, furthermore, does not go without comment in the film itself. The female characters refer to Hal's body in their dialogue; what's more, they look at him quite openly. Mrs. Potts initially encourages Hal to take off his shirt so that she can wash it for him. "You think anyone would mind?" he asks, to which she replies, matter-of-factly, "You're a man. What's the difference?" Her question is rhetorical insofar as she assumes that no one pays attention to a man working out-of-doors without his shirt; once bare-chested, however, he proves otherwise.

The scene in the yard, which begins with Hal taking off his shirt to work, is structured around a series of looks which Hal does not initiate and which focus on his body. To begin with, Milly stares at him from the next yard as he burns the trash: after she looks to see who is working there, he looks back at her in a reverse shot. Likewise, after Hal strips off his shirt to work, Rosemary initiates a secreted look of interest, turning away defensively when Hal returns it. "Working over there, naked as an Indian," she mutters scornfully after she looks, "who does he think is interested?" Rosemary's sarcastic comment leads Milly to take more notice of Hal's body ("*Who's* naked as an Indian?"), so much so that the newspaper boy, Bomber (Nick Adams), has to physically interrupt her voyeurism in order to get her attention.

Madge then appears outside on the front porch. When Hal walks over to rescue her from Bomber's pestering, he momentarily restores the familiar position of the male gaze. With Hal's entrance from Mrs. Potts's yard off screen, the camera now links its view of this scene to his, just as the imposing physical difference between Holden's body and Nick Adams's—marked by camera framing as well as commented on by the dialogue ("I'm biggern' you," Hal warns Bomber)—justifies Hal's possession of this feminine space in the name of the phallic male. But despite the attempt to reestablish a male gaze, this is also the point when Hal first sees Madge and she looks right back, their recip-rocated looks indicating their mutual sexual attraction. When Flo interrupts this visual exchange, she makes Hal embarrassed by his nakedness, which connotes his social inferiority as well as his immodesty. In acknowledgment of *her* visual positioning of *his* body, he looks down and covers his bare chest with his arms. And while Madge is still watching Hal as he leaves and shows off his virility on the basketball court, so is her mother, who has driven him out of the yard with her determined stare. After Mrs. Potts calls Madge over to the more neutral territory of the neighboring yard, Madge and Hal gaze at each other again. Madge then returns to her house, and her point of view closes this sequence as she looks back at Hal through the screen door.

Jackie Byars argues that this scene in the yard exemplifies how the film establishes a gaze "consistently under female control," and to the extent that she is talking about the viewing going on in the diegesis, I can agree. The looking that occurs in this scene collapses the scopic regime defined by Mulvey, since it places Hal in the same position of "to-be-looked-at-ness" occupied by Madge, who later complains that she is "tired of being pretty" and "tired of only being looked at." But it does not follow, as Byars goes on to claim, with reference to the end of the yard scene, either that "Madge's control of that final gaze is maintained throughout the film" or that "*Picnic* maintains Madge as its central focus and as its primary discursive agent." ("Gazes" 124).[3] First of all, the film allows Hal to be looked at from *multiple* viewing positions in the diegesis: Mrs. Potts's admiration, Milly's curiosity, Rosemary's hostility, Bomber's rivalry, Madge's attraction, Flo's suspicion, and, later in the film, Alan's identification and then jealousy. Second, all of this visual attention to Hal keeps turning the film's narrative around his masculinity, made problematic by the continuing sight of his body, and not Madge's sexuality, as in the play.

The film's shift of emphasis from Madge to Hal seems to have been a commercial decision on Columbia's part to turn the play into a star vehicle for Holden. He is the only star with above-the-title billing, and the film establishes the importance of his character with the first title card superimposed over an image of his body. The action occurring right before and then behind the opening credits, moreover, opens up the play to show Hal arriving by boxcar in the Kansas town. This prologue establishes a narrative frame that directs the viewer's attention to watch him serving as the catalyst of the film's action, first disrupting the stasis of the female community to expose its sexual desperation, and then unequivocally motivating the revised ending Joshua Logan insisted upon when directing the play on Broadway, with Madge leaving home to follow Hal to Tulsa rather than remaining in the town with her reputation as a "good girl" forever tarnished, as Inge had originally intended. The closure of the film thus occurs for audiences at the moment of Hal's decision to accept the proper breadwinner role (he proposes to Madge the morning after they make love, and then leaves for Oklahoma in search of gainful employment to support her), instead of her decision to break with her mother's hypocritical middle-class values (when she leaves to follow him). The adaptation, in short, gives the story to Hal and the film to Holden, which is how the review in *Photoplay* read *Picnic:* "Holden plays a light-hearted drifter who hits a Kansas town one summer day, lifting the spirits of many of its people (especially the women). . . . At the annual picnic . . . matters come to a climax. . . . And the picnic's last hours also bring Holden to a moment of decision" (Graves).

This reorientation of the film version of *Picnic* around Hal subordinates Madge's desire for independence to his growth as a "man." In effect, the studio redirected the play's emphases more along the lines of domestic melodrama, one of the favorite fifties genres for displaying American masculinity in crisis and then resolving it through the successful formation of a heterosexual couple. Much more so than in the play, Brandon French points out, "the film's subliminal message is that it takes *two* people to make a 'real man,' the man himself and the woman who sacrifices herself to his welfare" (119). To secure the conditions for turning Hal into such a "real man," *Picnic* "eliminates or changes most of the basis of the women's internal conflict," concentrating instead on Hal's longings and insecurities (116–17). Most notably, Daniel Taradash's screenplay discredits Flo's dreams for Madge by making them tantamount to pandering, it motivates Rosemary's resentment of Hal and Madge solely out of jealousy, and it uses the nonconforming, tomboyish Milly to validate Madge's choice to follow Hal. "In this way," French concludes, "the film makes room for Hal's considerable deficiency—his desperate lies and foolish dreams of grandeur and superficial bravado—without endangering his position as the romantic hero. In fact, it makes enough room to accommodate a hero whose vulnerability, beneath all those rippling muscles, is the basis of his appeal" (117–19).

But the film's considerable visual interest in Hal's body ends up subverting the kind of recuperation of conventional masculinity which French attributes to the narrative's closure. Thus, while the film version of *Picnic* may appear to be telling Hal's story, and valorizing him as "another [fifties] natural man" (Biskind 325) in a nostalgic yearning for an obsolete form of masculinity— that is, one made antiquated by the suburban American ranch house and back yard—it is still the spectacle of his bare chest, particularly as reinforced by the sight of Holden's oiled muscular body in CinemaScope, that sparks the action from scene to scene, continually attracting the camera's gaze and establishing the male body of the star as the film's primary image of sexual difference.

Hal's Masquerade

From the very moment that Hal/Holden first takes off his shirt behind the opening credits, *Picnic* challenges the fifties orthodoxy of a "real man." To start with, the spectacle of Hal's body immediately disturbs the social and sexual antitheses which upheld the era's hegemonic masculinity. If, as Richard Dyer comments about the male pin-up, "a man's athletic body may be much admired, but only on condition that it has been acquired through sports not labour" (*Stars* 43), then the sight of Hal working in Mrs. Potts's yard obscures the significant class difference between a male body praised for its athleticism (one of Hollywood's primary excuses for showing off a star's body, going back to Douglas Fairbanks), and a male body marked with the effects of hard physical labor. Originally a college sports hero with a physique appropriate for display, Hal now uses his body to work. Physical labor is the reason for his present fitness, as well as the occasion for the spectacle of his body in the yard scene, which positions him as an erotic object for the various female viewers.

Hal's "rippling muscles" may therefore signify phallic superiority in comparison to the other more diminutive male bodies on screen but it also reminds the female characters of his social inferiority as an itinerant laborer, which is, in turn, linked to his very unmanly capacity to be turned into a sexual object for them, into what one British reviewer called "a male Marilyn Monroe, halfway between a threat and a promise" (Brien). Or as *Time* put it, drawing a comparison that also suggests Hal's similarity to a female movie star, he "is a sex bomb" ("Conquest" 63). Indeed, a dozen years later *Variety* recalled the director's treatment of Holden as a kind of "camera-rape [of] the male body."[4] Since Hal's very appealing virility has its undeniable basis in the spectacle of his muscular body, the film encodes him with the value of "to-be-looked-at-ness." This marking then turns him, figuratively speaking, into a male version of the desirable female, the bombshell epitomized in the fifties by Monroe, as the only way the dominant culture could comprehend male spectacle. After all, during this period, as Kirk Douglas's comments about his audition indicate, a "man" simply didn't take off his shirt and strut in solicitation of another's gaze without calling into question his virility and, with that, his heterosexuality.

The problem which the spectacle of Hal poses for fifties hegemonic masculinity is made immediately apparent after the yard scene establishes the powerful erotic appeal of his body. Leaving Mrs. Potts's house, Hal goes to find his affluent college friend, Alan Benson, and entertains him with a bawdy account of his life since leaving college. The importance of this next scene lies in certain particulars of the story Hal tells Alan as they engage in frat-boy banter and physical play. Their exchange resonates more forcefully in the film than on stage because Hal's account of his past begins by calling attention to the spectacle of men in the movies. After working in a gas station and a stint in the army, Hal says he went to Hollywood to become a "big movie hero." Renamed "Brush Carter," he expected a big career but failed his screen test because of his teeth: "Out there you gotta have a certain kind of teeth or they can't use you," he tells Alan. "Don't ask me why. Anyway, this babe told me they'd have to pull all my teeth and give me new ones, so naturally . . ." Naturally, Hal refused (though both actors playing this scene on film probably had their teeth capped). Even more striking is what happened to Hal next. Hitchhiking in Texas, he confides, "two babes pull up in this big yellow convertible. And one of 'em slams on the brakes and hollers, 'Get in, Beefcake!' So I got in." The two "babes" get him drunk on martinis. Although he boasts, "they musta thought I was Superman," when he tires out before they do, "one of 'em sticks a gun in my back. She says, 'This party's goin' on till we say it's over, Buck!' You'da thought she was Humphrey Bogart!" Exhausted, Hal passes out and, while asleep, gets rolled of his life savings by the two women. To add insult to his injury, when he goes to the police they don't believe him but call his story "wishful thinking." "I'm telling you, Benson," he warns, "women are getting desperate."

Hal uses his autobiographical narrative to show off his virility to Alan, who responds with admiration and envy, wondering why such sexual adventures never happen to him. But notice that Hal gains Alan's attention by telling a story of male sexual *failure*, which he then turns into an allegory of the female desperation that jeopardizes virility. Hal's story of his misadventure with those two "babes" brings the film into line with the new discourses of sexuality that emerged from the Kinsey reports on sexual behavior in men and women. Viewed in the context of Kinsey's much publicized findings about the asymmetry of male and female desire, Hal's autobiographical narrative gives him a rather obvious ideological function: he translates the social and economic implications of the female characters' desperation into sexual and thus more personalized terms. His presence exposes the unhealthy repression of female sexuality so that the hostility of deserted wife Flo and spinster schoolteacher Rosemary appears as a symptom of what they "really" desire as women in the age of Kinsey; and he then cures female repression by liberating Madge's sexuality and, to a lesser extent, Milly's, from the oppressive feminine environment dominated by those older, unhappy women. In short, Hal reconfirms the power of the phallus to bring out the sexuality of the women in this matriarchal community, thereby implicitly regenerating exhausted male sexuality for American men past the age of nineteen. However, to do so Hal also ends up performing the role which Mulvey attributes to the female in Hollywood film: "Ultimately, the meaning of woman is sexual difference" (21). As Mrs. Potts declares to Flo after Hal's departure: "He clomped through the place like he was still outdoors. There was a man in the house, and it seemed good."[5]

Mrs. Potts's admiration is essentially unchanged from the play, which used Hal to define sexual difference around the phallus so blatantly that *New Republic* reviewer Eric Bentley accused Inge of waving, as a symbolic banner, "[t]he torn shirt of Stanley Kowalski," which "stands for the new phallus worship. . . . so much is made of the hero's body and . . . he has so little else" (71–72). This response was a common one. By now it's an unfortunate cliché that "the figure of the stud [in *Picnic* as well as in Tennessee Williams's plays and films] . . . is, like the sex-starved woman, largely a figment of male homosexual fantasy" (Haskell 250). So it is important to remember what Kinsey's research called attention to regarding sexual behavior and dysfunction in American men. Heterosexual masculinity, it turned out, was not quite the monolithic identity the culture supposed; and the figure of the stud—along with the movie stars who personified him—spoke compellingly of a fantasized masculinity to heterosexual men too, especially when they were told by the experts that female sexual desire exceeded male performance in direct proportion to the female body's resilience in outlasting the male's.

Given the discursive field supplied by the Kinsey reports, whatever sexual connotations fifties audiences read into Hal's sexuality were loaded, to say the least. He is by no means characterized as a homosexual in his sexual behavior (although his physical horseplay with Alan and their homosocial competition for Madge suggests such an undercurrent); and his muscular body refutes the effeminacy which the culture equated with homosexuality. Yet the film not only puts his body on display as an object of desire, turning him into "a male Marilyn Monroe," it also shows his attractiveness to all the characters, the other men (Alan, Howard Bevans, Mr. Benson) as well as the women. Hal, furthermore, is that most reviled and "unmanly" of fifties male figures, the bum, as exemplified by his many itinerant occupations: football hero, soldier, Hollywood "starlet," cowboy, and artist's model, he tells Milly, posing "almost in the raw." That these jobs are also all gender stereotypes is significant. Immature, insecure, and most of all an impostor, Hal's appealing virility turns out to depend upon his *posing* as a stud, lying and bragging to cover up his inability to make good on his muscles.

From the perspective of the dominant culture of breadwinning males, Hal encodes the failure of hegemonic masculinity, which is the specific meaning fifties America read into homosexuality, treating it as a question of gender inversion and social irresponsibility rather than as a difference of sexuality. With the breadwinning ethic made the unquestioned norm of heterosexual masculinity, "homosexuality" was the pejorative term encoding sexual immaturity, domestic irresponsibility, and professional failure, all covered up by the closeted homosexual's pretense of being a "real man." "Since a man couldn't actually become a woman (Christine Jorgenson was the only publicized exception throughout the fifties)," Barbara Ehrenreich comments, "heterosexual failures and overt homosexuals could only be understood as living in a state of constant deception. And this was perhaps the most despicable thing about them: They *looked like* men, but they weren't really men" (*Hearts* 26).

Once read as a form of social *deception,* the very category of "homosexuality" called into question the culture's assumption of a stable and automatic relation between male sexuality and masculine identity, implying instead that gender is an effect of social *reception.* Consequently, if Hal's adventure with the two women in Texas seems to encode a homosexual stud fantasy, it does so in large part because what he tries to conceal through the sexual bravado of that narrative ("they musta thought I was Superman") is the objectification of his body in the eyes of a desiring other, which results in the exposure of his sexual inadequacy. Instead of authenticating his virility, his body does just the opposite, letting slip its concealment of his failed manhood. Not only do the two women exhaust *him*, but one of them figuratively turns into a man, sticking a gun in his back to "motivate" his sexual services: "You'da thought she was Humphrey Bogart!" What does that make him, then? Lauren Bacall?

This troubling suspicion that Hal's virile brand of masculinity is bogus—nothing more than a series of poses, what with his frequent posturing and bragging and muscle-flexing—comes to the film from its source material in the play; and so does the ambivalence with which Hal is at once valued for his idealized manliness, particularly his ability to satisfy every kind of sexual fantasy, and rejected for turning masculinity into a public spectacle. From the very beginning of its try-out run outside New York, just how to pitch Hal caused difficulties for the stage production. Logan attributed the mixed reactions of the audience to discomfort—on the part of men even more than women—with the excessive posturing of Hal's character: "To them, a true hero wouldn't brag, wouldn't lie, wouldn't show off, wouldn't be a bit sweaty at times—but *they* think *we* don't feel that way. They think we believe everything he does is *attractive*." To solve this problem, the director inserted, with Inge's permission, a speech for Alan Benson, "the most reliable character," establishing explicit disapproval of his friend's exhibitionism (*Josh* 355). Alan tells Flo that, like the other boys in their fraternity, he didn't like Hal until they shared a room and he got to know him better, their intimacy giving him an opportunity to discover the genuine manliness that remained hidden beneath the bragging and posing. In the film this dialogue occurs as Flo and Alan drive to the picnic. Alan's criticism of Hal nevertheless seems only half-hearted at best since in both play and film he still responds favorably (and vicariously) to Hal's sexual bragging about those two "babes."

On film *Picnic* makes a greater effort to redeem Hal's masculinity through Rosemary's drunken attack on him, which occurs at the picnic and not in the shelter of the Owens' yard, as in the play. Visibly shaming Hal with her lascivious attentions when she pulls him away from Madge and rips open his shirt, Rosemary publicly emasculates him. With the curious crowd gathering on the bridge to witness his embarrassment and a searchlight illuminating his humiliating nakedness, Hal is made a public spectacle as the result of Rosemary's drunken outburst, which shows her up, in turn, as a hysterical, repressed, vindictive, sexually desperate woman. According to French's reading of this moment in the film, Madge must step in "to restore and sustain Hal's crumbling manhood; and making him 'something' makes her 'something' in turn. That is the symbiotic nature of 'real manhood' and 'real womanhood' which the film doggedly celebrates" (118). Yes, but . . . it's not easy to forget Hal's anecdote about those two "babes." That little allegory of castrating female desperation recounts how *he*, reduced to a sexual object by those two women, was unable to keep (it) up with them. He lacked the potency to begin with, so Rosemary's outburst cannot be dismissed simply as a spiteful and undeserved

Figures 24a and 24b.
The torn shirt: Hal (Holden) is made a public spectacle as a result of Rosemary's drunken outburst (top) and afterward he tells Madge (Kim Novak), "She looked right through me like an X-ray machine" (bottom).

belittling of his genuine masculinity, even though that's the inflection of Rosalind Russell's shrill performance in this scene.

When she cuts in on his dance with Madge, Rosemary treats Hal in the same way that the two "babes" and the camera have done, as an object of great erotic interest. "You know what?" she whispers, holding him so tightly that her earrings dig into his neck. "You remind me of one of those old statues. One of those Roman gladiators. All they had on was a shield!" Then, after he tries to get away, she tears his shirt in her effort to cling to him, and he tries to cover up his exposed chest. "You been stompin' around here in those boots like you owned the place," she yells, "thinking every woman you saw was gonna fall madly in love." Rosemary's beau, Howard Bevans (Arthur O'Connell), tries to defend Hal against her accusation that he got Milly drunk, saying, "The boy didn't do anything," but Rosemary goes on: "You think just 'cause you act young you can walk in here and make off with whatever you like. But let me tell you something—you're a fake! You're no jive kid—you're just scared to act your age!" Rosemary's accusation literally brings Hal to his knees. "She looked right though me like an X-ray machine," he tells Madge afterward, and what Rosemary exposes is the male masquerade—witness his muscle-flexing, his showing-off, his lying—that constitutes his virility. Based in spectacle from the start and then exposed as a fake, Hal's masculinity crosses gender lines because his masquerade puts him in what Hollywood has always identified as the feminine position in representation. His virility is nonetheless undeniably attractive to both women and men in the film, and for that reason, his masquerade is even more deeply disturbing, as first Rosemary's attack indicates and then Alan's repudiation of Hal before Flo immediately afterward bears out.

Rosemary's stinging accusation that Hal is "no jive kid" is made especially problematic in the film—much more so than on stage—because of the casting of the 37-year-old Holden in the part. The final draft of the script (May 2, 1955) repeats the text of Inge's script by describing Hal as "an exceedingly handsome, husky youth," and then adds: "sure of his attraction for women, but down deep, unsure of himself" (Taradash 1). To uphold this characterization, the film equates the sexual attraction and liberating value of Hal's masculinity with his youth and boyishness: he is called "a boy" several times by both Flo and Howard, and he is Oedipalized through his inheritance of his father's boots and criminal past. After Rosemary's attack, Madge attempts to reassure Hal of his youthfulness: "Don't pay any attention to her—you *are* young. . . . Not so young that you're not a man, too." With this kind of double-talk Madge hits the proverbial problem right on the nose: for in its visual register the film keeps representing Hal's masculinity in terms of his highly developed body, which does not look boyish at all. As a result, Rosemary's sarcastic admonition that he look into a mirror and see his real age rings far truer than the lines may have ever intended, suggesting an additional dimension of Hal's masquerade in the film. The Hal we see performed by William Holden is no jive kid at all but another kind of fake, a husky man masquerading as a youth and strutting before the fascinated gaze of the camera.

The Photogenic Chest

Picnic makes no pretense of disguising Holden's age since a great deal of the visual impact of his performance depends upon the sight of his physically mature body. The muscular definition of his build—with its clean lines, smooth surface, thick chest, lean stomach—differentiates Holden from younger stars like James Dean on the one hand and older stars like James Stewart on the other. In the photograph and poster art used to publicize the film, which produced the most famous image of *Picnic* (though it is not actually from the film), Holden stands with his shirt ripped open and hanging off his arms, his pectorals bared, biceps flexed, stomach held in tightly; while Novak, positioned to his side somewhat at knee-level, pulls at the sleeve of his torn shirt (see figure 25a, left). In addition, the studio produced a series of stills based on the same visual theme (for an example, see figure 25b, right). Holden's body dominates Novak's in every spatial variation of this scene. Her breasts are not ignored by any means, but his body functions just as much if not more than hers to draw the viewer's gaze toward the photograph. Indeed, as Will Holtzman, one chronicler of Holden's career, notes about *Picnic:* "The two [Holden and Novak] make a lusty pair, though it's a toss up for the more photogenic chest" (115). One could never make that claim of James Stewart in either of his two films with Novak (not after seeing him take off his shirt in *Rear Window*, 1954), nor of James Dean with Natalie Wood in *Rebel without a Cause* (1955).

Holtzman's sarcasm alludes to the unorthodox manner in which *Picnic* sets its two stars in a kind of visual rivalry, with the jibe at Holden's possibly having "the more photogenic chest" suggesting that the actor suffers some kind of embarrassing subjection to the camera as a result of his exposure. Because an open acknowledgment of the male body's erotic appeal confuses the gender orthodoxy of who looks as opposed to who is looked at, films of the studio era resorted to the same measures time and again in order to protect male stars from the demeaning implications of the spectator's visual interest in them as eroticized images. The conventions governing the male pinup, for instance, sought to minimize the troubling erotic implications of male spectacle: reciprocation of the viewer's gaze to imply dominance; an active pose; a tensed body to emphasize muscularity; and some sort of explicit motivation for the pose, such as sport (Dyer, "Don't"). On screen, male spectacle was just as conventionalized. As Steve Neale points out, action genres like the Western, the epic, and the war film encourage a reciprocal male gaze in the diegesis, implicitly inviting the spectator to look at the male body in similar terms, but they encode the spectacle as sadomasochistic ritual, a gunfight or hand-to-hand combat. Corresponding to the narrative motivations for displays of the female body as

Figures 25a and 25b.
Holden's photogenic chest received ample attention in publicity stills.

spectacle (for example, a nightclub or theater performance), in these genres the stock excuse for male striptease is some form of on-screen discipline, if not a beating or torture, then at least sport or manual labor. In the case of either the showdown between men or the stripdown by one of them, Neale comments, "We are offered the spectacle of male bodies, but bodies unmarked as objects of erotic display. There is no trace of an acknowledgment or recognition of those bodies as displayed solely for the gaze of the spectator" (18). Such

hidden traces, though, prove to be only skin deep at best. Inevitably, moments of sadomasochistic spectacle in an action film raise an unacknowledged look of homoerotic desire because of their function in orchestrating "a highly elaborated public show" of homosocial power relations among men (Hark 152). Regardless of the ideological intent and narrative cover for scenes of discipline and punishment—and some of the excuses offered to strip and whip a male actor can get pretty lame—"the *visual* point is the exposed body, passive—indeed, spread-eagled—and objectified" (Malone 70).

More so-called feminine genres such as the melodrama and romance, Neale notes, placed a male star much more openly on display as an object of desire.

In these films actors undress not to labor manually or be beaten but to incite desire in a viewer within the diegesis as well as off screen, and the effect is to effeminize them (18). The assumption is that one has to view with suspicion what is, quite literally in this context, a ladies' man—"the male who exists solely to seduce and be seduced by women" (Malone 3)—a male movie star lacking the narrative cover of sadomasochism for his erotic image. During the studio era, one recurring strategy to prevent the male body from appearing *too* desirable in these genres was to make the lover foreign (or if not foreign, then ethnic). Using his body to attract and manipulate the female gaze, sometimes to his advantage, sometimes to hers, a foreign lover—Valentino comes to mind, obviously, but so do, in the fifties, Yul Brynner, Rossano Brazzi, Louis Jourdan, Fernando Lamas, and Ricardo Montalban—helped to naturalize, by implication, the myth of the silent, rugged, and sexually innocent American male.

When *Picnic* makes a spectacle out of its male star without resorting to one of those defensive conventions, the display of Holden's body brings out the fundamental contradiction that, as an institution, cinema inscribes upon the photogenic chest of a male movie star. *Picnic* may therefore seem an exception to the rules governing male spectacle, but that is only because it follows a set of codes more specific to fifties representation, stylizing its visual treatment of Holden in a manner more befitting a biblical epic than a melodrama. Like the epic genre, *Picnic* draws on conventions of the bodybuilding exhibition and so-called "art" or "athletic" male photography for its representational codes, celebrating the muscularity of a hard, tensed, oiled, and hairless body in an ostensible if sometimes kitschy reference to antique statuary.[6] No wonder Hal reminds Rosemary of a Roman gladiator and a statue!

The bodybuilding subculture produced a panoply of erotic male imagery, some of it covert (as in the "physique photography" allowing homoerotic art to be sent through the mail without censorship), much of it overt, as in the Hollywood biblical epic and its spin-off, the Italian peplum cycle starting late in the decade, most notably with *Hercules* (1959) and its sequel *Hercules Unchained* (1960), which made a star out of American bodybuilder Steve Reeves (Mr. America in 1947, Mr. World in 1948, Mr. Universe in 1950).[7] Despite its Italian origin and classical settings, the peplum cycle of beefcake spectacles was instantly received on both sides of the Atlantic as celebrations of American masculinity because these films imported their leading men from the United States. Like the physique photography of the period, which supplied the conventions for representing the muscular body on screen, the peplum films dispensed with the pretense of disavowing the eroticism of the male body beautiful, openly glorifying the physiques of "All-American Boys, whose powerful bodies could be seen as symbolic of all that was best in the good old U.S. of A" (Foster 12).

Filling up the wide screen "with straining muscular flesh" (Foster 12), these

Figure 26.
Steve Reeves, the star of the peplum cycle of beefcake epics:
muscles replaced bosoms.

spectacles appeared to reinscribe a very orthodox understanding of masculinity, one which assumes "that it is precisely *straining* that is held to be the great
good, what makes a man a man" (Dyer, "Don't" 276). One feels compelled to
ask, though, straining for *whose* benefit? For the fact remains that, like the
bodybuilding and physical health magazines of the period, the Steve Reeves
epics and their imitators also provided a rare legal site for openly exhibiting
the muscular male body as erotic spectacle. "Muscles replaced bosoms," noted
one commentator about the Italian peplum cycle; "brawn didn't entirely
replace beauty but forced it into an inconspicuous corner of the screen"
(Whitehall 10–11). According to Richard Dyer, *Films and Filming*—where
this appreciation of the Italian epic (like many others) appeared—"quickly
established itself as a closet gay magazine" in Britain shortly after it first
appeared in 1954 (*Heavenly* 148). Consequently, I think it is safe to assume
that there was also a strong homoerotic component to the popularity of these
films in the United States as well, not to mention a crucial homosocializing
function for young adolescent boys at Saturday matinees.

What Antony Easthope observes about photographs of sports figures, who routinely make a public show of straining their muscles, applies equally well to the display of athletic physiques in epic after epic during the fifties: "these images of the hard, trained, disciplined body under rational control are not just there to be identified with—they are there to be looked at" (53). In *Champion*, Midge Kelly's manager, Tommy Haley (Paul Stewart), talks about what draws him to boxing in the very same terms:

> *Haley:* This is the only sport in the world where two guys get paid for doing something they'd be arrested for if they got drunk or did it for nothing.
> *Midge:* If that's the way you feel about it, what are you hanging around here for?
> *Haley:* Well, with some guys it's a bottle. Me, I like to watch a couple of good boys in action.

Though a trainer by profession, Haley defines his relation to boxing entirely as a question of spectating, and he does not try to justify his interest by expressing admiration for a fighter's skill, discipline, endurance, or grace, the usual explanation for the sport's attraction to male fans, but instead compares it to an addiction. Later, when Midge fires him in order to sign with a more powerful promoter, as Haley leaves, and he reiterates that the sport draws him to the ring as a compulsive viewer of the male body, a slight alteration in the wording of his original remark removes the gladiatorial context of a match to focus more intently on the individual fighter's performance as a form of spectacle: "I can't keep away from it. I like to watch a good boy in action."

In his 1958 satiric piece for *Playboy*, as he takes note of the increasing visibility of the male body in movies of the period to explain why the fifties should be considered "The Age of the Chest," Armour similarly comments that a straining, muscular body always implies a beholder. Contrasting the male chest to the female bosom, "which often benefits from being seen piecemeal," the humorist explains that "the chest needs to come on one with overpowering completeness. The chest, in other words, should leave nothing to the imagination and should simply be itself, there being little chance that it will be mistaken for anything else." For this reason, he continues:

> the chest is best displayed *au naturel*, which is French. Then the pectoral muscles stand out in stark relief and ripple like the flanks of a fly-bitten horse every time their owner makes the slightest motion, such as coughing gently to be sure everyone is looking. Then, too, observers are able to behold the beautiful mat of hair, with "Welcome" across it, hair that is curly and vibrant and would make superb filling for an invalid cushion or a softball. In a T-shirt all of this is lost. . . . (65)

Armour's jesting observation about the exhibitionism implied by displays of male nudity "on the beach, or in Hollywood" points out the comparable value of the muscular chest and the ample bosom in drawing the attention of an onlooker. The bare chest may "leave nothing to the imagination," thereby upholding the dominant fiction of a whole and unimpaired masculinity that is "overpowering [in its] completeness," but how can it follow that a chest is ever simply "itself"? What Armour actually points out is the way that the bare chest functions as such a transparent sign of masculine empowerment that it jeopardizes the fiction of the male body's invisibility. According to the humorist, Marlon Brando's appearance in *A Streetcar Named Desire* (1951) "made America chest conscious," but Burt Lancaster "has brought the chest to its height, as well as its breadth." His chest "is unmistakably male, and suggests brute strength, virile passion, and a tendency to perspire under the hot sun, or in a warm embrace" (65). Lancaster's "unmistakably male" chest can only carry those meanings, however, when it is stripped of its covering and turned into spectacle. Even when the straining body is sweaty, narrativized as physical labor, the movies' conventional disavowal of male spectacle cannot detract from its considerable erotic dimension.

In *Picnic*, Holden's star appeal on the screen, no less than Lancaster's, depends upon his being seen. Just as important, as *Picnic* also illustrates when it fashions Holden's body into a recurring visual reference to the epic genre's conventionalized style of male exhibitionism, the sight of his muscularity cannot help reminding viewers that a highly defined and developed build like his isn't natural at all but the transformation of the body itself into a mask. Strictly speaking, bulging, well-articulated muscles are not a natural condition of bodies but the result of repeated labor and discipline and, in a lot of cases, a careful regimen of diet and steroids. Even Tarzan, seemingly the most natural of all Hollywood he-men, is no exception: "To keep his torso in gleaming condition, Lex [Barker, the 1950s Tarzan] not only exercises in the morning, but in between scenes on the set you'll find him twisting and gyrating and chinning. It was fat around the middle that eliminated Johnny Weissmuller from the Tarzan series. Lex isn't taking any chances" (Armstrong 97).

Barker may have had to continue working out in order to keep playing Tarzan but his "twisting and gyrating and chinning" also suggests how the role put his masculinity on the line. As Margaret Walters comments, "paradoxically, body-building is the most purely narcissistic and, in that sense, most feminine, of pastimes. The body-builder's goal is appearance not action. He is less like the sportsman trying to improve on his time or performance, than he is like the woman, who sees her body as raw material to be pummeled, pounded, starved and even cut into better shape" (294–95). So for all his symbolic value in promoting the phallic power of the American male, the fifties bodybuilder could all too easily be turned into the male equivalent of a showgirl. In fact, on at least one occasion he actually was: in 1954 the 61-year-old Mae West performed in Las Vegas at the Sahara hotel with eight bikini-clad men—the reigning Mr. America and seven contenders for that title—in what she billed "the first bare-chest act for lady customers in history" ("People").

With its gender reversal, West's nightclub act played upon the transvestism implied by a bodybuilding exhibition, and this comparison is worth pursuing because it helps to clarify what *Picnic* puts at issue about fifties masculinity when it makes a spectacle out of its muscular male star. According to Annette Kuhn, to talk about bodybuilding as an "exhibition" actually misstates its cultural ground as an active and concerted performance—or impersonation—of gender. "For bodybuilding is more than placing the body on display, more than just passive exhibition," Kuhn explains. "The fact that bodybuilding is an active production of the body, a process of acting upon and determining its contours, is impossible to ignore." As the crucial element in the body's production of itself as spectacle, "muscles function in much the same way as does clothing in other types of performance." In the bodybuilder's performance, because muscularity is traditionally "constituted as 'essentially' masculine," when muscles enter the same cultural domain of clothing, the bodybuilder's physique turns out to function "rather like drag, for female bodybuilders especially" (56). Whereas Kuhn's point in equating *female* bodybuilding with drag is that it "implies a transgression of the proper boundaries of sexual difference" (57), thereby making a problem for notions about a proper "feminine" body, she formulates her comparison so as to implicate *male* bodybuilding in unorthodox gender performances, too. Bodybuilding is as much a performance art as any drag show; both activities theatricalize the body itself so that it becomes marked with gender signs, and they do so by inflating—to the point of crossing or even collapsing—the codes by which the culture differentiates "manliness" from "womanliness."

In the case of *Picnic*, rather than inflating Hal's importance as a physical symbol of patriarchal domination of women, as one might expect from all the attention lavished on his muscles by Joshua Logan's camera, the visual comparison implied between Holden's body and the bodybuilder keeps bringing to the foreground what in the Hollywood star system is perhaps most fundamental to the representation of masculinity on screen, and most disturbing to the symbolic support of male power: the extent to which an actor's appearance, no less than his female counterpart's, has to be artificially fashioned into an *image* of physical virility for the eye of the camera—with a little bit of help from toupees, shoe lifts, and Max Factor, that goes without saying.

Screen acting resembles transvestism because it likewise involves a star's masculinity in various levels of gender impersonation. A male star, for instance, has to wear makeup just like a female star does, and when he takes off his shirt, his body has to be made up, too. *Photoplay* reports that even John Wayne had to conform to this practice: "John Wayne held a power puff in one hand, a mirror in the other, and painstakingly dusted his nose. He grinned self-consciously when he caught someone watching. 'Have to take the shine off,' he explained" (Armstrong 52). Prompted by this picture of John Wayne, of all men, having to apply a powder puff to his face, and given the fifties' anxiety about masculinity becoming feminized, there was every reason—at the thought of such "big handsome he-men of the wide open spaces primping and prancing in make-up before they go into a scene"—for *Photoplay* to ask, "Are actors sissies?" (53). Not surprisingly, the magazine's answer was a resounding negative. According to the magazine, the job may require men to dress up, thus acting like sissies, but it does not undermine the essential manliness covered up by the pancake base. All those he-men, the article stressed, "try to compensate for the frills and furbelows of their film careers by leaning over backwards in private life to be very, very masculine. . . . the boys, embarrassed by the powder puff routine, spend a lot of time off stage proving they're as rugged as the parts they play. And that's very rugged indeed" (97).

Photoplay's question turned out to be purely rhetorical but it nonetheless indicates a disturbing suspicion about Hollywood masculinity that results from the spectacular value of the male body both on screen and within the star system. Dependent upon makeup and other features of the mise-en-scène, like lighting and costume, screen acting blows the cover of masculine rug-gedness because the technology of performance makes virility just another masquerade. The *Photoplay* article itself appears to be symptomatic of the unease which this revelation inspires, for it too cannot help pulling the rug out from under Hollywood ruggedness. At the same time that the article stresses the off-camera manliness of filmdom's he-men, it prominently fea-tures photographs of Burt Lancaster, Rock Hudson, Tab Hunter, Ricardo Montalban, and Tony Curtis, with captions emphasizing their favorite phy-sical activity but pictures displaying their seminude torsos. Thus, while trying to prove that male stars can transcend the effeminizing effects of their profes-sion, which, because the camera puts them on view, forces he-men to wear makeup and watch their figures—in other words, to act just like "women"— the article itself becomes another occasion for making a spectacle of male stars. This contradictory intent motivates the defensive tone with which the magazine goes on to survey the hypermasculinity of one major star after another as they all reportedly spend their offscreen lives in virile activities, compensating for the effeminacy of their careers.

As the *Photoplay* article makes evident, male spectacle sells movies and fan magazines, too, and in the process dispels the myth of a natural masculinity. This was especially evident in the fifties since the representational conven-tions of the day demanded a great deal of artifice in order to show a man in his most "natural" state. Although Armour proposed that a hairy chest functions like a "welcome" mat for the eye of the beholder, because it epitomizes the "*au natu-rel*" condition of being "unmistakably male," in fact the period's conven-tions for incorporating the body into representation, so that it could signify virility, displayed it as an object in culture, not nature, as Armour's own example of Lancaster bears out. "Can you tell me why big he-men like Burt Lancaster never have hair on their chests?" Mrs. R. C. Warner of Eureka, California wrote to *Life* after reading the article on male movie stars which I discussed in opening this chapter. The magazine's editor replied: "Lancaster has a hairy chest but shaves it for some roles."

In Hollywood, with the notable exception of Charlton Heston, baring the chest to represent the classical ideal of smooth muscularity generally meant that a hirsute actor, even a big star like Lancaster—or Douglas, or Brando, or Holden—had to shave or wax his body in observance of the "unwritten rule" of art photography: "male nudes should be smooth" as a way of suggesting "associations with marble and . . . painted nudes" (Foster 43). Even more specific to the codes of fifties representation, "[t]he tanned and oiled body," a convention of both bodybuilding and the cinema, "replaces the symbolic associations of marble with those of polished bronze: the glint of light on the rounded muscle-surface contrasts with the deep colour of the depressions, so that the musculature stands out in dramatic and highly tactile contrast . . ." (Dutton 315). As well as evoking the aesthetic ideal of classical statuary, denuding the male body of its hair, Kenneth R. Dutton explains, makes the skin texture appear smooth in order to give the bodybuilder "a more childlike appearance." The shaved body cancels out "the aggressive or intimidating message of the super-normal adult male body-shape," demonstrating "that this is not a body to be feared on account of its dominance, but rather to be looked at or touched—a body that places itself in the submissive role of 'object'" (306).

Whether the shaved body of a muscle man achieves the effect of seeming childlike is debatable, since the purpose of the exhibition is to show the skin's tautness as it stretches tightly over fully developed muscle, not its softness. But the point is still that the convention of shaving turns the body into a surface, with its musculature visibly inscribed on the skin. The shaved body therefore seems less "aggressive or intimidating" because it (literally, physically) accentuates a male body's phallic posturing while devaluing it as a masquerade. Removing body hair not only makes muscles look bigger and more sharply defined (or "cut"), but it also removes traces of secondary sex characteristics, "all that hair, which does not conform in texture or tonal value to the smooth monochrome of marble or bronze" (Davis 13), in order to render the male body a "safe" object of "aesthetic" contemplation by the eye of either men or women. Dutton therefore believes that the bodybuilder's torso is a "transfigured body": "not so much transcending sexuality as rendering it illegible, the bodybuilder's performance aims at a kind of sexual self-containment which sublimates de-sire" (300–301).

As deployed in films, where it interacts with a narrative system of regulating sexual difference, the fifties convention of shaving an actor's chest and stomach—and sometimes, as was required of Douglas for *Champion,* even his armpits, arms, and legs—makes a masculine ideal out of a smooth body that appears younger, less dominating, but, most importantly, not less differentiated as a *sexed* body because of this remodeling. The shaved body does not efface the muscular actor's physical prowess as a male but, in drawing attention to his body as a marked surface, it visibly equates the proof of his virility with a masquerade that makes the male and female body comparable in value for the film industry as constructed erotic objects. Hence Holtzman's passing remark, not meant as a compliment to Holden, that, in *Picnic*, it's a toss-up as to whether he or Kim Novak has "the more photogenic chest."

The Shaved Chest

When Holden took off his shirt to act in *Picnic*, the requirements of his performance meant he had to violate one of the most time-honored assumptions about sexual difference in our culture: the law of Samson's razor. Costar Susan Strasberg recalls that Holden "complained when he had to shave his chest" but, as she adds, "no hair was allowed in 1955" (46), so he had to submit to the razor (or to body waxing), no doubt more than once given the amount of screen time Logan devoted to his chest. This was not an unusual situation for Holden, by any means. His career began with Columbia's assumption that his screen performance was inseparable from the styling of his look. For *Golden Boy*, in which he played a violinist who gives up music for prize fighting, he had to undergo an extensive remaking of his body, getting his hair dyed, brilliantined and curled; his face and body covered with make-up; and his chest hair periodically thinned (Holtzman 28). And while in the 1950s he also had to shave his chest every time he took off his shirt, he was able to go hairy chested immediately after the war (in *Rachel and the Stranger*, 1948, and *Sunset Blvd.*, 1950, and even on the pages of *Photoplay* in 1951) and then again in the 1960s (in *Paris When It Sizzles*, 1964, and *The Wild Bunch*, 1969), when a full chest of hair, set against the androgyny of the counterculture youth movement, acquired new significance in connoting virility. The visual treatment of Holden's chest from decade to decade is a significant inscription of the changing cultural values regulating cinematic representations of the male body to determine its erotic value.

In this regard, it is worth considering why Charlton Heston, whose value for the screen I argued in the previous chapter also lies in the sight of his chest, could break the rules of fifties male spectacle and go hairy chested in *The Ten Commandments* (as well as in *Ben-Hur* and other epics). The obvious reason, as I pointed out, is that the DeMille film's differentiation of the categories of "Hebrew" and "Egyptian" according to the presence or absence of body hair was so ideologically powerful in its Orientalist stereotypes of Western/Asian masculinities that it could simply supersede the industry's sense of decorum. But more to the point of what I am arguing now, it is equally clear that *The Ten Commandments* also deviated from convention in order to position Heston's hairy (hence "natural" and more "primitive") body within the symbolic field of a conservative, highly phallocentric masculinity equated with "The Law." Heston's body thus carries a different meaning from that of other actors of his generation (Lancaster, Douglas, Brando, as well as Holden), all of whom had to have their bodies shaved, which is why they have not come to personify the epic genre as Heston has.

In one interview, Heston commented: "I don't look like a modern man, and I'm seldom asked to play contemporary parts. . . . My appearance qualifies me for historic characterizations, going back to the year one." Then he explicitly compared himself to Holden: "Bill Holden has just the opposite problem. His face is typical of the 20th Century. He'd be out of place dashing around in a tunic and waving a sword" (Scott, "Charlton"). Heston's hirsute appearance on screen in his various epics means to signify the intimidating, patriarchal body of conservative masculinity, in contrast to the more modern "look" of Holden's face. Nonetheless, even Heston was not entirely exempt from fifties decorum. After watching a later film, such as *Planet of the Apes* (1964), where the star's body is also on display for a considerable amount of screen time, one can see how his chest hair in *The Ten Commandments* was subtly trimmed and his stomach hair shaved to give his upper body more artful symmetry (and, it appears, sheared even more for the stills used in publicity)—and to focus as much attention on his pectorals as on God's two stone tablets.

In somewhat similar fashion, Holden's more modern "look," his face resonant of fifties hegemonic masculinity, as Heston's comparison implies (and as I shall discuss further in the next section), clashes with the way his smooth, hairless body functioned in representation as an eroticized alternative to the seemingly invisible body of the era's Man in the Gray Flannel Suit. The muscular features connoting Holden's "virility" in *Picnic* are no different than those connoting the "sexiness" of a female star like Monroe or Novak; they are as much an effect of Hollywood artifice and just as historically inflected to conform the star's appearance to popular tastes of the period, although the male star's body is cosmetically marked to produce the opposite effect, representing his maleness as a universal condition of nature. Male sexual identity on screen, however, is always the effect of an actor performing a historically specific version of masculinity, and *Picnic* makes this dimension of male star performance quite clear in the way it foregrounds the spectacle of Holden's body. His shaved body poses a particular problem for the film's delineation of sexual difference, in a way that Heston's body in *The Ten Commandments* does not, because it reverses and in so doing obscures the "woman/nature, man/culture dichotomy" which has always been central to visual representations of gender in American and European painting as well as sculpture, in another manifestation of the looked at/looking opposition (Saunders 91).

The visual treatment of Holden's body in *Picnic* may follow the conventions of the day in trying to evoke classical art, but the actual means of representation is neither marble nor paint but the camera. In a recent book on the male nude in contemporary photography, Melody Davis argues that a photograph can transgress the nature/culture gender division in ways that painting cannot, particularly when the camera does not disguise the natural texture of the male body. Because in our culture women still shave their bodies and men do not (or now they make a pretense of denying it), a photograph's revelation or even magnification of body hair can have the disrupting effect of "placing the male with the natural (where the female is supposed to be) and the female among the masculine and polished forms of culture" (14). *Picnic* achieves this same effect of destabilizing the differentiation of male and female bodies according to the culture/nature divide, but it reverses the procedure Davis describes. As both French's and Biskind's comments on the film's narrative suggest, Hal/ Holden's bared muscular body appears to position his masculinity within "untamed" sexual nature in opposition to the "civilizing" culture claimed for Madge/Novak's femininity. However, no matter how hard the film tries to naturalize Hal/Holden's maleness, the conventions of visual representation which it follows prove otherwise. The polished, phallic look of his "rippling muscles," achieved by the artifice of eliminating signs of his body's natural hairy state, actually means to improve upon nature, much as airbrushing removed blemishes and pubic hair from the bodies of 1950s *Playboy* pinups. Meant to be looked at on screen and off, the male body in *Picnic* calls repeated attention to its cultural status as an image. Far from authenticating masculinity, this muscular body is the most performative element in Hal's masquerade, and in Holden's too.

Just Another Red-Blooded American Boy

Even more so than Hal's account of his brief brush with Hollywood stardom, I have been arguing, the continual spectacle of Holden's body in *Picnic* challenges the film's ostensible project of recuperating Hal because it shows that his masculinity is constituted in a performance of virility. At the same time, because of his age, Holden's presence in the film also undermines the ideology of attractive male youth motoring the narrative of *Picnic* as part of the film's stage pedigree in what Bentley called "the new phallus worship" of Marlon Brando/Stanley Kowalski and what the industry dubbed that actor's "torn T-shirt style of acting." Brando, in fact, was first offered the part for the screen version, and Ralph Meeker, who had first come to prominence when he played Stanley on the road, originated Hal on Broadway and repeated his performance in Los Angeles. This is not to suggest, though, that the casting of Holden as Hal was a careless decision on the studio's part which worked against the impact of the film. On the contrary, "William Holden" was fundamental to the film's success in refuting what it simultaneously exploits in making (and marketing) the image of the male body as the primary stake of Hal's (and Holden's) masculinity. While Holden was criticized for being "terribly miscast," to quote Darryl F. Zanuck, it was, so to speak, the age of the chest that mattered in making the film a big hit—and Zanuck also predicted its success (Behlmer 257).

Holden's star persona as a "solid citizen on screen and off" ("Stronger" 93) helped to overcome the role's revelation that masculinity is constituted through masquerade. As Dyer notes in *Stars* (54–55), Holden's persona conforms to what fifties sociologist Orrin Klapp called "the good Joe" and what Holden himself referred to as his "Smiling Jim" screen image. In Klapp's words:

> The good Joe is friendly and easygoing; he fits in and likes people; he never sets himself above others but goes along with the majority; he is a good sport—but he is also a he-man who won't let anyone push him around where basic rights are concerned. Most of the time he is so modest that he is self-effacing: even if he is president of the company you can call him by his first name. . . . Joe is a native type, as distinctive of America as jazz and rock-and-roll; there is probably no correspond-ing type complex in any other country. (108–109)

While "Bill" Holden (as, true to the type described by Klapp, he was familiarly called by writers in the fan magazines and fans like Lucy Ricardo) played this type in films like *Dear Ruth* (1947), *Force of Arms* (1951), *The Bridges of Toko-Ri* (1954), and *Executive Suite* (1954), in his most famous roles—*Sunset Blvd.*, *Stalag 17*, *Sabrina* (1954), *The Country Girl* (1954), *The Proud and Profane* (1956), and *The Bridge on the River Kwai*—he actually performed the type's mutation. In its most nuanced inflection, Holden's star persona epitomized what Klapp considered to be "the new American character [that] is forming": "a composite" of the good Joe, "easygoing" and "with plenty of friends"; the smart operator, who "doesn't work too hard"; and the playboy, whose "wish to take part in a show . . . is a real incentive, for he is audience-directed and likes the limelight (especially when one considers that maximum effort is usually required only when the lights are on)" (121).

The star persona of William Holden was a considerable extratextual di-mension of *Picnic*'s complex attitude toward Hal and, more importantly, toward Holden's body as an object of cinematic fascination. Already signed to play Hal before Logan agreed to direct, Holden "was really too old for the part," Logan recalled, but "he was such a vital, virile, talented man and with such a youthful body, that I felt he would be strong in the part" (*Movie* 6–7). And indeed he was, since after the success of *Picnic*, Bob Thomas reports, "women everywhere dreamed of dancing in the moonlight with William Holden and being seduced by the railroad tracks" (109).[8]

Holden's star persona went to the opposite extreme of Hal in openly dis-claiming performance. Although he was not the only male star in Hollywood to disavow his craft because of its "unmanly" associations with fakery and spectacle, acclaim for the naturalness of Holden's performance style stands out in a period dominated by the discourse of Method acting. Unlike Brando, Clift, or Dean, say, in the words of Billy Wilder, his director on three major pictures, Holden "is beyond acting" (qtd. in "Conquest" 64). "He doesn't put on a mask the way Lon Chaney used to do," Wilder commented, "and play a monster one day and a bedbug the next" (qtd. in Holtzman 112). "Only actors who are ashamed to act are worth their salt," Wilder is supposed to have said as well. "[T]hat's why I'm fond of Holden. He dies every time he has to act" (qtd. in Malone 6). With this kind of press from his best director, it followed that a large part of the "authenticity" of Holden's star persona was based on his supposed transcendence of screen performance so that there could be no question about *his* masculinity even when the character's was in doubt. Consequently, the age and personality differences between "William Holden" and the character he plays in *Picnic* accentuate the actor's own safe distance from his impersonation of the bragging, swaggering Hal, while, from another perspective, the star's persona also suggests their similarity in the way both inhabit and implicitly market their body as spectacle. "Whatever the nature of his appeal," remarked a press release for one of his late-1950s films, "Holden is inclined to take a very practical view of it. 'The only thing I have to sell is myself,' he says. 'I'm glad that business is so good'" ("News").

The naturalness of Holden's performance style, which serves to ground the potentially explosive implications of the role of Hal, is a dominant characteristic of the Hollywood movie star generally. "Naturalness" supplies one of the key performance codes out of which the star system helps to structure an actor's relation to film. As Dyer explains:

> There is a whole litany in the fan literature surrounding stars in which certain adjectives endlessly recur—sincere, immediate, spontaneous, real, direct, genuine and so on. All of these words can be seen as relating to a general notion of "authenticity." It is these qualities that we demand of a star if we accept her or him in the spirit in which she or he is offered. Outside of a camp appreciation, it is the star's really seeming to be what s/he is supposed to be that secures his/her star status, "star quality" or charisma. Authenticity is both a quality necessary to the star phenomenon to make it work, and also the quality that guarantees the authenticity of the other particular values a star embodies (such as girl-next-door-ness, etc.). It is this effect of authenticating authenticity that gives the star charisma. . . .("*Star*" 133)

A male movie star's supposed authenticity as a nonperformer is what usually supports Hollywood's equation of "seeming natural" with "being male." However, since the apparatus promotes, as Dyer puts it, only an "effect of authenticating authenticity"—which, for an actor like Holden, amounts to the simulation of virility, deeply convincing perhaps but theatrical just the same—the screen actor's quite literal performance of masculinity on film always implicates male sexual identity and desire in a masquerade no less artificial, and no more natural, than the female star's—or Hal's, for that matter.

In the specific case of Holden's star persona, his discomfort with the artifice of screen performance is made evident in accounts of his temper, his drinking, and his daredevil stunts. Much like *Photoplay's* strategy in showing that actors are not sissies because they prove their masculinity with physical activity off screen, as part of the discourse surrounding *Picnic* at the time of its release and afterward, these characteristics were stressed in opposition to Holden's performance of Hal. Whether in feature articles written to promote the film or in autobiographies of the people who worked with Holden on it, every anecdotal account of the production not only mentions his discomfort with the role of Hal because of age and temperament but goes on to stress the actor's own display of youthfulness and virility off the set during the shoot in Kansas. Susan Strasberg, for one, remembers Holden being "very unhappy about his role. 'Christ, Josh, I can't swing around like a monkey. I'm too old for that crap. I'm going to look like an idiot'" (46). Yet it appears that Holden did more than his share of swinging around while on location. One repeated story has him hanging off the ledge of a tenth (or seventh, or fourteenth—the number varies in each account of the episode) floor hotel window in order (and, again, the point of the story varies with the source) to get Logan to apologize for something he said (Strasberg 47); or to prove his athletic ability with a daredevil stunt (Logan, *Movie* 16–17); or to show it off in a fit of drunkenness (Russell and Chase 186); or to convince Logan to let him play his final scene, when he jumps on to the moving train, without a double (L. Wilson, "Bill"); or to relax because, "[f]or some reason, Holden, a trained gymnast, likes to lower himself from outside a windowsill, hang there and look around" ("Conquest" 63). In recounting the incident three decades later, the version in a biography of Kim Novak even has the actor hanging from the window ledge in his "torn-shirt" costume from the film (Brown 98–99). Which version of Holden's behavior is truth? That's beside the point, of course. What matters, as Logan puts it, is that "[h]e was simply a red-blooded American boy who wanted to have a good time, and believe me, he did" (*Movie* 12).

Time's cover story on Holden, "The Conquest of Smiling Jim," timed to the national release of *Picnic* in February 1956, is an important document in this regard because it promotes his star persona as "a red-blooded American boy" by using criticism of his performance as evidence of the authenticity of his offscreen hegemonic masculinity, which, like Logan, the magazine also understands in national rather than erotic terms. Unlike Hal, Holden's "driving sincerity" and "his almost complete lack of pretentiousness" shine forth in the *Time* article as proof of his genuine virility on screen and off (67). "Holden's talent as an actor is not large, as he readily admits, but he uses it with an almost ferocious sincerity, and with an intelligence much keener than some men with greater gifts enjoy" (63). "Miscast" in *Picnic,* the article continues,

Bill was asked not only to portray a man far younger than himself, but to animate a type, completely opposite to his own—a feat especially difficult on the screen. For a good cinemactor, there is only one way to act: don't. The camera comes so close that the slightest insincerity can be seen. Bill's whole experience has taught him not to play a part, but to play himself in the part. . . .

In the *Picnic* part, however, the old way would not work, and Bill was made most mightily to stretch his soul. It would not always stretch. . . . Even so, in the balance, the lapses in Bill's acting weigh the most, and the greatest of these failures is emotional. In playing the part of a man who is little more than an animal, Bill seems unable to free the animal forces in himself. (63–64)

As *Time* accounts for it, the miscasting of Holden as Hal shows up most in the highly "emotional" acting required of him—which is to say that the *failure* of this star performance appears to guarantee the transparency with which Holden openly fakes Hal's brand of bogus masculinity in order to establish the authenticity of his own. To put it in fifties terms: "'The matinee idol of the Eisenhower era,' cracked a Hollywood reporter, 'is a man in a grey flannel suit'" (62). This description pithily summarizes the gap imposed between Holden's erotic star value and his masculine persona, and it underscores the performativity of both.

Figure 27.
Mr. and Mrs. William Holden at home on their suburban patio in the San Fernando Valley. Unidentified publicity photograph c. 1950s.

The "William Holden" which *Time* magazine reproduces as the man that Hal could not co-opt is an unlikely romantic movie hero: an ordinary American Joe with no pretensions toward high art, a long-lasting marriage, and a face resembling, in an often-repeated quotation, "A map of the United States. ... All those meaningless straight lines" (62). The adjectives that immediately stand out in the article's description of Holden are "likable," "forthright," and "suburban," words coming straight out of the fan magazines' homages to the ordinariness of Holden's middle-class life, from PTA and scout meetings to the Sunday barbecues with the family on the patio of their San Fernando Valley home.[9] These qualities were important to Holden's star persona as "an average guy" (Thompson), who was "too normal for comfort" (Bocca 28) and graced with "the All-American Face" (Hopper, "Never"), because, in linking the sincerity of his screen presence to his middle-class family life, they conform his masculinity to the hegemonic national identity: that all-American boy next door, who grew up, went to war, and came back to put on a gray flannel suit and live in the suburbs. Holden was by no means the only star whose persona was defined in such nationalistic terms. But it is revealing of what his persona signified that *Time* goes so far as to equate his screen appeal with his face, pictured as a kind of monument to postwar America, with its highways and waterways inscribed there as metaphors for the greater authority which age had brought to his indistinct pretty-boy looks, and not with his "athletic type [of body], with a graceful flow of well-conditioned muscle" ("Conquest" 62), which is what made *Picnic* a big hit.

In *Time*'s reading of Holden, the opposition between mature face and youthful body manifests a contradiction, etched into the very surface of the actor's star image, which catches his "tensions and complexities" to suggest a depth of personality off screen ("Conquest" 67). With this turn to Holden's "hidden" side, the magazine simply repeats the star's screen persona, indirectly documenting how the actor had indeed learned "to play himself in the part" as the reason for his great success as a "cinemactor" in the fifties. In the three starmaking films Holden made for Wilder—*Sunset Blvd., Stalag 17,* and *Sabrina*—his parts somewhat darkened his brash and earnest *Golden Boy* and *Dear Ruth* screen persona by exposing a cynicism and egoism lurking beneath the boyish charm, only to temper that nasty edge in the story's closure with a heavy streak of sentimentality posing as honor. As *Time* goes on to characterize Holden, revealing that "the grey flannel suit has a scarlet lining," it shows a man similarly divided: at home, a solid citizen and "civic booster," but at work, a boozing bad boy who grins and says, "Warm up the ice cubes" before *and* after performing a scene (63).

The cover story in *Time* reportedly "incensed" Holden because of what it revealed about his temper, recklessness, and heavy drinking (Thomas 111). As in his film roles, though, these two different sides to Holden's persona are not all that incompatible, because together they produce the particular masculine

Figure 28.
William Holden: "Just another red-blooded American boy."
Unidentified publicity photograph c. 1950s.

inflection of his star persona. With his "mature" side written all over his all-American face to inscribe his male identity quite clearly, his "boyish" side can then safely give expression to his body, as manifested in "his need for danger" ("Conquest" 63). Thus, even if motivated by heavy drinking, when cited as evidence of his athletic prowess, a grandstanding stunt such as hanging from a window ledge functions in several ways to define Holden's star persona in contrast to a character like Hal. It serves as proof not only of the expert physical control Holden has over his body, but also of his being in remarkably fit condition for a 37-year-old man. At the same time, in its impulsiveness as a prank, the stunt offers evidence that the American boy next door is still father to that 37-year-old man. Most of all, this type of reckless physical activity authenticates Holden's screen image as an action hero, since it is simply another version of what the star does professionally when he performs his own stunts for his films. Emphasizing male action over spectacle, reports of Holden's offscreen antics on the set serve to reproduce his manliness all the way down the line, denying his cinematic value as an object of desire in *Picnic* and insisting instead upon his attraction as an ego-ideal more consistent with the culture's understanding of masculinity conforming to four basic rules: "no sissy stuff," "be a big wheel," "be a sturdy oak," "give 'em hell" (Kimmel 238).[10] Holden's grandstanding performance of virility ensures that Hal remains "a type, completely opposite to his own," even though both of them *do* swing around like monkeys.

. . . and Looked at Again

"The All-American boy doesn't have a body," Marjorie Garber comments, "or didn't until recently. . . . Indeed, it could be said that a 'real male' cannot be embodied at all, that embodiment *itself* is a form of feminization" (*Vested* 372). If masculinity seems to resist embodiment because the male body has traditionally been understood to be exempt from representation, then the movies obviously put the lie to that cultural assumption. Hollywood has always made the bodies of men and women alike central to screen imagery, where embodiment does not turn actors into "sissies"; it is not "a form of feminization," at least not in the sense that *Photoplay* feared. However, visual spectacle does make the male star a potentially transgressive body—particularly when his exposure is as stylized as in *Picnic*, and its juxtaposition to a normative star persona as bracing as in Holden's case—because this is a *male* body collapsing the boundaries between performance and authenticity.

Fifties beefcake may therefore give the impression of inviting viewers to identify with a powerful, muscular male body as a phallocentric ideal ego, but it just as openly supplied the conditions for rupturing that identification. The era's characteristic attention to male spectacle, which *Picnic* exaggerates in its continual display of Holden's bare chest but also exemplifies as a product of the fifties star system, has the noticeable effect of positioning the viewer, female or male, as just that: a spectator of the male body. This spectacle was overtly directed at women in the audience, as Armour noted at the time in his satiric account of "The Age of the Chest" and *Life* in its "Album of Male Appeal." But it was just as much put on view for "the Average Man, now hunched self-consciously in his seat while his best girl drools over the massive chest muscles of Marlon or Burt" (Armour 65)—or Bill Holden, the movies' "Smiling Jim." As Armour recognized, one possible solution for the Average Man's discomfort at watching an eroticized male was to turn away, refusing to look at the bare, oiled, gleaming, and posed torso of a movie hero. Refusal to look would confirm the Average Man's exclusion from this unorthodox representation of masculinity in order to resecure his identification with hegemonic masculinity. Given the popularity of beefcake at the time, though, there is every reason to suppose that many an Average Man looked just as intently at this eroticized male imagery, not drooling necessarily, but still compelled to watch, as Tommy Haley says in *Champion*, "a good boy in action."

So if the fifties was indeed The Age of the Chest, as Armour proposed, then the visual exploitation of muscular stars like Holden produced a range of conflicted meanings for the exposed male body. The convention of shaving the body as the requisite condition for its representation on screen associated the visual embodiment of an ideal, physical masculinity with culture, not nature, as a means of establishing its claim to dominance. However, in following the conventions of bodybuilding and rendering the male body as a mask, this visual aesthetic called into question the phallic terms by which muscularity had traditionally functioned as the guarantee of male entitlement. The conventionalized artifice with which a fifties film like *Picnic* incorporates Holden's exposed body into its diegesis openly eroticizes it as spectacle, configuring the possibility of an alternative masculinity through the image's solicitation of an assortment of possible gazes across a continuum of gendered/sexed viewing positions: female, male, heterosexual, homosexual.

Because it is melodrama and not an epic, *Picnic* certainly exceeds the terms by which films of this era made a spectacle of their male stars. Generally speaking, fifties movies most blatantly exploited the bodies of their male stars on screen for only a scene or two, as when Lancaster stripped to swim and make love in *From Here to Eternity*. In comparison, the spectacle of Holden in *Picnic* is unusually revealing of the problems which the star system itself caused for the fifties embodiment of a "real man" through an actor's muscularity. Logan's camera subjects the star to a steady gaze, placing Holden in the position of exhibitionist and focusing on his body with the kind of unrelenting visual interest supposedly reserved only for a female star like Novak. This objectification of Holden as an image of "to-be-looked-at-ness" collapses the difference between star and part, between the "real man" and his representation; and while his star persona tried to differentiate the actor's embodiment of masculinity from Hal's phallic imposture, that persona itself repeated the very performative dimension of masculinity it disclaimed in the name of Holden's being just another "ordinary Joe." Anyway you look at it, the masculinity Holden embodies as a muscle man in *Picnic* all too easily turns out to depend upon performance, not authenticity, just as Hal's does—and just as the star's persona itself did, too.

6

Why Boys Are Not Men

The current movie heroes are boys trying to do a man's work. Most of them are adolescent, and this applies regardless of age. These heroes include boys who'd like to be men. Some play tough guys, like Paul Newman and Marlon Brando. Some are rebels like the late James Dean and the current Sal Mineo and Elvis Presley. Others, like Tony Perkins . . . play it shy and boyish. What's wrong with this new look in Hollywood men? Why are the old reliable favorites—Clark Gable, Jimmy Stewart, Gary Cooper, John Wayne and company—still carrying the big box-office burden and running away with the heroine at an age when they might well be settling down to pipe and slippers? Does the fault lie in the way these stars are being handled, or in the stars themselves? To each his own, and every generation has its own heroes. Let's face it: The actor is never isolated from what is happening around him. (Skolsky, "New" 41)

With these comments, introducing a feature story in the July 1957 issue of *Photoplay*, columnist Sidney Skolsky compares the old guard of Hollywood male stars to the new generation who emerged during the postwar era. According to Skolsky, the new Hollywood star is *young*, and his youth summarizes his visible difference from Hollywood's traditional representation of American manliness. "Clad in T-shirt and blue jeans, serious, moody, an individualist to the core, Montgomery Clift was a far cry from any of the previous screen-hero styles," Skolsky observes about the beginning of what he names, with a probable nod to Dior's equally radical "New Look" of 1946, "the new look in Hollywood men" (42).[1] Clift, the columnist recalls, "became a popular idol overnight . . . [after] just one appearance in a more-than-good Western called 'Red River,'" because his youthful persona spoke so loudly to postwar audiences, who "had little use, with the war won, for the physical heroes, the Gables and Waynes." As Skolsky follows the trajectory of stardom traced during the decade first by Clift, and then by Brando, Dean, Presley, Newman and others in their mold, he concludes that the new star persona is "a hero with neuroses" (111), a diminished version of the rugged, physical masculinity still being personified on screen by those old working war horses, Cooper, Gable, Stewart, and Wayne.[2] In contrast, these new stars are, as Skolsky states at the start of his article, "boys who'd like to be men"—meaning, of course, that they are boys who are *not* men.

In a 1960 interview John Wayne voices the same complaint. Deploring "the psychotic weaklings depicted as heroes in modern down-beat movies," the star points out: "Ten or 15 years ago audiences went to pictures to see men behaving like men. . . . Today there are too many neurotic roles." As part of the publicity preparing for the release of Wayne's production of *The Alamo* later that same year, this interview reassures all of Duke's fans that, "by his very appearance," the "big guy" is "disqualified automatically" from playing one of those "trembling, torn T-shirt types" himself. With a not-so-veiled homophobia, Wayne attributed their popularity to "the Tennessee Williams effect both on Broadway and in the movies" ("Modern"). The actor's well-known hostility to the psychologically conflicted heroes of the period implies how much his own on-screen personification of virility depends upon the subordination of male youth in one form or other. In the binarized system of representation enhancing his masculinity on screen, more often than not (the exceptions are usually when he costars with Maureen O'Hara and tames *her* flashing Irish temperament in the final reel) Duke's opposite turns out to be, not a Duchess but a Dauphin, so to speak: a young man, often nicknamed the "kid" from one Western town or another, whom Wayne guides to manhood, usually in a displacement of his own character's sexual repression.[3]

Generally speaking, the new young male actors of the fifties still stand out as different from "old reliable favorites" like John Wayne because their star imagery on and off screen played up the performative elements of their youth: the uniform of black leather jacket, T-shirt, and jeans; the mumbling diction emphasizing inarticulate (and uneducated) speech and deeply rooted (and unresolved) emotionality; an association with New York theater, particularly the style of Method acting learned at the Actor's Studio; and an irreverent attitude toward a studio career. The characteristics read off from this imagery in the fifties—their self-conscious posing, grungy clothing, lack of formal education, working-class identity, urban background, emotional immaturity, alienation from corporate America—immediately coalesced around the star personae of Montgomery Clift and Marlon Brando, vividly coming together in such roles as Clift's George Eastman in *A Place in the Sun* (1951) and Brando's Stanley Kowalski in *A Streetcar Named Desire* (1951).

With its key note of social disengagement, the new star's rebel persona paralleled the nonconformist beat movements in Greenwich Village and San Francisco, making a deliberate contrast to the era's hegemonic masculinity. The Hollywood studios, however, repeatedly positioned their new male stars in a variety of settings—narrative films, magazine articles, publicity releases, photographs—that put forward one set of meanings for them (their open personification of sexual self-expression) in place of another (their implicit articulation of class differences). Joan Mellen attributes this substitution of meanings to the industry's own anxiety before the second wave of HUAC investigations. Turning away from the social-problem films of the late 1940s, she explains, "Hollywood replaced social dissent with a fascinating and serious examination of *sexual* politics. The assumed definitions of the male sex role were challenged as films discovered the male capable of sensitivity and an open expression of tenderness, feelings which in the forties were ridiculed as effeminate" (192). The derogatory depiction of the "torn T-shirt types" as "trembling" in John Wayne's interview condenses into that single, engendered adjective the new stars' interiorization of masculinity, the signal effect of their distinct performance style, which translated the social nonconformity connoted by their rebel pose into the psychological terms of inner torment and emotional excess. Gossip about the private lives of the biggest names like Clift, Brando, and Dean crystallized all the more solidly their sexual disengagement as "trembling, torn T-shirt types" from the "hard" masculine personae of older, established stars like Wayne. Thanks to numerous tell-all biographies, this view has become much more pronounced four decades later. But even at the time strong hints of sexual uncertainty in the personae of the new young stars were already the inescapable messages of their visual treatment on screen and in publicity shots. One has only to recall the galvanizing early screen appearances of the young Clift and Brando to see how readily imagery of a youthful male body, not only beautiful to behold but also highly theatricalized, marked out the erotic appeal of these new young actors within the star system, underscoring their alienation from the screen's more traditional representations of masculinity.

That the new young stars gave an important, influential, and very sexy new look to postwar masculinity is by now a truism of the period. What I emphasize in this chapter is how their youth was interpreted, both on film and in the fan discourse, through the trope of boyishness which mainstream American culture repeatedly drew upon after the war when representing deviations from hegemonic masculinity as a boy's impersonation of manhood, as a performance that always falls short of the original. Far from following the critical consensus, then and now, that the new stars were simply feminized (and hence "lesser") males in contrast to big "he-men" like Wayne, I claim that their disruptive status as "boys who are not men" summarizes an important reconfiguration of masculinity in movies of this period because their "new look" challenged the conflation of "gender" and "sexuality" underwriting the symbolic economy with which "boys" were made legible as the opposites of "men." In response, as Skolsky's *Photoplay* article implicitly recognized, "John Wayne and company" likewise served the fifties star system because their personae contained the most subversive element of that "new look": the eroticism implying youth's open rejection of hegemonic norms.

A Soft Boy and a Hard Man: *Red River*

The generational difference that structures Skolsky's portrait of "the new look in Hollywood men" in *Photoplay* was, as he himself notes, signaled by the popular and influential Western *Red River* (1948). Critics after Skolsky have also noted how this film's conflict between a rancher and his foster son on a cattle drive explicitly sets established star John Wayne against new screen personality Montgomery Clift.[4] Cattleman Tom Dunson (Wayne), as sidekick Nadine Groot (Walter Brennan) remarks in the first scene, is "a mighty set man—when his mind's made up." Dunson's foster son, Matthew Garth (Clift), on the other hand, is flexible, intuitive, contemplative, and initially respectful of Dunson's commanding authority. Whereas Dunson exercises his control of the cattle drive by instilling fear in his men—and when that doesn't work, driving them to exhaustion so that they are too tired to rebel—Matthew earns their camaraderie, loyalty, and trust. Midway through the film, Dunson wants to hang two cowboys who have quit the cattle drive, and this abuse of his power motivates Matthew's rebellion. With the support of all the other hands, including Groot, the younger man takes control; left behind, Dunson vows he will catch up with them and kill Matthew to avenge the theft of his cattle. However, with his different, more humane style of leadership, Matthew finishes the job that Dunson started and, as if in vindication of his achievement, in the last section of the film, the youth becomes romantically involved with Tess Millay (Joanne Dru), again setting up a contrast to the older man, who remains a bully and a bachelor to the very end.

From the perspective of its closure, which achieves a reconciliation between the two men through Tess's intervention, it is at first easy to agree with Mellen's claim that *Red River* offers "a composite portrait" of postwar masculinity, half John Wayne, half Montgomery Clift—as she puts it, "a gentle superman" (175). The film even makes the continuity between the two men visible in Clift's own face, since, as a result of his final showdown with Dunson, Matthew carries the former's mark, a bullet scar on Clift's cheek much like the one on Wayne's throughout the main narrative. However, while *Red River* may close with the visualization of Dunson and Matthew's resemblance in its final shot, the opposition between the two men is what keeps propelling the film forward, from the founding of the ranch in the prologue, to the epic adventure of the cattle drive in the main narrative, to their final showdown in Abilene in the climax. In fact, the very cattle on which Dunson stakes his fortune and, ultimately, his relation to Matthew, condenses both the symbolic and historical contexts that inform the film's representation of their difference, working against the credibility of that "composite portrait."

To start with, the great herd is the actual by-product of the original union of Dunson's bull and Matthew's cow. As Gerald Mast observes, this portentous coupling tropes the difference between "man" and "boy" as a binary opposition equating the boy with the softness of femininity through his cow and

Figure 29.
Red River closes with a reconciliation of Dunson (John Wayne) and
Matthew (Montgomery Clift), but their opposition is what keeps
propelling the narrative forward.

the man with the hardness of masculinity through his bull (302). But far from
letting this hard/soft opposition serve simply to polarize the two men, the
narrative of *Red River* sets it in the years immediately following the Civil War,
a historical context which, as in most Westerns of the fifties, instantly evoked
for contemporary audiences a clear parallel to the end of World War II. In
Red River, the parallel gives the difference between Dunson's hardness and
Matthew's softness a timely resonance as a commentary on postwar masculinity. After all, Matthew is himself a veteran whose return home announces a
shift in cultural expectations about hard, masculine aggression. While four-
teen years earlier Dunson could build a ranch from practically nothing
because of his hard attributes, in the postwar setting his inflexible masculinity
has to be reevaluated as the historical product of economic conditions; as
those conditions change, so does the measure of his manhood.

The sweep of time that occurs between the prologue and the main narrative
shows how Dunson's hard masculinity belies historical change in a way that
Matthew's softer version does not. Appropriating the land from its Mexican
owner, Dunson delivers a stirring speech, a personal avowal of American
manifest destiny in the West, that turns into a voiceover accompanying a

montage of his empire building to mark the transition to the film's main narrative: "My land. We're here and we're going to stay here. Give me ten years and I'll have that brand on the greatest ranch in Texas. . . . Ten years and I'll have the Red River D on more cattle than you've looked at anywhere. I'll have that brand on enough beef to—to feed the whole country." After more than a decade of Dunson's hard work, however, the end of the Civil War has made his cattle worthless unless it can reach a Northern market. Groot comments to Matthew upon the latter's return from the war, "Dunson learned that a ranch isn't just beef—it's money, too. He never knew anything about money." As a result, Matthew confirms, the rancher, now faced with the prospect of losing the entire value of his herd, "doesn't know who to fight." Dunson's inability to deal with the South's depressed economic conditions on the terms he understands (i.e., gunplay), Matthew then adds, is what accounts for "the look [of fear] on his face." While in the prologue Dunson can shoot the men who threatened to take away the land he himself appropriated from someone else (and seven graves remain on the ranch as visible evidence of his mastery with a gun), in the main narrative capital is what sustains—and endangers, when his cash flow dries up—Dunson's leadership, his dominance over the other men as a cattle baron and their employer.

Even as *Red River* lays out this economic explanation of the rancher's masculinity, however, its narrative also evades full recognition of the historical conditions that produce a hard man like Dunson before a war and then diminish his value afterward. The cattle come into play here as well since the herd supplies Dunson with an epic adventure—crossing the newly forged Chisholm Trail northward to establish Texas as the United States' prime source of cattle—that helps to restore the authenticity of his old-fashioned masculine valor. According to the narrative, what finally determines the price of the herd is the men's collective heroic achievement in bringing the cattle to Abilene, not the quality of the beef or its value in a depressed market. "How can a man deal with someone who's done what you've done?" asks Melville, the agent at Abilene, as he negotiates with Matthew, standing in as Dunson's representative, to buy the entire herd at top-dollar price. Fortitude, courage, perseverance, loyalty, sacrifice, and honor—these traditional manly virtues, when stripped of their economic motivation as an ideology supporting prewar entrepreneurial free enterprise, rescue Dunson's empire from the threat of postwar corporate capitalism, particularly since the narrative now clearly identifies for Dunson whom he has to fight: Matthew. With Matthew's usurpation of his command, Dunson finds a discernible antagonist who allows him (and, for the most part, *Red River* too) to discount the historical reasons for his earlier look of fear—and to reify the myth of the individualistic Western hero. As validated by Melville's respect for what Matthew has accomplished, the youth's success in leading the drive to its successful conclusion ultimately testifies to the way that Dunson, his aggression and paranoia notwithstanding, still embodies the gender code against which the masculinity of every other man in the film is overtly measured, Matthew's most notably (Tompkins 119–20).

As far as Dunson is concerned, manhood *is* ultimately proved through action not capital. In the prologue, for instance, before Dunson takes on the orphaned Matthew (initially played by Mickey Kuhn), he first tests the fourteen-year-old's mettle, acknowledging to Groot afterward, "He'll do." Matthew's status as a boy who is not a man is shown first by the ease with which Dunson disarms him and then by the youth's readiness, despite his defensive demeanor, to capitulate to the older man's authority following the loss of his gun. When Dunson then takes Matthew's cow to sire his own bull's progeny, in effect making the boy a silent, subordinate partner in his enterprise, the elder man also demands that the youth earn his position on the ranch's brand, the Red River D. Over two hours later, in the film's climax, as he tries to bait Matthew into a showdown, Dunson still taunts his foster son, who at this point *can* outdraw him although he refuses to fire. "You're soft," Dunson snarls. "Won't anything make a man out of you?" According to the logic of this question, in Dunson's eyes Matthew becomes a "man" only when the latter finally accepts the former's own gender code and participates in a showdown. The confrontation does not result in a conventional Western standoff, but the terms of aggressive male interaction forced upon Matthew nonetheless allow Dunson to regain his authority. Dunson gives Matthew license to become the breadwinner that he himself is not ("You better marry that girl, Matt," he orders). What is more, to acknowledge his parity with Matthew as partners in the Red River D, Dunson finally adds the younger man's name to the brand ("You've earned it," he observes, referring to Matthew's accomplishment in standing up to him as a "man").

In legitimating the manhood of the younger Matthew, Dunson fulfills what Virginia Wright Wexman considers to be the proper generic function of the Western movie hero, namely, to serve "as a model for young boys" (84). This role defines masculinity as a product of male expertise (whether sheriff, rancher, or gunfighter, the Western hero is a consummate professional) and homosocialization (he is more comfortable around other men, not women, maintaining the dominant position in a variety of same-sex relations that end up distinguishing among masculinities, ranking them according to age, race, ethnicity, class). Of all the big stars who have performed in Westerns, Wayne's postwar persona has most consistently been read in this light as the screen's exemplary male role model for American men. In the mid-fifties Wayne himself attributed his dependability at the box office to two related factors: "He explains that everybody loves a hero; therefore he has never played a villain"; and "he plays exclusively to men and boys. . . . He plays to his own sex by being simple, uncomplicated, and completely unaffected" (Scott, "John" 27–28). The appeal of Wayne's star persona, especially for young boys, was that, in film after film, he was never in doubt as to the manly course of action even when, as in *Red River,* he is proven wrong. As Hollywood journalist Lloyd Shearer put it at this time, Wayne "plays the ruthless hero who must drive his men to accomplish some dangerous but honorable mission. His men may hate him, but moviegoers always understand that beneath the granite exterior beats a heart pure and noble" (156). According to Mast, the source of this familiar persona, repeated in most of the star's postwar Westerns and best dramatized by his Ethan Edwards in *The Searchers* (1956), is the character Wayne plays in *Red River* (302–303).

Commentators on Wayne have tended to filter the less stable meanings that the actor bore in his postwar films through the lens of the actor's own right-wing patriotism, which became more public in the wake of his own overtly politicized productions of *The Alamo* in 1960 and *The Green Berets* in 1968 and then dominated his star persona in the 1970s and after. Wayne has been remembered simply as "a kind of folk-hero, his name an idiomatic expression, a metaphoric formula or cliché that instantly invoked a well-recognized set of American heroic virtues—or, from a different perspective, inflated American pretensions" (Slotkin 518–19). However, in building their narratives so as to reconcile the "ruthless" and "noble" sides of his star persona, Wayne's postwar Westerns usually make a problem out of his hard masculinity, an important point forgotten by critics and moviegoers alike when they conjure up the monolithic star image of "John Wayne" almost fifty years later. The postwar Westerns that kept Wayne at the top of box-office polls throughout the fifties actually used his aging star persona to register, albeit indirectly, a break with traditional representations of hard masculine ideals like Dunson's.

The highly charged contest between the soft boy and the hard man in *Red River* dramatizes such a shift in the mainstream culture's demands upon masculinity; this is certainly how Skolsky recalled the film's impact on postwar audiences a decade after its release. Whereas the film interprets Dunson's masculinity as an issue of gender, making a narrative problem of his behavior as a hard, unbending cattle-man, it defines Matthew's as an issue of sexuality, calling attention to his desirability as a soft, self-reflexive cow-boy. Matthew's "feminine" characteristics do not emasculate him in the eyes of others to make him a tamer version of the rancher; on the contrary, in articulating his difference from Dunson, those characteristics actually intensify his attractiveness to everyone in the film, including Dunson. As Melville says to the cowboys who nervously await Dunson's return and the inevitable showdown with Matthew, "I like that boy, too." If any sentiment in *Red River* summarizes the difference between Matthew and Dunson, it is, finally, this one.

The Cowboy and the Cattleman

Even though both generic convention and the Wayne star persona may encourage otherwise, it would be imprecise to assume that Dunson's hard masculinity nostalgically refers to the myth of the movie cowboy: that undomesticated, pure, red-blooded example of prime American masculinity. The diegesis of *Red River* plainly identifies Dunson as a cattleman, not a cowboy; moreover, as his inflexible treatment of his men shows, Dunson is emotionally, morally, and socially alienated from the cowboys working his ranch, and that includes Matthew, his foster son, right-hand man, and, as his foreman (the younger man's implied role on the Red River D), his head cowboy. Matthew's position as a cowboy is in fact why the other men look to Matthew for leadership—and why they like him, too.

No more than any other Western, *Red River* cannot be said to faithfully reproduce the conditions of ranch life in the nineteenth century, but it is worth pausing for a moment to consider more fully the historical basis of ranch hierarchy as it organized the gender meanings of the men who worked under a cattleman like Dunson. In nineteenth-century Western society the cattleman and the cowboy were just what their names designated: a man and a boy occupying vastly different economic positions within a ranch's class structure. Their difference was then made legible in the symbolic system governing the social conventions of ranch life. According to Blake Allmendinger's account of cowboy culture, a cattleman valued his ranch hands because of their marginal status as "unattached, deprived single men" (6). Confined to the all-male community of a ranch, and so cut off from the socializing influences of marriage and women, cowboys were given an ambiguous gender identity, not properly male in their gender positioning yet not properly female in their sex. To be sure, from the perspective of town life at least, cowboys were stereotyped as "sex-starved men" who threatened the propertied class and its morality when they rode into town on payday, ready to raise hell, seduce women, and brawl in barrooms (7). But while this assumption of the rowdy, virile cowboy persists, both in nineteenth-century literature and the movies, Allmendinger's point is that the socioeconomic structure of the ranch "transformed [cowboys] into nonmen, partly because they were socially and economically 'powerless'" (67–68).

Ranch culture represented the cowboys' disempowerment in sexual terms that identified them with the cattle they tended, making them an extension of the cattleman's capital (6, 51). For a cattleman's own purposes, the castration and branding of calves twice a year—the task around which a cowboy's livelihood on a ranch turned—was to claim property, leaving scars on the animal (the sutured cut and the burn mark) that inscribed his ownership. Metaphorically speaking, cowboys were likewise castrated and branded because their economic subordination to a cattleman rendered them "sexually nonfunctional," in a word, boys (50). The cowboys' emasculation was regularly acted out in square dances held after roundups. These were often but not always stag affairs, the rituals of which identified a cowboy's gender ambiguity in same-sex partnering (to compensate for the absence or scarcity of women) and mandatory transvestite costuming (taking the female position even when some cross-sex partners were present, cowboys had to wear a "heifer brand," a handkerchief tied around the arm, and sometimes even "ruffled skirts, which they borrowed from women"). Putting the cowboys' marginality on symbolic display in a public spectacle, same-sex dancing and cross-dressing "made them act out in gendered disguises what they experienced, on ranches, as a denied access to power." Such treatment extended to cowboys in town gatherings as well, which used the conventions of livestock castration to reiterate the cowboys' marginality as a means of containing their threatening sexuality in a domesticated environment: dancers were called a "herd"; women, "heifers"; and men, "'steers' or castrated bulls" (66–68).

In response, a cowboy subculture developed its own rituals of manhood that, in "contesting the premise that they were like members of the opposite sex or like castrated men with no gender at all" (55), subverted the codes by which employers diminished their workers' identities as vital heterosexual men. Cowboys turned their castration and branding of livestock into a symbolic disavowal of their emasculation: making an elaborate aphrodisiac rite out of eating a bull's castrated testicles (6), for example, and appropriating the intricate semiotics of the brand's markings to create a lore of spiritual elevation (29), all to celebrate the evidence of their own virility and independence as "uncastrated men who subdued weaker, castrated animals" (56). But that is not to say that cowboys simply reproduced among themselves the rigid man/boy hierarchy imposed upon them by above. Rather, the all-male cowboy society of a ranch was a carnivalesque display of gender mobility, in effect an ongoing masquerade, with a "constant reversing and reassigning of sex roles . . . representations of western male gender were problematic and prone to revision, depending on who was defined as acting out what kind of role" (55). Unlike the mandatory cross-dressing that their bosses forced upon them at public events like a square dance, in his own all-male society, a cowboy's identity ranged across a gender continuum. At one extreme, ranch hands willingly and inconsistently took on "names, roles, and costumes" that represented themselves "as eunuchs or women" when performing functions traditionally designated as feminine, such as cooking; while at the other, these same cowboys often portrayed themselves as "sexually engorged men" (59). Cowboys carried their role-playing off the ranch, as well. Outside of square dances, which held them in check as "nonmen," they consciously used their ranch clothing in town to call "attention to their cowboyishness and quintessential maleness," continuing this masculine masquerade in brothels, where the noise of their spurs, worn even while having sex, gave audible testimony through the very tool of their trade that they were neither steers nor heifers (70).

Whether viewed from the perspective of the cattleman or his hands, nineteenth-century ranch culture reveals how a cowboy was made to identify with the cattle that symbolized his own economic subordination, social marginality, and gender ambiguity. While I don't want to argue for a direct correlation

between Allmendinger's historical analysis of cowboy culture and its representation in *Red River*, in dramatizing the rites of ranch labor, the film does draw
on the symbolic coding of the cowboys' marginal status as "nonmen," their
masculinity subordinated to and negated by the cattleman's economic power.
Even when the film does not follow the structure of ranch culture exactly—
for instance, Dunson carries married men on his payroll, and he himself is
unmarried—this coding still identifies who among the rancher's men are not
proper cowboys, accounting for their exclusion from the drive early on. The
one married man who signs on is the first to die, for example, and the sugar
thief, who accidentally starts a stampede and destroys Dunson's property, is
driven off, his contract voided. More to the point, the terms by which Allmendinger explains how ranch life symbolically enacted the cowboy's emasculation through the castration and branding of livestock helps to identify the
historical materiality of the symbolism with which *Red River* dramatizes
Matthew and Dunson's asymmetrical relation in its branding scene.

In the prologue, when he designs the Red River D logo that will go on the
cattle produced by the union of his bull and Matthew's cow, Dunson calls it
"a mark, a brand to show they're mine too." Now that he is rounding up his
cattle to drive them to a northern market, he wants to take possession of
"every steer, cow, and bull I can lay my hands on," even if they bear the sign
of another owner. Dunson therefore chastises Matthew, who is trying to sort
out stray cattle from other ranches, for disobeying his orders.

> *Matthew:* You're gonna wind up branding every rump in the state of Texas ex-
> cept mine.
> *Dunson:* Hand me that iron, Keeler. . . . You don't think I'll do it, do you?
> *Matthew:* No, I don't.

But Dunson *is* serious. In making this challenge to Matthew, cattleman Dunson uses the branding iron, the tool overlaid with symbolic significance for a
cowboy, to establish his authority as a "man" over his "boy." Dunson equates
Matthew with his own cattle, so that one rump is like another, and all bear the
inscription of his ownership, a brand signifying their castration by his hands:
"So closely associated are the acts of branding and castrating cattle," Allmendinger observes, "that one task sometimes stands in for the other one" (48).

Matthew's own orphaned background, carefully established by the prologue, further helps to explain Dunson's treatment of his cowboy in this scene.
Allmendinger explains that "ties between cattle*men* and cow*boys* . . . were
phrased as bonds between fathers and sons, or as signs of family duty and kin-
ship" (126). But the economics of ranching undercut such a bond; the pater-
nalist rancher fired cowboys when times were bad, and cowboys left for better
paying positions elsewhere when opportunities arose. Cowboy poetry and
song thus imagined a different familial bond, linking ranch hand and cattle
through the figure of the "dogie," the orphan calf that the cowboy both parents

(as nurturer, not castrator) and identifies with (as a fellow orphan and castrato). The dogie condenses both the myth of the lonesome cowboy and the symbolism of his metaphoric castration, since in usage it meant not only "personified children," but also "consumable beef in a western cattle economy" (126–27). That Matthew enters Dunson's life as an orphan, emerging from out of the brush leading his cow, links his youthful figure to the dogie—an orphaned calf, something to be objectified through its possession as well as personified through identification. Dunson therefore makes his threat to Matthew without skipping a beat because, through the scar that inscribes the cattleman's ownership of a cow or a boy to make it legible on the subjugated body as a castration, branding the orphan's rump would signify the cattleman's possession of his dogie before the rest of the cowboys. At the same time, though, Dunson himself bears a scar of his own over his cheek (it does not appear on his face in the prologue but, along with his graying hair and stiff limbs, marks the tracing of age on his body at the start of the main narrative). Given what scarring means to a cattleman, this mark can be understood as a brand too, a sign of Dunson's own subjection to the economic conditions that determine his success or failure as a cattleman. His inability to master capital, which motivates the urgency of the roundup, jeopardizes the economic ground of his patriarchal authority over the cowboys. Hence Dunson must resort to the symbolism of ranch culture to act out his domination of Matthew in the branding scene. Similarly, in the film's climax Dunson does not reconcile with the younger man in Abilene without first putting his mark on his dogie when his bullet grazes Matthew's cheek, this scar confirming the older man's paternity as the condition for adding Matthew's initial to the ranch's brand.[5]

Within the social hierarchy of the ranch, Matthew himself occupies something of an ill-defined position: working the herd with the other men while also overseeing their labor to ensure that they carry out Dunson's orders. Matthew's indeterminate status evokes an analogy to the gender continuum in which a cowboy played out his identity as a mobile, ongoing performance of masculinity. The branding scene establishes Dunson's authority over Matthew by defining him more clearly as another one of the cowboys taking his orders, and the sequence that follows that scene then illuminates how Matthew's being a cowboy actually gives him a position from which to resist the gender code imposed upon his masculinity by Dunson. Matthew engages in a shooting match with a cocky new recruit, cowboy Cherry Valence (John Ireland), and their interaction establishes a new set of terms by which the film will go on to differentiate Matthew from Dunson, depicting the youth as a desirable boy by revealing the ground of his masculinity in performativity and bisexuality.

Most viewers of *Red River* instantly recognize that the shooting match between Matthew and Cherry is homoerotic, making much more explicit what had been the sexual undertone of Dunson's eagerness to place his branding iron on Matthew's rump. Like adolescent boys engaged in mutual masturbatory play, with Cherry leading Matthew into a moment of sexual intimacy ("That's a good-looking gun you were about to use back there," he tells Matthew), they take out their guns ("Can I see it?"), admire each other's equipment ("Maybe you'd like to see mine?"), fondle each other's weapon ("Nice, awful nice"), and then try to outshoot the other with it. (Later Cherry says he joined the drive because he took "a liking" to Matthew's gun.) "They was having some fun," Groot, who has been watching, tells one of the other hands afterward. "A peculiar kind of fun. Sizing each other up for the future. Them two is gonna tangle for certain." But in fact, they do not "tangle," an omission in the narrative that has always puzzled critics of the film.

Because, narratively speaking, it goes nowhere, the exchange between Matthew and Cherry does indeed stand out as "a peculiar kind of fun": an isolated, self-contained moment of erotic spectacle, rather like a number in a musical, during which the two cowboys compare their masculinity and sexualize it through performance, acting out as play the very gender code that makes Dunson inflexible and hard. Not only does Groot watch the two "paw at each other," but he follows the pair precisely because Dunson tells him the shooting will be "worth seeing"; afterward the cook reports on it as a show, "two of the best men with a gun you've ever seen together." Furthermore, just like any duet in a musical, this performance displays the parity of the two shooters, both in their expertise and their admiration for each other. Whereas Dunson's tactic when drawing against Matthew—whether in the prologue, or upon Matthew's return from the war, or the confrontation in Abilene—is always to stare his opponent down, here, as the two cowboys size each other up, the shooting contest grounds their boyishness in their gender masquerade, and then implicates that masquerade in the homoerotic effect of its performance, which stages their attraction to each other: when it is over, we see two men of equal build and coloring, smiling at each other in mutual admiration. Their reciprocal desire negates the aggression and paranoia motivating Dunson's own gunplay throughout the film, and it explains, finally, why these "boys" cannot be "men" by the cattleman's standards—and also why this scene cannot develop narratively into the showdown Groot anticipates.

The detachment of the shooting contest from the narrative development of *Red River* should not detract from its significance for the film. To start with, the scene dramatizes the performativity that defines Matthew as a soft, flexible boy who critiques Dunson's hard, inflexible manhood for disavowing its own reliance on theatricality and spectacle. Dunson's many showdowns with Matthew are all staged before an audience. Like the branding scene on the ranch, each of their confrontations on the drive takes place before the spectatorship of the other cowboys, performed in an area marked off as a stage by the framing of the wagons and the fire, which designates where the two actors stand and the audience sits to watch. In these public scenes, whereas Dunson tries to subdue Matthew—for the cattleman understands masculinity as a demonstration of his authority, meant to objectify and possess a subordinate male—the youth, by contrast, excites desire in his beholder, which is why Cherry takes a liking to his gun and instantly changes from rival to ally, as do the other cowboys, even the two Dunson tries to hang, when they take Matthew's side over the cattleman's.

The theatrical setting of Matthew's steady resistance to Dunson's authority in the mise-en-scène of *Red River* casts their confrontations in performative terms as a staging of their growing antagonism; and it begins to suggest, too, why the cowboy radically differs from the cattleman. From Dunson's perspective the shooting contest merely shows how Matthew has to prove his masculinity to Cherry because it *is* in doubt, as the branding scene has just established. Dunson does not bother to watch the scene himself because, in his eyes, Matthew has nothing more to prove; publicly emasculated, his boy can assert his masculinity only over another boy. However, if the gunplay of these two cowboys establishes their lack of masculinity by linking boyhood (and "emasculation") with "performance," and manhood (and "virility") with "authenticity," then performance is also what ultimately enables Matthew to rebel against Dunson's oppressive authority, which similarly exercises power by theatricalizing it.

Dunson's rigid gender code naturalizes his superiority as a man dominating boys by disavowing its own investment in performance. He nonetheless establishes his command over Matthew in the branding scene by staging a scene of empowerment before all the other cowboys, and he tries to do so again when, before the same audience, he announces his intention to hang the two cowboys who have deserted. "Who'll stop me?" he dares, and this time Matthew accepts his challenge. In effect taking center stage away from Dunson, Matthew coopts the former's authority and the gender code supporting it because he assumes command as a "boy," basing his decision to change course for Abilene, where there might be a railroad, entirely on intuition, a feminizing trait by Dunson's standards, since the cattleman believes only what can be visibly proven and no one can testify to having actually been in Abilene. "He was wrong," Matthew says after Dunson departs. "I hope I'm right and that there's a railroad in Abilene." Thus, even after he displaces Dunson, Matthew still remains a "boy" within the symbolic terms through which *Red River* differentiates them from the beginning. The film continues to trope Matthew's masculinity as "soft" and "feminine"—which is also to say, flexible, fluid, and mobile—in contrast to Dunson's "hard" manliness, only by this point it is clearer that what such an opposition dramatizes is the difference between avowing or disavowing the performative basis of masculinity.

The contrasting acting styles of Wayne and Clift also effectively underscore how performance differentiates the man from the boy in *Red River*. The camera work framing the two stars, not to mention their vastly different body types, visualizes their asymmetrical relation as cattleman and cowboy. Direc-

Figure 30.
Camera setups like the one recorded in this still emphasize
the physical difference between Wayne and Clift.

tor Howard Hawks repeatedly places them in spatial opposition, with one actor standing and the other seated, to establish their lack of parity and also to compose his shots along the diagonal axis indicated by the gaze of one man on the other. My sense is that the two stars rarely occupy the same frame on equal terms until the last shot of them in medium close-up, which gives the false impression of their equal physical stature. When addressing his costar (or any other actor in the film, for that matter), Wayne holds a concentrated stare, the conventional male gaze connoting power. Clift, on the other hand, seldom holds a steady look; even when being addressed, his eyes move about the space implied by the shot to indicate his thinking (what Dunson calls Matthew's "figuring"), as he listens to what someone else says. In contrast to Wayne's stolid, monolithic stance, Clift repeatedly shifts his position, darts his eyes, turns his face, particularly when in the background of the frame and when he has no dialogue. At such moments, the actor gives the impression of reciprocating the nondiegetic spectatorial gaze drawn to him wherever he wanders within the frame. He likewise uses physical gestures to draw attention to his presence in a shot, rubbing his face, caressing his nose, holding his chin, sitting side-saddle on his horse to show his relaxing of tension as the cattle cross the river. When speaking, Clift's delivery of dialogue has a similar effect. He frequently hesitates, shifts his body, or plays with a prop, as if to throw away his lines; or, less often, he lets his words flow out in an inarticulate torrent. As Clift uses his body to rivet attention on his character, his acting implies Matthew's passivity as erotic spectacle and with that, his desirability as a boy who is not a man like Dunson. During Matthew's first love scene with Tess, as they lie together on the grass in the mist, it is Clift who faces the camera, talking rapidly about his emotions, his face alive with movement, and Joanne Dru, angled above him, who watches him with the fixed, concentrated look of desire, her body stable and motionless save for one gesture that articulates her attraction: her finger caressing his lips as he speaks.

In this regard, the shooting contest between Matthew and Cherry accrues even greater importance in articulating the boy's difference from Dunson because it provides the film's diegesis with a scene that takes account of the erotic effects of Clift's performing style. The interplay with Cherry brings out Matthew's own sexuality, thereby negating the previous impression of the boy's emasculation by Dunson in the branding scene. Furthermore, because the performative dimension of his gunplay with Cherry allows Matthew's sexuality to be dramatized, it draws a link between sexuality and performance, suggesting another reason why performance will provide him with a powerful means of disturbing Dunson's oppressive cattleman/cowboy gender hierarchy. The sexual coding of the cowboys' gun "play" manifests the desire that Matthew elicits in his beholder as the fundamental effect of his performativity; and in openly eroticizing Matthew as a desirable boy, the homoerotic overtones of this exchange establish how his desire is bisexual in its address. "It is

not only the 'performer,' but also the 'performance,' which can be bisexual,"
Marjorie Garber observes (*Vice* 142). Because his desirability is based in spectacle, Matthew himself does not act upon desire but excites it in the person
who looks at him, thereby soliciting a male gaze just as readily as a female one.
As a result, Matthew's eroticization through performance implies a bisexuality on his part that repudiates an aggressive male desire like Dunson's. Much
as Cherry leads Matthew into the shooting contest, Tess, not Matthew, takes
the initiative in their lovemaking. In fact, prior to going after him, Tess first
seeks out Cherry, with whom she may have had a sexual liaison, suggesting the
ease with which the two exchange places as Matthew's sexual partner.

Matthew's relation with Cherry reaches no aggressive, climactic "tangle" as
the narrative develops because the proper heterosexual couple (Matthew and
Tess), which *can* be successfully narrativized, replaces the improper homosexual one (Matthew and the aptly named Cherry), which is, by Hollywood convention, unnarratable. As these two successive relations establish Matthew's
rather mobile sexual positioning within the diegesis of *Red River,* their symmetry also supplies the film with a means of containing the homosexual
dimension of his most intense bond in the entire film: his coupling with Dunson. As Mast says of *Red River,* using Hawks's own description of his *El
Dorado* (1967), "this [is a] 'story of friendship, which is really a love story
between two men'" (300). Matthew and Dunson do not act on their love for
each other but Tess herself recognizes how it informs and structures her
relation to both men. She stops the final showdown by forcing them to admit
their love: "Why, anyone with half a mind would know you two love each
other." Her first love scene with Matthew also begins with her realization of
the men's strong bond: "You love him, don't you? He must love you. That
wouldn't be hard." Loving Matthew "wouldn't be hard" because he excites
desire in Tess and Dunson alike. She tells Dunson that, after Matthew left her
to complete the drive, "I wanted him so much that—" and the older man
finishes her thought: "That you felt like you had knives sticking in you." "How
did you know that?" Tess asks, adding, "Well, I suppose other people have felt
that way before." Dunson replies, "They have." While his response alludes to
his dead sweetheart, Fen (Colleen Gray), who made the same declaration
when he left her behind at the start of the film, it could as easily be taken as
a confirmation that he himself feels the same way about wanting Matthew.

Crucial in this regard is the film's insistence upon Dunson's sexual repression as it marks his difference from Matthew's appealing bisexuality. In the
prologue, as Dunson prepares to leave the wagon train to strike out on his
own, Fen begs her inflexible lover to take her along. He will need her sexuality,
she warns, and not only in order to breed the heirs he will someday want. "Oh,
listen to me, Tom," she implores. "Listen with your head and your heart, too.
The sun only shines half the time, Tom. The other half is night." Dunson's
refusal to change his course of action prevents him from hearing what Fen is

telling him about his nighttime desires. While he responds to Fen's speech as if she were describing a separation of fundamental boundaries (day from night, head from heart, light from dark, male from female), what she tries to get Dunson to see is how desire blurs those lines. Unmoved, Dunson leaves her on the wagon train and she dies in the Indian attack that young Matthew survives. When Groot later tells Matthew that the Red River D ranch "cost [Dunson] dear, too—cost him a woman," this kind of accounting names the price the cattleman has had to pay to realize his great ambition: the denial of his own sexuality. That Matthew and not another woman replaces Fen as Dunson's love object indicates the erotic value of the cowboy in personifying the collapse of the dualism on which the cattleman depends for the mainte-nance of his power and his male identity.

The homoerotic undercurrent of Dunson and Matthew's relation has been recognized and yet discounted by most critics. Mast, for example, reads against it through Hawks's auteurism, making their gender difference another example of the director's overturning of sexual stereotypes (302). Donald Spoto similarly casts the Dunson/Matthew bond in auteurist terms, citing Hawks's fascination with "the theme of bonding" as the basis for proposing that the "metasexual affinity" of the two characters makes theirs "a deeper relationship than the men realize, a relationship beyond sex and even beyond paternity and filiation: it's a spiritual need, based on the irreplaceable some-thing that only men can share together" (*Camerado* 210). In a less defensive response, Wexman notices the "homosexual subtext" of the Western generally but, with reference to *Red River*, interprets it "as a developmental interlude in the life of the young man that eventually gives way to a narrative resolution in which these characters are paired off with a woman" (87–88). While this view may follow the ideology governing the generic function of marriage in the Western, it doesn't see how *Red River* problematizes that convention. Instead Wexman herself effectively contains the bisexual desire that Matthew sets into circulation for the film through her own reference to the fifties' psycho-logical discourse of maturation, which rationalized hegemonic masculinity for all men. In her discussion of fifties masculinity more generally, she likewise claims that homosexuality "was rather sympathetically depicted as a normal phase of maturation . . . a developmental problem of a divided protagonist" (169). In other words, a symptom of a boy who is not a fully fledged man.

On the other hand, when Richard Lippe touches briefly on *Red River* in an article on Clift, he begins to recognize what the film stakes on its homo-eroticized man/boy opposition. Mentioning Dunson's proposal of marriage to Tess if she will bear him a son, a biological heir to replace Matthew, Lippe notes, "the offer suggests that Dru's body will provide access through which [Wayne] can indirectly express both his anger and love of Clift, who has aban-doned him" (38). Whereas Wexman believes that the coupling of Matthew and Tess in the closing of *Red River* restores the straightforward heterosexual pairing of man and woman that Dunson originally jeopardizes in the prologue when he deserts Fen, Lippe contends that Tess triangulates Dunson's relation with Matthew. Mellen puts the matter even more directly, stating that the two men are the ones "getting married," with Tess "looking on as if she were the best man" (179).

Lippe's and Mellen's remarks imply why the homoeroticism of *Red River* cannot simply be written off either as that "irreplaceable something that only men can share together" or as a "developmental interlude." Matthew's desirability, the effect of his being a soft boy who is not a man, manifests the important structuring role of bisexuality within the homosocial economy supporting Dunson's hard masculinity. Just as boys and women are equally made the objects of his subjugation, so they are also substitutable as objects of his desire: Dunson gives his mother's snake bracelet to Fen as a love token, and after her death, gives it to Matthew, who gives it to Tess, who then provides the man and the boy with an acceptable means of expressing their desire. Tess's presence in the last part of the film thus allows for the full recuperation of Dunson and Matthew's intense, eroticized bond so that it can be restructured in more acceptable terms as homosocial desire. In fact, Tess literally unites them in the diegesis, stopping their fight to remind them of their mutual love, and confirming that, her own relation to Matthew notwithstanding, the cowboy and the cattleman still comprise the film's dominant couple. Even though Dunson then tells Matthew, "you'd better marry that girl," thereby anticipating the heterosexual union that Wexman emphasizes, *Red River* actually ends with the shot of Clift and Wayne smiling at each other, making the heterosexual pairing secondary in importance to the union of the man and the boy that originally seeded the story—and the ranch.

Ultimately, as I said to start with, the closure of *Red River* appears to reconcile Dunson's and Matthew's opposing masculinities in the name of their resemblance as heroic men, so that, as Lippe also claims, "Clift is a young adult male who represents a *healthy* alternative to the aging Wayne" (39). But the characterization of Matthew as a boy who is not a man can also be seen to resist, in its avowal of the bisexuality and performativity which Dunson represses, the full recuperation of the homosocial gender code that the cattleman diegetically inscribes and that Wayne's persona brings to the film. The closing shot of *Red River* thus does not necessarily guarantee what precise sense audiences can make—and, indeed, historically have made—of the softboy/hard-man opposition and the stars embodying it. For if Matthew connotes the performativity and bisexuality I am attributing to his character, that is because Clift's star persona interacts with the text of *Red River* to the same measure that Wayne's does. Even though *Red River* was Clift's first film (produced in 1946, it was held up for legal reasons and actually followed his second film, *The Search*, into theaters in 1948), the key features of his persona were already operating on his youthful screen image and, as Skolsky's commentary

indicates, inspired "the new look" in screen masculinity. Indeed, Elsa Max-
well, a gossip columnist, reportedly announced after watching a rough cut of
Red River that "Monty had 'persona'" (Bosworth 125). Just what comprised
that persona deserves careful attention.

Clift's "Intensity"

On the surface, as Lippe points out, Clift's characters tend not to deviate all
that much from "the traditional expectations of what constitutes a 'real' man."
In other key films such as *The Search* (1948) and *From Here to Eternity* (1953),
the Clift character is as principled, courageous, and determined as Matthew
is in *Red River*, "embody[ing] traits which are societally perceived as being expressions of a masculine strength" (37). One of Clift's biographers explains
that the star's "obsession with acquiring exaggerated machismo" as a cover for
his own sexual ambivalence made him self-conscious of how he appeared on
screen. He chose parts that allowed him to parade his virility and he resisted
using words or mannerisms stereotypical of homosexuality, going so far as
to demand a retake of a scene in *The Search* because he unconsciously referred
to child actor Ivan Jandl as "dear" (LaGuardia 71).

Nevertheless, Lippe believes that Clift's persona broadened the period's accepted definitions of masculinity, because, in direct contrast to the type of
"primitive masculinist moral code" that Wayne embodies in *Red River*, a Clift
character "doesn't display negative masculine strength—the Clift persona isn't
authoritarian, aggressive, brutish." As important, Lippe continues, echoing
Mast, Clift also displays many "feminine characteristics" which identify him
with the screen's treatment of women: he is passive, silent, reflective, emotional, fallible, vulnerable, and, most of all, masochistic and victimized, "subjected
to bodily pain [when he undergoes a physical beating, as in *Red River* and *From
Here to Eternity*] because he has defied a masculinist authority figure." This
side of Clift's persona, which *Red River* brings out in Matthew's softness, adds
an important "neurotic dimension" to his screen presence, "undercutting an
idealized hero-figure image." Furthermore, when amplified by Clift's intense
on-screen bonding with other males, it implies a bisexuality that the films
themselves, regulated by the dominant social and sexual ideology of the time,
leave undeveloped. The feminine, neurotic, bisexual qualities connote the boyishness of Clift's persona on screen; and his distinctive performing style, which
appears to inscribe upon his diminutive body symptoms of its own disturbing
interiority, then makes this boyishness appear as a deliberate criticism of whatever verbal approvals of machismo a script puts in his character's mouth. Lippe
therefore concludes that "the Clift characterization seems to offer almost contradictory personas: he is portraying the personification of the 'average' young
adult male but simultaneously he is, and Clift's presence encourages this

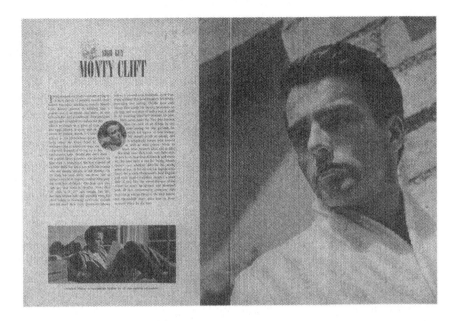

Figure 31.
Postwar "sigh guy" Monty Clift.

reading, decidedly 'different'" (37–38). In one of Clift's later films, *The Young Lions* (1958), Hope Plowman (Hope Lange) describes the shy, insecure, and fumbling Noah Ackerman (Clift) to her father in terms that try to articulate this difference: "He's gentle and he's clever. He's not just a man—he's a boy."

Fan magazine articles promoting Clift in the fifties clarify more exactly what his star presence connotes as his decidedly different persona interacts with his film characterizations. A 1949 one-off magazine album entitled *Movie Glamour Guys* included the new young star in a section entitled "Sigh Guys":

> The denizens of Hollywood are trying to wrap a sheath of mystery around their hottest box-office attraction, moody Monty Clift. Rumor persists in labeling him a poseur and a sourpuss, but none of this criticism has any foundation. The gossipers just haven't troubled to analyze the guy who is as simple as a plate of ham and eggs. Monty is quiet and reserved by nature, which is a hindrance to his tremendous popularity since he won't bend to ordinary rules to which the stars are subjected. . . . (4)

Here Clift's mystery and moodiness, the effects of his nonconformity, connote "a poseur," someone playing a role, but underneath he is "as simple as a plate of ham and eggs," which is to say an ordinary Joe; at the same time, driven by his integrity, he refuses to follow the ordinary rules of stardom, which consequently reinstates the pose and the mystery. Particularly in the way that performance is implicitly made the key to penetrating but also intensifying Clift's enigmatic personality, the more authentic self hidden by the star persona (and the "sourpuss" label), this excerpt summarizes how the fan magazines in general elaborated upon Clift at the point of his greatest popularity (that is, from the release of *The Search* and *Red River* in 1948 to *From Here to Eternity* in 1953).

In 1950 *Modern Screen*, for instance, also glossed Clift's posing and mystery as the proof of his integrity as an actor. As this article explains, he may show up on the set looking like "a derelict," wearing "a pair of tattered blue jeans, a T-shirt and a jacket full of holes," but when he puts on his "suave, elegant" period costume for *The Heiress* (1949), Clift is completely transformed. Likewise, he battles over scripts and directors because in contrast to older, established actors he is not interested in making money but instead has "artistic conscience" as his primary goal. Furthermore, because he disdains the exhibitionism of Hollywood, "Clift's insistence on maintaining his integrity has been the despair of publicity men." While he says he likes girls, he refuses "to drag any particular girl I like into the spotlight by talking about her to reporters." At the same time, his popularity keeps putting his private life under scrutiny. After starring in only three films, "his fan mail is second to none in volume (and probably intensity) and exhibitors everywhere will tell you he's an actor who attracts more profit than even their popcorn machines." Thus, *Modern Screen* concludes in its tag to this article, "Hollywood accepts Monty Clift's individualism. It's the only way they can have him." Significantly, while the article means to appreciate his individualism, it interprets Clift's difference from mainstream Hollywood through his youth, calling him "a barefoot boy" in the opening paragraph to pit his integrity against his inexperience, so that his sixth-floor walk-up flat in New York City, sloppy dress, and wreck of a car—the possessions of a rebellious youth flaunting his lack of conformity to middle-class values—are an "embarrassment" to his studio and associates. But is the "derelict" look of the "barefoot boy" really all that different from the "suave, elegant" period costume worn in *The Heiress*? Each is equally performative; and that this young man is a "barefoot boy with shows on," as the article's title playfully puts it, has the ultimate effect of collapsing Clift's youthful "lone-wolf" true nature into his performativity as an actor (Charles 137–38).

Robert LaGuardia reports that, early in his career, Clift actually fabricated "the true story of his life" for the kind of articles described above. "He gave them an elaborate construct, an honest picture, not of himself, but of the sloppy, bohemian World War II veterans filling New York's acting classes. . . . The image was powerful, as interesting to read about as to see, and it was Monty's own creation" (75). While this anecdote may appear to show how Clift skillfully manipulated the media to protect his private life, it seems to me to offer greater testimony of what the fan discourse emphasized in its descriptions of the intensity with which he blurs the difference between actor and character when working on a film. In effect, the fan discourse turns LaGuardia's point about "Monty's own creation" inside out, showing that, far from maintaining the integrity of his private identity in contradistinction to his posing, performance supplies the *only* ground of authenticating his identity, regardless of whether it is factual or fabricated.

At the height of his success in 1953, Clift himself stated to Maxine Arnold in *Photoplay* that he was perhaps "too transparent" (87). His comment sought to dispel the legends, many apparently started by himself, that had quickly sprung up around his eccentric and reserved behavior, but it is also a quite telling (if not intentional) revelation about what performativity means to his star persona. As Arnold explains of this "maverick," "I had come to realize that for Monty to put down *Prewit* or any other character in whom he's currently embodied is psychologically impossible" (52). Transparency, this is to say, does not result in Clift's transcending a part; on the contrary, it confirms the actor's fusion with whatever persona he adapts for a film role (or an interview, for that matter). Every new role submerges him further in the performance as a result of his intensity, which the fan discourse appreciates as the proof of his integrity, both in himself and in moviegoers. Small wonder that *Modern Screen* said his fan mail was second to none in intensity! "He's also one of the most intense people," Arnold comments, quoting costar Deborah Kerr in support: "Such intellectual purity, Monty's. His mind is so clean and uncluttered—like a very pure flame inside him" (87). Clift's intensity, the source of his integrity as an actor, causes him to disappear into his roles so completely that, Kerr continues, "You have the strangest feeling he's actually experiencing the scene." The effect of Clift's performing with such intensity, director Fred Zinnemann concurs in this article, is that "he gives the feeling he isn't even acting. That he's just being himself" (89). In a later *Photoplay* article on Clift, writer Richard Gehman similarly notes how "his ability to concentrate, to lose himself in a part and yet maintain an individualism which pervades his acting, is the envy of every performer who has ever worked with him" ("Flight" 35).

The fan discourse on Clift reverses the customary relation of mask and person, of theatricality and authenticity, that operates in accounts of a traditional star like John Wayne, who is made to epitomize the absolute clarity, stability, coherence, and above all else, the naturalness of masculinity in the American male. This persona, however, was not without its own problematical basis. As Wexman points out, Wayne's personal life belied the media's portrait of him as the exemplary American because he spent the World War II years "establishing his image as a fictional war hero" on screen, instead of serving in the military, emphasizing the gender performativity that authenticated his powerful postwar star image as America's supreme patriot (74). Likewise, in the early 1950s, Wayne and his second wife, Esperanza, engaged in a messy and much publicized divorce that revealed, not only his adultery and abusive behavior, but his own emasculation at her hands as well. As newspaper headlines about his being "woman-handled" summarized his legal defense that he, not she, had been the victim of abuse in their marriage, this loaded phrase implicitly caught both the fictiveness of his unimpeachable male screen image as a "man's man" and the streak of misogyny that supported the suspicion of women and all things associated with femininity—like the Hispanic women whom he romanced and married in private life, or the boyishness of his young male costars, beginning with Clift—that underwrote his virile screen presence.[6]

Wayne's star persona succeeded in fusing his own offscreen identity with his film roles, thereby obscuring the significance of his much less admirable private life on the meanings attributed to his conservative masculine image, because he repeatedly denied his performativity as an actor. "I don't try to act," the star told Sidney Skolsky, repeating what he said in many of his interviews, "I re-act" ("Hollywood" 1953). Obviously, Wayne's considerable stature on screen depends upon his theatricality, too (after all, he *says* he plays to men and boys), particularly his deployment of the specific star signs that connote "John Wayne" from film to film: his large size, his sturdy walk, his clipped speech, his quick draw with either a revolver or a rifle, his cavalry costume. But taking him at his word when he says he does not act, the fan discourse collapses the difference between his performing and his being, noting, for instance, how his "personal mannerisms"—such as the particular way he lights a match by flicking it with a fingernail, his own "slow, husky drawl," his own "rolling, shambling gait," all "show up on screen unchanged" as the mannerisms, speech, and walk of the various characters he plays (Scott, "John" 28).

What authenticates Wayne's virile persona in the fan discourse, then, is not his biography, which the fan discourse appears to draw on with its references to his origins in the industry as a prop and stunt man before he became an actor, but the lack of artifice in his professionalism, which purifies the troublesome biography. Guest spots on television programs during this period (such as the two-part episode of *I Love Lucy* in which Lucy Ricardo steals Wayne's footprints from the forecourt of Grauman's Chinese Theater) reproduce the performance style of his films within the diegesis of a fictional narrative that itself confuses the private identity of a star with his persona, to further reinforce the impression that he transcends "acting." At the same time, though, such appearances as "himself" reiterate his value as a star to fans like Lucy, thereby reinvesting his personal traits with their performative value for the movies.

In Clift's case, the fan discourse refers to the star's intense screen performances, not his private life, using his dedication to his craft to authenticate his personality as a rebel male youth: "sensitive, forthright and possessed of great independence of spirit" (Steele 78). Clift's integrity and intensity—the traits repeatedly evoked by the fan discourse to summarize both what distinguishes him from the traditional movie star (to make him different) and what authenticates his persona as genuine (to make him appear more ordinary, by cutting through the layers of Hollywood pretension)—also erase the line separating star performance from star authenticity but for a much different effect than in the comparable example of Wayne. For Clift, the qualities of integrity and intensity make "acting" and "being himself" equivalent terms, as the syntax of Zinnemann's comment reveals. One accounts for the other as its origin, and their equivalence turns him into a cipher, which then causes the fan magazines to reinscribe his indecipherability as his most authenticating feature. "[T]here will always be two points of view about Montgomery Clift," Arnold remarks, "that of those who know him and that of the many who in all probability will never understand him" (87). This explanation of Clift's enigmatic nature produces the kind of contradictory characterization that Lippe describes, and the fan discourse repeatedly evokes the star's intense integrity as its principal means of obscuring its own demonstration that Clift's authenticity is, in the final analysis, performative.

Although the fan magazines always refer to Clift's psychological complexity, articles written at the very height of his career do not explicitly address the neurotic dimension that Lippe claims is so central to the star's significance in breaking with traditional expectations about masculinity. However, following Clift's near fatal car accident in 1956 while making *Raintree County* (1957) after a three-year absence from the screen, the fan discourse more explicitly began to unravel the enigma of "this complex, fascinating personality" by reading it symptomatically: "Clift seems to be faced with the choice of growing up or cracking up" (Gehman, "Monty's" 59, 87). At this point in his career, too, the star's immaturity, made manifest in a host of neurotic symptoms, explains "his inability to form a permanent, lasting relationship with any woman approximately his own age" (85). Since gossip also suggested a link between his wasted appearance and his private life as an unhappy bisexual, the more pronounced neurotic dimension of Clift's persona as "a tense, confused, young man" (59) underscores even more strongly the levels of masquerading which had originally enveloped his integrity and intensity as a performer. One anonymous actress, who confesses that she always gets crushes on her leading men, confides that she could never get close to Clift while working with him: "He uses his acting as an excuse for living" (Gehman, "Flight" 110).

Even more significantly, at this point Clift's intensity as a performer, once the hallmark of his (implicitly masculine) integrity, became more explicitly feminized. "In acting instinct, intuition, and intensity," *Photoplay* quotes Eva Marie Saint, Clift's costar in *Raintree County*, "he is the equal of some of the great female stars" (Gehman, "Flight" 109). With the fan discourse's feminization of Clift's intensity, neurosis replaces integrity as the key trait focusing the contradictions that his persona had previously raised. For example, *Photoplay*'s 1958 account of "Hollywood's Most Shocking Rumor" appears to allude to scandalous details about Clift's tumultuous private life—his nervous breakdowns, his alcoholism, his drug addiction, his bisexuality—but the rumor "most shocking" to Hollywood turns out to be "accounts of [his] tottering antics" during the troubled production of *Raintree County*. With a frail, drug-addicted Clift no longer recuperable as a purist battling writers and directors over artistic achievement, *Photoplay* first infantilizes him as an irresponsible boy to start with and then, in conclusion, feminizes him as a diva. An editorial note prefaces the story with this statement: "Says writer [Cameron] Shipp, I am now convinced after ten years of writing about Monty: He's as unconcerned about being a problem as a boy with a toad in his pocket" (75). In the article itself, as Shipp confidently predicts that the star will, as he has in the past, surmount his difficulties to continue his career, the writer equates Clift's persona with a performance that will vary but never end. "On his endurance record," Shipp explains, "Clift is tougher than he looks. Like Judy Garland, he will—I am persuaded—go on for many years staging apparent collapses, disappearing, but always rising again to perform better than ever" (87). The comparison to Garland repeats the collapse of authenticity into performativity that had always been central to the Clift persona. Furthermore, when we recall the significance for fifties fan discourse of Garland's deviant female body—frail, overweight, unstable, stoned, in short, resistant to studio control—it helps draw attention to what the earlier fan discourse had repeatedly circled around through its allusions to the "intensity" of Clift's performativity but without being able to address directly, namely, Clift's own deviant body as a beautiful, bisexual young male.

It seems clearer in retrospect that all the attention in the fan discourse to the enigma of the "tense, confused, young man" was in fact alluding to the gender masquerade that covered up his private life as a bisexual. A 1950 piece in *Photoplay* reports that, all the while Clift was filming *The Big Lift* (1950) in Berlin, "he was called a lot of contradictory things; 'a shy, modest, retiring sort of guy,' 'an egotistical fraud,' 'a very warmhearted generous man,' and 'an anti-social snob.'" According to this article, "exactly three people really got to know him": his driver, his secretary, and his housekeeper (Leiser 43–45). As each witness reports on the authentic Clift underlying his contradictory star image, they reiterate the integrity, the lack of pretension and ceremony, and the reserve that were the offscreen incarnations of his principled, introspective screen characterizations. At the same time, through these revelations, the article reinstates the mask that it claims to dislodge. For company he hangs out with "some GI companion"; while on the way to the studio, "Monty would speak wistfully of a girl back home and the driver overheard the word 'marriage' pop into the conversation more than once"; "because of his lack of pretension," he earned the respect of the various technicians and artisans who worked on the film, "and a good many of the GIs and airlift guys," too (89).

One does not need to know of Clift's own bisexuality to read between the lines, sensing the displacement of one performance (temperamental star, Hollywood poseur) by another (GI Joe, average American).

However, such masquerading *was* a constant factor in the lives of fifties gay men, as Clift's biography dramatizes, and it helps to explain why his star persona, with its great dependence on constituting an "ordinary" masculine identity in performance, so readily yields a queer subtext. According to Jack Babuscio, "intensity" encodes the emphatic theatricalization of stardom that is central to the gay following of performers like Garland, whose "popularity owes much to the fact that she is always, and most intensely, herself" (46). In Garland's case, as in Clift's, the star's "intensity" also dominated the fan discourse's effort to define her difference years before her offscreen collapses then added the neurotic dimension that forced a revision of her earlier MGM persona (Staiger 166–67). For this reason, what Richard Dyer says in explanation of Garland's attraction to gay male fans applies almost equally well to Clift's persona. While originally "the image of heterosexual family normality" in her MGM musicals, as revelations in the fifties made evident, "[t]o turn out not-ordinary after being saturated with the values of ordinariness structures Garland's career and the standard gay biography alike" (*Heavenly* 159). Whereas, with the termination of her contract at MGM and the disclosure of her addictions and breakdowns, Garland's fifties persona retrospectively and abrasively counterpointed her difference off the screen to her ordinariness on it, Clift's persona overlays the two through the performativity that keeps displacing his authentic identity in the name of his intensity, on screen as well as off. Whether we see him in the fan discourse as a rebel posing as GI Joe, in the film criticism as a neurotic posing as a healthy, youthful alternative to John Wayne, or in the biographies as a queer posing as a straight romantic lover, the point is still that such masculine masquerades straddle the line between being ordinary and being different. The Clift persona, in sum, swings both ways.

With this claim I do not intend to evoke Clift's biography as my own means of authenticating his persona in the ultimate "truth" of a private life that was fully disclosed to the public after his death. Rather, I am claiming that unmistakable intimations of bisexuality in his star persona were already legible in the fan discourse's repeated attention to his intensity and performativity. In its repeated allusions to "the mystery of Montgomery Clift—for, without exaggeration, Clift is an enigma" (Gehman, "Flight" 108)—the fan discourse evokes the ambiguous sexuality that he brought to his film roles and that became synonymous with his portrayal of male youth. For instance, in her *Photoplay* article on Clift, Arnold portrays the star as being feminine and boyish without ceasing to be masculine: "He has strength which belies his boyishness," and yet is himself undeniably boyish in his "lyric strength," which combines a masculinizing "tough mind" with a feminizing "tender heart" and a "kid-like zest and eagerness to explore" that "[draws] children to him like a Pied Piper" (87, 89). When the fan discourse engenders Clift's persona as masculine *and* feminine in this way, it attributes to his boyishness an androgyny that invests his performativity with a bisexual resonance.

Perhaps, as Gerald McCann proposes, the fan discourse's concentration on his integrity and intensity alludes to what is now recognized as Clift's groundbreaking representation of "the 'new' kind of man for the 1950s; a man who refused to make judgments on sexual preference" (47).[7] More likely, given the censorship and gentlemen's agreements that determined the fan magazines' reticence to out a big star at the time, the characterizing of Clift through his intensity reveals how his persona was primarily legible in the fifties as giving body to a reflexive, narcissistic masculinity poised—and, I cannot help adding, *posed*—between agency (his own active desire) and passivity (his costars' and his fans' desire for him). The discomfiting ambiguity that results from such equipoise gives his persona its strong intimations of bisexuality, "of being simultaneously all-desiring and all desired" in a "heightened performative state" (Garber, *Vice* 140). Consider a comment Richard Gehman makes in *Photoplay* about Clift's acting: "The intensity he brings to each role is, at times, terrifying to his colleagues, some of whom feel that each part he plays takes a severe toll of his nervous system. He has a rare charm; men and women alike are attracted to him in large numbers" ("Flight" 35). Insofar as Gehman first finds Clift's intensity "terrifying" and disabling, and then links it to the star's attractiveness to both men and women, I don't think it is stretching things to conclude that "intensity" functions in the fan discourse as a code word, elliptically referring to—by substituting for—his eroticized, neurotic body and the ungovernable, unnamable bisexual desires it excites in his viewers, whether in the cinema auditorium or the diegesis of a film.

If, as Garber states, "'bisexuality,' which is difficult to pinpoint 'in life,' is perfectly recognizable as a performative mode" (*Vice* 142), then the bisexual performativity structuring Clift's persona is what determined his value—in the fan discourse and, hence, in the star system as a whole—as the representation of a boyishness different in kind from the seemingly unproblematic, literally straightforward masculinity of an older star like John Wayne. "Montgomery Clift is the most motile subject this writer has ever interviewed," Joseph Steele commented in an early *Photoplay* article, adding, "he is all over the room, slouching, sprawling, shifting, stirring" (78). The motility of Clift's body, which his screen presence continually emphasizes in his characteristic performing style and the fan discourse interprets as the primary sign of his burning intensity, epitomizes the way his persona exceeds the strict heterosexualization of male desire as active, aggressive, and in complete command of the gaze. Clift's persona consequently identifies him as a boy who is not a man because he represents masculinity as a condition of unorthodox desiring. As Steele's description suggests, the desiring subjectivity Clift at once embodies and solicits through his "motile" body is not only performative but sexually indeterminate in both its origin and its aim, hence, bisexual in its implied effect as well.

A Place in the Sun: Performing Desire

Of all Clift's films, *A Place in the Sun* gave his star persona its fullest, most powerful and memorable expression on screen. George Eastman (Clift) embodies the inarticulate longing of working-class youth, what the film's trailer refers to as "a boy fighting for his place in the sun." However, the film itself depicts this boy's ambition through a melodramatic romantic triangle. While having an affair with coworker Alice Tripp (Shelley Winters), George meets the girl of his dreams, wealthy Angela Vickers (Elizabeth Taylor), who desperately wants to marry him. When Alice discovers she is pregnant, George can either do the right thing, forsaking Angela and forfeiting his place in the sun, or find some way of getting Alice out of the picture. Although Mellen does not even mention this film, as compared to its source, Dreiser's *An American Tragedy,* *A Place in the Sun* aptly demonstrates her contention that fifties Hollywood cinema interiorized social dissent to focus instead on male sexuality. More importantly, the film shows how the boyish persona of a young star like Clift was also the means, not only of effecting this thematic transformation, but of disturbing the narrative containment of the male desire that structured it.

George's desperate, romantic passion for Angela obscures the social factors that produce his driving ambition, but it does not strip them away entirely to leave in their place a romance in which cinematic style replaces social content, as Clift's biographers charge (LaGuardia 87, Bosworth 181–82). Director George Stevens's use of Clift in the film's opening is particularly important in this regard, both in condensing social commentary and in mediating it through the star's persona. Following the credits, which have rolled over a shot of Clift standing with his back to the camera, the star turns to show his face, the camera moving in for a long close-up of his contemplating look. In this first shot of Clift, what had already become the trademark rebel uniform of the new star—leather jacket (a high-school club emblem apparently removed), grayish white T-shirt, dungarees—marks George's position in the working class, just as George's contemplation and costume evokes Clift's star status as a "poseur" exciting the intense desire of his fans, male and female.[8] A reverse shot then identifies the object of George's contemplation: a roadside billboard featuring an attractive girl in a bathing suit—not too unlike Elizabeth Taylor in appearance—to advertise the swimwear that his uncle manufactures. George's ambition to rise above his working-class status, signified for him by his mother's life as a kind of Salvation Army missionary, depends upon

his getting a job at his uncle's factory. The billboard displays the economic relation of sexual desire and consumerism that supports the affluent postwar
society to which George seeks admission: his uncle's world (and not Angela
herself) is presumably the place in the sun toward which he aspires. Then a car
horn sounds, and George turns around as Angela speeds past him in her convertible. He watches intently—and it is not clear whether he is admiring her
or her automobile—as she becomes an elusive, blurred object in the distance.

That image of Angela driving away in her expensive convertible predicts
how the film's entire mise-en-scène supplies George with a landscape of sexual
desire that overwhelms his social ambition. Angela appears in her flashy car at
many points in the film. Particularly when contrasted to the clumsy, older one
George drives with Alice, the convertible signifies Angela's mobility, modernity, affluence, and most of all the freedom her social position gives her to act
on her own desire in a way that George himself cannot. The car's distinct horn,
moreover, sounds remarkably like the oboe repeatedly playing on the film's
soundtrack in later scenes to signify George's desperate longing for Angela,
and it is a fitting correlative. As George sits in his darkened room after listening to a radio account of a drowning, which inspires his scheme to solve the
problem of Alice's pregnancy, Angela signals her unexpected arrival outside
his boarding house by hitting her horn. The familiar sound interrupts his
reverie and also gives materiality to what Clift himself has only implied about
George's emotions in his silent close-up. Similarly, in almost every scene set in
his rented room, the Vickers sign lights up the night through the window as if
to visualize the desire motivating George's actions. In like fashion, when he
takes Alice out rowing with the intent of drowning her, the rippling water of
Loon Lake can be seen reflected in Clift's eyes, and the editing keeps reverse
shots of Shelley Winters to a minimum in order to concentrate on the background's absorption into George's conflicted, inarticulate emotional state.

The film even makes the diegesis a reflection of his subjectivity when
George himself does not formally focalize the narrative. He admires a tweed
suit in a clothing store window, indicating his intention to buy it so that he will
be properly attired when he goes to his uncle's house later that evening, and
this image dissolves into a shot of his wealthy cousin, who closely resembles
George, adjusting his black tie in a mirror. At another point later in the film,
after a phone call to his mother while at his uncle's party, Angela takes George
into the ballroom, and over a montage of the couple dancing is superimposed
a shot of Mrs. Eastman tenderly caressing the telephone. In these dissolves
George's desire is not object oriented but a potentially uncontainable condition
of desiring that, in its self-consuming negation of his individuality, evokes
the fan discourse's discussions of Clift's own intensity as a performer who
disappears into his roles so completely that he ceases to act, "he's just himself."
However, far from internalizing the external world through his ego, as Robert
Kolker suggests (74), George rather appears to disappear into it. As George

Stevens repeatedly positions Clift in relation to the mise-en-scène to achieve the effect I am describing, the diegesis functions as a mirror expressing George's desiring better than he can. "If I could only tell you how much I love you," he moans to Angela, "if I could only tell you all." "Tell momma," she croons, cradling his face in her neck, "tell momma all." Commentators on Clift use this dialogue to show how Stevens exploits "[the star's] image as a man in search of a mother" (LaGuardia 91), underlining the boyish immaturity of the sexuality he projected. However, I think *A Place in the Sun* invokes this aspect of Clift's sexual persona to make an even stronger point about George's passion for Angela: like an infant's for its mother, his desiring exceeds a stable subject/object relation, casting it in the performative mode of bisexuality.

To be sure, in the direction, camera work, and editing of *A Place in the Sun*, Stevens exploits the radiant, erotically charged appearance of teenage Elizabeth Taylor, focusing her image through Clift's gaze as a means of inscribing a traditional heterosexual male position of desire fixated on a spectacular female object. But Stevens also uses Taylor to register how George's desire for Angela disrupts that traditional positioning of heterosexual male desire

Figure 32.
The lobby card for *A Place in the Sun* incorporates the tight close-ups
of Montgomery Clift and Elizabeth Taylor into its ad design.
Note the frames at the top left.

around a stable voyeuristic gaze. Revealing the intended prominence of gazing in *A Place in the Sun*, biographer Patricia Bosworth reports that during rehearsals Stevens often had Clift and either Taylor or Winters first run lines for him, after which he made them act out the scenes "without speaking—just looking at each other" (183). Even more tellingly, Bosworth mentions that, in coaching Taylor on her role, Clift sometimes "would demonstrate by acting the part of Angela Vickers himself" (186). Within the film, the repeated presence of Angela's convertible in the mise-en-scène suggests how her own desire for George is a reflexive metonymy of his; and so does Stevens's repeated use of extremely large close-ups to structure the lovers' private encounters. As George and Angela each become increasingly excited by the sight of the other at his uncle's party, soft, tight close-ups of Taylor's face initially set her apart from the fuller, sharper ones of Clift's, marking her as the object of his desiring gaze. However, once George declares his love for her the next time they go out, their close-ups become perfectly symmetrical in size, and one beautiful, similarly featured face becomes almost indistinguishable from the other. In a cinematic corollary to what the fan discourse describes as Clift's intensity, the tight camera work and shot/reverse-shot editing visualize how George's desire is reflexive in its aim, entirely bound up in his being desired by Angela.

While the most famous moment in *A Place in the Sun*, this love scene's depiction of George's reflexive, narcissistic desire is not an isolated one. George's great passion for Angela cannot be easily differentiated from his solicitation of desire in everyone who looks at him, beginning with his uncle, who first notices him working as a hotel bellhop and ultimately promotes him to management so as to "keep a closer eye" on him. The factory girls whistle at George as he walks by them his first day on the job; while at work Alice eyes him; so does Angela as she stops to watch him playing pool by himself at his uncle's party. She asks why he is so aloof and alone: "Being exclusive? Being dramatic? Being blue?" She repeats her comment a few moments later but, significantly, omits the second possibility, though George's performativity—both in action (he's an expert at pool) and in impression (he's decidedly different from the other young men in Angela's class)—is clearly what drew her gaze, causing her to stop in her tracks and enter the room to look at him more closely. According to Bosworth, "[Clift's] cruising sexual swagger (which Brando and Dean picked up on)," while actually held for only a few moments on film, serves to underline an almost complacent sense of his own beauty. "Few audiences in the 1950s were aware of the meaning of that androgynous swagger" (214), but Angela herself certainly catches it. When George says he may not be able to take his vacation at her family's summer house on the lake, she declares that she will wait outside the factory every evening and pick him up in her convertible: "you can be my pickup." Despite his passivity, which makes him do what anyone asks of him—his mother, his uncle, Alice, Angela, finally the law and the church—one cannot underestimate how frequently

George's apparent willingness to capitulate to another's desire is actually a means of soliciting it through performance. As Angela puts it to George, when commenting on how her parents are starting to like him, "You've worked them over with your boyish charm."

Significantly, when George goes on trial for Alice's murder, a crime he planned but did not commit as intended, his unsuccessful defense rests entirely on the immateriality of his desire, its distinction from action. "The boy is on trial for the act of murder, not for the thought of murder," his lawyer tells the jury. "Between the idea and the deed there's a world of difference. And if you find this boy guilty in desire but not guilty in deed, then he must walk out of this courtroom as free as you or I." On the stand, after George explains how, although he had planned to murder Alice, her death by drowning was an accident, his lawyer asks him to "solemnly swear that it was an accident undesired by you." By contrast, District Attorney Marlowe (Raymond Burr) bases his prosecution entirely on the incriminating fact of George's desire: the youth's deception, first in concealing his affair with Alice, then in covering his tracks as he began to carry out his plan to murder her on the lake. "Isn't it a fact," Marlowe charges in cross-examination, "that every move you made was based on a lie?" This accusation determines Marlowe's entire prosecution. George's lawyers try to persuade the jury that, while he wanted Alice to die, it was purely an unconscious desire on the young man's part. Marlowe, on the other hand, asks the jury to see George's desire made manifest in action (his deception), thereby portraying it, to turn around the defense's own term, as a kind of unaccidental desiring. As George's lies anticipate and, according to Marlowe, authenticate the prosecution's account of what happened on the lake, they supply the evidence that proves the youth's guilt by virtue of their performative value.

After George testifies, in a very dramatic (and overplayed) performance of his own, Marlowe brings a rowboat into the courtroom and goes on to direct him in a reenactment of Alice's death. Marlowe stages the performativity of George's desire in order to prove its materiality as evidence. The prosecutor's reasoning implies, first, that George's desire only acquires its authenticity before the eyes of the law as an event through its performance, which makes it legible as action; and second, that, since the action on trial in this case is George's deception, the performativity enabling him to desire is tantamount to a sexual masquerade. Even before the trial Marlowe indicates that his prosecution will take this direction when he interviews the Vickers family. He pointedly asks them, "And none of you knew this boy was leading a double life?" The question clearly intimates that the sexual complications of George's life, as he tried to keep one relationship secret from the other, required him to masquerade as a serious lover of each woman. George, in other words, just wasn't playing straight with them.

I don't want to exaggerate what Marlowe's phrasing may imply about George's double life, but I don't want to ignore it either. Obviously, George's

Figure 33.
At the trial the prosecutor directs George (Clift) in a reenactment of Alice's death in order to stage the performativity of the boy's desire.

desire is characterized as heterosexual; but the secrecy of his affair with Alice, which enshrouds their sexual relation in deception even before he becomes involved with Angela, nevertheless has a transgressive resonance because it has to be kept in the closet, so to speak, forcing him to lead a double life. Because his uncle forbids dating among employees, their trysts evoke comparison to the furtive encounters of homosexual men in the fifties: meeting in the darkened auditorium of a movie theater, in the shadows of a deserted parkway, and most often, in the confined and cramped quarters of a dingy rented room.

The characterization of Alice, moreover, poses something of a problem for the film which is also related to what I am getting at. Given that she and George begin dating out of loneliness and that he seduces her after he tricks his way into her room, why does she end up exerting such a hold on him? George is not in love with her; and he is skillful enough at manipulating Alice (after all, he persuades her to go out boating with him on Loon Lake despite her great fear of water) to suggest that he might have found other solutions. Why couldn't he have convinced Alice to return to her family farm to have the baby—as the doctor she consults about an abortion advises her to do? or have asked his uncle for money to buy her off? or even sold his car to get the funds for that purpose? To compound the weight of Alice's demands on George, Shelley Winters's performance makes her "so horrifyingly, naggingly pathetic," Pauline Kael recalls, "that when Clift thinks of killing her he hardly seems to be contemplating a crime: it's more like euthanasia" (462). However, when one reads Alice *as if* she were a male lover and George's "double life" *as if* it were concealing an implicit bisexual desire, then it may be much more understandable why he cannot end their relation easily and cleanly, how she can blackmail him with the threat of full exposure to the newspapers, and why his only solution is to contemplate murder. The full implications of George's "double life," in short, explain why his sexual history with Alice is so transgressive for the narrative that it gives the impression of stain or contagion—as Kael intuits—which George needs to eradicate from his sexual past in order to preserve his sense of being "decent," decent enough to be worthy of Angela's love.

Obviously, such inferences have to go against the intent of George Stevens and his screenwriters, but they nevertheless do help to account for the contradiction in *A Place in the Sun* when the film makes George innocent, because the killing only existed in his mind as a desire, while condemning him to death at the trial because of that desire. To motivate this ending, the screenplay has to bend over backward to convince audiences that George is not an innocent boy unjustly condemned to death for wanting his place in the sun. With George awaiting execution in the electric chair, a priest urges him to confess. George replies: "I don't believe I'm guilty of all this. But I don't know. And I want to know." The priest then urges the convicted man to look inside his heart. "Perhaps you've hidden the truth even from yourself," the priest says. "There's one point in your story that holds the answer to what you are looking for. . . . Who were you thinking of just at that moment [when the boat capsized]? . . . Were you thinking of Alice? Were you thinking of that other girl?" George does not answer, but he doesn't have to; music swells on the soundtrack, and the film's romantic theme supplies the missing piece of the puzzle. "Your heart was murder, George," the priest concludes, and George accepts this verdict. When Angela comes to his cell to take a last farewell, he informs her, "I am guilty of a lot of things, most of what they say of me." The apparent conclusiveness with which the priest gets George to admit the guilt that justifies the law's pound of flesh tries to make his desiring determinate; the priest's extralegal verdict thus effectively seals over what the trial itself reveals about the performative ground of George's desire. This conclusion still rings false, though, because it cannot explain why his intense passion should have been justifiably condemned simply because he showed too much "undesired" desire—that is, unless we realize what his desire fully implies about the crossing of sexual as well as social boundaries.

What I am proposing is not at all inconsistent with the status of George's desire in *A Place in the Sun* because the film exploits Clift's star persona to pull against the incoherence of its ending. Particularly in the closing section, *A*

Place in the Sun shapes its view of George's desire in much the same way that the fan discourse constructs Clift's persona through the star's intensity as a performer. In his interview with George, the priest, trying to sound the depths of the young man's heart, sounds remarkably like the fan magazine articles when, in their own quest to answer the mystery posed by Montgomery Clift, they use the star's intensity to authenticate the performativity of his persona. But then the entire trial gives this impression. While in jail awaiting the trial, Clift's costume—the same white T-shirt and dungarees worn in the opening—and the framing of his diminutive, vulnerable body behind the prison bars evoke the performativity of his youthful rebel posture in the fan discourse. George's lawyers, moreover, are "sold" by his story, as one of them puts it, because his sincerity functions as Clift's integrity does in the fan magazines; it convinces them that George is not a poseur but an unaffected youth, mistakenly accused of being a maverick simply because of circumstantial evidence. Before calling George to the stand, in fact, one of his lawyers identifies him to the jury as "the only one who knows the truth, the whole truth," just as the fan discourse turns to Clift. Finally, the effect of Marlowe's prosecution in using George's performance in the courtroom to authenticate the latter's desire as an incriminating deed makes essentially the same point as the fan discourse's revelation that Clift's authenticity as an intense actor lies in his performativity.

Perhaps most importantly, *A Place in the Sun* ends with quotations from its own erotic imagery that overlays the narrative closure with unabashed visual references to Clift's star persona. As George hears the priest say that murder was in his heart, the film dissolves to a slow-motion replay of the tight close-up of Clift and Taylor, their faces moving as they kiss. This screen memory then dissolves to Angela's unexpected appearance in George's cell, making one wonder if her presence has in fact been provoked by his desire. After he con-fesses his guilt to her, she declares: "All the same, I'll go on loving you." Like the visual quotation of the love scene, her response renews the open-endedness of George's desiring, establishing a counterweight to the closing determination of his guilt. As George marches to his execution, the film quotes from his love scene with Angela a second time, the slow-motion imagery of Taylor and Clift kissing now superimposed over a close-up of the latter's face, which moves progressively toward the camera, filling up the screen. On this image *A Place in the Sun* ends, dissolving into its final title and the Paramount logo, and effectively displacing the closure of the narrative through its reiteration of Clift's star persona.

A Place in the Sun goes much further than *Red River* in exploiting what had already become, only three years after that Western's release, Clift's iconic status as the personification of desiring youth—"rebelling against his fate without knowing how and questioning why"—which explains why "*A Place in the Sun* was tremendously relevant to the youth of the early fifties" (Morella and Epstein 58). The success of the Stevens film transformed Clift from "teenage idol" to "the most important young star in the movie industry" (LaGuardia 91), and it pretty much established the basis for Hollywood's treatment of its new young stars for the rest of the decade, too.

Why Can't Boys Be Men?

The framework that Skolsky invokes in his *Photoplay* article, which opposes "manhood" to "boyhood" to describe the asymmetry of old and new male stars like Wayne and Clift, evokes a long-standing tradition in American culture of securing the position of hegemonic masculinity by representing it as the top of a generational hierarchy. Historically speaking, for Skolsky's readers in the late 1950s his reference to grown men as "boys" had a more timely resonance than usual because, just more than a decade earlier, the term had signified all the young men who had been forced to find their manhood in the Second World War. For instance, when interviewing people for his oral history of the war, Studs Terkel found that "'Boys' was the word invariably used by the combat-protagonists of this book. The references were to enemy soldiers as well as our own" (3). On both sides of the battlefield, many of these soldiers were literally boys who never became men, so the term "boys" evoked innocence and loss as well as immaturity and lack. But while the war years saw the radical disruption of the culture's understanding of a male youth's normal transition into manhood, the referential field named by the category of "boy" was by no means unique to a postwar mentality.

The opposition of boys to men, central to the gender hierarchy of ranch culture, was just as significant for the middle class in nineteenth-century America. According to historian E. Anthony Rotundo, Victorian culture likewise believed that if a male was not a man then he had to be not like a woman, but "like a boy" (20), wild, impulsive, lacking in self-control. A visible "boy culture" differentiated young males from the domestic sphere of women and girls on the one hand, and the public sphere of adult men on the other. Yet because the term did not correspond to an actual age group, but included school children, adolescents, college students, and bachelors, "boy" was also an indeterminate gender category functioning, through its absorption of all the male "vices," to regulate the masculinity of "grown" men. More than just the period in a young male's life when he wore short pants and knickers and caused hell in the neighborhood, boyhood was a "time of transition . . . [which] was variable in length and loose in the definition of its boundaries. This period of flux, when it received any name at all, was called youth. It began in a boy's teens and lasted until his twenties or even thirties"—until, that is, the time when a young man had earned a stable place in his chosen profession, married, and begun a family (56). By the end of the century, however, the revised definition of masculinity stressed the continuity of boyish impulses and manliness. As a result, the categories of man and boy, and their distinct social spaces, converged (256–59). The former opposition of manhood to womanliness and boyhood shifted, with the third term no longer male youth but male homosexuality (276–79).

In the fifties, since the meaning of what counted as "manhood" had further changed in accordance with the shifting configuration of U.S. society following the end of World War II, the "boy" condensed all those earlier meanings and became even more of an indeterminate gender category. The term was regularly invoked, as in Skolsky's *Photoplay* article, to critique grown men who failed to live up to the culture's standard of hegemonic masculinity. "If adult masculinity was indistinguishable from the breadwinner role, then it followed," Barbara Ehrenreich reports,

> that the man who failed to achieve this role was either not fully adult or not fully masculine. In the schema of male pathology developed by mid-century psychologists, immaturity shaded into infantalism, which was, in turn, a manifestation of unnatural fixation on the mother, and the entire complex of symptomatology reached its clinical climax in the diagnosis of homosexuality. . . . Fear of homosexuality kept heterosexual men in line as husbands and breadwinners; and, at the same time, the association with failure and immaturity made it almost impossible for homosexual men to assert a positive image of themselves. (*Hearts* 20, 26)

The 1950s boy who was not a man differed from his 1850s counterpart because the marked implication of homosexuality—laid out, as Ehrenreich suggests, by the clinical discourses of the social sciences to legitimate the domestic mystique—linked an inability (or unwillingness) to conform to hegemonic masculinity more explicitly with sexual deviancy, thereby interpreting a "boy's" social transgression, which marked his difference from men, as a form of male impersonation: a gender masquerade concealing his inability to perform his proper social or sexual obligations as a "man." It is in this context, too, that "boy," could so easily be used to reinscribe a racial hierarchy among men.

At the same time, particularly given Kinsey's revelation that a male reaches his sexual peak during his teen years, the fifties "boy" also personified the nation's promise and potential, the very antithesis of *Look*'s fear of a declining manhood, especially in times of a hot or cold war. Boyishness may have connoted the deviant social position of an incomplete man, regardless of his actual age, but it also had an undeniably attractive quality, fostering the postwar youth culture and exciting the admiration of the grown men who were not boys themselves. In *Mister Cory* (1956), the title character (played by Tony Curtis) is a busboy at a resort who moonlights as a gambler while posing as a man of means in order to impress Abby Vollard (Martha Hyer), one of the rich guests. After Abby introduces Cory to her father, the latter observes: "Seems like a nice boy to me." Abby, however, feels obliged to correct dad: "He's *hardly* a boy." But Mr. Vollard then explains: "Sweetheart, anyone under forty is a boy to me." In his indeterminacy, the fifties version of the "boy" registered the ambivalence with which postwar culture insisted upon the breadwinner ethic of hegemonic masculinity. A "boy" personified not only the failure to achieve manhood but also the price of a man's maturity: youth, "anyone under forty" and still unmarried, able to move with relative ease through the social strata with all the fluidity and masquerading of a "Mister" Cory.

The new stars of the fifties were read through this double-sided lens in both the fan discourse and the Oedipal narratives Hollywood fashioned for them to promote their "new look" as boys. Although the obvious intent was to represent the new stars as inchoate men, the effect of their appearing to be "either not fully adult or not fully masculine" was to implicate their rebel personae in the same gender masquerading that informed the construction of Clift's. In the case of the new young male stars who succeeded Clift as teen idols, the fan magazines' authentification of their private lives inevitably tried to replace whatever seemed untamed and uncommon about them in their screen imagery with a more conventional and safer persona that conformed to expectations about hegemonic masculinity—and, as I want ultimately to argue, that also tried to suppress what Ehrenreich suggests were the homosexual overtones of their failure, as boys, to live up to those expectations.

Recognizing the inevitable, that "the 'rebel' craze is here to stay," *Photoplay* at first criticized "this new 'heel worship'—this worship of all that is rebellious, unconventional, rude, even brutal." However, the magazine went on to show, the authentic "truth" behind the rebel screen image reveals another side to the teenage public's fascination with the new stars:

> But the admirers of this whole school of young "rebels" overlook one fact: While Presley, Brando, Mineo, Dean and the others are idolized for appearing to fight against society and authority, in their private lives every one of these young men is a complete conformist. They are hardworking, church-going and home-loving, ambitious for fame and success. In other words, in their personal lives the rebellious feelings which they share with all young people have taken the perfectly acceptable and even admirable form of working hard in order to become the masters rather than the victims of their environment. It is unlikely that any of them would ever be found in a screaming mob of young people, working themselves into a frenzy, while reaching for a torn scrap of an idol's clothing. Each one of these young men, in fact, has an amazingly deep sense of responsibility toward his family and friends, and their rude or shocking behavior is reserved strictly for the occasions when they are in front of a camera or a microphone. (Lane 121)

Like the fan articles on Clift, in showing how a fundamental respect for the breadwinner ethic of hard work and family values lies beneath the surface of the new stars' nonconformity, this piece substitutes one masquerade for another. The teaser headline summarizes in big capital letters the legerdemain which the article tries to achieve: "THE REBEL HEROES—ON-STAGE SHOCKERS, OFF-STAGE SOFTIES" (58). Only with this kind of reasoning can the article then accommodate the impact of Elvis Presley, to cite just one of its examples, describing his politeness, sincerity, and respect for his mother to counter how, as one fan says in a quoted letter to the magazine, he "demonstrates a wild, free emotion" when he performs. What this article therefore "exposes" is that Presley's boyishness ("he is no child," the fan continues, "yet he still is not an adult" [59]), no less than that of all the other young rebel stars, is a gender masquerade realized only through performance, since this pose, particularly disturbing given its borrowings from black singers, is so bound up in its theatricality, "reserved strictly for the occasions when [he is] in front of a camera or a microphone" (121).

In his article on the stars' "new look," Skolsky follows the same recuperative strategy, ostensibly to show how "the rebel has been cleaned up—literally." New stars such as Anthony Perkins, Sal Mineo, Paul Newman, John Kerr, and Ben Gazzara prove how "the leather jacket brigade"—"a new mob of boys" on screen that addresses "a new one in the audience"—is a masquerade, with their outward defiance of authority concealing an inward readiness to conform. This "group of actors," Skolsky contends, ". . . are intelligent, sensitive, confused; but in reality [their] weakness is their strength. . . . The new movie heroes may not be as rugged as the old favorites, but most of them are smarter. They fight their battles in the mind, not by slugging it out in dirty T-shirts." To prove that these boys, all of "similar cut, from the standpoint of individualism and nonconformity," are actually neophyte men, Skolsky goes on to describe, in case after case, how their private lives follow the standards of the hegemonic professional class: these young men have gone to or are attending college and "their education shows" in their seriousness and intelligence, not to say in their laundered, properly fitted Oxford shirts (111–12).

In closing, though, Skolsky repeats the ambivalence with which he first describes these young stars as "boys who'd like to be men." He qualifies his recuperation of "the new look" by suggesting that "smarter" may not necessarily be more virile. He asks: "Who, in the new crop, is strong enough today to lift a woman into romance? Got you stumped, huh?"[9] To formulate his question, Skolsky has to discount the erotic overtones of the new stars by attributing their sex appeal to performance, not charisma. Going for the most likely target in 1957, Skolsky also emphasizes Presley's theatricality in order to point out its lack of authenticity. "Don't be fooled, Elvis is a natural actor, and he is always acting. He knows what he's doing every second of every wiggle. Elvis studied Jimmy Dean. He decided to be Dean with a guitar and a song." As Skolsky describes it, the result is rather like a musicalization of Clift's persona even more than Dean's: "Elvis, in his act, closed his brooding eyes and shook his body—sent himself—when he sang." Skolsky ignores what Elvis's "always acting" may imply about the significance of his smoldering star presence: a narcissistic sexual performance that, far from being "natural," is a "carbon copy" of what was already a copy. Instead, the columnist claims that, while the star's performance may encourage his fans "to rebel against their parents for him," Presley himself "is a model son, who obeys his parents" (112). Skolsky's comments about Marlon Brando, "the first of the modern movie heroes," likewise seeks to domesticate this star's "mumbling, brooding, scratching, sexy, and confused" image of boyish masculinity. In his persona ("A moody, introspective type that was hardly calculated to set hearts fluttering") and widely imitated performance style ("he produced a new model and they soon began coming off the assembly line"), Brando "cleared the road for the others." "While the pack was following," however, Skolsky reminds his readers, "Brando grew up and matured. He visually went from T-shirt to a tuxedo," and even "joined the ranks of the business-actor," confirming that a change of clothes is easily what makes the proper man (111).

Brando, however, *did* "set hearts fluttering," his body functioning even more blatantly on screen as a sexual objectification of spectatorial desire than Presley's wiggling or Clift's intensity. With a career whose brilliance, notoriety, inconsistency, and longevity rivals that of every other major film star from any period of Hollywood's history, Brando has perhaps been analyzed more thoroughly than any actor to emerge from the fifties, with the exception of Marilyn Monroe. But, particularly in the light of Skolsky's challenge to find a new star who appeals to a female audience, it is still worth examining how the fan discourse of this period initially characterized Brando, like his rival Clift, as a boy masquerading as a man, and to see what role performativity and bisexuality play in this depiction.

Brando's "Authenticity"

Throughout the fifties, Brando made good press because—from his publicized refusal to wear ties and jackets and even to wash regularly, to his practical jokes on and off the set, to his pet raccoon Russell, to his temperamental dedication to his craft, to his pseudointellectualism, to his interracial love life—he flaunted his nonconformity. The fan discourse contained his rowdy offscreen behavior by situating his persona against Rock Hudson's. As paired opposites, Brando and Hudson came to personify, respectively, the "dangerous" and "safe" sides of youthful male sexuality (Klinger 99, 104–16). Profiling Hudson in *Photoplay* in 1957, for example, Joe Hyams wanted readers to see that "[u]nlike Rudolph Valentino, who was the sex-boat of his day, Rock Hudson is not the lover type. He has sex appeal, but his older fans want to mother him. Young girls want to marry him, and men want to emulate him" ("Rock" 90). Brando, by contrast, *was* "Hollywood's New Sex-Boat," as Hedda Hopper exclaimed. "Is sex appeal his secret?" *Time* asked, following up on the kind of coverage given to Brando by the fan magazines. To answer, the magazine quoted a producer ("No doubt about it. . . . He's a walking hormone factory") and an exhibitor ("He's the Valentino of the bop generation, and he's bringing the kids back to the movies"). Noting his nickname, "The Slob," as well as his difficult, abrasive manner, *Time* went on to conclude: "He is a hit with the ladies . . . despite the fact that (as one of his girls panted) 'he does things to you in public that you hardly expect even in private.' Still, as a lover boy, Marlon is almost more sinned against than sinning. Many women find it hard to keep their hands off him" ("Tiger" 58–59).

Today we may remember most the difference between Brando, the quintessential fifties Method actor, and Hudson, the quintessential fifties Hollywood fabrication, too easily forgetting that, despite their contrasting personae in the fan magazines as sexboat and pureboy, they were comparable in value for the star system as eroticized young men. Hudson was the perfect male pinup, not only for his big, strapping, muscular body—"and an eye-pleasing shape it is," an anonymous editor of *Photoplay* commented ("Meet" 43)—but also for his handsome face.[10] Hyams reported in *McCall's:* "Bud Westmore, his make-up man, says the main trouble with Rock's face is that it is almost too pretty. Westmore has to put in character lines, whereas he has to take them out with most other stars" ("Why" 85). But Hudson's was not the only pretty new face on the block. With his "intensely male and vital" appearance (Hopper, "Hollywood's" 108), the young Brando was also something splendid to look at. According to his acting teacher, Stella Adler, "It wasn't difficult for a professional to see that he showed a good deal of promise. For one thing there was his great physical beauty—not just good looks, but that rarer thing that can only be called beauty" (Jacobi 91). Brando also easily enough met the beefcake requirements of *Photoplay*'s "Hollywood men of muscle," showing that he could compete with the likes of Rock Hudson in the same photo spread when the occasion demanded: "Marlon Brando (5'10", 170, 42", 30") scored his most sensational hit in a thoroughly torn shirt, and his toga in 'Julius Caesar' grants an excellent view of the bulging Brando biceps" ("Meet" 43).

In their comparable status as muscular pinups, Hudson and Brando marked the poles of the continuum along which the fan discourse defined the erotic appeal of the other new stars as boys fashioned in their respective images (Dean and Newman in the mold of Brando, for instance, and Tab Hunter and John Gavin in the mold of Hudson), which explains why the considerable differences of these two star personalities could so easily be collapsed through pinups on the pages of *Photoplay*. Hudson was a big man—so tall, in fact, that he was supposedly self-conscious about his size, which reportedly made him keep readjusting his actual height from article to article ("Meet" 43)—but he was still read as a "boy." His boyish star image was narrativized in the many melodramas he made during the first decade of his career at Universal-International; and his successful casting opposite the older Jane Wyman in his star-making parts in *Magnificent Obsession* (1954) and *All that Heaven Allows* (1955) underscored the actor's youthful appearance on screen all the more. Brando similarly connoted immaturity on screen since he played on the "adolescent beauty and pathos" (Naremore, *Acting* 205) of characters who are actually much older in *A Streetcar Named Desire*, *The Wild One* (1953), and *On the Waterfront* (1954). Moreover, the actor's well-publicized nonconformity was taken as evidence of his own immaturity. "I emphatically won't go along with those who say Marlon is eccentric," Adler was also quoted as saying about her most famous pupil. "He's high-spirited and full of fun—perhaps a little reckless at times, true— but he's always been very young and I don't particularly see where this makes him so different from millions of other American boys" (Jacobi 90). Other articles described him as a "child of nature" (Berg), "the theatre's 'brilliant brat'" (Bacon), "a strange boy" (Parsons, "Marlon"), "a grubby Peter Pan" (Hopper, "Hollywood's" 108), "Bad Boy Brando" ("Tiger" 58).

More importantly, Brando was characterized as a boy through the psychological profiling that, in stressing a neurotic dimension similar to Clift's, made his immaturity conform to the etiology of homosexuality as understood in the fifties: the gender confusion of a sissy boy resulting from an overdominating mother who had jeopardized her son's identification with his father.

> First, like all great actors . . . he was born with an abnormally keen sensitiveness to everything around him. He felt things more deeply than his sisters. He reacted more violently than they did.
>
> Secondly, being a boy, Marlon naturally tended to identify himself with his father. But Mrs. Brando, being the dominant force in the family, pulled him in the opposite direction. She made it almost impossible for him to develop a sense of security about being a man.
>
> All his life Brando has oscillated between the polar attractions of his parents and has had a difficult time finding out what he, himself, is. (Zolotov, 20 Jan.: 18–19)

Brando appears to have actively cultivated this understanding of his oversensitivity in the mid-1950s for two reasons. First, it was consistent with his legal defense when Twentieth Century-Fox sued him for breach of contract in 1954. At the time, his own psychoanalyst described him as "a very sick and mentally confused boy," a phrase which the fan discourse then recycled (Zolotov, 27 Jan.: 22). Second, after he starred in *On the Waterfront* (1954), playing a boy who is himself pulled between identifying with masculine and feminine authority figures, Brando made a point of publicly disentangling his persona from the character of Stanley Kowalski in *A Streetcar Named Desire*, which had launched his career on Broadway and in the movies, and would continue to supply the iconography of his screen image throughout the decade.[11] The mainstream press and the fan magazines alike quoted Brando's repudiation of the Tennessee Williams character: "Why, he's the antithesis of me. He is intolerant and selfish . . . a man without any sensitivity, without any morality" ("Tiger" 60). Attributing his "realization that he was hiding behind Kowalski's anti-social personality . . . to the hours spent with an analyst" ("Temporary"

43), these interviews stressed that, when "he put on as his own the personality which belonged to Stanley Kowalski in 'Streetcar,'" he had been wearing a mask (Ager 24).

Both the suggestions of sexual ambiguity, arising from the fan discourse's revelation of Brando's oscillation between male and female "attractions," and of gender impersonation, drawn from his insistence that the public's long-standing identification of him with Stanley Kowalski was the product of a masquerade on his part, were important in crystallizing the dimensions of bisexuality and performativity that shaped Brando's fifties persona in the wake of *Streetcar*, despite the competing impression, still current today, of the transcendent authenticity with which he personified masculinity in his acting. "Looking at Brando in a movie," Cecelia Ager wrote in 1954, "the screen vanishes, Brando vanishes, acting vanishes, and there's nothing left between you and the naked truth" (33). Four decades later, in a piece inspired by the actor's autobiography, Harold Brodkey repeats this refrain: "he asserted that he was *playing a role*. But to me it seemed that Brando was only playing himself, in an autobiographical epic about an American soul. . . . Brando taught me something about maleness . . . Brando is a self-invented, one-character actor who does the separate selves in himself as characters" (80–81).

However, although Brodkey's italicizing of the phrase "playing a role" should underscore the point for him, the critic glosses over the extent to which, even in the fifties, Brando's celebrated naturalness signified the theatricality of his acting, not as technical expertise, but as the ground in which he performed "maleness" and wore it on his body as a masquerade. Brodkey's own description of the actor's performance in *Streetcar* responds to this theatrical dimension, just as it registers what director Elia Kazan called "the 'bisexual' effect of Brando's image" (Naremore, *Acting* 194). "I am not discussing Brando's androgyny," Brodkey explains. "I take androgyny for granted in everyone. But Brando took over the vanity and posing and sheer willfulness of a good-looking woman and developed a deconstructed version—an anti-version of a diva's romantic sexuality. He gave it a male twist, using the rigorously male energy of his director, Elia Kazan" (82).

If Brando taught male fans like Brodkey "something about [their] maleness," the lesson had to do with the theatricalized, indeterminate sexuality underlying his macho posturing as Stanley, which focused on his body as the crucial prop of this masculine masquerade. *A Streetcar Named Desire* made Brando's physique a central element in his personification of youthful male sexuality for the fifties, most famously when, his wet T-shirt clinging to his body and torn open to reveal the expanse of his muscular back, Stanley Kowalski (Brando) summons his visibly aroused wife, Stella (Kim Hunter), back to their apartment following a violent quarrel. According to the fan discourse then and now, in this scene Brando "made the torn undershirt a symbol of male virility" (Zolotov 6 Jan.: 15). With its obvious contrast to the gray flannel

Figure 34.
Brando, the torn T-shirt, and THE scene.

uniform of hegemonic masculinity, Brando's torn T-shirt appeared to signify a more authentic expression of "pure" masculinity: "He stands for everything that is primitive and untamed in the masculine psyche and that will survive in spite of a repressive and ordered society" (Spoto, *Camerado* 141).[12] In effect, this view follows the sympathetic perspective of Stanley's victim, Blanche Du-Bois (Vivien Leigh), whose warning to her sister, Stella, "Don't hang back with the brutes," is confirmed when Stanley rapes Blanche, enacting what Tennessee Williams himself described as "the ravishment of the tender, the sensitive, the delicate by the savage and brutal forces in modern society."[13]

Actually, Kazan's film version of *A Streetcar Named Desire* takes a much more multilayered view of Stanley. Competing with Blanche's recognition of the threat that his "brutal" masculinity poses to her fragility, a recognition tinged with repressed attraction to his body, Stella's open avowal of sexual desire for her husband, like her appreciation of her sister's desperation, structures the film through her conflicted viewpoint. Stella pointedly tells Blanche, who seems shocked that her sister would want to return to Stanley after the previous evening's violence, "I wish you'd stop taking it for granted that I'm in something I want to get out of." Even before we get to see Stanley, Stella points him out to her sister, asking, "Isn't he wonderful looking?" After showing Blanche his photo—and caressing it as evidence of the affect his physical appearance causes her to feel—Stella then confesses that Stanley excites her so much that "I can hardly stand it when he's away for a night. . . . When he's away for a week, I go nearly wild."

Stella's desire for Stanley, more than his rape of Blanche or the latter's promiscuity, is what forced Warner Bros.—following protracted negotiations over the shooting script that involved the studio, Kazan and Williams, and the Production Code Administration—to censor *Streetcar* before releasing it. After viewing the completed film and meeting with the Legion of Decency, PCA official Jack Vizzard wrote to Joseph Breen:

> The clue & key to fixing this picture lies in the character of Kim Hunter—Stella, who is married to Marlon Brando. Generally speaking, there is no problem with the man, nor the rape. . . .
>
> But Joe, a very strange thing has happened. In concentrating on our two leading characters, with whom most of the problems lay, we completely missed what this bastard Kazan was doing with Stella. It is so vivid & clear now with the picture all edited & polished & strung together as to be almost unbelievable. . . . The result is to throw into sharp relief in the finished film the purely lustful relationship between Stella & Stanley, that creates a totally different impression from the one we got when we saw it.[14]

The censors' attention focused in particular on the scene when Stanley bellows his wife's name and, her body visibly shaking with excitement as she pushes Blanche away, Stella leaves Eunice's upstairs apartment to join him in the courtyard below. Without consulting Kazan, to avoid Legion of Decency condemnation, Warners agreed to cut several lines of offensive dialogue at various points throughout the film and, more notoriously, to shorten, re-edit and rescore this particular scene for the theatrical print, eliminating close and medium shots of a sexually excited Kim Hunter in favor of "several long-shots, to get away from the very sexy 'register' on the countenance of Stella as she returns to Stanley."[15]

Even though the tamer version (the only one audiences saw until the director's cut was finally released in 1994) plays down Stella's desire for her husband by minimizing Hunter's close-ups and entirely cutting the sight of her body undulating with desire before she begins her slow walk down the stairs, the substitution of shots does not disguise the eroticization of Brando's body; the long shots actually heighten it because they keep the bodies of both actors in the image. Thus, despite the cuts, the imagery of Brando clinging to Hunter in his revealing torn T-shirt, which supplied the art for the film's publicity as well as the iconography of his star persona, cannot be easily extracted from the gaze that finds his body so desirable and, for that reason, problematizes its received meaning as an image of authentic, primitive masculinity. (Indeed, that Brando's "primitivism" is no more than a masquerade is Billy Wilder's very point when he parodies this scene from *Streetcar* in one of his hapless hero's daydream fantasies of being sexually desirable and potent in *The Seven Year Itch*.) Stella not only objectifies Stanley whenever she looks at him in *Streetcar,* but he himself acknowledges the female gaze and uses his body to solicit it, thereby jeopardizing the conventions by which a Hollywood film typically secures the heterosexuality of its leading man. When Blanche finally meets her exciting brother-in-law in the flesh, her gaze as she eyes his entrance into the apartment is made as emphatic as his because of matching medium close-ups of Leigh and Brando. As if to flaunt his awareness of Blanche's attention, Stanley removes his sweaty T-shirt and, before replacing it with a clean one, turns toward her in an unashamed display of his lean, damp, muscular chest. Whereas in *A Place in the Sun* the bisexuality and performativity of Clift's persona are internalized as "intensity" through repeated close-ups of his desiring face, in *A Streetcar Named Desire* similar elements of Brando's persona are externalized in his eroticized body, which, far from authenticating his masculinity, theatricalizes it as a series of poses much in the manner that Brodkey describes. *Life*'s coverage of *Streetcar* even demonstrated Brando's emotional range by featuring a series of photographs that literally pose him "in expressions of gluttony, childish grief, anger, annoyance" ("Movie").

Given the posturing in the characterization of Stanley, it is important to notice how Kazan frequently emphasizes the exciting boyishness of Brando's physical appearance in *Streetcar* too, as when, dressed like a dead-end kid, Stanley returns from the garage the morning after his fight and reconciliation with Stella, his grinning face framed by a cap and streaked with grease.

Blanche, moreover, calls Stanley "a boy" whenever she flirts with him or refers to his boorishness, moodiness, and inability to understand her feminine wiles. Sexy *and* boyish produce a cocksure pose that qualifies Blanche's reduction of Stanley's physicality to mere brutality (though he *is* brutal, to be sure) by using the body to exaggerate the posturing of male youth, as crucial for Stanley's swagger and bluster as it is for his pretensions and naiveté. For Stanley, masculinity is highly theatrical. He likes colored lights when he and Stella make love, and he pulls out his silk pajamas for special occasions, like his honeymoon night or the birth of his child. A similar flair for performance motivates his display of boorish manners and the unexpected violence with which he then clears the table by breaking dishes after Stella scolds him for making a pig of himself at Blanche's birthday dinner. Strictly speaking, Brando's masquerade in *Streetcar* is not, as Brodkey imagines, a deconstruction of "a diva's romantic sexuality," because Stanley does not mimic and invert the binary terms (truth/illusion, realism/magic, naked/veiled, primitive/civilized) by which Blanche gentrifies her own sexual desire as a feminine masquerade. Rather than appropriating the posturing of femininity, Stanley's masculine masquerade draws on the narcissism and aggression that, in openly sexualizing his body—whether the effect produced in his audience is desire or fear—give it the homoerotic impact of a boy posing as a "man."

Brando's costuming in *Streetcar* is also especially important in emphasizing that performativity and sexuality interact to make Stanley legible as a boy whose masculinity impersonates maleness in its various postures. David Shipman points out how comparison of stills from the stage and film versions of *Streetcar* "demonstrates the extent to which [Irene] Sharaff redefined the 'slob' image, rendering it more powerful, individual, sexy" (54). The sweaty T-shirt and blue jeans, far from being the random attire of someone who does not care how he looks, is actually a "look" (as it indeed proved to be for Brando) arranged by a famous designer to produce a calculated effect, both dramatically and cinematically, in the way it veils and exposes the male body with the kind of attention conventionally given to costuming a female star. Figure 35a (left) illustrates how the T-shirt and jeans comprise such a costume; and as just one of a series of wardrobe tests released as stills to promote *Streetcar*, it also records how his different costumes (not only the T-shirt but his suits, work clothes and pajamas, too) keep modifying Brando's appearance in the film to underscore the performativity of his body as the setting for Stanley's masculine masquerade.

Figure 35b (right), another publicity still, shows how Brando's body is incorporated with the torn T-shirt costume to convey the eroticism of Stanley's masquerade. His "cruising" stance here is a product of several interrelated elements in the photograph: the sexual narcissism implied by Brando's face as it solicits a viewer's gaze; the pronounced theatricality of the photograph's lighting, which emphasizes the torso and darkens the face in shadow, as if Brando were standing under a streetlamp; and the pose itself, which pushes the body into the light, where details of Brando's chest, revealed against the white T-shirt, are set against the density of his pelvis and crotch, the contrast breaking down the male figure into zones of erotic interest. That Brando's body is in a relaxed state, moreover, brings out the sensuality of its musculature, not its phallic tightness; the raised arm with the cigarette pushes the pectorals forward, while the thrusting hip makes the line of his body appear loose and shapely, like a woman's only in the sense that the photo celebrates this body, too, as a sexual object. The pose draws on studio conventions of female and not male portraiture, but there is nothing in Brando's stance to suggest effeminacy. On the contrary, the whole point of this photo seems to be to eroticize his virility.

Both stills of Brando typify the performativity and erotic objectification that cohered around his persona because of *A Streetcar Named Desire*. Even when Stanley is most brutal and violent, Brando always appears to be impersonating his virility rather than embodying it, which is why he registers as a boy, his gender masquerade implying, too, though more obliquely in the film than in the photographs, the bisexual shadings of his eroticization. Although later films do not blatantly eroticize Brando to the extent that *Streetcar* memorably does, there, too, his performance style links his masculinity to a gender masquerade through his body. Indeed, for a star who is remembered as epitomizing the naturalistic performing style of Method acting, what is remarkable is the extent to which, with a tendency "to hide behind changes of accent and makeup" (Naremore, *Acting* 196), masquerade turns out to be the central motif of Brando's career. "In this respect, Marlon is a real ham," Adler observed. "He loves to fool around with make-up, putty, false noses, beards and wigs. And he has a wonderful ear for inflections and accents, along with a natural gift for mimicry" (Jacobi 91).

For most writers on the fifties, the moment from his films that summarizes Brando's impact as a young rebel star challenging traditional masculinity occurs in *The Wild One* when Kathie (Mary Murphy) asks Johnny (Brando) what he is rebelling against: "What have you got?" he replies. Far more telling to me is her earlier comment that Johnny resembles her father: "He's a fake—like you." Unlike other stars of his stature, Brando radically changed his look from film to film, often relying on dramatic displays of makeup, costuming, and diction. His fakery is most obvious when he plays a Mexican in *Viva Zapata* (1952), Marc Antony in *Julius Caesar* (1953), a biker in *The Wild One*, Napoleon in *Désirée* (1954), a Gene Kelly styled song-and-dance man in *Guys and Dolls* (1955), an Asian in *The Teahouse of the August Moon* (1957), a German in *The Young Lions* (1958), or a Brit in *Mutiny on the Bounty* (1962)—but that about sums up his entire output during this period! "Most of the time," Brando was quoted as saying about his performance in *Désirée*, "I just let the make-up play the part" ("Tiger" 65). While meant to be dismissive of this film,

Figures 35a and 35b.
Publicity photographs of Brando in his costume of T-shirt and jeans
used to promote *Streetcar*.

if taken as a recognition of the theatricality of his performance style, his statement aptly summarizes how all his characterizations are, to varying degrees,
inflections of a deliberated masculine masquerade. Even *On the Waterfront,* his
performance most celebrated for its authenticity, has this dimension. While
critics have focused on the subtext indicated by small, improvisational gestures, as when Brando takes Eva Marie Saint's glove and puts it on his hand
during their first long talk together (Naremore, *Acting* 193–94), what strikes
me about his acting when I watch this film is its more calculated use of performance signs centered on his body: the way he acts with his make-up (a scar
cutting into his right eyebrow as evidence of his boxing days) and costume (the
plaid jacket) as effectively as with his stooped posture, anguished facial expressions and soft, mumbling voice, all this theatrical fakery exceeding the
naturalism of Method acting's psychological subtext.

Brando is still the new male star of the fifties who, in his acting style, most
strongly connotes not theatricality, but authenticity; and he continues to personify Method acting for film critics, leading Brodkey to conclude that all of
the star's roles were "the separate selves in himself as characters." Nonetheless,
a masculine masquerade, with its implications of performativity and bisexuality, was the recurring theme of Brando's career as well as the dramatic extension of his early star status as a transgressive boy. Despite the macho iconography that he himself disavowed in the press, the erotic and performative
dimensions of Brando's fifties persona mark its continuity with Clift's more
neurotic, interiorized persona, and it is just as revealing of how the boy who
is not a man could cross the binarized axes of masculinity/femininity, straight/
gay, authentic/theatrical, young/old that structured the virility of a traditional
"he-man" movie star like John Wayne.

The Censored Boy

In their star personae, both Clift and Brando illuminate how "the new look in
Hollywood men" brought to the foreground of cinematic representation what
was, for postwar culture, a very unstable signifying relation between "gender"
and "sexuality." In the passage from Ehrenreich quoted above, for example,
her account of what "homosexuality" meant to fifties assumptions about
errant masculinity has to do with how a man behaved, making an issue of his
gender (his identity as a recognizable "male"), not his sexuality (his desire as
one male for another male). However, since a "boy" was not a "man" because
he failed to conform to the standards of hegemonic masculinity, and "fear of
homosexuality kept men in line" with cultural norms for masculine behavior,
the figure of the boy who is not a man all too easily evoked the homosexual
desire that his gender deviance censored.

For instance, in *Rebel without a Cause* (1955), the fifties rebel movie featuring the one new star who would forever remain a boy in fans' memories, Jim Stark's (James Dean) alienation from his middle-class family turns out to be symptomatic of his masculinity crisis. "What can you do when you have to be a man?" Jim asks his emasculated father (Jim Backus), who can neither supply a direct answer nor offer a viable role model himself. Jim initially thinks like John Wayne, that manhood is a matter of honor, of not backing down when his peers call him "chicken." But his girlfriend, Judy (Natalie Wood), teaches him otherwise: "What kind of person do you think a girl wants?" she asks. "A man," he answers. "A man?" Judy replies in turn. "But a man can be gentle and sweet, like you. He's someone who doesn't run away when . . . like being Plato's friend when no one else liked him. That's being strong." Judy offers Jim the kind of direction for his masculinity that his father fails to provide. She shows him how to reconcile courage, honor, and loyalty with sensitivity and tenderness without impugning his masculinity. And in the film's closure, when his introduction of Judy to his parents coincides with his father saying, "I'll try to be as strong as you want me to be," she provides Jim with a way back into the middle-class family as the containing structure for his maturation into a "strong" man himself.

What this resolution of Jim's gender confusion achieves, however, is the erasure of the bisexuality brought out in his undisguised affection for Plato (Sal Mineo), which triangulates his relation to Judy as it develops through the course of the film—and which she pointedly uses as her example of Jim's manly strength: he likes Plato even when none of the other kids do. As Vito Russo notes about the three misfit youths of *Rebel without a Cause,* "the pressure to conform, to hide any secret sensitivity out of fear of the word *queer,* was a popular subtext [of homosexuality]" (108). An early moment in *Rebel* brings this subtext to the surface in a way that is hard to ignore. On Jim's first day at his new high school he tries to find a bathroom before going to class and first enters the girls' room by mistake; as he rectifies his error, walking across the hall to the proper room for boys (and he checks out the sign to make sure before entering), his action is intercut with shots of Plato opening his locker to comb his hair, catching sight of Jim in a mirror fastened to the inside of the door, angling the glass to get a better view, and staring at him intently. To be sure that we do not miss the point of Plato's look, the camera angle slyly puts forward Jim's image in the mirror so that it displaces a pinup photo of Alan Ladd, which initially can be seen in Plato's locker as this sequence begins.

At the level of its narrative, *Rebel without a Cause* treats Jim's inability to read sexual difference correctly as an anecdote dramatizing his disorientation in an unfamiliar setting. Plato's desiring look at Jim, however, which establishes the homoerotic ground of the friendship that will begin in the next scene at the planetarium, sexualizes the boy's masculinity crisis. The erotic implication of Jim's gender confusion suggests that his rebellion may well have a cause in his alienation from the oppressive heterosexuality that his parents, who tear

Jim apart with their fighting and hypocrisy, represent in their asymmetrical re-lationship. Plato's eroticizing viewpoint of Jim, comparable to Judy's, enables the film to dramatize the bisexuality underlying this rebel boy's difference from his parents as well as the other teenagers (and Dean's own bisexual star persona certainly cultivates the attention drawn to the queer subtext of *Rebel* by almost everyone who comments on the film). Similarly, Plato's death, the final link in the chain of events that leads to Jim's romance with Judy and his reconciliation with his parents, then disavows that early implication of sexual rebellion; as far as the narrative closure is concerned, the desire of one boy for another literally amounts to a dead end.

Actual censorship of homosexuality in film adaptations of Broadway plays from this period more candidly displays the logic by which gender confusion was made a substitution for transgressive sexuality in Hollywood's representa-tions of the boy. The most notable example is the compromise forced upon the film version of *A Streetcar Named Desire* when Kazan and Williams refused to eliminate Blanche's monologue about her dead young husband, Allan Gray. "There was something different about the boy," she remembers in the play, "a nervousness, a softness and tenderness which wasn't like a man's, although he wasn't the least bit effeminate looking—still—that thing was there." "That thing" was the teenager's bisexuality. In her monologue, Blanche reveals how she ac-cidentally found out about her husband's double life: "By coming suddenly into a room that I thought was empty—which wasn't empty, but had two people in it . . . the boy I had married and an older man who had been his friend for years" (Williams 70, ellipsis in original). Her undisguised revulsion at what she saw in that room drove her young husband to suicide, and the point of Blanche's monologue is to show how this traumatic memory explains, for the action of the play in the present, both her fragility and her compulsive sexual attraction to young boys.

The sensitive dead boy who never became a man, Allan Gray still haunts the screen version of *A Streetcar Named Desire* as Stanley Kowalski's opposite. However, while supervising the preparation of a shooting script, the PCA in-sisted not only that the film contain no suggestion at all of the boy's homo-sexual desire, but that some other explanation be put in its place as the source of Blanche's rejection of her husband: "because of the reputation of the play, it will be necessary for you, *affirmatively,* to establish just what it is that was wrong with the young husband," meaning "that the element of the story can-not be left 'open' to the 'guessing' of the audience. It will be necessary, affirm-atively, to establish that he was *not* a sex pervert."[16] As a result of this interdic-tion, Allan's gender deviance as a "boy," rather than his sexual transgression as a bisexual, becomes the problem that Blanche could not face in her past. "There was something about the boy," she now remembers in the film—with the word "different" significantly excised from her speech along with the ex-plicit refutation of his effeminacy—"a nervousness, a tenderness, an uncertainty," which she could not "understand" at the time of their marriage. Rather than sensing the boy's unnamable sexuality that she would go on to discover by accident in the play, in the film Blanche confesses that she could not deal with her young husband's inability to function as a proper breadwinner. He "wrote poetry," she now says, and "didn't seem able to do anything else. [He] lost every job." What subsequently caused Blanche to lose all "respect" for her husband is not her sudden confrontation with his double life but her growing realization that he was too "weak." An accusation of debility—"You're weak! I've lost respect for you! I despise you!"—is all that the film version of *Streetcar* can put forward, somewhat incoherently, as the boy's motive for taking his own life.

Turning Allan Gray's desire for an older man into a gender problem, the revision of Blanche's monologue erases the boy's sexual transgression from representation, following the culture's own encoding of homosexuality as a gender deviation, as signaled by the film version's more explicit revelation of the boy's effeminacy: his sensitivity, his creativity, his weakness (Larson 22–23). In the script approved for shooting, Blanche's new monologue, cobbled together through phone dictation by officials at Warners and the Breen office, was actually longer than it is in the finished film, and it culminated in an even more explicit castigation of young Allan's manhood for failing to hold down a steady job. During shooting Kazan cut the monologue to make it less talky; and when word got back to Code officials that the speech had been changed without prior consent, the director had to reassure Breen that "I wouldnt [*sic*] put the homosexuality back in the picture, if the Code had been revised last night and it was now permissible. I dont want it. I prefer the delicately suggested impotence theme; I prefer debility and weakness over any kind of suggestion of perversion."[17]

It's no surprise that Kazan took this approach with Breen. Knowing full well that a return to the original text was not permissible, he denied any intention of restoring the boy's bisexuality, although he did take the time to point out to Breen that he shortened the speech because it lacked the impact of Blanche's discovering her husband with another man. Kazan's implicit recognition that the boy's "impotence" functioned as a cover for his "perversion" indicates the shrewdness with which the censored monologue, particularly as abbreviated in an ad-hoc move by the director, effectively plays the cultural coding of the boy's gender problem, his "weakness" in Blanche's eyes, against the institutional Code, which forbade reference to what that "weakness" connoted about an "unmanly" boy's homosexual desire. In this way, the revised speech as filmed ends up foiling the PCA's insistence that what "was wrong with the young husband" had to be explicitly acknowledged in order to prevent audiences from recalling the fuller explanation offered in the play.

Although he does not mention *Streetcar,* Chon Noriega documents how film reviewers often guided fifties audiences to read into the censored adaptations of Broadway plays and novels the homosexual characterizations that had to be cut to satisfy Code restrictions. "Thus the original source could be brought to bear on the ambiguous or unexplained parts of the film," he explains. In effect such reviews instructed audiences how to decode what was Hollywood's routine pattern of substituting a deviation from gender norms for a forbidden sexual desire. For example, when *Tea and Sympathy* (1956) premiered, Noriega reports, "all reviewers agreed that the effeminate student feared that he might be homosexual, a motive that was supposed to have been censored and changed" (28). In Robert Anderson's play, Tom Lee (John Kerr) is explicitly presumed to be queer because he has been seen sunbathing in the nude with one of his male teachers. Even though the outing was perfectly innocent, the other teachers and students believe the rumor because the boy's effeminate behavior readily connotes homosexuality. "Everything I've been doing all my life makes me look like a fairy," he complains to his roommate Al in the play, when the latter tries to teach him how to appear more manly (Anderson 426). For the film version, MGM had to omit the overt homophobia of Tom's persecution and hit instead "the sissy angle,"[18] and the PCA required that "these changes should be so definitized that there should be no spot where it could be inferred that anybody is afraid that he is a homo-sexual [*sic*]."[19] Thus in the film version the event that sets off the persecution of Tom occurs when two students see him on the beach sewing with a group of faculty wives, one of whom jokingly tells Tom that he will make somebody a very good wife. Nevertheless, after Anderson's screenplay received the go-ahead from the PCA, Pandro S. Berman, the film's producer, told the *New York Times:* "We never say in the film that the boy has homosexual tendencies—I don't believe the word homosexual was actually spoken in the play either—but any adult who has ever heard the word and understands its meaning will clearly understand the suspicion in the film" (Pryor).[20]

Because of the notoriety that resulted from the studio's difficulties in clearing the play with the PCA, *Tea and Sympathy* has been remembered as a film that severely compromises its gay subject matter. But actually, as Russo points out, "people forget it is the story of a shy heterosexual.... The subject here is the accusation of homosexuality, not the presence of it" (112). Though in outward appearance he evokes the fifties stereotype of gay youth as "the sad young man" (Dyer, "Coming"), the sissy boy in the film version of *Tea and Sympathy* does not stand in for the latent homosexual. Simply put, Tom's effeminacy marks a gender confusion that challenges the machismo which headmaster Bill Reynolds (Leif Erickson) exemplifies both in his rugged athleticism and the close physical bonds he forms with his hunky students through sports. In the play Reynolds torments Tom because of his own homophobia, and he orders his wife, Laura (Deborah Kerr, in both the play and film), to leave when she hurls in his face her suspicion that "you persecute in Tom, that boy upstairs, you persecute the thing you fear in yourself" (Anderson 460). By contrast, in the film Laura elaborates upon Tom's threat to her

Figure 36.
While Tom Lee is off screen sewing with faculty wives, the other boys act manly on
the beach to win the headmaster's approval—and attention.

husband's "outward show of manliness." "This boy is different," she tries to get
her husband to understand in a speech written for the screenplay by Anderson: "[He] doesn't conform to your idea of what a man is. . . . You wanted to
humiliate the boy in the eyes of the school. Because if he was right then you
had to be wrong. If he could be manly then you had to question your own
definition of manliness. Well, Bill, he's right. . . . Manliness is not all swagger
and swearing and mountain climbing. Manliness is also tenderness and
gentleness and consideration."

Laura revises manliness in accordance with the domestic mystique of fifties hegemonic masculinity, but the film version of *Tea and Sympathy* shows
through its sissy boy that, whether its effect is swagger or gentleness, heterosexual masculinity is performative. Bill's "outward show of manliness" is just
that, a masquerade; and Tom's difference as an "off-horse" results from his
failure to internalize the terms by which all the other boys in the school strut
their stuff to masquerade as men like Bill—and to solicit his interest in their
performances of virility, as when they hand-wrestle on the beach before the
headmaster's admiring gaze. As a result, the scene in which Al (Darryl Hick-

man) instructs his roommate on the proper carriage of manhood acquires even greater resonance for the film as a pointed demonstration of the performativity required to be what Tom's father calls a "regular guy." "That's a good walk," Tom comments as he watches Al stride across the room as if he were John Wayne, "I'll try to copy it." As well as realizing that masculinity is something a boy has to copy from his elders in order to be convincing as a "man," Tom recognizes the arbitrariness of the gender conventions guaranteeing a man's virility: "Why should a guy with a crew cut look more manly?" he asks Al, and then explains that such a haircut simply does not suit his hair or his face. With his effeminate body inscribing his resistance to the regulation that Al willingly accepts in conforming to the headmaster's masculine code, Tom's lack of conventional manliness has the effect not of revealing the latent homosexual desire in the sissy boy, but of undermining the gender authenticity of the virile heterosexual man.

Tom's effeminacy threatens the manliness of his persecutors—Bill Reynolds, the other male students, even his own father—because it forces them to confront the slippery, unstable alignment of gender and sexuality which is so crucial to their masculine masquerade. By the same token, Tom's difference from a "regular guy" like Al also marks his own inability to perfect the proper masculine masquerade. "*Tea and Sympathy* is the ultimate sissy film," Russo points out; "it confirms what the creators and portrayers of sissies have always sought to deny, that the iconography for sissies and for sexual deviates is the same and that the one has come to *mean* the other" (113). This is why Tom's effeminacy—as indicated by his gardening, his sewing, his poetry, his chintz curtains, his walk, his style of playing tennis, his willingness to do drag to be in a school play—still connotes "homosexual tendencies," as producer Berman suggested to the *Times,* even though the film eliminates all of the play's references to such suspicions and the virulent homophobia fueling them. However, because of that omission, even more so than in the play, in the film Tom's effeminacy does not belie the heterosexuality that drives his doe-eyed infatuation with Laura, who ultimately sleeps with the boy in order to eliminate any doubt that he is indeed "a man." It is therefore important to appreciate how carefully the film version contains the sissy's implication of sexual transgression so that it can be understood more directly as a deviation from gender norms: Tom is persecuted not because he may been fooling around with an older man but because he has been caught sewing with older women.

What makes this sissy boy such a transgressive figure for the film, then, is the fact that his effeminacy does *not* connote homosexuality within the diegesis—the PCA saw to that. As a consequence, Tom disrupts the logic of inversion that produces the sissy as the exemplary homosexual according to "a long tradition of viewing gender and sexuality as continuous and collapsible categories—a tradition of assuming that anyone, male or female, who desires a man must by definition be feminine; and that anyone, male or female, who desires a woman must by the same token be masculine" (Sedgwick, *Tendencies* 157). In turning out to be a cultural oxymoron—i.e., a *straight* sissy—the effeminate boy of *Tea and Sympathy* disturbs the ease with which gender is supposed to function as an authentic index of sexuality.

Although the Breen office did not notice the difference, the transgressive straight boy in *Tea and Sympathy* and the transgressive queer boy of *Streetcar* presented the PCA with flip sides of the same cultural coin. Whereas with Allan Gray the censorship erased the boy's actual bisexuality by representing it in gender terms as a failure of masculinity, with Tom Lee the censorship repressed the "obvious" but inaccurate intimations of homosexuality all too easily read into the sissy boy's failure to conform to the regulating fiction of gender norms. In their different ways, both censored films expose Hollywood's logic in using gender as a displacement of forbidden sexual themes, and, as importantly, they exemplify how the boy who is not a man personifies the disavowal of homosexuality that legitimates this thematic legerdemain at the level of narrative content.

The "Transvestite Effect" of the Boy

In pressuring a gender ideology that could represent sexual difference only in binarized terms, and whether incarnated in troubled adolescent characters or, much more complexly, in the eroticized star personae of Clift and Brando, the "passing" boy of fifties films calls to mind the comparable figure of the transvestite. Not only does the transvestite cross gender boundaries and disturb the culture's equation of gender and sexuality, but the figure of the boy is central to transvestic iconography, too. In fact, according to Marjorie Garber's examination of cross-dressing throughout the history of American, British, and European representations of sexual difference, the transvestite occupies the same indeterminate gender position that fifties culture attributed to the boy who is not a man. Like a transvestite, the boy in Garber's account is an "elastic and gender-conflicted concept" because he crosses sameness and difference (*Vested* 286).

Garber refers to the figure of the boy as "the third . . . that which questions binary thinking and introduces crisis" (11). "The third" is not a distinct category per se (i.e., not a "third" gender) but, much like the cowboy in ranch culture, the indeterminate figure that exceeds, displaces, and co-opts the various symbolic binaries that maintain hierarchies of power. The boy therefore epitomizes what she calls "category crisis"—"a failure of definitional distinction, a borderline that becomes permeable, that permits border crossings from one (apparently distinct) category to another. . . . The binarism male/female . . . is itself put in question or under erasure in transvestism, and a transvestite figure, or a transvestite mode, will always function as a sign of overdetermination—a mechanism of displacement from one blurred boundary to another" (16). The "transvestite effect" of the boy is "to mark this kind of displacement, substitution, or slippage: from class to gender, gender to race; or, equally plausibly, from gender to race or religion" (36–37). Or from gender to nationalism: recall what I mentioned earlier about Terkel's observation that the category "boys" confused ideological boundaries by crossing the ally/axis binary in veterans' accounts of World War II. Or, as I have been emphasizing, from gender to sexuality.

In his personification of the boy who is not a man, as the new male star of the fifties likewise passes between binarized categories (masculine/feminine, straight/gay, young/mature), he disturbs the ease with which Hollywood's representation of masculinity collapses sexuality into gender. The new stars did not cross-dress literally, of course, but their association with melodrama gave their boyish personae an unmistakable "transvestite effect" nonetheless. While older and more established stars such as Gary Cooper, James Stewart, Robert Mitchum, Kirk Douglas, Gregory Peck, and William Holden appeared in melodramas at this time, their personae never became as identified with this one genre as was the case with the biggest of the new stars as well as the less luminary.

Drawing on Oedipal narratives of generational conflict, the melodramas of this period dramatize the category crisis that results from the displacement of sexuality onto gender. These films often follow the example of *Red River,* pairing an emerging male star like Clift against an older actor, using the casting to eroticize the boy as a means of disturbing the ground of gender representation. In the melodramas, though, the patriarchal figure lacks the obvious stature and history that John Wayne bears for the representation of masculinity in the movies. Instead of the lean, mean Tom Dunson, the aging patriarch in these films is now flabby and crabby, played by Raymond Massey (in *East of Eden,* 1955), Jim Backus (in *Rebel without a Cause*), Orson Welles (in *The Long, Hot Summer,* 1958), or Burl Ives (in *Cat on a Hot Tin Roof,* 1958). Consequently, while the conflict between old and young becomes even more intensely Oedipalized as melodrama, as far as star power goes there's very little contest. Even more so than in *Red River,* the casting of these films blatantly foregrounds the sexuality of the younger leading man (Dean in the first two films I listed, Paul Newman in the last two), whose youth has the crucial effect, as Skolsky's commentary implies, of marking out his specific value within the Hollywood star system—namely, his difference as an eroticized boy. "Son, why should I be scared of you?" Will Varner (Welles) asks Ben Quick (Newman) in *The Long, Hot Summer.* Cocking his body as if to cruise Varner, Ben replies: "'Cause I've got a reputation for being a dangerous man." "Hmmm," Varner replies in turn. "You're a *young* dangerous man. . . . I'm an old one." When Ben tells Varner that he's a young man in a hurry, the elder replies, "You're wasting your time. Job at the top is already taken." But Ben warns,

Figure 37.
In *The Long, Hot Summer*, Ben Quick (Paul Newman) and Will Varner
(Orson Welles) confront each other, and the boy's virility
marks the crucial difference between them.

somewhat ominously, "Like you said—you're an old man." For all of Varner's
considerable economic power over Ben as the patriarch of Frenchman's Bend,
the visual contrast between Welles (corpulent, red-faced) and the aptly named
Newman (slim, sweaty, and in an athletic shirt that shows off his lean torso)
immediately confirms that, cinematically speaking at least, youth has the distinct advantage. What makes Ben Quick potentially dangerous to Varner is the
boy's eroticized body, which the old man admires and covets, seeking to perpetuate his threatened dynasty by marrying off his daughter (Joanne Wood-
ward) to "that blue ribbon bull! . . . Quick, that big, stud horse!"

I have quoted Varner's unabashed appreciation of Ben Quick's virility because the industrial setting of new stars like Newman in melodrama has encouraged critics to read their eroticized masculinity much as Skolsky and
Wayne did in the fifties: as a "feminization" of the virile Hollywood film hero.
But in adapting the language of domestication voiced by characters in the
films themselves, such as Judy in *Rebel without a Cause* and Laura in *Tea and*

Sympathy, commentators on the new stars of the fifties indirectly point out their "transvestite effect." For example, Peter Biskind collapses the considerable difference among stars like Clift, Brando, Dean, Newman, Peck, Holden, Hudson, and Ford in order to attack the period's hegemonic masculinity. Biskind argues: "The new generation of actors who came to age in the late forties and early and mid-fifties were well suited to the new masculinity. . . . Men . . . were sensitive, in close touch with their feelings (or could be made to be). . . . Men, in other words, were becoming more like women. They were becoming 'feminized.' When they put down the gun, they put on the apron" (257). Among his many examples, most of which are melodramas like *Rebel without a Cause* (and he cites Judy's speech about manliness to supply evidence of his argument), Biskind also includes *Red River,* which the critic claims is driven by "the imperative to feminize men" (284).

Even when they do not go as far as Biskind in depicting the new stars' difference as a lamentable, transvestic emasculation, other critics still position them according to a strict masculine/feminine dualism. For instance, Nora Sayre calls attention to the new stars' excessive emotionality as an appealing feminization, particularly as personified by James Dean: "At a time when both sexes were over-awed by the period's concept of masculinity, his freedom to unfetter every emotion, to shriek or sob or thrash out conflicted feelings, was enviable as well as exhilarating. . . . In the best sense, Dean was unmanly, and an adolescent girl or a young woman could identify with him, as I did" (111). In similar fashion, as Wexman describes the Oedipal narratives that featured the new stars, with their "highly charged scenes in which a young man attempts to assert a model of virility different from that of his elder," she explains that "[s]uch scenes call forth the Method actor's ability to indulge in the kind of emotional outpouring traditionally associated with feminine behavior" (170).

As their rhetoric of feminization indicates, what all three of these critics describe is the new stars' "transvestite effect" as boys in displacing binarized terms from one ground of representation (i.e., gender) to another (sexuality). Each critic's characterization thus emphasizes the emotional excess that marks the new stars' confusion of gender positions. "Excess," Garber comments, "that which overflows a boundary, is the space of the transvestite" (28). Crossing and so disturbing the masculine/feminine dualism that conventionally structured gender as a means of censoring sexual content, the new male stars projected a different "look" for Hollywood's men without ceasing to signify maleness. Far from calling into question their sexuality as men, the erotic imagery that promoted their stardom celebrated it, putting forward the excess that provoked the new stars' "transvestite effect" in disturbing what, at the level of narrative, was the collapse of sexuality into gender.

As the first of Hollywood's postwar boys who were not men, Montgomery Clift best exemplifies the transgressive dimensions of "the new look" of the era's young male stars. Through the performativity and bisexuality that co-alesced in his star persona to signify his mercurial boyishness, Clift crosses the boundaries structuring the virility of a "he-man" star like John Wayne, causing a disturbance in the traditional ground of gender representation. A similar category crisis can be sensed in the fan discourse's efforts to recuperate the new stars' boyishness as a gender masquerade, in Brando's eroticized star icon-ography, and in the PCA's censorship of the homosexual boy when this figure explicitly appeared in narrative. Viewed from any of these industrial vantage points, the new stars' status as "boys who'd like to be men" clearly stood for their disruption of the hierarchy in which a "boy" functioned in representation as the subordinated opposite of a "man." This is also why, when so blatantly eroticized by the young stars who portrayed him, the figure of the boy who is not a man evoked such unmistakable intimations of bisexuality in the nar-ratives that Hollywood produced to feature the new actors. When, in both those narratives and the fan discourse, Hollywood then justified its portrayal of new stars like Clift as boys who were not men by dramatizing or analyzing their "feminization," this restoration of gender as the ground of representation reinstated a masculine/female dualism as a means of containing their disturb-ing intimations of sexual transgression. The new stars could not dismantle the dualism that upheld the period's hegemonic masculinity, but their popularity testifies to the ways in which audiences did indeed sense if not fully articulate the category crisis they personified as boys who are not men.

The Bachelor in the Bedroom

This career girl had everything but love.
This bachelor had nothing else but.
They had absolutely nothing in common except a party line.
They believed passionately in the motto, "Hate thy neighbor."
Then he met the body that went with the voice he hated.
What would you do?
That's what he did . . . Pretend he was two other guys.
And then the wooing got frantic.

The opening voiceover narration in the theatrical trailer for *Pillow Talk* (1959) well describes this film's comic take on the fifties battle of the sexes. Career girl Jan Morrow (Doris Day), an unmarried interior decorator with only work on her mind, and bachelor songwriter Brad Allen (Rock Hudson), a bachelor with only sex on his, repeatedly clash on the telephone over his dominance of their party line; he uses the telephone morning and night to serenade women, and Jan cannot get through to make or receive her business calls. As if their animosity did not complicate matters enough, these two antagonists are connected by more than the phone company's failure to upgrade its technology in Manhattan. Jan, it turns out, is also being relentlessly but unsuccessfully wooed by Brad's best friend and her client, Jonathan Forbes (Tony Randall). Inevitably, Brad accidentally comes face to face with the other end of his party line and instantly decides to make a play for her, masquerading as "Rex Stetson," wealthy oilman from Texas, in order to prevent Jan from discovering his real identity as her nemesis on the telephone. His ruse works and she falls for him. Just as inevitably, Jan stumbles upon Brad's real identity and, furious at his deception, breaks off all further contact. Now realizing that he is in love himself, in an effort to win Jan back Brad hires her to redecorate his bachelor apartment while he, confident of a reconciliation, goes through his little black book to inform all his old girlfriends that he is getting married. But Jan de-

Figure 38.
Jan Morrow (Doris Day) inspects the technology of Brad Allen's (Rock Hudson)
apartment before redecorating it.

cides to retaliate for the trick he had played on her by posing so successfully
as Rex Stetson. She remodels Brad's apartment into a travesty of the bachelor
pad, turning it into what looks like a cross between a Turkish bordello and the
tent setting of *Son of the Sheik*, all done up in lurid, clashing colors. A furious
Brad finally convinces Jan that he sincerely loves her, and the two get married.

When *Pillow Talk* opened in 1959, its enormous success was notable for a
number of reasons, not the least because it glamorized the star persona of
Doris Day and established Rock Hudson as a romantic comedian on a par
with Cary Grant. However, since it is now remembered primarily for being
the first in a long line of hypocritical sex comedies about the unassailable
virgin, most of them starring Day, the film's influence has also obscured the
shrewdness with which it sizes up the cultural tensions inhering in the figure
of the bachelor playboy. For example, perhaps the most striking feature of
Pillow Talk, which still does not fail to elicit laughter from an audience, is that
it so wittingly situates Brad Allen's sexuality against the theatrical backdrop of
his bachelor apartment, a fantasy playpen which uses modern technology to
promote a single purpose for his domestic space: seduction. Flip a switch and

the front door locks, the lights go out, and a record player starts to play mood music. Flip a second switch and the sleeper sofa opens out into a double bed, already made up with baby blue sheets. Late in the film, when Jan reluctantly agrees to take the job redecorating Brad's apartment, she examines its technology and asks, "Why redecorate? It's so functional for your purposes." Her sarcastic remark views the bachelor apartment solely as a den of seduction, and her garish redecoration job means both to punish Brad for his deceit and to critique his playboy lifestyle for its adolescence as defined by the standards of domestic ideology.

But the bachelor apartment in *Pillow Talk* is much more than the spider web (another description of Jan's) where the male traps the unsuspecting female. After Jan observes the functionality of his apartment, Brad replies: "Not anymore. That's why I want you to redecorate. And that bed is the first thing I want you to get rid of. And anything you think is in bad taste, throw it out." His reference to "taste" indicates a forgotten dimension of the fifties bachelor apartment, particularly as represented every month in *Playboy* magazine: the bachelor pad was not a den of iniquity but a site of consumerism. Historically, the bachelor apartment marked the single man's marginal position within the domestic ideology of the period, but it also indicated his recuperation as a consumer whose masculinity could be redeemed—even glamorized—by the things that he bought to accessorize his virility.

Whether in the pages of *Playboy* or in Hollywood comedies, representations of bachelorhood in the fifties condensed the culture's deepest anxieties about the stability, coherence, and normality of heterosexual maleness, underscoring the homophobia that positioned "masculinity" in strict opposition to "femininity." Jan's stinging comment that Brad's playboy residence is so functional for his purposes should cause us to wonder just what his purposes are, and the answer is not the obvious one. Given the elaborate masquerading which this bachelor has to undertake to move the film's seduction plot along, it quickly becomes clear that Brad is not doing all of that work simply to get Jan to bed. As *Pillow Talk* theatricalizes heterosexual masculinity through Brad's impersonation of Rex, the film turns on its head the conventional narrative of the virgin's seduction by the predatory male, revealing the gender performativity of the bachelor's sexuality at every stage of his game.

Examine the text of the film's trailer again to see what I mean. Despite what I said a moment ago, the trailer is technically imprecise as a summary of the seduction plot because the voiceover refers to *two* masquerades on the bachelor's part ("That's what he did . . . Pretend he was two other guys"). Who is the second "other guy" that Brad Allen pretends to be in *Pillow Talk*? Could it be the playboy's own persona of hyperactive heterosexuality? This slip of the text in the trailer (the correct phrasing should be "two *different* guys") suggests that "Brad" and "Rex" are both pretenses and, what is more, that straight masculinity itself has no origin outside of a gender masquerade, no point of reference outside of its multiple representations. The carefully crafted heterosexual masculinity of Rock Hudson's star persona is the perfect case in point. When the trailer states that the bachelor in *Pillow Talk* has to "pretend to be two other guys," the phrasing acknowledges, even if only accidentally, that Hudson, a gay star pretending to be two straight guys, also depends upon an elaborate and doubled pretense of heterosexuality for *his* projection of masculinity on screen. *Pillow Talk* itself appears to appreciate this fact of Hudson's stardom with great wit and audacity. In both its screenplay and mise-en-scène, the film quite knowingly incorporates Hudson's star persona into its masquerade plot, and many of these references center on his playboy apartment. With Brad and Rex each alluding to specific elements in the fan discourse's construction of "Rock Hudson" as the exemplary and desirable tall, dark, and handsome unmarried male, these "two other guys" divide the monolithic masculinity which the star represented as a fifties romantic screen idol.

Placing *Pillow Talk* alongside both *Playboy*'s celebration of bachelorhood and Hudson's star persona helps to bring out more fully the problematic orientation which this romantic comedy takes toward its representation of the single man as the culture's icon of active, desiring heterosexuality. It is a very queer orientation indeed: the bachelor's multiple masquerades in this film—as Brad Allen, Rex Stetson, *and* Rock Hudson—dramatize numerous possibilities of gender instability and sexual transgression. My close attention to the film's queer slant on masculinity, let me also add, is motivated by much more than retrospective knowledge of Hudson's own homosexuality. The queer male had a significant history in the fifties, one based in the effective erasure of his homosexuality; because of his marginal position in domestic ideology as an unmarried (and, thus, potentially nonheterosexual) man, the bachelor figured into that history in important ways, as both *Playboy* and Hudson attest—and that history, in turn, figures into *Pillow Talk*.

Sex and the Single Man

Particularly as played in fifties romantic comedies, the playboy bachelor was cast as the breadwinner's opposite: not the asexual male "spinster" of nineteenth-century military societies but a glamorized "bum" who personified some of the most deeply felt anxieties about male sexuality, anxieties which the era's domestic ideology tried to mask in its representations of the breadwinner as the norm of masculinity. Interpreted with suspicion for his refusal to embrace the whole package of privileges and responsibilities that marriage was supposed to offer the male in compensation for his regulated sexuality, the bachelor cut a highly ambiguous figure: on one hand, a lady killer, but on the other hand, a woman hater; on one hand, a party animal, but on the other, a lonely guy. His single status was assumed to signify a fundamental "immaturity," "irresponsibility," "insecurity," and "latent homosexuality" that simultaneously needed correction (to promote a man's maturity as the family breadwinner) and expression (to confirm his heterosexuality as the errant playboy). For this reason the bachelor was a reversible figure, at once placed on the margins of domestic ideology and central to its perpetuation. While made the primary symptom of arrested development according to the standard of domestic ideology, the bachelor could just as easily be turned around to critique the breadwinner ethic for its emasculation of married men and to offer an alternative style of masculinity. He could be, in the words of Hugh Hefner's *Playboy* magazine, "sophisticated, intelligent, urban—a young man-about-town, who enjoys good, gracious living" ("Playboy" 36).

Launched in December 1953, *Playboy* represented bachelorhood as the male's liberation from domestic ideology through his sexuality (Nadel 129–36). The magazine packaged the single life as an alternative representation of masculinity—Barbara Ehrenreich goes so far as to call its agenda a "male rebellion" (*Hearts* 50)—with the aim of resisting the stifling ethic of the breadwinner by asserting that "responsibility" was *not* inherent to a male's nature. On the contrary, *Playboy* took as its motto the axiom "Woman wants to be a wife long before man wants to be a husband" (Zollo 37). The centerfold in each monthly issue, which gave *Playboy* its instant notoriety, visibly confirmed its male readers' heterosexuality, guarding against any suspicions just as to why a bachelor might want to remain single.

Playboy represented the bachelor as a figure whose overactive heterosexuality could resolve the ambivalence with which the culture viewed the unmarried male. But the magazine itself raised doubts about the bachelor's sexuality early on with the following "party joke":

> Then there was the playboy who suddenly decided to live a strictly moral life. First, he cut out smoking. Then he cut out liquor. Then he cut out swearing. Then he cut out women.
> Now he's cutting out paper dolls. ("Playboy's Party")

This joke plays with the possibility that bachelorhood signifies some form of gender transgression, though it does so with a high degree of ambiguity. The joke can be read as being "pro-bachelor" in its intent, demonstrating that the straight-laced moral man, the breadwinner, is a sissy, with a coded implication of castration by his wife. Or it can be read as an "anti-bachelor" joke, indicating that if you take away all the outward signs of the lusty playboy, you also get a sissy, though now with a coded implication of his latent homosexuality. But doesn't a man "cutting out paper dolls" also describe the *Playboy* reader himself, removing the magazine's three-page centerfold for mounting on a wall? From any perspective, the playboy of this joke calls into question the naturalness of one form of straight male sexuality (the bachelor) as opposed to another (the breadwinner). Any interpretation of the joke thus has to conclude that bachelorhood is all an act, as readers of *Playboy* would have had to suspect, once they bought into the lifestyle designed for them by Hugh Hefner.

The lifestyle, though, provided the means through which the marginalized bachelor was successfully brought back into the fold of dominant culture as an unmarried consumer. What Richard Dyer calls "the playboy discourse," with its presumption that "sex is for the man," with women serving simply as the vehicle for male sexuality (*Heavenly* 41), functioned to prevent unsympathetic readers from asking why the bachelor didn't want to get married. The playboy discourse went to a great deal of trouble to disavow the possibility that there was trouble in paradise, the bachelor's bedroom. In the process of promoting the evasion of marriage, which was usually the point of its jokes, cartoons, and articles, *Playboy* made the bachelor synonymous with the sexual predator whose ambition is to bed but not wed every attractive woman he meets. "When a fellow first meets a girl, a lot of questions run through his mind, among them, can she be had? And, if so, with how much—or how little—promotion? Being an efficient sort of guy, you don't want to waste a lot of promotion on a pushover" (Archer, "Will" 13). Armed with the Kinsey report ("You can prove almost anything with this book" [F. Smith 50]), *Playboy* turned the predatory bachelor into a child of nature simply acting on his impulses. "Like the little bee, he flits from flower to flower, sipping the sweet nectars where he finds them, but never tarries too long at any one blossom" (Zollo 38).

The bachelor's promiscuous behavior did not make him immoral or indecent in *Playboy*'s view. On the contrary, it was always the female, stealing home all the while the male was simply trying to get from first to second base, who turned out to have the upper hand in the magazine's running account of the battle of the sexes. "More bachelors than you would suppose have a tender conscience about the seduction of females," one article informs the magazine's readers, continuing with this reassuring bit of news: "Today's bachelor can enjoy much more peace of mind if he realizes that the girl he thinks he has persuaded to sleep with him has made up her mind to do same long before he throws her a pitch" (Archer, "Don't" 21). With this kind of logic, it's no surprise to find the magazine persuading the playboy bachelor that he really has the woman's own interest at heart when trying to seduce her, because he is helping her to discover her feminine nature according to Dr. Kinsey: "you are actually doing the girl a *service*," readers are assured. "Actually, you are *giving* them a new freedom" (F. Smith 9).

However articulate it was in advocating a philosophy that "the true playboy can enjoy the pleasures the female has to offer without becoming emotionally involved" (Zollo 38), *Playboy* influenced but never seriously undermined or revised the domestic ideology of the period. True, in the public idiom *Playboy* became synonymous with the consumption of sex outside the regulation of marriage; but by its third year of publication, when it started to accept ads, it had already become clear even then that the magazine had recognized the value of being "a prime advertising medium" (Ryan 14). More than just participating in the public discussions of sexuality that Kinsey's published research had inspired, which was the justification offered for its erotica in the first issue, *Playboy* turned out to be a major factor in the postwar effort to enlarge the leisure-time consumer market to include men. In its advertising but also in its articles, *Playboy* pitched to readers the desirability of purchasing high-fidelity stereo equipment, stylish clothing, appealing aftershaves, bathroom accessories, virile liquors, fine wines, exotic vacations, controversial books, hip jazz music, all with the aim of intensifying *their* sexual attractiveness to women.

Playboy's most radical effect on fifties American culture, in fact, may well have been to encourage married men not to leave their families in defiance of the breadwinner ethic of responsibility, but to go shopping, to purchase all those products associated with the single man's pleasures. The magazine addressed its readers in such a way as to conflate their sexuality, their membership in the professional class, and their tastes as consumers. Since masculinity had not traditionally been associated with consuming—prior to the fifties, that had always been considered the economic and social province of femininity—the position *Playboy* invited its readers to occupy as a means of identifying with bachelorhood in spirit if not in license was a conflicted one. Textually, the *Playboy* reader's gender confusion was already apparent in the first year of the magazine's publication. In the September 1954 issue, the conclusion of an article on virginity ended up being placed next to the end of one explaining the use of a chafing dish and offering men various recipes, and the juxtaposition of instructions for a successful bachelor playboy (how to seduce a virgin) and another for an expert bachelor chef (a recipe of "Welsh Rabbit for Four Males") typifies what would become a continuous interplay of sexuality and consuming in every issue of the magazine.

The clash of gender codes soon became evident even within single articles, as the magazine tried to negotiate the tension resulting from its equation of playboy masculinity with both seduction and consumerism. *Playboy* tried to overcome the ideological conflict of its rhetorical address through a monthly promotion asking readers as well as potential advertisers the crucial question: "What Sort of Man Reads *Playboy*?" The answer every time was always a young, educated, urban male who himself could see no conflict between earning money and spending it, and thus see no folly or vanity in treating expensive clothes, furnishings, or recreational travel as investments on a par with his stock portfolio. Noting the success of this "very impressive" campaign directed "at the young executive group," one reader from North Dakota wrote the magazine in 1958 to complain about the narrowness of its target audience, suggesting that "more young men would buy *Playboy* if you were to aim your campaign at Mr. Average a little more" (Peterson). But he was sharply rebuked: "*Playboy* is edited for a special sort of guy—a bit above average in taste, education and income." Defined through his consuming, the playboy bachelor and, more importantly, his values have by now become so pervasive in contemporary advertising—to epitomize professional middle-class aspirations and achievements generally—that today we may forget just what kind of impact that figure had in the fifties as a new, very different, and potentially incoherent representation of hip, sophisticated, liberal masculinity in the postwar marketplace.

Playboy's Bachelor Apartment

Imagined as the site for liberating masculinity from the constraints of domestic ideology, the bachelor apartment was fundamental to *Playboy*'s representation of bachelorhood as a viable alternative to married life from the very beginning of the magazine's history. The bachelor apartment served as the primary setting of a playboy lifestyle that absorbed the single man's sexuality into the more important activity of his consuming. The significance of the bachelor's living space in *Playboy* began with the first issue, where Hefner's lead editorial called attention to his magazine's difference from other male-oriented publications, "which spend all their time out-of-doors." By contrast, Hefner wrote, "We like our apartments. We enjoy mixing up cocktails and an *hors d'oeuvre* or two, putting a little mood music on the phonograph, and inviting in a female acquaintance for a quiet discussion on Picasso, Nietzsche, jazz, sex" ("Volume I"). The playboy pad may have epitomized sexual freedom but, in supplying the perfect setting for uninterrupted consumption of Picasso as well as cocktails, it also served to regulate the bachelor, who was now expected to find his sexuality by consuming the whole repertoire of new products and technologies promoting masculine glamour.

In 1956 *Playboy* ran a two-part article with a blueprint for the perfect bachelor digs, a penthouse apartment: "a high, handsome haven—pre-planned and furnished for the bachelor in town" ("Playboy's Penthouse" Part I, 53). The purpose of this apartment, described in elaborate detail, is to engender as virile and then to unify the bachelor's domestic space, projecting an alternative to the gender strife that characterized the spatial layout of the typical middle-class home. The interior of this ideal bachelor pad is holistic, and so, one infers, is the masculinity it contains. "[T]he apartment is not divided into cell-like rooms but into function areas well delineated for relaxation, dining, cooking, wooing and entertaining, all interacting and yet inviting individual as well as simultaneous use" (60). The kitchen, for example, can be closed off from other rooms or, "since the urban male prides himself on his culinary artistry it may, more often, be opened onto the dining room, so the host can perform for an admiring audience while sharing in conversation." The kitchen turns the playboy pad into a stage on which the bachelor "can perform for an admiring audience" (60). And what does he perform? His masculinity *as* a bachelor: no female cohabits with the playboy in this apartment to compete with him for domination of his domestic space. Technology replaces the need for a female homemaker in this kitchen (although, as a reminder of the bachelor's affiliation with the professional class, it still retains a broom closet for "your once-a-week servant"). Thus the bachelor host can, when entertaining, integrate the cooking and dining spaces in order to show off his culinary skills: "For this is a bachelor kitchen, remember, and unless you're a very odd-ball bachelor indeed, you like to cook and whomp up short-order specialties to exactly the same degree that you actively dislike dishwashing, marketing and tidying up. All that's been taken care of here" (60), and in such a way as to associate the kitchen's modern appliances with masculine recreation (the dishwasher uses "inaudible hi-fi sound to eliminate manual washing") while projecting virile associations for the room ("a unique kitchen stool [is] constructed from rugged, contoured tractor seat") (58).

This ideal playboy pad does end up dividing space, however, reflecting how the bachelor's masculinity is itself divided. Another way the apartment does not follow "the conventional plan of 'separated rooms for various purposes'" is by re-creating within the apartment the traditional separation of public and private spheres. In the Victorian era, Lynn Spigel observes, "the doctrine of two spheres represented human activity in spatial terms: the public world came to be conceived of as a place of productive labor, while the home was seen as a site of rejuvenation and consumption" (73).[1] This polarization of public/private spaces posited the workplace as a masculine province governed by men, and the home as a feminine one dominated by women. As Spigel shows, fifties domestic ideology repositioned that gender binary, and the sexual politics informing it, entirely within the private sphere. Playboy's bachelor apartment, in its turn, interiorizes that older division of public and private spheres to make it a condition of unmarried masculinity: "there are two basic areas, an active zone for fun and partying and a quiet zone for relaxation, sleep and such" ("Playboy's Penthouse" Part II, 65). As described in the article, the "active zone" of the apartment (kitchen, dining, and living rooms) is an arena for performing bachelorhood before an appreciative audience of friends and guests, while the "quiet zone" (bedroom, bath, and study) is a space for authenticating it in private.

The "quiet zone" re-creates the "active zone" as a more private, more singularly male version of bachelor heaven. References to the "active zone" appear in the bedroom, among them "the mate" to a "Saarinen chair" from the living room, and even a second eating and drinking area "cannily concealed [in] a built-in bar and small refrigerator, just large enough for ice cubes, mixers and midnight snacks—a boon to the barefoot bachelor in PJs who's reluctant to trek to the kitchen for his good-night potation, or perhaps unwilling to interrupt the dulcet dialogue he's been sharing" (Part II, 67). In the bedroom, "multiple controls" on the bed "control every light in the place," as well as fastening the locks on doors and windows, and drawing the drapes. The control panel even operates the appliances in the kitchen: if the bachelor plans wisely before retiring, he can start his breakfast from his bed the next morning. The bed, in fact, is so laden with technology—built-in speakers for the remote-controlled hi-fi system located in the living room, storage cupboards that convert to bedside tables, a telephone, "and miscellaneous bedtime items" (68)—that it seems more like a bachelor apartment all unto itself, exceeding the ostensible purpose of a bed in this context, which is to have sex.

The rest of the "quiet zone" confirms the impression that this self-contained half of the bachelor apartment means to forge a more private counterpart of the public "active zone." By means of a sliding translucent glass screen, "the outsize bathroom" can be divided into its own "active" and "quiet zones," forming a master bath and "ensuring total privacy" for the host, who can dress while guests on the other side of the impromptu wall freshen themselves up. Special amenities in the private lavatory ("a bidet, magazine rack, ash tray, and telephone") guarantee a long stay, too, in recognition, the article confides, of the bachelor's inclination "to spend quite a lot of time in the throne room—maybe as a hangover from younger days of living at home, when it was the only place to get away from it all" (70), and to do you know what.

Of all the areas in the "quiet zone," the study is the most private room of all, extending the self-contained aura of the bathroom to function as "the sanctum sanctorum, where women are seldom invited, where we can work or read or just sit and think while gazing into the fireplace." Nested in a haven of walled bookcases, comfortable furniture, a fireplace, and, of course, the requisite "binaural hi-fi speakers," the bachelor satisfies the need to relieve stress from on the job and off; no need to be a playboy, with its emotional alienation and burden of hyperactive heterosexuality, in this room. "With a study like this, even the most dedicated pub crawler or theatre and nightclub buff will be tempted to stay at home of an evening, content within his own surroundings and savoring the city's glamour view via the enchanted view from the window wall" (70). Even more than his bedroom or bathroom, the bachelor's study enables its occupant to return to an imaginary state of complete and perfect self-unity, overcoming the division of male subjectivity laid out by the actual design of the apartment.

The centerpiece of the study is "an enormously comfortable upholstered, contoured Herman Miller armchair with footstool, a lord-of-the domain chair reserved for you alone, which holds all of you evenly supported in the right places and fits in with your relaxed posture so that you and the chair are like twin spoons nested together" (70). The "spoon" metaphor used to describe the bachelor's physical pleasure in this chair, with its erotic implications of necking or "spooning," as well as its visualization of two people sleeping together crotch to ass in spoon fashion, makes it seem like the bachelor is having sex with his own double when he sits languidly in his study and idly daydreams. Whether in his bed, his bathroom, or his study, the function of the "quiet zone" is to create a space for a bachelor's erotic self-stimulation, so it follows that the *object* of desire signified by *Playboy*'s apartment is the bachelor himself, and that the overall purpose of the apartment's design is to turn his domestic sphere into a site of uncontained but nonetheless consumable auto-erotic fantasy. The flexible walls, which, true to a fantasy landscape, open and fold to keep dissolving the boundaries separating rooms—so that the entire apartment can "hold a real big shindig"—create an impression of liquidity, particularly in the "quiet zone." With the accordion wall separating the study and bedroom folded back, the two can be "merged into one magnificent room," creating "a grownup's playground for rollicking, fancy-free fun" (70). The article does not exactly state whether this new arrangement of space means to turn the "quiet zone" into an extra-large bedroom, the place for a sex romp, or an extra-large study, with its implications, as I have been suggesting, not only of the bachelor's adolescent self-absorption but of his ultimate transgression as well: consuming his own body as a source of pleasure and site of fantasy. Either way, the apartment's division of space into two zones serves as a trope for designating conventional sexual activity (occurring in the bachelor's "active zone") and differentiating it from the unconventional (occurring in his "quiet zone"). The "quiet zone" does not invert the "active zone" in the way that the culture believed a sissy, the effeminate man who cuts out paper dolls, inverts the virility of the playboy wolf, so much as it remodels that "active" public space into a more private, even secret articulation of a "quieter"—and hence different—sexuality of the bachelor.

The "quiet zone's" implications of a hermetically sealed psychic unity for the bachelor is important. For if the outer sphere of the apartment, with its orientation toward entertaining and exhibitionism, can be said to theatricalize bachelorhood as a public spectacle, then the inner sphere, with its connotation of shelter and security, can as easily be seen enclosing bachelorhood in a closet, that invisible edifice constructed to contain homosexuality entirely within the "quiet zone" of culture, so to speak. The closet, as Eve Sedgwick has remarked, sits on a boundary that effects only to obscure the seemingly clear-cut difference between hetero- and homosexual signs. Sedgwick argues that the closet does not limit so much as pluralize sexual definition, so that, when it comes to queer masculinity, ignorance about it is as important as knowledge, just as silence about it is as vocal as speech, and its absence is felt as keenly as its presence (*Epistemology* 67–90). The closet does not hide homosexuality but instead actively pivots around an axis of symmetrically paired gender values (virile/sissy, dominant/submissive, visible/invisible, normal/deviant, authentic/fake, disclosure/secrecy) that keeps queering masculinity so that it cannot possibly be read as "straight."

As the mainstay of heterosexual regulation of masculinity, the homosexual closet needs to be understood as constructing much more than a stable place of refuge. The closet maintains a sliding signifying relation—rather like the sliding walls in *Playboy*'s ideal bachelor apartment, which establish the borders between the active and quiet zones. The *Playboy* bachelor pad, while obviously committed wholeheartedly to heterosexual masculinity, ends up evoking the specter of the homosexual closet because of the way the layout simultaneously seeks to theatricalize (in the "active zone") and contain (in the "quiet zone") male sexuality within a single domestic space. When *Pillow Talk* sets Brad Allen's masculinity against the backdrop of his bachelor apartment, with its own "active" and "quiet zones," the locale implies something similar about the ambiguously divided sexuality of its playboy hero, whose masculinity the film represents as an ongoing and multiple masquerade that positions him even more uneasily between sexual secrecy and sexual spectacle.

The Bachelor and the Virgin

The captivating story of what happens when . . .

A CAREFREE BACHELOR WHO BELIEVES IN "TOGETHERNESS"

tangles with

A CAREFUL CAREER GIRL WHO INSISTS ON "SINGLENESS"!!!!

(Pressbook for *Pillow Talk*)

Whenever American romantic comedies of this period draw on the cultural currency of the bachelor playboy, they always begin by valorizing his "natural"—which is actually to say "undomesticated"—virility, only to critique him for his immaturity in resisting marriage. Most typically, the "carefree bachelor" sexualizes the "careful career girl," while she in turn refashions him into proper husband material. This pattern applies to films such as *Susan Slept Here* (1954), *Sabrina* (1954), *The Tender Trap* (1955), *Marty* (1955), *Indiscreet* (1958), and *Teacher's Pet* (1958), even though the social milieu each represents differs from the others quite dramatically. The result, in the light of the history of American romantic comedy, was a shift from courtship and playfulness, the primary tropes of 1930s screwball comedies, to seduction and antagonism, the primary ones of 1950s romantic comedies, with a corresponding reduction of the sexual relation to a conflict between a male's virility and a female's virginity (Krutnik, "Faint" 59–60).

The Tender Trap, made four years before *Pillow Talk*, exemplifies the fifties' "taming of the bachelor" scenario. In this film, women stream in and out of playboy Charlie Reader's (Frank Sinatra) apartment, to have sex with him (in fifties parlance that translates into making out on the couch), of course, but also to bring him food, clean his apartment, and walk his dog. Charlie's best friend, married man Joe McCall (David Wayne), visiting from Indianapolis, admiringly asks how he can "rate" so highly with all these "tomatoes." "It's not what I've got," Charlie replies. "It's what I haven't got. A wife." New York City, unlike their home town, Charlie continues, is teeming with "dames," all enthusiastically descending upon *him* because of his unmarried status. "And you mean all I got to be is a bachelor?" Joe asks in reply, envying his pal's "setup."

Although *Playboy* was still a very new publication when *The Tender Trap* was produced, Charlie's bachelor existence already anticipates what would quickly gel in the popular imagination as the *Playboy* lifestyle where, in the bachelor's apartment, sex and consumption are comparable sources of pleasure for the single man. Charlie's privileged status as a "carefree bachelor," which gives him the upper hand with single women and makes him the envy of married men, rationalizes his sexual irresponsibility as a defiance of domestic ideology. Likewise, his excessive spending on his apartment and nightclubbing (he tells Joe that he makes almost as much as he spends), means he has no plans to save for a future like Joe's. But Charlie's attitude, in turn, encourages the women in his life to infantilize him, undercutting his virile position. As Joe later puts it to his friend, women pester Charlie day and night because they all want "to feed you, caress you, burp you." Charlie's punishment for taking advantage of his mistresses' good natures occurs when they each leave him for boring but more reliable prospects. Eventually, too, the envious Joe sees through Charlie's callow behavior, condemning him as a "louse" for his "indecent" treatment of women. In the meantime, Charlie's means of reformation arrives on the scene in the female body of pert, young Julie Gillis (Debbie Reynolds), who tells anyone who will listen that a woman is not complete until she is married. When the philandering bachelor falls for this earnest virgin, she ensnares him in the "tender trap" of love and marriage. After breaking up because of his dishonest treatment of women, Charlie and Julie reconcile at a mutual friend's wedding in the final scene, when *he* catches the bridal bouquet and sheepishly offers it to her as a sign of his repentance. As *The Tender Trap* tells it, all you have to be is a bachelor to discover that what you *really* want is to be married.

Early in *Pillow Talk*, a conversation between Brad and Jonathan cites this axiom as a basis for placing the former's bachelorhood in the era's domestic ideology. Jonathan, inspired by his own love for Jan, enthusiastically advises Brad to give up his playboy life. Their exchange is worth quoting in full:

> *Jonathan:* Brad, as a friend, sit down, boy, as a friend, I only hope you'll find a girl like this. You oughta quit chasing around and get married.
> *Brad:* Why?
> *Jonathan:* Why? You're not getting any younger, fella. Oh sure, it's fun, it's exciting, dancing, nightclubbing with a different doll every night. But there comes a time when a man wants to give up that kind of life.
> *Brad:* Why?

Jonathan: Because he wants to create a stable, lasting relationship with one person. Brad, believe me, there is nothing in this world so wonderful, so fulfilling as coming home to the same woman every night.

Brad: Why?

Jonathan: Because. That's what it means to be an adult. A wife, a family, a home. A mature man wants those responsibilities.

Brad: Why?

Jonathan: Well, if you want to, you can find tricky arguments about anything. I gotta get out of here. What have you got against marriage anyway?

Brad: Jonathan, before a man gets married, he's . . . uh . . . like a tree in a forest. He—he stands there, independent, an entity unto himself, and then—he's chopped down, his branches are cut off, he's stripped of his bark, and he's thrown into the river with the rest of the logs. Then this tree is taken to the mill. And when it comes out it's no longer a tree. It's a vanity table, a breakfast nook, baby crib, and the newspaper that lines the family garbage can.

Jonathan: No, no. If this girl weren't something extra special, then maybe I'd agree with you. But with Jan, you look forward to having your branches cut off.

Frank Krutnik uses this scene to illustrate how *Pillow Talk* invokes a fantasy of bachelorhood as phallic omnipotence and marriage as castration ("Faint" 60). But like the joke about the playboy going straight, the wit running through this conversation is multilayered, creating an ambiguous effect in its double-edged representation of the sexual relation according to domestic ideology. The tension that gives the exchange its punch here comes from the way it divides masculinity: male viewers may admire Brad's resistance because of the humor in the picture of castration that he draws, but they also have to empathize with Jonathan's capitulation because of the position in domestic ideology from which he speaks. But that latter position is itself divided because Jonathan is a witness whose evidence is tainted. He has been married three times already, so to what extent can he say that he knows the fulfillment of "coming home to the same woman every night," and *really* get us to believe it? Clearly, he speaks in the glow of his own (futile) desire to marry Jan. And the look on Tony Randall's face after he delivers the last line of this exchange recognizes his character's acceptance of—even desire for—a castration that Brad claims to have escaped in remaining "independent, an entity all unto itself," in a word, a bachelor. Nonetheless, viewers who might side with Brad and deride Jonathan's faith in marriage and maturity must also know that the irresistible logic of the Hollywood couple supports what the latter says and will eventually undermine the bachelor's inflated image of independence from marriage.

Implicitly acknowledging that the breadwinner and the bachelor are male positions in ideology, so that the uncastrated bachelor is no more natural an expression of masculinity than the responsible, emasculated husband, the exchange between Brad and Jonathan establishes the terms by which *Pillow Talk* will go on to dramatize the bachelor's successful conversion to domestic ideology. After he tricks Jan and she spurns his apologies, Brad discovers, much to his chagrin, that Jonathan is right twice over: there *is* "nothing in this world so wonderful, so fulfilling as coming home to the same woman every night," and, if he can ever reconcile with Jan, he *will* "look forward to having his branches cut off." From the perspective of Brad's conversion, the sexual relation seems straightforward enough: the female convinces the male of the need to be more responsible (her condition for going to bed with him), and he loosens up her inhibitions (so that when they go to bed, it will be mutually orgasmic). Ideologically, this view of sexual difference reinscribes the double standard that, contrary to the revelations of Kinsey's 1953 report on women, men are sexually active and aggressive and so entitled to premarital sexual experience, while women, being sexually passive and timid, are not. This hypocritical axiom further assumes that the Day character is not only sexually inexperienced and objectified but also repressed; she therefore needs the touch of the big, strong, strapping male—his branches tall, outstretched, and intact—to stir her up. As *Pillow Talk* actually goes about working out this view of sexual difference, however, it turns out to be the other way around. The ad copy quoted at the start of this section already hints at the way Brad and Jan invert the gender conventions of heterosexual coupling in fifties America. He may be "a carefree bachelor" and she "a careful career girl," but he is also the one "who believes in '*TOGETHERNESS*'," and she the one "who insists on '*SINGLENESS*'," the advertisement quoting, underlining, and capitalizing these two words to insist upon the irregularity of their unexpected sexual innuendo.[2]

Sex and the Single Woman

Doris Day herself reportedly "did not feel she was playing a virgin" in *Pillow Talk*, although she was quite aware that audiences projected such a reading onto Jan Morrow (Hudson and Davidson 116). To be sure, the lyrics to the title song, played over the opening credits, frame the film to support the assumption that Jan will guard her virginity to the death—or until she finds the right marriageable "boy." In the song's refrain, Doris Day complains that she is tired of "hearing myself talk, talk, talk," and she wonders "how it would be / To have someone to pillow talk with me." The verse describes her nightly situation as an unmarried female: "All I do is talk to my pillow / Talk to my pillow. . . / Talk about the boy I'm gonna marry / Some day, somehow, some time." Taken at face value, the lyrics bind female desire entirely to the goal of a companionate marriage. To encourage this reading, during the opening credits a man and a woman appear on opposite sides of the wide screen, each talking on the phone while lying on their backs in bed with their legs up, tossing pillows back and forth over the space where the credits appear (and causing one to wonder why the film isn't called "Pillow Fight").

However, it is hard to discount the more unorthodox implications of the song in supplying the pretext of Jan Morrow's characterization as a single woman. Day's vocalized rendering of her character's desire dramatizes Jan's subjectivity as an act of nocturnal fantasy, not crying into her pillow but imagining what it would be like to "pillow talk" with someone and then going further to articulate a sexual desire as yet in excess of an actual person, thereby moving it beyond the scope of love and marriage. When Day sings of talking into her pillow every night in solitude, her "pillow talk," which she is doing alone to compensate for not being able to do it with "a pillow-talking boy," is surely a euphemism for masturbation. Reiterating this implication, the advertising campaign exclaimed in the posters and the trailer that "pillow talk" is "what goes on when the lights go off!" If that's the case, then what does a single woman do when the lights go off and, as the song says, she is all alone with her pillow? This question gives the title "Pillow Talk" its strong connotation of a female sexuality comparable (if not actually, as Kinsey revealed, superior) to the male's in its urgency, its power, and its fantasizing.

To reinforce the song's implication of Jan's active sexuality, *Pillow Talk* consistently adopts her focalizing position, at many times making it superior to Brad's (even though she does not know about his masquerade and the audience does) through point-of-view shots gazing at his body, through periodic voiceover commentary about his attractiveness and her desire to know him better, and through Day's singing another song, "Possess Me," as her interior monologue played over their drive to Connecticut, where they go, both intending to consummate their relationship. The film's device of splitting the CinemaScope screen whenever Jan and Brad are on the telephone also makes her sexuality comparable to his so that each character's desire drives the narrative along with equal force At one point, as Jan talks to "Rex" on the telephone in her bedroom, an inserted shot of Brad in his bed appears in the upper right-hand portion of the wide screen over her reclining body, as if to visualize her erotic fantasy and explain the glowing expression on her face while lying in bed in the dark moments prior to the phone's ringing. Regardless of what fifties viewers may have thought about her being a virgin or not, then, *Pillow Talk* does not imagine Jan lacking sexuality. On the drive to Connecticut, Jan thinks in voiceover, "You know, you've gone out with a lot of men in your time, but this—this is the jackpot," and her remark indicates both the superlative value of Rex's masculinity and the experiential ground by which she rates him so highly.

With its characterization of Jan as an active, attractive, unmarried, professional woman living alone in New York City, *Pillow Talk* portrays the same sexualized career woman that *Cosmopolitan* editor Helen Gurley Brown would celebrate in print just a few years later in her bestseller *Sex and the Single Girl:* "There is a more important truth that magazines never deal with, that single women are too brainwashed to figure out, that married women know but won't admit, that married men *and* single men endorse in a body, and that is that the single woman, far from being a creature to be pitied and patronized, is emerging as the newest glamour girl of our times" (3). Reducing Jan (and the Day persona) to the perennial virgin misses this important coding of the single career woman, which the mise-en-scène of *Pillow Talk*—particularly in Jan's costuming and apartment, often color coordinated to reflect her rapport with and domination over her own interior space—emphasizes. The mise-en-scène lays out a potential ground of feminine identification with her professional success that resists what would otherwise be the containment of her single state by the comedy of the bachelor out to seduce the virgin.

It is the bachelor narrative, in other words, which clouds the liberated status of this single woman "as the newest glamour girl of our times." When sparring with Jan on the phone in the first part of the film Brad accuses her of being "a woman who lives alone and doesn't like it," despite her protestations to the contrary. "I happen to like living alone," she avers with a clarity that Brad does not hear since he confuses "living alone" with "not having sex," what he describes as *her* "bedroom problems."

> *Brad:* I don't know what's bothering you, but don't take your bedroom problems out on me.
> *Jan:* I have no bedroom problems. There's nothing in my bedroom that bothers me.

Jan's maid (Thelma Ritter)—the acerbic, alcoholic, and love-starved Alma—has been eavesdropping on this conversation, and she validates Brad's viewpoint to maintain the focus on Jan's supposed virginity. "You know, he makes pretty good sense," Alma observes.

> *Jan:* What did he say that makes such good sense?
> *Alma:* If there's anything worse than a woman living alone, it's a woman saying she likes it.
> *Jan:* Well, I do like it. I have a good job. A lovely apartment. I go out with very nice men to the best places. The theater. Finest restaurants. What am I missing?
> *Alma:* When you have to ask, believe me you're missing it.
> *Jan:* Well, what is a girl supposed to do? Go on out in the street and ask the first man she meets to go home with her?
> *Alma:* No, don't do that, ma'am. It don't work.

Alma influences Jan to doubt her self-confidence so that, following the close of their conversation, Jan goes into her bedroom, which Brad defined as a site of lack (because there's nothing in her bedroom to bother her), where she looks in the mirror, asking in voiceover to internalize his charge of frigidity: "Bedroom problems?"

Viewers—most of the film's academic critics included—tend not to take Jan's defense of her single life seriously because it is filtered through Brad's and Alma's perspectives, with their privileging of a fantastic phallic masculinity. As a consequence, what gets lost in this particular scene, which overtly functions to let viewers think, like Brad, that Jan is a frustrated and repressed virgin, is her outspoken claim that she happens to like living alone. And why shouldn't she? *Pillow Talk* characterizes her liberating modernity—her sophistication, her glamour, her sexuality—through the spectacle of her style of living: her Jean-Louis gowns, hats, furs, and jewels; her elegantly furnished and artfully decorated apartment; her familiarity with New York City's exciting night life; her access to rich people, which gives her great social mobility, through both her job and her dating. In *Pillow Talk,* Jan's significance for the battle of the sexes is that she appropriates for femininity what the culture had accepted, in large part through the influence of *Playboy* magazine, as a proper sexual identity for the bachelor. Day's Jan Morrow is not impersonating the bachelor as a transvestite, in the style of the star's tomboyish roles in the earlier *On Moonlight Bay* (1951) and *Calamity Jane* (1953), say, but feminizing what the bachelor represented, much as Helen Gurley Brown was to do a few years later, following the success of *Sex and the Single Girl,* when she remodeled *Cosmopolitan* and addressed it to the single woman in the workplace, the "Cosmo reader," along lines obviously inspired by *Playboy*—and, no doubt, by *Pillow Talk,* too.

There is no reason, then, *not* to take Jan at her word when she tells Alma she is satisfied with her life, any more than there would be if she were Brad speaking to Jonathan—or a male reader writing in to *Playboy.* If we are to believe *Playboy,* for that matter, unmarried career women like Jan, far from being virgins or prudes, were in fact as sexually experienced as their male counterparts. When *Playboy* told bachelors not to feel guilty about seducing virgins because these women were using them to get sexual experience, the magazine could well have had Jan in mind: "This is particularly true of the bachelor girl who is out of her teens and who is career-minded." Trained for a career either at university or an art school and then moving from a small town to the big city, these educated single women "choose sexual freedom as well as freedom to think out their own choice of profession or life style. . . . Up to 22 or 23, they may abstain from any sexual life, but after that they generally have sex. . . . Many women are beginning to adopt the sexual attitude of bachelors in that they want physical pleasure—or relief, if you prefer—without having to pay for it by signing up for a lifetime" (Archer, "Don't" 21, 32).

If anyone worried about female virginity it was not the single career woman but the bachelor. "All sophisticated playboys are interested in virginity," begins one article on the topic in *Playboy.* "We trust that the matter of your own virginity has already been taken care of. You must now face up to the problem of virginity in your female friends and acquaintances" (F. Smith 9). Another article remarked: "Bachelors are frequently sentimental about virginity, because they consider this the trademark of the 'nice girl'" (Archer, "Don't" 38). Such masculine "sentimentality" covered over the extent to which virility more than virginity was at issue in the culture's overvaluation of the "nice girl." Female virginity paved the ground for a cultural fantasy of male plenitude and power, that phallic image of a "whole" man, "an entity unto himself," conjured up by Brad in his response to Jonathan about why he does not want to get married. The tree metaphor in Brad's defense of his "independence" verbalizes how the playboy's interest in virginity plays out a social comedy of castration, so that the intact female body is made the central issue of his sexual identity: the physical penetration of her body displaces what Brad fears will be the symbolic cutting up of his. In this way, "virginity" functions as an eminently safe figuration of "virility," sustaining, as the ground of representing a sexually potent masculinity, a male psychology of the hunt that repeatedly defers sexual gratification by idealizing as a love object, not a thirty-something sexualized woman like Jan, but an unobtainable nonwoman, "the virgin" who remained a girl until she became a wife.

Pillow Talk dramatizes the male's strong investment in female virginity after Brad is unmasked in Connecticut and Jonathan takes a hysterical Jan back to New York City. When they stop at a roadside diner for coffee, two truck drivers, overhearing Jan sob out her story, incorrectly assume that Jonathan has seduced her, made her pregnant, and now refuses to marry her. Jonathan slaps Jan's cheek to stop her crying, and one of the truckers retaliates, defending her honor by punching him in the jaw. In this exchange, the actual purity or impurity of the female body matters little except as a sign of male power in the eyes of other men. The scene reaches its big laugh when Jonathan receives the punishment that Brad deserves; and even though audiences—laughing as Jonathan slumps down into the booth at Jan's feet, causing her to sob even harder now—recognize the mistake, in order to get the gag they have to view it from the position of those two truckers, who are being excessively sentimental about female virginity, to say the least. The big laugh here secures a perspective on Jan's position at this point in the plot, which, while punishing the absent playboy through a surrogate, still assents to the seduction fantasy that motivates his playboyishness to begin with. By the same token, because Jan *is* there and Brad is not, the scene in the diner has a satiric edge to it sharp enough to expose the playboy's fantasy of the virgin as a myth shared by men of all classes. Jan is crying excessively because she has been deceived by the playboy, not because she has been deflowered, abandoned, or impregnated, as the truckers think. Although sobbing to the point of incoherence, she herself shows no signs of being sentimental about her virginity one way or the other. The purpose of the gag with the truckers is to maintain a male's "sentimental" perspective of Jan's sexuality, thereby smoothing over the real reason for her hurt response—because Brad, a.k.a. Rex, the sexual jackpot for a single woman, turns out to be, as she says, a "big phony."

The scene in the diner typifies how Brad Allen, the bachelor playboy, mediates the representation of Jan's sexuality throughout *Pillow Talk* to the point where her virginity, real or imaginary, functions as the screen on which he projects *his* bedroom problems. The picture Brad initially draws of Jan as a sexually repressed spinster "living vicariously in what you think I do" not only gratifies his ego, it also reflects his own narcissistic investment in the ongoing display of his heterosexuality as a bachelor playboy. This is why Jan's redecoration of his apartment so offends him. When he breaks into her apartment after seeing the redecoration job, he drags Jan screaming from her bed and then, like a "contemporary caveman" (Babington and Evans, *Affairs* 200), carries her back to the scene of the crime, where he confronts her with her dirty deed. His aggression produces closure for the sexual comedy by putting Jan in her proper place, literally so, first in his arms and then in his apartment. Or at least this is how the scene is played to spectators *within* the film. Seeing Brad carry Jan into the elevator inspires the operator Harry "to do something I should have done a long time ago," which is to propose to Alma: "What you need is a man to take care of. Then you wouldn't have so much time to drink." Moreover, the sight of Brad carrying Jan down a busy midtown Manhattan street on a weekday morning results in titillated approbation of his virile behavior by onlookers of both genders and various ages, even by a cop who does not arrest her kidnapper, as Jan requests, but cheers him on.

This climactic scene restores traditional active/passive gender roles to the film but only because it is self-consciously framed by Brad's admiring audience: Harry and Alma, to start with, then the pedestrians, finally the policeman.[3] Brad does not simply carry off Jan to his "cave" in an implied rape; he does it in full view, making a spectacle out of his chest-thumping virility, much like the truckers depicted in the diner scene. If Brad's aggressive behavior at the end of the film consequently seems perfectly acceptable as the "natural" response to what Jan has done to him, that is only because it is being performed for spectators who legitimate it as such. And that was exactly Jan's point when she redecorated his bachelor apartment to call attention to his investment in the apparatus of seduction that makes his domicile a playboy pad.

Too Many Bedrooms

From Jan's perspective, Brad is a "sex maniac" because he does nothing but seduce women on the phone. When, seething in anger, she leaves him in Connecticut, she taunts him with the promiscuous implications of his insincerity: "Bedroom problems! At least mine can be solved in one bedroom. You couldn't solve yours in a thousand." Actually, Brad appears to be solving his nicely enough in *two* bedrooms, thank you, or at least in two beds: his electronically operated sofa-bed downstairs in the spacious living room, which functions as the "active zone" of his bachelor apartment, and his double bed in his bedroom upstairs, which functions as the "quiet zone." As far as we can see from what the film shows him doing there, all he does in this upstairs room is talk on the phone to Jan in his two voices of "Brad" and "Rex." The primary setting when he is in his apartment, Brad's quarters downstairs comprise a perfectly self-contained living space with a bathroom (which we see) as well as a place to sleep (the sofa-bed). Given Brad's barbed comment about Jan's bedroom problems, that automatic sofa-bed is a striking piece of furniture for this bachelor to own. When he sheepishly demonstrates how the sleeper sofa works as Jan inspects his apartment, and this piece of respectable furniture automatically unfolds into a bed designed for having sex, this visual joke gets a laugh because we assume he *does* have sex there. For Jan to be shocked (and audiences amused) at the way he has gotten seduction down to a science, as she remarks afterward to her assistant, that sofa-bed has to register as the ultimate destination whenever he entertains a woman in his home.

But if, as we see at various times in the film, Brad also has a perfectly good double bed upstairs—and the spiral staircase leading there is almost always present in the mise-en-scène of his living room to remind us of the second story in his apartment—why does he need to use the sofa-bed downstairs to have sex with his mistresses? Surely not because he's too lazy to walk upstairs or too inept a seducer to guide a woman up there. Let me put the question more directly: why does *Pillow Talk* need to include Brad's upstairs bedroom, with his own bed distinguished from the one where he (presumably) has sex in his living room, as part of its representation of a bachelor apartment? And in showing the bedroom, why erase any implications of the sexual activity that surely must occur there? Just what does Brad *do* in the bed upstairs?

The bachelor apartment in *Pillow Talk* clearly needs further sorting out, particularly in terms of its mise-en-scène, which displays the same signifying relation of decor and gender that characterizes Jan's. Brad's two-level bachelor pad is far more stylish in its furnishings and expansive in its layout than, say, the comparable setting of *The Tender Trap*, where the playboy lives in a one-bed-room apartment that is decorated in a very functional and slapdash manner. As well as displaying Brad's consumption of expensive commodities encoded as "masculine" (the living room, in addition to having many paintings and books, also boasts hi-fi equipment, a well-stocked bar, attractive—and matching—furniture, a piano, a fireplace), the decor of the bachelor apartment in *Pillow Talk* complies with the style in the rest of the film and with the conventions of fashionable interior decoration generally. According to *Playboy*, for instance, "juxtapositions of textures" of the sort characterizing the various painted and unpainted, smooth and rough wall surfaces of Brad's apartment—which Babington and Evans incorrectly assume shows the absence of a decorating style (*Affairs*, 210)—were designed with the intention of producing a "sense of masculine richness and excitement" ("Playboy's Penthouse" Part I, 57). The wall of paintings behind the sofa ("Men are usually much taken by them," Helen Gurley Brown observed, when recommending that the single girl follow the style [119]) was not just conspicuous consumption but another element of decor: the many neo-modernist paintings connote Brad's contemporary tastes as well as his affluence.

As significantly, the color scheme of Brad's living room, its round white furniture and reddish accents standing out against the warm earth colors of the walls, evokes the furnishing of Jan's (where similarly colored furnishings stand out against bright pastel walls), visually forging a link between the masculine (earth colors) and feminine (pastel colors) domestic spaces in the film. Similarly, the red pillows on Jan's sofa rhyme with the red bolsters on Brad's bed upstairs, as do the pale blue quilted headboard on her bed and the pale blue sheets on his sofa-bed. In their colors, as well as their furniture, both apartments conform to 1959 notions of smartness to signify contemporaneity along with the money needed to commodify good taste. The same month as *Pillow Talk*'s national release, *Life* reported on the way that interior decoration could overcome the "bland similarity" of apartment living. With accompanying color photographs of five sample rooms, the magazine commented, "The only thing these rooms have in common is opulence. There are ankle-deep carpets, original paintings, special tile floors. Rich colors are used—purple, orange, electric blue, stop-light red" ("Opulence" 76). Admittedly, the decorators doing these sample rooms for *Life* were told to mind no expense (and they didn't), while the two apartments in *Pillow Talk* are somewhat sparer to reflect the social status of their occupants as professionals working for the genuinely wealthy class, i.e., millionaires like Jonathan. Nevertheless, Jan's and Brad's apartments each use many of the same type of furnishings and visual motifs that appear in the *Life* photos, most notably those "rich" colors accenting the furniture.

Brad's apartment does differ from Jan's, though not in its style but in its usage. Of the two, the career woman's apartment is the more functional for its occupant's purposes (to sleep, to dress, to have breakfast). Whereas in her domestic space Jan maintains a strict distinction between her professional and personal lives (even when she wants to make business calls from home, his monopolization of their party line prevents her from doing so), Brad does just the opposite, working at the piano (where he writes his songs) and also playing it as a tool of seduction (when he serenades his various mistresses with the song "Inspiration"). His automated sofa-bed epitomizes the blending of public (the sofa) and private (the bed), but then so does the entire first floor of the apartment. Brad's "active zone" serves to visualize the ease with which this playboy combines work and play. As a result, the first floor of this apartment does not draw boundaries between the bachelor's labor and his leisure, his producing and his consuming. Many shot setups in Brad's living room make the piano figure prominently in the mise-en-scène because this instrument represents the ease and the means with which Brad, composing songs for a new musical that Jonathan is backing, plays in order to work and, as a playboy, works hard at his playing.

Visually, then, the film differentiates Brad's apartment from Jan's, engendering it as masculine through the various instruments that allow his apartment to function so well for his purposes. His success as a playboy greatly depends upon the technology of seduction installed in his apartment to the point where his virility is signified primarily by his impressive equipment—I mean the piano, the telephone, the hi-fi, the fireplace, the control panel behind the sofa-bed, in short, the instrumentation that turns Brad's living room into a theater so that he can perform his masculinity for an audience, particularly when he talks on the telephone. Designed as a setting that theatricalizes his virility as the quintessential bachelor playboy, the implications of which Jan's redecoration pushes to an extreme, Brad's living room functions to bring out the performative basis of his heterosexuality. The telephone, his primary mode of seduction, also figures prominently in the mise-en-scène of his apartment because, even more than the piano, it is the central prop of his playboy performance, enabling his pose of sincerity when he sings "Inspiration" to go undetected as a performance. Not a traditional male symbol, the telephone guarantees Brad's virility since, much to Jan's chagrin in the opening scenes, it is the prosthesis that lets him keep going and going, morning and night.[4] Even when Brad has a woman in his apartment (we see him there with one of his mistresses, Marie), he is still "on," singing insincerely of his "inspiration" during their tête-à-tête before the fireplace. And since the automated sofa-bed suggests that Brad has sex downstairs rather than in his bedroom, it is reasonable to assume that when in that piece of furniture with one of his mistresses, he really *is* expected to perform.

Brad's bedroom upstairs, which the film takes pains to show at several points once he begins impersonating Rex, visually signifies the spatial division of his apartment, expressive of the divided masculinity that Brad himself comes to represent for the film because of his masquerading. Given the rakish characterization of this playboy, one would expect Brad's bedroom to have a revolving door, so the quieter use to which *Pillow Talk* puts this upstairs room is surprising, unless one recalls how the bedroom similarly establishes the "quiet zone" of *Playboy*'s ideal bachelor apartment. The resemblance is not quite exact, however. While Brad's bachelor apartment shares the two-part layout of *Playboy*'s, it inverts the purposes of the latter's division into "active" and "quiet zones." In its imaginative rendering of the ideal bachelor apartment, *Playboy* meant to organize a safe space for a single man, differentiating public and private areas of the apartment in order to represent in the spatial terms of the "quiet zone" the underlying unity of his masculinity. That unity is imaginary, a means of sealing over a male subjectivity divided between work and leisure. The bachelor apartment in *Pillow Talk* repeats the spatial dualism of "active" and "quiet zones" but it produces the opposite effect. Its multilevel layout transforms the seeming unity of the playboy's "carefree" bachelor existence into spatial recognition of his divided subjectivity. The "active zone" of Brad's apartment makes his work and leisure comparable (an equivalence imagined through his piano), suggesting that the bachelor playboy can achieve in his home space a natural unity lacking in other men, particularly when they are married. But every time we glimpse the bedroom upstairs, that "quiet zone" exposes his apparent unity as a false front, a masquerade enabled by the excessive theatricality of the "active zone" downstairs. Producing a more jarring sense of the bachelor's sexual contradiction than on the pages of *Playboy*, the bachelor apartment in *Pillow Talk* is a much more transgressive place— dangerous both for the bachelor and his culture.

I therefore find it highly significant that *Pillow Talk* does not imagine Brad's bedroom as a place where he has sex with women. For one thing, confining his romantic liaisons to the apartment's "active zone" means that his heterosexuality never transcends theatricality; despite the way that the bachelor playboy has been read by critics of the film, no natural "caveman" ends up seeping through the multiple layers of performances and deceptions that Brad relies upon to personify virility. For another, whenever the film shows Brad alone in his bedroom talking to Jan, he impersonates both Rex and himself to keep his charade going, thereby experiencing exactly what he told Jonathan he was determined to avoid—being cut up and multiplied. Brad's upstairs bedroom consequently has to keep appearing in the film as Brad becomes more and more embroiled in his masquerade, because it is, ultimately, the site from which *Pillow Talk* queries the singularity, stability, and authenticity of the playboy's heterosexual masculinity; and the view from that private world upstairs, the film strongly implies, is the critical vantage point of the closet.

Pretending to Be Two Other Guys

Actually, Brad has still another bedroom he doesn't use for sex in *Pillow Talk*: the room at the Plaza Hotel that he rents as Rex Stetson in order to begin his seduction of Jan. His strategy is to gull her into making all the aggressive moves, and he does this by setting his playboy and pureboy personae off of each other. Rex calls Jan to arrange their first dinner date and Brad gets on the line afterward, pretending to have overheard and telling her not to trust Rex's gentle demeanor. Like all men, he'll find some excuse to take her to his hotel room, Brad warns, "and that, Miss Morrow, is when the payoff comes." Sure enough, after dinner Rex brings Jan up to his hotel room, ostensibly for his topcoat, where she stands stony-faced, waiting for the "payoff" Brad has led her to expect. However, Rex puts on his coat and is ready to leave after showing

her the lovely view of Central Park at night. Jan professes surprise at his
civility. "I should have known you were not like the others," she confesses. "But
I had to be sure."

If he's "not like the others," doesn't that mean that Rex is, well, different?
After first meeting Rex, Jan considers him a potential suitor as she falls asleep,
thinking in voiceover: "Obviously he respects you. He didn't even try to kiss
you. Or maybe you don't appeal to him." Or maybe he respects women *so*
much that he swings the other way? That's Brad's line the second time he
goads Jan. After she boasts on the phone that he was wrong about the gallant
Rex Stetson leading her on for the quick payoff, he wonders aloud if Rex is
"worse" than he thought. "There are some men who just . . . are very close to
their mother. You know, the type who like to collect cooking recipes, exchange
bits of gossip." Jan replies: "What a vicious thing to say!" Brad snidely persists:
"Don't you think you'd better make sure?" Later that evening, at a piano bar
aptly named the Hidden Door, Rex lays on the effeminacy pretty thick, first
asking Jan about her work, which allows her to deal with all those "colors and
fabrics and all," and then, his pinkie up in the air, tasting the dip on the bar
and mentioning how much he'd like to bring the recipe back home to his
mother. In response, Jan takes the initiative, asking Rex if he is or is not
sexually interested in her. They kiss for the first time in the film, and then kiss
again, after which Jan goes to the powder room (she calls it the "powder
moon," her slip of the tongue indicating her sexual arousal).

While Brad and Rex are the same "marvelous-looking man"—to quote Jan's
voiceover, as she sits with Rex in a taxi on the night they first meet, her gaze
scanning up his torso from his waist to his face—the contrasting personae
polarize the masculinities they represent for the film. Playboy Brad's urbanity,
self-confidence, sexual aggression, dishonesty, disrespect for women, and im-
morality heighten pureboy Rex's opposing qualities: a rural background, insecurity, gentleness, sincerity, gallantry, ethics. More to the point of the film's
romantic energies, Brad seduces women while Rex courts them; Brad objectifies them sexually while Rex makes friends with them. True, Jan marries Brad
in the conclusion, but Rex is the man she falls in love with, and the film shows
how his courtship exceeds Brad's seduction to make evident that the joy the
couple feels when together is a more complicated and rewarding view of the
sexual relation than the *Playboy* fantasy of deflowering the virgin. Until the
scene at the Hidden Door, Rex and Jan do not kiss, let alone consummate their
relationship. Nonetheless, in a montage of day and night scenes of their going
about New York City together, *Pillow Talk* shows the two enjoying themselves
tremendously, and their continual laughter gives their dating relationship its
strong sense of sexual energy in the middle portion of the film.

Following the conventions of romantic comedy, *Pillow Talk* implies in its
closure that when Jan marries Brad he somehow integrates the two opposing

sides of his personality. But to what extent can Brad and Rex be satisfactorily unified into a whole male identity? Rex's gentle persona effectively critiques Brad's wolfish playboy bachelor, offering an alternative figuration of unmarried masculinity, which is why Jan thinks she's hit "the jackpot" with Rex. Furthermore, *Pillow Talk* does not differentiate between the contrasting male personae of Brad Allen and Rex Stetson simply on the basis of one being a truthful identity and the other a disguise. On the contrary, through the persona of Rex, whose attractive masculinity we witness being constituted out of a series of gender performances for an appreciative audience in Jan Morrow, *Pillow Talk* implies that every expression of masculinity is theatrical and not natural, surely not natural in the sense evoked by Brad's image of himself as a tree. Because the success of Brad's performance as Rex is ample evidence of the playboy's own gender trouble, the question of Rex's being queer, of his not being "like all the others," hangs over his persona from the moment he fails to kiss Jan goodnight for the first time. Rex does not register as queer simply because Brad drops several homophobic clues in Jan's path. Rather, Brad's masquerading as Rex evokes a sense of the ongoing gender performance that was expected of closeted gay men in the fifties, when a bachelor like Rex often had to pretend he was another guy: someone virile and outwardly heterosexual, someone just like Brad.

Pillow Talk turns around the masquerade required of the closet, so that the virile male made in the image of all the others (the confirmed bachelor) is the one who poses in public as the different kind of male, the one not like the others (the queer man). Brad, in this regard, comes out of his upstairs bedroom as Rex, the man Jan falls in love with for his very *un*phallic masculine characteristics. Originally, Brad's intention in posing as Rex confirms his heterosexuality: he wants to get back at Jan for her rude behavior on the phone, add another notch onto his sofa-bed, and steal her from his best buddy, all in one crafty maneuver. "I don't know how long I can get away with this act," he thinks in voiceover as he sits next to Jan in the taxi after they first meet. "But she's sure worth a try." The film shows that Jan *is* worth the effort to get to know; but more to the point, the effort, not to say expense, that Brad undertakes in wooing her indicates that he has more of an investment in his masquerade than he ever realizes. If Rex's interest in the minute details of Jan's work as an interior decorator implies his gayness (as Brad himself states), what are we to make of Brad's own interest in the fine points of *his* masquerade, right down to taking the time and expense of renting a room at the Plaza Hotel simply for the dramatic effect of not putting the moves on Jan? Or what about the pleasure he evinces in the details of Rex's fictional biography, as when he tries to get Jan to visualize his mountain in Texas, using the objects on the restaurant table as props? Clearly, the masquerade acquires an importance for Brad that exceeds his original rakish intentions and is in that sense liberating for him, not only because he doesn't have to play the wolf with Jan, but because his sheep's clothing allows him to come out of his bachelor apartment with the truth about his heterosexuality, which is that it is neither whole nor natural but an ongoing performance.

The Masculine Masque(e)rade

As a defense against the queer coding of Brad's masquerading as Rex, *Pillow Talk* provides him with a more gentle, effeminate male counterpart in Jonathan, whose neuroses deflect attention from the denting of the playboy's virility by the masquerade plot. In the friends' exchange about marriage, Jonathan's willing subjection to domestic ideology measures Brad's potency in having evaded the buzz saw of marriage. The string of divorces, his dependency on his psychiatrist, and his mother fixation—in short, his inability to digest the fruits of domestic ideology—characterize Jonathan as a failed heterosexual, not so subtly making the indirect point that his best friend, who suffers from none of those problems, is just the opposite, a successful heterosexual. Brad is quite literally made the straight man to Jonathan's fey foil.

Pillow Talk by no means originated the comic convention of having an effeminate rival or confidante serve to authenticate the virility and normality of the leading man. Aside from its source in stage comedy, this was a convention of the Astaire-Rogers musicals and screwball comedies in the 1930s (i.e., the Ralph Bellamy part, as it became known), as well as the inspiration for shading the Hope-Crosby and Kelly-Sinatra pairings in musicals of the 1940s. Furthermore, as Barbara Klinger notes, the pairing of Hudson with Robert Stack in the Douglas Sirk melodramas *Written on the Wind* (1956) and *The Tarnished Angels* (1957) anticipates the latter casting of Hudson with Randall in the Doris Day comedies (109). However, with its witty use of Hudson and Randall, *Pillow Talk* did set the standard for the sex-comedy cycle in the following decade. In the sixties films, which already begin responding to the impact of various counterculture movements in resituating gender and sexuality, the playboy bachelor critiques a rival expression of masculinity in an effeminate male, and this critique, in its turn, is made the unquestionable measure of the playboy's heterosexuality.[5] *Pillow Talk* differs significantly from its later imitators because it does not turn this convention into an outright rejection of effeminacy or homosexuality. The pairing of Brad and Jonathan complements the doubling of Brad and Rex, with the result that Jonathan, who mirrors Rex's persona in many respects (both are millionaires, both are gentle with Jan, both talk about their mothers), is more much than the fey foil working to enhance the playboy's virility.

Hudson's buddy relation to Randall was repeated in all three of his films with Day, suggesting that the pairing of the two big stars as a hugely popular romantic couple, one still famous enough to evoke the period and its contradictory sexual values, was somehow inconceivable without the third performer's support. For this reason it pays to notice what the follow-up comedies dropped from *Pillow Talk* when it came to reproducing its apparent formula for success, namely, the best friends' sexual rivalry over Day. In both *Lover Come Back* (1961) and *Send Me No Flowers* (1964), Randall is Hudson's best friend and fey foil, but he no longer intersects with or complicates the Day-Hudson sexual relation as he does in *Pillow Talk,* where he functions as the third figure in a homosocial triangulation of male sexuality.

Jonathan's double duty as Jan's suitor and Brad's best friend, in contrast to Randall's simpler role in the later two Hudson-Day comedies, prevents him from occupying a single, stable position in *Pillow Talk*'s homosocial plotting of heterosexual desire. Jonathan's description of the woman he wants to marry is what initially makes bachelor Brad think of his telephone nemesis as a potential erotic object, so it is the rivalry between the two best friends that lays the foundation of Brad's desire for Jan once they meet in the flesh. By the time Brad replaces his best friend as the more suitable sexual partner for Jan, *Pillow Talk* also makes clear through Jonathan that the three positions in its homosocial triangle are interchangeable, with one character perhaps *too* easily replacing the other. Aside from the obvious ways that one man fills in for the other (as when Jonathan receives the blow really meant for Brad in the diner, or when Brad takes Jan to Jonathan's place in Connecticut), Jan and Jonathan are also interchangeable in this structure, as the similarity of their names suggests. Jan's beau on the one hand and Brad's buddy on the other, Jonathan straddles both sides of the battle of the sexes, sustaining an affective connection to each member of the romantic couple. Consequently, in the structural terms of the homosocial triangle he can be seen competing with Jan for Brad's affection just as much as he vies with Brad over her.

This queerer version of the more orthodox homosocial triangle emerges most plainly after the scene in the diner, when a bruised Jonathan reveals to Brad that he has given Jan up on the advice of his psychiatrist. Imagine: even though his buddy has stolen his girl and indirectly caused him to suffer a broken jaw, Jonathan *still* remains best friends with Brad, choosing the man over the woman. Nor has the aborted effort to steal Jan away from his best friend cooled Brad's feeling for Jonathan. As Brad tries to win Jan back, he discusses his strategies with Jonathan; as Brad waits for Jan to redecorate his apartment, in Jonathan's presence he calls all his old girlfriends to tell them he's getting married; Brad takes Jonathan with him to see the remodeled apartment; and the film's coda testifies to the success of the couple's marriage because Brad is on his way to tell Jonathan that he and Jan are expecting a baby. Given the fact that Brad's desire for Jan originates, even before he lays eyes on her, in the thought of his cuckolding Jonathan, the importance of the men's friendship outlasting their sexual rivalry indicates that, for Brad as well as

Figure 39.
When Jan meets Brad in his persona of Rex, there follows a series of gags about
Hudson's large body. Here he slings the unconscious Tony Walters
(Nick Adams) over his shoulder like a side of beef.

Jonathan, the homosocial bonding is more fundamental to their masculinities
than their heterosexual desire. Brad may consequently appear to enjoy a sexual
entitlement to Jan that the more effeminate Jonathan lacks; nonetheless, their
bonding, the film shows, is what makes the heterosexual desire of either man
possible.

Far from simply supplying a means of preserving the supposed authenticity
of the bachelor playboy's virility, a convention that implies a homophobic suspicion about alternative forms of masculinity like effeminacy, the friendship of
Brad and Jonathan also provides the ground for a running gag through which
Pillow Talk voices suspicions about the authenticity of the male body itself as
a "natural" guarantee of heterosexuality. To be sure, in appearance the film
gives every sign of doing just the opposite, since it verbally and visually fetish-
izes the body of the bachelor playboy; but that turns out to be another way of
describing how the male body becomes so thoroughly implicated, for the performer as well as his audience, in a masquerade of masculinity. After listening

to Jan describe Rex in height as well as manner, Alma urges her on: "Six foot six inches of opportunity doesn't come along every day, you know." As Richard Meyer points out, Alma's comment about Rex's size "leaves little doubt that the length of Hudson's body is to be measured as phallus" (260). Elsewhere in *Pillow Talk* camera setups follow the convention of other Universal-International films with Hudson, which show him crouching in the frame, again to emphasize his phallic proportions. The visual comparison to the more diminutive Randall achieves the same effect, as does the great difference in height between Hudson and Nick Adams. Adams plays Tony Walters, the college-age son of Jan's wealthy client who forces his attentions on her but passes out from too much drink while they are dancing. When Jan and Rex meet over the body of the unconscious Tony, their encounter initiates a series of visual gags about Rex's size. He slings Tony over his shoulder like a slab of beef and sends him back to Scarsdale in a taxi, and then cannot get his giant body in or out of Tony's foreign sports car to drive Jan home, the visual point being that this is an *American* phallus that does not bend very easily.

On one hand, these jokes about Rock Hudson's size all glorify how Rex's body signifies the unmistakable presence of the phallus as the surefire guarantee of his underlying virility as Brad. The bachelor's body isn't naturally manly because it is *like* a tree—it turns out that his body *is* a tree. But on the other hand, the visual gags also implicate Rex's/Brad's/Hudson's phallic body in gender performativity since they make the bachelor playboy the object of spectacle, someone who is being watched erotically by another on screen and off. Note how often Randall has to look up at Hudson because the camera setups play upon their contrasting heights. The result, as Mark Rappaport's video essay *Rock Hudson's Home Movies* observes, is to suggest an erotic gaze on Randall's part similar to Day's. The body of the bachelor in *Pillow Talk*, whether we are talking about Brad, Rex, or Hudson, turns out to be too deeply problematic for conventional straight coupling because of its erotic value as the support of a gender performance.

Pillow Talk marks the male body's transgressive potential with a running gag that takes the breakdown of the masculine/feminine binary to its queerest extreme: the pregnant male. At one point during his masquerade as Rex, Brad almost runs into Jan in Jonathan's office; to avoid an untimely meeting, he dashes into a nearby doctor's office. Unaware that the doctor is an obstetrician, Brad blithely walks into a waiting room of pregnant women and asks for assistance. "I haven't been feeling too well," he tells the nurse. "It's probably just an upset stomach. But a fellow can't be too careful." After the surprised nurse goes to get the doctor, Brad decides he can now emerge from his hiding place and leaves the office. When the doctor finds Brad gone, he turns on the nurse: "The man said he was going to have a baby, and you let him get away?" She responds: "But he was obviously a psychopath." Later, when Brad and Jan run into each other in Jonathan's office after the exposure of the masquerade, Brad chases her into

Figure 40.
In the coda, Brad exclaims, "I'm going to have a baby!" and is dragged off by the
doctor and nurse who suspect he may have crossed "a new frontier."

the ladies room; the nurse sees him emerging and goes to get the doctor, who chides her disbelief by announcing that Brad may be a man who has "crossed a new frontier." Finally, in the coda, which occurs three months after Brad and Jan reconcile and marry, he goes to Jonathan's office one more time when the doctor and nurse, as if lying in wait all this while, grab him. Brad tries to explain that he's on his way to his best friend to give him the good news: "I'm going to have a baby!" The doctor and nurse nod knowingly in agreement, as they drag him yelling down the hall.

The coda not only picks up and runs with the queer implications of Brad's masquerading as Rex but, textually speaking, it also displaces the heterosexual couple from the very end of the film's narrative, turning the homosocial triangle on its head to reemphasize the bachelor's bond with his best friend. True, in the very last moments the film anticipates the new married couple's great fertility, indicating that Brad will go on to sire many more children (and that Jan will no doubt have to give up working to become a baby-making machine)

to show that he is clearly not castrated as a result of marrying; but this information is relayed extradiegetical during the closing credits. For this reason, as
far as *Pillow Talk* is concerned, I find it hard to agree with Klinger when, in her
generalization about Hudson's comedies, she sees the bachelor's ultimate absorption into domestic ideology—"with marriage and a passel of kids"—easily
confirming both "the inevitability of heterosexual monogamy as a social norm"
and "Hudson's manliness" (115–16). Clearly, if that were the only goal of *Pillow Talk* at this point, there would have been other, more straightforward ways
to announce the impending product of Brad and Jan's marriage.[6] Because the
sexual comedy of *Pillow Talk* is, in narrative terms, perfectly closed with the
bachelor's marriage, the very presence of the coda in the text, with its gag about
a transgressive male body, signals some sort of excess of meaning arising from
his ungovernable sexuality. That excess, which the doctor tries to literalize as
the body of a pregnant male, the nurse to expel as psychopathology, and the
closure to recuperate as the married man, points to the way Rock Hudson's star
persona figures into this film.

"But a Fellow Can't Be Too Careful"

Rock Hudson is more of a romantic figure today than at any time in his life. His
divorce from Phyllis Gates became final in August, and he joined the ranks of the
eligible Hollywood males. (Parsons, "Rock")

Louella Parsons's observation about the timing of Rock Hudson's huge popularity at the moment of *Pillow Talk*'s release in 1959 catches the essential paradox of his star persona, particularly as highlighted by retrospective knowledge of the actor's homosexuality. If, as most of Hudson's fans now know,
his 1955 marriage to Phyllis Gates was arranged by his agent (and her employer), Henry Willson, in order to preserve the actor's heterosexual persona,
why was it that he became *more* of a romantic figure at the exact point when
his marriage publicly failed?

Meyer believes that Hudson's popularity as a screen idol depended upon
the recurring tension between the actor's representation of attractive heterosexuality in his films and his own active if closeted homosexuality in his private
life. According to Meyer, the quiet, gentle, and unthreatening masculinity that
Hudson personified for the fifties was a crucial effect of his homosexuality,
which "—however disavowed by Hollywood, by the film viewer, or by Hudson
himself—registered in his star image, in the sexual immobility of his masculinity, in the way that women really *could* count on him to maintain his erotic
distance" (279, 282). Meyer goes on to explain that what audiences perceived
as attractive in Hudson's heterosexuality—on screen in the melodramas that
made him a big star, intertextually in the beefcake imagery of fan magazines

(which openly eroticized his body as his films themselves rarely did), and off screen in the short-lived marriage to Phyllis Gates—was actually the dividend of his living in the closet: the homosexual's expertise in passing as straight, the "(gay) knowledge of how to construct an ideal heterosexuality for, and in, representation" (272).

Meyer's reading of Hudson's star imagery registers an undeniable and disturbing undercurrent generated by the well-known artificiality of the actor's persona, starting with the fabricated name. In a *Look* cover story on the star, one anonymous naysayer was quoted complaining that Rock Hudson was nothing but artifice, "completely an invention of his agent. His name, his voice, his personality were all made up for him." But fans of the star's screen appeal and talent did not defend him by denying the circumstances of his transformation at the hands of agent Willson; on the contrary, they simply accepted the fabrication of an apparently blank façade as part and parcel of the Hollywood star system.[7] In fact, according to *Look*, Hudson's "greatest asset— not counting his looks—has been his very blandness," because of what it connoted: the absence of angst, neurosis, rebellion, decay. "He's wholesome," *Look* quotes one "Hollywood veteran" to explain Hudson's success. "He doesn't perspire. He has no pimples. He smells of milk. His whole appeal is cleanliness and respectability—this boy is pure" (Harris 48). Nor was *Look* alone in making this observation. It was the strategy behind the studio's promotion of Hudson on film and off.

Pointing to the *Look* article, Klinger argues that the wholesome male persona was crucial to Hudson's star function, which was to embody "sexual normalcy" (99) as a conservative alternative to the psychological profile of the "disturbing new trends in male stardom" (106). Set in contrast to the likes of Brando, Clift, Dean, and their many imitators, Hudson personified a safer and more manly version of masculinity than was personified by those boys who were not men because of his own apparently "uncomplicated virility" (99), an image carefully and consistently built up by the studio's publicity mill. This kind of meaning is made most apparent in the oppositional casting of Hudson and Dean in *Giant* (1955). However, though the star system set Hudson's persona against that of the more neurotic and "dangerous" young stars, as I also explained when comparing him to Brando in the previous chapter, his virility was not, strictly speaking, all that "uncomplicated" or "conservative." Hudson was not Clift, Brando, or Dean, to be sure, but then neither was he John Wayne. Indeed, if any star emerged at this time to check the rebel boys by personifying "a historical throwback, a quasi–Paul Bunyan figure who has maintained innate masculine characteristics unpolluted by fame or civilization" (104), it was not Hudson but Charlton Heston. Likewise, the more powerful containment of the new stars' "abnormalcy" was not Hudson but, as I showed in the previous chapter, a more genuinely conservative star like Wayne.

Hudson's persona actually implied an alternative to the traditional "normalcy" with which he was overtly associated, and *Pillow Talk* brings out this element of his masculinity through its masquerade plot, which satirizes his star image as an icon of seemingly unproblematic virility. At the very least, the success of his own passing as straight confirms what *Pillow Talk* proves through Brad's masquerade, namely, that convincing heterosexual masculinity is itself merely a question of "proper" representation. A closeted gay man like Hudson could make the best straight man, precisely because he (and his agent) had learned to mime—and to mine—the part so well. To be sure, in 1959 audiences at *Pillow Talk* were aware of Rock Hudson's failed marriage but not of his homosexuality, which is no doubt why the film could be bold enough to embed his bachelor character in so much queer innuendo. For as Hudson himself put it years later, America just didn't want to know.[8] Given the widespread assumption that the studio, Willson, and Hudson wanted to conceal his homosexuality at all costs, it's revealing of the sexual tensions that his star persona could not completely reconcile that the comedies he made after *Pillow Talk* all build upon this film's masquerade plot in one form or another. Although *Pillow Talk* was recognized, as *Life* observed at the time, as widening his talents beyond the expanse of his impressive 43-inch chest ("Rollicking" 73), this hit comedy did not, as Klinger maintains, simply reinvent the star persona of Rock Hudson for the sixties—by projecting a "heterosexually fixated" (115) masculine bachelor image "at odds with his earlier, pristine image" (101)—so much as build into its plot a perceptive self-consciousness, if not outright critique of the pureboy star persona that had been carefully cultivated by the collaborative efforts of the melodramas made by Universal-International, his agent Henry Willson, and the fan industry.

In 1955, as Hudson was shooting *All that Heaven Allows*, *Life*'s first ever cover story on the star describes him in a way that already makes apparent the divided masculinity in his persona shown to brilliant effect in *Pillow Talk*. The magazine comments: Hudson became a star "on the strength of his amiable good looks and, even more, on a determined bachelorhood. But now [fans] are beginning to grumble. . . . Fans are urging 29-year-old Hudson . . . to get married—or explain why not" ("Simple" 129). Though the demand for an explanation is instantly disavowed in the text of the article (readers are quickly informed that he was too busy making movies to find time to get a haircut, let alone a wife), it reverberates throughout the magazine's portrait of his "determined bachelorhood" with the same effect that Brad's innuendoes about Rex have for *Pillow Talk*.

What the public wanted from Hudson in the period when he became a big star was, as *Life* put it, an explanation of his bachelorhood, which is not the same as a confirmation of his heterosexuality, and this desire persisted even after he married Phyllis Gates in 1955. With a fervor analogous to today's TV tabloids, the fan magazines continued to scrutinize every detail of this union, largely because it took them by surprise and lasted for so short a dura-

Figure 41.
In 1958 *Screen Album* asked the question on everyone's mind, if not
their tongues, after Rock Hudson's divorce.

tion. Refuting rumors of trouble, *Movieland* observed that "MARRIAGE is what every man needs, even Rock Hudson." When the marriage hit the rocks and the couple separated, *Photoplay* asked, "Can Rock's marriage be saved?" offering "Her Side" and "His Side" versions of the split in *Rashomon*-like style. Once the marriage headed for the divorce courts, in 1958 *Screen Album* screamed on the cover of its August-October issue, "Rock Hudson: What kind of romance *does* he want?" Repeated as well in the short article on the star, this seems to have been the question on a lot of minds if not tongues.

Pillow Talk can be seen attempting to answer that baiting question through the cleverness with which it braids allusions to Hudson's star persona into the texture of its masquerade plot. It is easily recognized, for instance (almost everyone writing on the film or on Hudson mentions it), that when Brad masquerades as Rex, every woman's jackpot, he impersonates a Texas oilman much like the role Hudson himself played in *Giant,* his only Oscar-nominated performance. The masquerade that occurs in the plot of *Pillow Talk* underlines Hudson's own persona to emphasize its basis in a gender performance, too. Additionally, the script makes playful reference to another Hudson film through the tree metaphor in Brad's speech to Jonathan, which recalls his role as a gardener in *All that Heaven Allows,* just as the very premise of the irresponsible playboy hiding his real identity in order to romance a woman who hates him is borrowed from *Magnificent Obsession* (1954), and the rivalry of neurotic Jonathan and virile Brad over a New York career girl reiterates the opening plot gambit of *Written on the Wind.*

Pillow Talk's allusions to Hudson's star persona go beyond such obvious in-jokes, moreover. Playboy Brad and pureboy Rex are each carefully composed of identifiable and repeated elements of Hudson's fifties star persona. Because the traits that the playboy manipulates in fashioning his disguise all refer to Hudson himself as characterized by the fan magazines, "Rex Stetson" is much more than a simple jesting allusion to *Giant* as a means of instantly acknowledging the lack of authenticity in Brad's masquerade. Like Rex, Hudson was supposed to be "basically shy, conservative and tolerant," "a devoted son," who, while perhaps not interested in dip himself, did make his own "famous barbecue sauce." And as unlike playboy Brad as could be, Hudson, it was said, like Rex, "hates phonies and has learned to recognize them and keep them out of his life. He has also learned that he wants an uncomplicated girl who can adapt herself to his simple way of life" ("Would" 25). At the same time that he knew what he wanted from the Hollywood rat race, the actor, again like Rex, was just the opposite: "shy, self-conscious and so utterly unsure of himself, his six-feet-three inches were actually a hindrance instead of a help" ("Rock, the New" 39).

In another article on the star that anticipates what would become the Rex persona of *Pillow Talk,* Hedda Hopper interviewed Hudson while he was busy opening a crate from England containing Wedgwood he had ordered for his mother ("Big"). This demonstration of his devotion as a son obviously serves as an allusion to the Wedgwood that signifies Ron Kirby's sensitivity in *All that Heaven Allows,* the film in production at the time of the interview, so it is very telling when it reappears four years later as the trait Brad warns Jan to be on the alert for. The bond between Hudson (then unmarried) and his mother was so close, in fact, that—another article on the star mentions in passing—when he worked overtime at the studio, she would stop by his bachelor house "with a baked ham or a lamb roast" so that he would be sure to have supper (L. Wilson, "How"). On one hand, the accounts of Hudson's strong relationship with his mother mean to evoke his gentle nature, the proof that he was as pure off screen as on; but on the other hand, since a son's dependency on his mother was also well known as a symptom of homosexuality, such evidence of Hudson's wholesomeness is contrived and confused enough to be turned into its own ironic sendup, as *Pillow Talk* points out, precisely for having such a queer shading.

In appreciating the satiric representation of Hudson's pure and wholesome masculinity in *Pillow Talk,* though, we also need to keep in mind that this persona was still in place when he made the comedy. *Pillow Talk* could satirize Hudson without in any way demeaning his significance or damaging his marquee value as its romantic lead because the film also incorporates an element from the fan magazines that was even more crucial to the star's persona than his purity: his status prior to his marriage, in *Life*'s phrase, as "Hollywood's most handsome bachelor" (3 Oct. 1955: cover). *Pillow Talk* was released at the time when Hudson, his marriage over, resumed his bachelor ways and became even "more of a romantic figure today than at any time in his life," as Parsons observed. It is safe to surmise that, at least as far as the studio was concerned, *Pillow Talk* was crucial in reestablishing his star persona as a heterosexual bachelor following the divorce, which is Klinger's point about its consistency with the other comedies. Hence the film's outward strategy of jeopardizing Brad's masculinity through the masquerade plot only to recuperate him for domestic ideology at the end when he and Jan start producing one child after another as evidence of their marriage's bountiful harvest.

But while it may be tempting to conclude that *Pillow Talk* ironizes only Rex, in effect forging a distance between an old and new Hudson, it treats Brad in much the same way and with the same effect of grounding key elements of Hudson's persona in a gender masquerade. Whereas with Rex the allusions to Hudson's persona cluster around his film roles and the wholesome characteristics they reinforced, with Brad the allusions center upon the bachelor apartment. One of the central means through which the fan discourse characterized Hudson's persona was his own bachelor living arrangements since, when he became extremely popular before his marriage, he publicly maintained what was unthinkable according to domestic ideology: "a house without a wife!" (Townsend 53). But then so did many unmarried male stars (like Hudson's own gay friend, George Nader) and without much comment in the press at all.

Highly indicative of the pressures that bachelorhood exerted upon Hudson's star persona is the fact that, as soon as he became a big star in 1954–55 following the success of *Magnificent Obsession*, articles describing his bachelor home appeared in an assortment of venues: *American Weekly*, a newspaper Sunday supplement, and *Life*, as well as movie magazines such as *Photoplay*.

These accounts of the star's bachelor digs illuminate just how carefully *Pillow Talk* incorporates Hudson's offscreen persona into the character of Brad Allen through the latter's high-tech playboy apartment. Recurring details in these articles would go unnoticed now except for the fact that, when placed alongside *Pillow Talk*, they acquire specific resonance as signs of "Rock Hudson." In the same vein, details about Brad in the film appear entirely self-contained until the fan discourse about Hudson's bachelor home reveals an added significance as a reference to his star persona surpassing the diegesis. Thus, for instance, the articles appearing in *Life*, *American Weekly*, and *Photoplay* all take pains to mention how Hudson's piano, his one big piece of furniture, has pride of place in his bachelor home. When *Pillow Talk* subsequently characterizes Brad as a wolfish playboy through his piano playing, this detail metonymically links the playboy with Hudson's offscreen persona in exactly the way that Rex's characterization as a "giant" Texas oilman does.

The piano is not the only metonymy of Hudson's publicized bachelor persona that later appears in *Pillow Talk*. One article includes a photo of him talking (bare-chested) on the phone, with a caption indicating that, as "a popular young bachelor" he phones a lot of women; the magazine then asks the reader to guess which popular young starlet he is calling. The real capper, though, comes with the revelation in the same piece that, like Brad's apartment, Hudson's house is wired! "Push a button in Rock's house and strange things happen—stoves cook, coffee perks, garbage dispenses, glass walls slide, garage doors open, hidden lights come on, and music floods the room" (L. Wilson, "How"). This description of Hudson's new house anticipates both the spatial fluidity of *Playboy*'s ideal bachelor apartment and the technology of Brad Allen's in *Pillow Talk*, which is to say that his bachelor pad is functional for his purposes in every possible way, as the *Photoplay* article also indirectly makes clear. The caption for a photograph of Hudson and "new date, Phyllis Gates" enacts how the bachelor's pad serves as a closet disavowing his homosexuality. "Usually voluble," *Photoplay* comments about Hudson, "he now clams up about dates, switches conversation to his new house!" (Townsend 53). On the one hand, the caption can be taken at face value: he no longer chats about his dates because with Phyllis he's really serious, as his marriage would soon prove. On the other hand, as his marriage does soon prove, Gates was used to cloak his homosexuality—as Meyer puts it, the "marriage [to her] was sufficient to secure and emit the sign 'heterosexuality' . . . [that] would remain publicly affixed to Rock Hudson's body for the following three decades" (274)—and so does the new house. In substituting for his heterosexual dates in conversations with the press, the bachelor home, that "house without a wife," becomes the public sign that displaces Hudson's homosexuality, recognizing what his bachelorhood signifies in the act of refuting knowledge of it.

Through the masquerading bachelor (at once Brad *and* Rex) and his apartment (at once theater *and* closet), *Pillow Talk* may appear in its closure to be reconciling the sexual contradictions informing the movie industry's production of "Rock Hudson" as the ideal unmarried male of fifties American cinema, with the specific effect of reestablishing his star persona as an eligible straight "bachelor" following his divorce (which became final just weeks before the film's premiere); but it is equally clear that the film does not completely seal over the sexual instability in the star's masculine persona. The ongoing references to Hudson as a source for both Rex and Brad divide the rocklike masculinity he represented, and this splitting then subverts the star's male persona by heightening its performativity. As *Pillow Talk* envelops the playboy's heterosexuality so thoroughly in masquerade, its comic plot then gives Brad's (and by implication Hudson's) bachelor apartment additional significance as the homosexual closet, a gloss reiterated in the film's use of that setting to evoke Rock Hudson's own persona and the fan discourse that mediated it.

The appropriateness as well as the mechanism of *Pillow Talk*'s subversion of Hudson's heterosexual bachelor persona may seem more obvious today than in the fifties because of the revelations about his private life following the actor's very public death from AIDS. As Babington and Evans remark, in the light of later knowledge about Hudson's homosexuality, "there is a particular irony about a great heterosexual icon of the cinema whose fabrication includes even the nature of his sexuality" (*Affairs* 205). Such a revisionist account of Hudson is the point of Rappaport's *Rock Hudson's Home Movies,* which illustrates the queer undercurrent of Hudson's divided persona—Rappaport calls it "macho Rock" versus "homo Rock"—by taking scenes from his films out of their narrative contexts for a camp recoding. "It's not like it wasn't up there on the screen if you watched carefully," the actor (Eric Farr) impersonating Hudson tells the audience early on. With *Pillow Talk*, however, Rappaport doesn't have to camp up his clips very much, since this film already incorporates a revisionist view of Hudson's masculinity into its own masquerade plot.

While fifties audiences may have, paradoxically, caught all the jokes in *Pillow Talk* and yet missed what may or may not have been their intended punch line—those many ongoing allusions to Hudson himself as a gay man posing as a straight lover—that does not necessarily mean that the subversion of *heterosexual* masculinity in *Pillow Talk* was not intentional, not perceived, and not pointed directly at the authenticity of the star's persona and the masculinity he exemplified for the fan discourse. After all, the pureboy characteristics chided by Brad for their queer implications were the very elements of Hudson's star persona that the magazines celebrated. But even if one does not think about Hudson's private life while watching the film, because *Pillow Talk*'s masquerade plot divides the playboy's masculinity into "Rex" and "Brad," it is difficult to see how domesticity can possibly accommodate, let alone straighten out this bachelor's riven sexuality. The romantic narrative may therefore close in typical fifties fashion, promising the bachelor's fulfillment as a heterosexual husband through his own personal baby boom; but the coda, with its gag imagining him as a pregnant male, undermines that closure with its joking revelation of the bachelor's ultimate subversion of hegemonic masculinity—a crossing of biology achieved by the queer body that does not lie behind the mask as the definitive truth of sexual difference. Rather, the bachelor's body *is* the mask, which is *Pillow Talk*'s whole point.

Epilogue: Who *Was* That Masked Man?

A publicity still for *Some Like It Hot* (1959), reproduced as figure 42, perfectly visualizes what I have been arguing throughout *Masked Men*. This photo shows Tony Curtis posing in full drag with William Holden, apparently visiting the set and dressed in more normal attire—if it isn't actually a gray flannel suit, when next to Curtis's lady-like Roaring Twenties ensemble, it surely signifies as one. Curtis faces the camera, his lips puckered in mimicry of a woman's, with one arm linked through Holden's and the other touching his shoulder. Holden looks on with a decidedly ambiguous smile that is simultaneously readable as stifled amusement at and extreme discomfort with Curtis's drag costume. Does Holden want to laugh? or is he trying not to gag? This photograph pairs two of the fifties' biggest male stars in a teasing suggestion of gender transgression (in Curtis's costuming, which connotes femininity but does not disguise his Adam's apple) and homosexuality (in his physical intimacy with Holden), and the whole point of the gag (in either sense of the word) depends upon the juxtaposition of queer and normative masculinities. The photo gives the appearance of drawing attention to Curtis's theatricality, literally so, since he apparently is in the middle of shooting a scene from *Some Like It Hot*, and to Holden's greater naturalness, since his lit cigarette suggests that the star has been caught in a candid moment of relaxation as a nonperformer and spectator; but the juxtaposition just as easily leads one to conclude that each man's costume is comparable as a masculine masquerade.

The Billy Wilder film dramatizes this double-edged masquerade with great aplomb. Having witnessed a gangland killing, two buddies, Joe (Curtis) and Jerry (Jack Lemmon), flee Chicago by posing as women (Josephine and Daphne, respectively) and, while sustaining this first impersonation, Joe also poses as another man (Junior, the Shell oil heir) in order to seduce an unsuspecting Sugar Kane (Marilyn Monroe). He even persuades Jerry to go out dancing as Daphne with millionaire Osgood Fielding III (Joe E. Brown) so that he can borrow the latter's yacht as the setting for his second masquerade. Commentary on the film has concentrated on the cross-dressing of Jack Lemmon's character more than Curtis's, emphasizing the androgyny (Bell-Metereau 54–64), or the transvestism (Garber, *Vested* 7), or the homosexuality (Sikov 128–48), or the polymorphous sexuality (French 137–52) suggested by Jerry's masquerade as Daphne. All the attention paid to Jerry is not surprising. He takes to his feminine persona so thoroughly and, ultimately, so happily that he

Figure 42.
William Holden visits Tony Curtis on the set of *Some Like It Hot*
in this publicity still.

even considers the prospect of marrying Osgood—that is, until Joe reminds Jerry he is really a guy, and this fact makes Jerry wish he were dead, a striking confession for a man to make in the age of The Man in the Gray Flannel Suit. But as Osgood observes in the film's justly famous last line, "nobody's perfect."

By comparison, *Some Like It Hot* characterizes the Curtis character in more conventional terms as a conniving, lying wolf with women, a confirmed heterosexual even when in his drag costume. Particularly as viewed against the backdrop of 1920s Chicago, which negates the "manliness" of prewar movie tough-guys George Raft and Pat O'Brien by associating it with violence and death, the cross-gendered disguise of Josephine redeems Joe's heterosexual masculinity—in direct proportion to the way that the cross-gendered persona of Daphne unsettles Jerry's—by giving the rakish bachelor a dose of his own medicine. His feminine perspective as Josephine teaches Joe to act, as he tells his buddy, "on the level" in a relationship with a woman for the first time in his life. This appears to be the case, when, impersonating Junior, Joe relinquishes his customary bravado with a woman, allowing Sugar to take the initiative in seducing him and inverting the aggressive/passive binarism that has previously defined his heterosexual behavior (French 148–50; Bell-Metereau 55, 58).

In playing the "straight" and "queer" masculinities of Joe and Jerry against each other, *Some Like It Hot* follows the convention of buddy comedies like the Hope and Crosby "Road to" series and the Martin and Lewis vehicles, where the pairing of a straight leading man with a comic serves to contain, and therefore give greater license for, the latter's outward subversion of gender norms. True to this convention, Curtis ends up with Marilyn Monroe while Lemmon gets Joe E. Brown. But while the "perfect" mating of one couple, set in contrast to the "imperfect" matching of the other, may appear to reinstate the heterohomosexual binarism organizing fifties masculinity, it does so in parodic fashion, since the indeterminacy of this closure does not resolve the instabilities of "gender" and "sexuality" that *Some Like It Hot* sets in motion when it puts both its male stars in drag. At least one offended viewer from Rochester wrote to the *New York Times* during the film's first-run engagement, complaining about this "utterly tasteless and puerile film designed as a holiday for transvestites," adding: "One gets an awfully uncomfortable feeling watching Tony Curtis and Jack Lemmon have too good a time cavorting as female impersonators" (Rabkin).

As that angry *Times* reader suggests, Curtis's cross-dressing is just as disruptive of traditional feelings about masculinity as Lemmon's, perhaps even more so. After all, *Some Like It Hot* allows Curtis to cavort as a male *and* female impersonator. His character's reformation as a passive, straight lover occurs because the "liberating" confidence Joe gains with Sugar is doubly invested in masquerade. Not only is it acquired through one disguise (Josephine), but it is available to him only through the other (Junior). Junior makes a performance out of what Sugar has told Josephine she wants from a man, her description quoting from the earlier Wilder-Monroe collaboration, *The Seven Year Itch:* "Men who wear glasses are more gentle and sweet and helpless," Sugar confides, "haven't you noticed?" When Joe poses as Junior, the masquerade allows him, not exactly to inhabit the social position of hegemonic masculinity (since he is pretending to be a millionaire), but to adopt its "more gentle" domesticated characteristics nevertheless. Junior's passive heterosexuality amounts to another act of cross-dressing for Joe, and not just in the obvious sense of its being a ploy that disguises his seduction of Sugar. This masquerade "feminizes" him through its declaration of unmanliness, when, to prove his helplessness before her, Junior confesses he is "harmless" with women. "Girls do nothing for me," he says, and his explanation suggests that he not only cannot perform with her, he may not want to. His performance of impotency—and *Some Like It Hot* proposes that such phrasing is not an oxymoron—then results in *his* uttering the cliché that movie heroines are supposed to say after a steamy love scene: "I never knew it could be like this." And the masquerading does not stop here. Because Joe's impersonation of the "frigid" Junior also draws upon the star persona of Cary Grant, the multiplication of personae in this scene (Tony Curtis as Joe as Josephine as Junior as Cary Grant) creates an effect even more dizzying than the one *Pillow Talk* produces through its masquerade plot. In this film, too, the wolfish bachelor's pretense of failed virility, with its intimations of nonheterosexual passivity, ends up implicating his heterosexual aggression in his masquerading, suggesting that Joe's hot and cold male identities are just as performative as his Josephine persona.

Joe, Josephine, and Junior establish the continuum of masquerades along which Curtis oscillates throughout *Some Like It Hot,* thereby calling into question the stability of his character's "straight-man" masculinity. As Ed Sikov points out, "Joe's female identity preexists his cross-dressing" (133), an important detail in the film that viewers do not always catch. Whereas Jerry initially resists the disguise and takes a while to adapt to it, even before he puts on the wig and costume, Joe assumes the voice and puckered expression of his Josephine persona immediately upon realizing that the only way he and Jerry can leave Chicago alive is by joining an all-female band on its way to Florida. Sikov explains that Curtis's impersonation of Josephine can undergo such an instantaneous transformation even without benefit of drag costuming, and without startling moviegoers, because it draws upon the actor's "reputation for being not only handsome but beautiful." The feminine mask (much like the Cary Grant one, let me add) "simply builds in both appearance and performance on a foundation audiences had already perceived in the star's persona. . . . Curtis could move from male to female to male without any violence being done either to his own image or to the general image of masculinity he represented" (133–34). In illustration, Sikov cites a comment made about a Curtis character in another film, *Sweet Smell of Success* (1957), when a starlet guesses that Sidney Falco (Curtis) must be an actor because "he's so pretty." Other characters in this film similarly refer to Falco's good looks. Rita, the cigarette girl, calls him "Eyelashes," and Harry Keller, the corrupt cop, sarcastically dubs him "the boy with the ice cream face." In reality, Falco is the corrosive underside of fifties hegemonic masculinity, a hustling public relations man. As columnist J. J. Hunsecker (Burt Lancaster), explains to the starlet, "Sidney has forty different faces, none of them pretty," although to be more precise, one should say that being pretty is just one of the many different masks Falco wears with the agility and inconsistency of a trained actor—or a male impersonator.

Actually, *Some Like It Hot* builds upon Curtis's unstable masculine persona even more closely than Sikov appreciates. Unlike other new stars of this era, while under contract at Universal-International, Curtis, who was Rock Hudson's rival in importance for the studio, played in a variety of genres (thriller, Western, musical, comedy, as well as melodrama), though he was initially associated with Arabian Nights adventures, such as *The Prince Who Was a Thief* (1951) and *Son of Ali Baba* (1952), in which, as he later put it, "I was a sort of male Yvonne de Carlo" (Mann). As his star meanings deepened and box-office allure increased in the late 1950s, when commenting on his success at the time, Curtis invoked the transvestite comparison to describe his position in the star system even then. In an interview appearing almost a year before *Some Like It Hot* went into production, the star attributed his newfound financial and professional success to his playing "the second lead, which used to go to glamour girls" opposite costars like Burt Lancaster (in *Trapeze*, 1956, as well as *Sweet Smell of Success*) and Kirk Douglas (in *The Vikings*, 1958): "'There are no leading ladies left in Hollywood,' Tony explained. 'So I co-star with other guys'" (Scott, "2nd Banana").

Although *Some Like It Hot* obviously has a fifties "glamour girl" in its cast, and Lemmon, not Curtis, plays the second male lead, the film's publicity exploited Curtis's glamour boy-girl image, as in the photograph with Holden. During production, one newspaper article described the scene in which Joe hides his Junior costume from Sugar and Daphne by donning Josephine's wig and jumping fully clothed into a bubble bath, giving movie star Curtis the opportunity to compare his tub scene to that of wife Janet Leigh's in their previous costarring venture, *The Perfect Furlough* (1958): "We're the only couple I know competing with one another for the most exciting movie bath." Elaborating upon this intent of drawing attention to the transvestic connotation of Curtis's persona, the article concludes with Lemmon complaining about the rigor of putting on the drag makeup, to which Curtis, given the last word, replies: "You're just sore 'cause you're not as pretty as I am" (Scott, "Glamour").

Curtis could make his rather audacious claim about taking over the glamour girls' parts in films, figuratively when he talked about his flourishing career and, it appears, much more literally when he discussed his role in *Some Like It Hot,* because he and Janet Leigh were the darling star couple of the fan magazines throughout the decade. As in the case of Bogart and Bacall in the 1940s,

their marriage and frequent on-screen coupling throughout the period mediated the transgressive implications of such unorthodox remarks by projecting
an overriding heterosexual image that put Curtis's bending of gender norms in
quotation marks, as it were. However, while readable simply as a tease, particularly in the publicity for *Some Like It Hot,* Curtis's own allusion to his transvestic position in the star system recognizes the performativity that underwrote his "feminizing" pretty-boy good looks, investing his persona with an
undeniable sense of gender mobility. Regardless of his very straight private
life, after the enormous success of the Wilder film the queer implications of
the performativity structuring Curtis's persona were not lost on the press, as
an Earl Wilson column from 1968 records, with its baiting headline: "Come
Out of the Closet! . . ." While it turns out that Curtis has simply invited the
columnist into his clothes closet for the interview, his theatrical display of
male vestments, "the finery that cost him thousands," reiterates the transvestic
meaning that had already informed his star persona in the fifties.

When taking on what he stated was "the glamour girl's" part opposite male
stars like Lancaster and Douglas, Curtis's transvestic status allowed him to
enact many of the variations of masculinity that competed with the hegemonic
norm of The Man in the Gray Flannel Suit. In the second half of the 1950s
alone, Curtis played an epic hero in *The Vikings* (a big-budget version of the sex
and sand adventures that had first made his reputation); a boy who was not a
man in *Trapeze, Spartacus* (1960), and *Operation Petticoat* (1960, opposite Cary
Grant); a bachelor in *The Perfect Furlough* as well as *Some Like It Hot;* a hustling
bum in *Mister Cory* (1956), *The Square Jungle* (1955), and *Sweet Smell of Success;*
and a criminal in *Seven Bridges to Cross* (1955) and *The Defiant Ones* (1958).
Masquerade supplied the narrative theme focusing this mobile screen persona,
from the master of illusionism in *Houdini* (1953), to an imitation Scarlet
Pimpernel in *The Purple Mask* (1955), to Ferdinand DeMara, Jr. (who imper-
sonated a prison warden, navy physician, school teacher) in *The Great Impostor*
(1960).

Curtis's imitation of Cary Grant in *Some Like It Hot,* moreover, accents
(literally so) what was perhaps the most crucial dimension of male impersonation underlying this mobile persona: the male movie star. A 1957 feature in
Photoplay calls attention to the performativity of Curtis's persona off screen,
and it highlights the shifting discursive positions of his various masquerades.
This article first introduces Curtis as a "rebel in a button-down collar," noting
how he is dressed "in the best Madison Avenue style," which gives him the look
of "an aspiring young bank executive," and describing how his home with Janet
Leigh is a palace of consumption which even *Playboy* would envy (Jessup 55).
The article then traces the stages through which Curtis reached this position.
It notes his origin "as a kid who barely skinned out of a boyhood of juvenile
delinquency"; his arrival in Hollywood "fresh from a GI education," when,
because of his friendship with Marlon Brando, he was viewed as another rebel

star, albeit "not a torn-shirt rebel" but one who "doted on clothes, [and who] collected shoes as other men collected pipes"; his initial success "as an exuberant, devilishly handsome beefcake hero with curly black hair"; his idolizing of Cary Grant, which was "so great" that, almost a decade before *Some Like It Hot*, Curtis "used his idol to cover up a bit of shyness when he first began courting Janet Leigh," mimicking Grant's voice when he telephoned her at home for the first time; and finally, his marriage to Leigh, which takes fifties togetherness to its logical economic conclusion through the formation of Curtleigh, a "family corporation" for producing films. The article closes by citing Curtis's recent outspoken criticism of "copycat" Method acting, made with some controversy while shooting *Sweet Smell of Success* in New York City, as proof of the star's "exuberant honesty, which is sometimes misunderstood" (92).

The point of this "picture of a rebel of a very special sort" is to show how, in his own way, Curtis is an original of his kind, a man of multiple faces. What the *Photoplay* article ends up recounting, though, is the transformation of one copycat, "Bernie Schwartz of the Bronx," who "admits that he used to save Cary Grant's pictures, at a time in his life when other boys were collecting ballplayers," into another: Tony Curtis, movie star, a fabricated identity that does not exactly unify these various personae comprising his biography so much as delineate their sequential unfolding and reiteration in masquerade. Thus the "boy who wears his pin-striped suit and button-down collar with authentic flair" transcends his Bronx origins while, at the same time, that "authentic flair" for male fashion refers to his father's profession as a tailor, to remind us that, in the fifties, clothes made the man just as much as T-shirts made the boy (92). As a movie star, Curtis is himself a great impostor, and his masquerading works against a straightforward reading of his persona as the "dimpled pretty-boy" transformed into "a solid citizen on all accounts. . . . A good professional man, too" (Zunser 10, 15). Many of Curtis's roles in the late 1950s simply turned this persona inside out so that it became, on one hand, the manipulator of other-directed performance signs, as in the hustling, cynical PR man he plays in *Sweet Smell of Success,* or, on the other hand, the pretty boy crossing gender boundaries, as in the female/male impersonator he plays in *Some Like It Hot.*

Curtis's persona incorporated performativity into his fan biography more explicitly than any star I have analyzed in *Masked Men.* His screen image as a glamour girl-boy became not just comparable to, but identified as a transvestic masquerade. If his cross-dressing in *Some Like It Hot* did not do violence to the masculinity he represented, as Sikov claims, that was because the Curtis persona already posed a disturbance to the cultural coding of masculinity. The Earl Wilson interview appearing almost a decade later, its headline intimating the opening of a closed closet that turns out to be an invitation into a clothes closet, reveals even more directly how the slippages measured by Curtis's fifties star image as a glamour girl-boy prevented gender and sexuality from being perfectly or accurately legible in the other. Masculinity and femininity, heterosexuality and homosexuality, the Curtis persona put into play a disruption of both binaries, but without making them equivalent. As exemplified by his long-standing interest in clothes, the persona's identification with transvestism collapsed the difference between glamour boy and glamour girl, but it could register an analogous distinction between heterosexual and homosexual only in metaphoric terms (in the Wilson interview, through the trope of the closet) that broke down their presumed correspondence: gender provided a figure for representing sexuality—the attractive "Tony Curtis" star persona— but not a stable, let alone transparent, referent in sexuality.

Some Like It Hot makes the same point. Gender signs circulate through the film much like the jokes built around one character's borrowing of phrasing from another as they perform their masquerades, Sugar included, such as their references to blood-type O. This particular running gag occurs repeatedly in the dialogue because it verbalizes the inability of biology to guarantee sexual difference absolutely. At first Jerry is convinced that their cross-dressing will not work, and Sugar's appearance at the train station seems to confirm his recognition that there is an immutable difference between men and women. "We'll never get away with it," he warns. "It's a whole different sex." "No one's asking you to have a baby," Joe replies. By the film's end, however, their cross-dressing has put gender in an entirely new light. Trying to explain to Osgood why they cannot get married, Jerry first reasons as if he were a woman (he smokes, he's not a natural blonde, he has a notorious past), then appeals to biology (he can never have children), and only after that fails to work does he invoke gender ("I'm a man!"). Osgood's indifference even to this last, seemingly most definitive reason for their not getting married then pushes beyond gender to suggest the homosexuality that may or may not be signified by his attraction to Daphne—and by the latter's own eagerness to tie the knot. "Why would a guy want to marry a guy?" Joe asks Jerry, who answers with the single word summarizing the fifties domestic mystique: "Security." When elaborating, he draws a parallel between his motives and Sugar's: "This may be my last chance to marry a millionaire." Coupling with a millionaire at the end of the film, Jerry fulfills what had been Sugar's ambition, successfully taking her place in a way that he had *never* expected to be able to do at the train station.

Some Like It Hot puts an entirely different spin on the basis of gender in reproduction. As the publicity photograph pairing Curtis with William Holden visualizes, the film confirms *Look's* worst fears when it analyzed the decline of the American male in 1958. The first article in the series concludes with this warning from a psychiatrist: "We are drifting toward a social structure made up of he-women and she-men" (Moskin 80). Confusing gender to the point where one does not know whether to call Joe/Josephine/Junior and Jerry/ Daphne "he-women" *or* "she-men," the cross-dressing in *Some Like It Hot* pushes the implications of the masculine masquerade to its limits. The masquerading in this film recognizes that gender ("women" and "men") and sexuality ("he's" and "she's") are aligned in performance. Even more outrageously, it shows how this performativity can just as easily cross as construct the mutually signifying relation of gender and sexuality necessary for maintaining the hetero-homosexual binarism that naturalized masculinity. That *Times* reader had every reason to feel "awfully uncomfortable" when watching Wilder's comedy!

Taking the performativity of masculinity literally as an act of transvestism, *Some Like It Hot* condenses the ideological tensions which produced the era's masculinity crisis—and its masked men. Masculinity was a focus of great concern for fifties America because it brought together in representation the binary thinking that organized the culture's sense of social, political, and historical realities: manly or womanly, straight or queer, manhood or boyhood, husband or bachelor, normal or deviant, inner-directed or outer-directed, blonde or dark, white or black, free state or slave state, American or alien—in short, with a nod both to global warfare and Billy Wilder's film, hot or cold. The ideological function of masculinity made it inseparable from representation, and its place there was highly contested, unstable, and disturbing. As the era's films and its movie stars document, the unity of gender and sexuality, necessary to authenticate those oppositions in the figural, uniformly dressed body of the American male, could be achieved only in performances of masculinity that called its authenticity into doubt. The photograph of Tony Curtis and William Holden, which juxtaposes the era's glamour girl-boy and its "Smiling Jim," captures this masquerade in its full complexity, vividly recording why it inevitably had the effect of underscoring the performativity of men, whether they were in full drag or in gray flannel.

NOTES

1. The Spy in the Gray Flannel Suit

1. Interestingly, this scene was a turning point for the film in more ways than one since "the idea of Eve's shooting Thornhill with blanks" appears to have been the catalyst that started Ernest Lehman writing again in late 1957 after writer's block had stalled his completion of the last quarter of the screenplay (Leff 105).

2. Modleski suggests that in both *Vertigo* and *North by Northwest* "fear of heights" is associated with "femaleness"—more specifically, with femininity as a construction of symbolic male lack (*Women* 90).

3. Wood reprints his 1965 book within *Hitchcock's Films Revisited* (55–236). For his analysis of *North by Northwest* as a growth narrative, see 131–41.

4. In order of their publication in *Look*, the three pieces were by Moskin, Leonard, and Attwood. They were then republished later that same year in book form under the title *The Decline of the American Male* by the editors of *Look* (New York: Random House, 1958).

5. Geoffrey M. Shurlock, Letters to Joseph Vogel, 2 Oct. 1958 and 16 Oct. 1958; *North by Northwest* PCA file.

6. George M. Wilson also refers to the film's thematic defense of illusionism, but rather than historicizing it, as I am doing, he interprets this theme as an instance of Hitchcockian metacinema: a "wry apologia for the sort of illusionistic art—more specifically, for the sort of illusionistic cinema—that Hitchcock, paradigmatically, has always practiced" (64). But this film is just as much an Ernest Lehman screenplay as it is an Alfred Hitchcock classic. With its adept and knowing positioning of Roger within the social milieu of the media professional, *North by Northwest* bears a strong similarity to Lehman's previous film, *Sweet Smell of Success* (1957), a film noir depiction of the night life of newspaper columnists and publicity mongers. I don't think it is an understatement to say that Lehman's contribution to the film's thematic preoccupation with illusions and performances is probably what helps to give *North by Northwest* the historical context I am emphasizing.

7. 20th Century-Fox Press Release, Oct. 1957, Grant file, Herrick. This press release was used to publicize the production of *An Affair to Remember,* in which the star reportedly wore "all his own clothes," but the characterization of Grant's fashion sense applies as well to *North by Northwest.* The description was boilerplate, since it appeared in a studio press release from 1952 as well.

8. Naremore comments on the way the gray color of Roger's clothing has caught the eye of many fans of the film, though his concern is to talk about the suit as it accentuates Grant's body in support of the star's performance style (*Acting* 214–16).

9. For a related discussion by Butler, see her essay "Imitation and Gender Insubordination."

10. The major articles applying Riviere to film, which I allude to in my comments here, are Doane, "Film and the Masquerade: Theorizing the Female Spectator" (1982) and "Masquerade Reconsidered: Further Thoughts on the Female Spectators" (1988–89), both reprinted in *Femmes Fatales* 17–43; and Fletcher. See also Irigaray, who describes the feminine masquerade as self-effacement "imposed upon women by male systems of representations" (84), while also seeing it as a form of mimicry, a "play[ing] with mimesis" (76).

11. See Holmlund's critique of the limits that have been placed on the masquerade as a

conceptualization of male sexuality (216–19). For a survey of the scholarship in various disciplines that go beyond Riviere's formulation to conceptualize masculinity as a masquerade, see Harry Brod's introduction to Perchuk and Posner (13–19). Likewise, for examples of the emerging centrality of the masquerade as a framework for analyzing masculinity in both cultural criticism and visual representation, see the entire volume, which includes an early version of this chapter.

12. See also Butler, *Gender* 136–37, "Imitation" 24, and *Bodies* 1–16. Modleski wants to distinguish between "the concepts of the 'performative' and the masquerade," with the latter compensating for a female's usurpation of masculine power (as in Riviere's explanation), thereby unsexing herself as it were, and the former containing "no such disavowal" (*Feminism* 54), but I think it is more useful not to make such a neat binary pairing out of "performance" and "masquerade" in order to recognize their imbrication: the effect of performativity is the masquerade, and the masquerade is constituted through performance, making it as much an action as an object (or a persona).

13. "They were easy to drip dry when one was traveling," Grant reportedly told reporter Joe Hyams in explanation about five months before the release of *North by Northwest* (Higham and Moseley 280).

14. That the problem of impotence was crucial to an understanding of the social and sexual pressures faced by men was a theme stressed in popular accounts of the era's masculinity crisis, as in discussions about the American male's decline in the magazine articles already cited. I discuss the significance of the Kinsey reports on the representation of masculinity at greater length in the next chapter.

15. For a more detailed analysis of the technique behind Grant's seemingly effortless performance style in *North by Northwest,* see Naremore, *Acting* 213–35.

16. In my allusion to the screwball comedies, I am following Andrew Britton's argument about Grant's "male femininity" (50). These films, Britton explains, "use Grant to formulate a type of masculinity which is valuable and attractive by virtue of the sharing of gender characteristics with women" (43).

17. Naremore also notices that both Kaplan and Roger are similar to Cary Grant the star as fabricated identities (*Acting* 221–22).

2. The "Paradox" of Hegemonic Masculinity

1. Connell elaborates upon this point in *Masculinities*, 76–81.

2. See also Carrigan, Connell, and Lee 180 and Connell, *Masculinities* 70.

3. *Boxoffice* 7 Aug. 1948, n. pag., *Pitfall* file, Herrick. I am quoting from the trade magazine's description of the film's selling angles. For contemporary reviews that discuss the film as a domestic melodrama about an errant husband, see, for instance, "New Films" and Scheuer, and for a summary of the New York critical response, see "Honesty."

4. Lucy Fischer discusses this fear of momism—first voiced to a large audience by Philip Wylie in *Generation of Vipers* (originally published in 1942 and reprinted with some fanfare in 1955)—as it intersected with discourses about the returning veteran. On the fear of momism producing a generation of men vulnerable to communism, see Rogin 242–46.

5. "Copy of a letter from Gadge Kazan to Mr. J. L. Warner," 15 Nov. 1955, *Baby Doll* PCA file.

6. See the reviews of *The Seven Year Itch* in *The Hollywood Reporter* (Moffitt) and *Variety* ("Land"). The *Variety* reviewer specifically complained that the film was an "emasculation" of the play.

7. Interestingly, in an interview included on the Republic Home Video laser disc of *Invasion of the Body Snatchers,* Kevin McCarthy explains that, in his mind, the body snatchers represented not McCarthyism (as is typically assumed), but the conformity typified by the era's Man in the Gray Flannel Suit.

3. Tough Guys Make the Best Psychopaths

1. I am quoting from the running head of the second page of the obituary (Laro 8). Another Los Angeles newspaper featured a photograph of the memorial service with the headline "Pay Last Tribute to 'Tough Guy' Bogart."

2. For example, when filling in vets on their missing years, Paul Gallico summarizes what the gossip columns had reported, year by year, in their chronicles of Bogart's much publicized meeting with, courtship of, and marriage to Bacall (53–54, 58, 61–62).

3. See also D'Emilio's discussion of the war years in *Sexual* 23–39.

4. For descriptions of the way *Dead Reckoning* borrows from those other Bogart films, see Krutnik, *Lonely* 256–57n and Telotte 110–11.

5. Krutnik also makes this point, but he then immediately turns the social threat posed by their returning to civilian life back into the question of sexual difference as posed by Coral (*Lonely* 166).

6. Polan documents the various changes that occurred in the screenplay and includes the text of the original ending, which appears to have been shot and immediately disliked and discarded by the star and the director, Nicholas Ray (*Lonely* 54–61).

7. Bacall then adds her own viewpoint: "And despite how wonderful he was, there were times when I would have liked to do the same thing to him" (176). Polan also notes the similarity between Bogart's behavior off screen at El Morocco and Dix Steele's on screen, and he too cites Bacall's explanation, though without noting its source in *Dead Reckoning* (*Lonely* 25).

8. Polan claims that "the publicity machine did what it could to keep it quiet" (*Lonely* 25), but judging from the L.A. papers (well represented in the Bogart file, Herrick), which most likely fed the story to the wire services and syndicates, the altercation at El Morocco made more noise than he presumes. Moreover, it was well known enough to be referred to again by the L.A. papers in their obituaries on Bogart over seven years later (for example, see Laro 9, which devotes four short paragraphs to "the panda expedition").

9. According to James W. Palmer, the element of surveillance in the film also evokes an allusion to the HUAC investigations of Hollywood in 1947, in which Bogart himself had become embroiled, first as a vocal and visible supporter of the Committee on the First Amendment, then, after the Washington hearings, as a critic of the Hollywood Ten's tactics.

10. The transformation of the landing on Iwo Jima into cultural myth, not only during the war but afterward in the 1950s too, makes for a fascinating story since the memorable iconography of this victory, the marines hoisting up the American flag, was actually based on a photograph restaging the event. See Marling and Wetenhall.

11. *Los Angeles Daily News* 16 Apr. 1953: n. pag, Ford file, Herrick.

12. In fact, just prior to making *The Desperate Hours,* Bogart reminded fans of his star-making role in *The Petrified Forest* by performing with Bacall and Henry Fonda in a television production of the play (Bacall 221).

13. Sklar assumes that the "it" in Hilliard's statement ("you put it there") is indeterminate in its antecedent, which could refer to "backbone, or courage, or a tinge of evil" (249). But it seems to me that Hilliard's declaration refers to his earlier identification with Griffin's anger and capacity for violence ("I have the same thing in me").

14. At the same time that she documents its repressive effects, Freedman claims that the discursive construction of the psychopathic personality by the legal and psychiatric institutions also had the indirect effect of legitimizing more liberalized attitudes toward sexuality. The psychopath stigmatized "extreme acts of violence," she argues, but he also was the occasion for the entrance into public discourse of previously forbidden sexual topics (most notably, sex with children or with other men), and in this way he helped to "legitimize nonviolent, but nonprocreative, sexual acts, within marriage or outside it" (200).

15. Freedman also notes that, while the term "psychopath" retained its popular currency, the American Psychiatric Association officially adapted the newer term "sociopathic personality" in 1952 (218n). For discussions of the way the discursive construction of the psychopath shaped the public's understanding of homosexuality as a disease and a crime, see D'Emilio, *Sexual* 16–20, 40–53; Bérubé 255–65; and Chauncey 359–60.

4. The Body in the Blockbuster

1. See "'10 Commandments' Much More Sexy" and "Cardinal Spellman's Condemnation."

2. For a history of the genre, see Elley, and Babington and Evans, *Biblical.*

3. This is Biskind's reading of the 1950s cycle of low-budget sci-fi invasion films (102–59), for example, as well as Rogin's (245–46, 264–67).

4. Warner's speech is included in *Hollywood on Trial* (1976; dir. David Helpern; Corinth Films).

5. Vernet suggests some of these parallels (66–68).

6. To give another example of the way Nadel coerces details from the film's representation of Egypt to find support for his claim that it is a transparent recreation of 1950s America, he states more than once that the Egyptian women wear their hair in imitation of Mamie Eisenhower's bangs (97, 98, 99), not appearing to recognize the style's source as a coding of "Egyptianness" in past Hollywood representations of Nile queens, such as DeMille's earlier *Cleopatra* (1934) or *The Egyptian* (1954).

7. According to Sobchack in "Surge and Splendor," it is characteristic of the Hollywood epic generally to collapse its reproduction of history into accounts of the history of its production.

8. See "British," "DeMille Makes," "Naguib," and DeMille 417–18, 421–23.

9. On events leading up to and following from the Suez crisis, see Yergin 479–98 and Oakley 222–25.

10. On Iran's nationalization of Anglo-Iranian Oil, see Yergin 450–78.

11. Even after the Suez crisis had abated, Nasser was still perceived as an enemy of the West. When *Look* published the Egyptian president's "first hard-hitting American interview since the Suez war," the cover exclaimed: "Exclusive! Nasser Tells Why He's Anti-American" (25 June 1957). The interviewer, incidentally, was *Look* editor William Attwood, later to write one of the articles, the one with the cold war slant, in the magazine's series on the decline of American manhood.

12. Similar treatment in the news media can be found in these sample clippings (all of which were written for various news syndicates like UPI or Hearst): Mosby, Manners, and Buchwald.

13. I am indebted to the late Bill Readings for insisting that I see the word "chest" embedded in the name "*Ch*arlton H*est*on."

5. The Age of the Chest

1. Robert Francis, the male ingenue in *The Caine Mutiny* (1954), died in an air crash a year later, which is why his name is unfamiliar today.

2. In a 1951 beefcake spread in *Photoplay*, Ruth Waterbury asked a jury of female stars to rank their male counterparts on sex appeal. After the results came in, she noted that, while Holden placed fourth (behind Burt Lancaster, the undeniable front-runner, Kirk Douglas, and Alan Ladd), the star was something of a "dark—or should I say clothed—horse," since "Bill, who started his career showing his chest in 'Golden Boy,' now rarely appears in anything less than a tailored suit" ("Jury" 70). That situation changed, however, when Holden appeared bare-chested in *Love Is a Many Splendored Thing* and *Picnic* and became *Photoplay*'s male star of the year two times running.

3. Byars makes much the same argument in her expanded reading of the scene in *All that Hollywood Allows* 171–78, although she modifies her claim to say that Madge is only "frequently the agent of the gaze" (178).

4. The comment by *Variety*'s reviewer is worth quoting in full. Complaining about the way Logan introduces Franco Nero as Lancelot in *Camelot*, "Land" remarked: "he [Logan] seems about to camera-rape the male body in the hokey style of 'Picnic'."

5. In the final revised script, as in the play, Mrs. Potts continues, making the point even clearer: "And that reminded me—I'm a woman. And that seemed good, too" (Taradash 153). This line is not in the release print of the film.

6. On the development of physique photography both before and particularly after World War II, see Foster 9–12 and 27–30. For a more comprehensive history, see Hooven.

7. For a brief history of the peplum cycle, see Elley 21 and, for a contemporary account, Whitehall. On Steve Reeves's sudden importance for the film industry in the late 1950s, see J. Lane.

8. My mother was one of those fifties women, and not ashamed to admit it either. A few years after Holden's death, she happened to meet Stefanie Powers, his last partner, at a charity event in Palm Springs. My mother remarked how much she had loved Holden in her youth, and Powers is said to have replied: "Oh, so did I—and honey, I had him!"

9. For an example of this type of domestic discourse about the actor, see Dee Philips's profile of Holden, published at around the time of his first award from *Photoplay* as male star of the year.

10. Kimmel is summarizing the conclusions of psychologist Robert Brannon regarding the components of "the dominant traditional male sex role."

6. Why Boys Are Not Men

1. For a brief discussion of Dior's "New Look" and its influence on fifties culture, see Marling 9–12.

2. Arguing that Stewart acts out "the psychic trouble and oppression proliferated by phallic masculinity" (11), Bingham offers an account of this star's persona that would seem to distinguish him from the company of John Wayne and the others mentioned by Skolsky. However, while clearly resonant, as Bingham shows, in the films Stewart made in the fifties with Hitchcock and Anthony Mann, these elements in the star's persona were ignored by the fan discourse, illustrating the complexity with which the personae of all the established male stars were continually being renegotiated following the end of World War II.

3. For instance, after the war, Wayne starred opposite Clift in *Red River;* Harry Carey, Jr. in *3 Godfathers* (1948); John Agar in *Fort Apache* (1948), *She Wore a Yellow Ribbon* (1949), and *The Sands of Iwo Jima* (1949); and Claude Jarman, Jr. in *Rio Grande* (1950); then in the late fifties, following the success of the young star at the box office, opposite Jeffrey Hunter in *The Searchers* (1956), Ricky Nelson in *Rio Bravo* (1959), Frankie Avalon in *The Alamo,* and Fabian in *North to Alaska* (1960). While these films do not narrativize it in so dramatic (or complicated) a fashion as *Red River* does, they all reveal how Wayne's representation of masculinity relies on the subordination of a boyish costar to his authority.

4. See, for example, Mellen 175–79; Spoto, *Camerado* 207–10; Mast 301–303; Biskind 278–84; Pettigrew 95–96; and Lippe 38–39.

5. On the function of scars in the phallic economy of traditional movie masculinity, see P. Lehman 55–69.

6. The Wayne clipping file in the Herrick library contains reports of the 1953 divorce suit in the Los Angeles newspapers, and the articles are too numerous to list here. But one account is worth quoting to indicate how the coverage made public the difference between Wayne and his persona: "Rugged-looking John Wayne, a scourge of the bad guys in scores

of movies, glumly admitted in court yesterday that in his private life he was 'woman-handled'" ("Wayne").

7. McCann's book is a pastiche of what biographers, reviewers, and critics have said about Clift, some of them not always clearly cited, so I assume we can take this statement, like the book as a whole, as representing more or less a consensus of the way Clift is now being read.

8. Kolker also notes how the opening of *A Place in the Sun* works to make a viewer desire Clift.

9. According to Skolsky, the significant exceptions to his generalization were Yul Brynner and Rock Hudson, the two new stars who supposedly appealed to adult women as well as teenagers.

10. For an insightful analysis of Hudson's body in his pinup photographs, see Meyer.

11. These revelations about his sexual ambiguity and gender performativity may also have been Brando's oblique way of acknowledging his bisexuality and even of responding to the underground circulation during this time of a forged pornographic photo showing him having sex with former roommate Wally Cox (Higham 129; Anger alludes to it in *Hollywood Babylon II* 285). Though reticent about his private life, and extremely heterosexual in his publicized romantic involvements throughout the fifties, Brando revealed he had "dabbled in homosexuality" in a French interview given to *Ciné-Revue* in 1975 (qtd. in Shipman 34). In 1991, after Christian Brando was sentenced for voluntary manslaughter, ex-wife Anna Kashfi blamed their son's troubles on Brando's bisexuality, charging in the *National Enquirer* that "it was Marlon's affairs with men that hurt and confused Christian" (Brenna 36–37), even suggesting that their son, born in the late fifties, had been named after one of Brando's gay lovers, actor Christian Marquand.

12. Allen Larson likewise claims, though with more theoretical sophistication, that in this scene Brando's "body functions specifically for the purpose of establishing its privileged masculine status" as a way of disavowing whatever homoerotic implications derive from its "erotic presentation" (27). I take a different view, as I shall explain momentarily.

13. Tennessee Williams, letter to Joseph Breen, 29 Oct. 1950, *A Streetcar Named Desire* PCA file.

14. Jack [Vizzard], letter to Joe [Breen], 12 July 1951, *A Streetcar Named Desire* PCA file.

15. Jack [Vizzard], letter to Joe [Breen], 22 July 1951, *A Streetcar Named Desire* PCA file.

16. Joseph I. Breen, letter to Irene Selznick, 19 July 1949, *A Streetcar Named Desire* PCA file. The point was then stressed throughout the correspondence between the studio and Breen as the screenplay was being written.

17. Gadge Kazan, letter to Joe [Breen], undated but stamped 14 Sept. 1950; *A Streetcar Named Desire* PCA file.

18. Pandro S. Berman, letter to Geoffrey M. Sherlock, 5 Aug. 1955, *Tea and Sympathy* PCA file.

19. "Memo for the file by G.M.S.," 26 Aug. 1955, *Tea and Sympathy* PCA file.

20. Actually, Berman remembered incorrectly, since Tom's father is told his son is "a fairy. A homosexual" (Anderson 412).

7. The Bachelor in the Bedroom

1. On Victorian America's separation of masculine and feminine spaces through the doctrine of separate spheres, its establishment in the early nineteenth century, and its collapse starting in the 1920s, see D'Emilio and Freedman; and for an account of the impact of the doctrine of separate spheres upon Victorian masculinity, see Rotundo.

2. In an essay which I read in draft form after I had completed this chapter, Cynthia J. Fuchs also argues that *Pillow Talk* "scrambles," as she puts it, the binarized positions in

which fifties culture tried to fix gendered identities and normative sexual desires, and she too cites this advertising slogan in illustration. Though we mention some of the same issues, such as the star personae of its cast and the masquerade plot, her analysis considerably differs from mine in the historical context she supplies for her reading of the film. Fuchs approaches *Pillow Talk* through the significance which new technologies bore for fifties culture, as evident in this film's innovative deployment of the CinemaScope screen as well as in the effect that technology has in destabilizing sexual binaries within the diegesis, whereas I am reading the film through its representation of bachelorhood. See "Split Screens: Framing and Passing in *Pillow Talk*," *American Culture in the Fifties*, ed. Joel Foreman (Urbana: U of Illinois Press, forthcoming). I thank her for sharing the essay with me.

3. Hudson, in fact, reports in the biography of Day that the whole scene had to be rigged, because he wasn't strong enough to hold her, which adds to the theatricality of Brad's behavior at this point in the film. "Doris is a tall, well-built girl," the star confesses, "and I just couldn't tote her around for as long and as far as was required, so they built a special shelf for me with two hooks on it and she sat on the shelf and all I did was hold her legs and shoulders." The actor playing the cop kept confusing the character with the star, blowing his line by referring to "Rock" instead of "Brad," so they ended up doing the scene on the street twenty times: "That's why the shelf for Doris to sit on" (Hotchner 187).

4. *Pillow Talk*'s playboy bachelor became so firmly associated with his telephone, in fact, that on the Academy Awards show the spring following the film's release, when Doris Day (a best actress nominee for *Pillow Talk*) appeared alone to present the song award, she made a scripted joke to emcee Bob Hope about Rock Hudson not being on stage with her (though he would later appear to present the best actress award) because he was still talking on the phone.

5. For commentary on this convention as a recuperation of heterosexual masculinity in American sex comedies, particularly the ones with Day and/or Hudson, see Russo 159–61; Babington and Evans, *Affairs* 212–13; and Klinger 115.

6. Indeed, the "At a glance synopsis" submitted to the PCA indicates that the original shooting script of *Pillow Talk*, then titled *Anywhere the Wind Blows*, did not include the coda or mention children, but instead ended with Jan trapping Brad in his redecorated apartment and then inviting him to have sex with her: "As he turns toward her she smiles, turns out the light, and says, 'All apartments look alike in the dark'" (*Pillow Talk* PCA file). With Jan's last line presumably censored and the coda added, the revised screenplay shifted the film's ending to focus on male sexuality as a force of biological as well as cultural transgression.

7. For example, *Movieland* devoted a large part of its April 1955 issue to show "how Hollywood improved" a number of big stars, male as well as female, placing Hudson in a group of men that included John Wayne, Tony Curtis, William Holden, and Alan Ladd.

8. While hidden from the public, Hudson's homosexuality was an open secret in Hollywood at this time. According to Hudson's autobiography, a future lover is quoted as saying that, when he came to Southern California in 1962, he had already heard about the star. "In the gay subculture, he was talked about all the time—about how he was gay and very handsome and a kind person, well liked" (Hudson and Davidson 133). In *Rock Hudson's Home Movies*, Rappaport surmises that the various masquerades in the star's comedies was the industry's punishment of Hudson for being an open homosexual in Hollywood. Hudson himself said in a candid interview with Boze Hadleigh in 1982 that there was "built-in protection" for a gay actor—"*You* know that no one's going to want to print the truth" (199)—because, as he had said moments earlier, "Trust me, Boze, America does not want to know" (195). Hudson goes on to confirm that the problem a gay actor like himself encountered in the industry was not public exposure but the industry's own homophobia:

"Everyone knows about everybody in Hollywood—who sleeps with whom. . . . And some of those guys just don't like fairies" (199). Commenting on his comedies at the start of the interview, and he does not distinguish *Pillow Talk* from the others, Hudson acknowledges their "homophobic subplots" (Hadleigh's phrase, not his) and comments, "I just did my job" (182). He seems set up to take this position by Hadleigh, who, in asking questions about the comedies with Day and in his own accompanying commentary, gets details from them wrong (as in Hadleigh's references to Nick Adams's role in *Pillow Talk*, used to prod Hudson into admitting that his films had homophobic subplots). Hudson either does not catch or does not bother to correct Hadleigh. At other points in the interview, Hudson talks about his teaming with Day and *Pillow Talk* with more affection.

SELECT FILMOGRAPHY

This list includes only films from which I quote my own transcriptions of dialogue.

The Big Heat. Dir. Fritz Lang. Columbia Pictures, 1953. RCA/Columbia/Image videodisc.

The Big Sleep. Dir. Howard Hawks. Warner Bros., 1946. MGM/UA videodisc.

Blackboard Jungle. Dir. Richard Brooks. MGM, 1955. MGM/UA videodisc.

Champion. Dir. Mark Robson. United Artists, 1949. Republic videodisc.

Dead Reckoning. Dir. John Cromwell. Columbia Pictures, 1947. RCA/Columbia videodisc.

The Desperate Hours. Dir. William Wyler. Paramount Pictures, 1955. Paramount videodisc.

Father of the Bride. Dir. Vincente Minnelli. MGM, 1950. MGM/UA videodisc.

Father's Little Dividend. Dir. Vincente Minnelli. MGM, 1951. LVA Film Classics videodisc.

In a Lonely Place. Dir. Nicholas Ray. Columbia Pictures, 1950. RCA/Columbia videocassette.

Invasion of the Body Snatchers. Dir. Don Siegel. Allied Artists, 1955. Republic videodisc.

Kiss Me Deadly. Dir. Robert Aldrich. United Artists, 1955. MGM/UA videodisc.

Laura. Dir. Otto Preminger. 20th Century-Fox, 1944. CBS/Fox videodisc.

The Long, Hot Summer. Dir. Martin Ritt. 20th Century-Fox, 1958. Fox videodisc.

The Maltese Falcon. Dir. John Huston. Warner Bros., 1941. MGM/UA videodisc.

The Man in the Gray Flannel Suit. Dir. Nunnelly Johnson. 20th Century-Fox, 1956. Fox videodisc.

Marty. Dir. Delbert Mann. United Artists, 1955. MGM/UA videodisc.

North by Northwest. Dir. Alfred Hitchcock. MGM, 1959. MGM/UA videodisc. Includes trailer.

Panic in the Streets. Dir. Elia Kazan. 20th Century-Fox, 1950. Fox videodisc.

Picnic. Dir. Joshua Logan. Columbia Pictures, 1955. Pioneer Special Editions videodisc.

Pillow Talk. Dir. Michael Gordon. Universal-International, 1959. MCA videodisc. Includes trailer.

Pitfall. Dir. Andre de Toth. United Artists, 1948. Republic Pictures videodisc.

A Place in the Sun. Dir. George Stevens. Paramount Pictures, 1951. Paramount videodisc. Trailer cablecast on American Movie Classics.

Rebel without a Cause. Dir. Nicholas Ray. Warner Bros., 1955. Warner Bros. videodisc.

Red River. Dir. Howard Hawks. United Artists, 1948. MGM/UA videodisc.

The Seven Year Itch. Dir. Billy Wilder. 20th Century-Fox, 1955. CBS/Fox videodisc.

A Streetcar Named Desire. Dir. Elia Kazan. Warner Bros., 1951. Warner Bros. videodisc. Original and restored versions.

Sweet Smell of Success. Dir. Alexander Mackendrick. United Artists, 1957. MGM/UA videodisc.

Tea and Sympathy. Dir. Vincente Minnelli. MGM, 1956. MGM/UA videodisc.

The Ten Commandments. Dir. Cecil B. DeMille. Paramount Pictures, 1956. Paramount videodisc.

The Tender Trap. Dir. Charles Walters. MGM, 1955. MGM/UA videodisc.

Teresa. Dir. Fred Zinnemann. MGM, 1951. Turner Classic Movies cablecast.

Them! Dir. Gordon Douglas. Warner Bros., 1954. Warner Bros. videodisc.

To Have and Have Not. Dir. Howard Hawks. Warner Bros., 1944. Warner Bros. videodisc.

Vertigo. Dir. Alfred Hitchcock. Paramount Pictures, 1958. MCA videodisc.

The Violent Men. Dir. Rudoph Maté. Columbia Pictures, 1955. Pioneer Special Editions videodisc.

Where the Sidewalk Ends. Dir. Otto Preminger. 20th Century-Fox, 1950. American Movie Classics cablecast. Included trailer.

The Wild One. Dir. Laslo Benedek. Columbia Pictures, 1953. RCA/Columbia videodisc.

The Young Lions. Dir. Edward Dmytryk. 20th Century-Fox, 1958. CBS/Fox videodisc.

WORKS CITED

In quoting from periodicals published in the fifties, as well as using my own copies and the collections in the Library of Congress and the library of my home institution (with invaluable assistance from Interlibrary Loans), I have drawn on files in the New York Public Library for the Performing Arts, Lincoln Center, New York City (abbreviated as NY Public), and, more extensively, in the Margaret Herrick Library, Academy of Motion Picture Arts and Sciences, Los Angeles (abbreviated as Herrick). The Herrick collection divides its files according to person or production, and I have followed that distinction here. (I should also note that the Herrick library often identified the *Los Angeles Citizen-News* by the name of its regional editions, such as the *Hollywood* or *Beverly Hills Citizen*, and I have followed their citations.) The Herrick library has, as part of its holdings, the Production Code Administration files in the Motion Pictures Association of America Collection, and these are designated as a PCA file here and in my notes.

Ager, Cecelia. "Brando in Search of Himself." *New York Times Magazine* 25 July 1954: 24, 33. Brando file, Herrick.

"All About Eve: Kinsey Reports on American Women." *Newsweek* 24 Aug. 1953: 68–71.

Allmendinger, Blake. *The Cowboy: Representations of Labor in an American Work Culture.* New York: Oxford UP, 1992.

Alloway, Lawrence. *The Long Front of Culture* (1959). Qtd. in Pacific Film Archive program notes. 14 Apr. 1991. *North by Northwest* file, Herrick.

———. *Violent America: The Movies, 1946–1964.* New York: Museum of Modern Art, 1971.

"The All-Time Film Blockbuster." *Hollywood Reporter* 5 Apr. 1957: 1, 8. *Ten Commandments* file, Herrick.

Anderson, Robert. *Tea and Sympathy.* 1953. *New Voices in the American Theatre.* New York: Modern Library, 1955. 377–463.

Anger, Kenneth. *Hollywood Babylon II.* New York: Dutton, 1984.

Archerd, Army. "Who Needs Hair?" *Photoplay* Feb. 1957: 64–65, 109–10.

Archer, Jules. "Don't Hate Yourself in the Morning." *Playboy* Aug. 1955: 21, 32–33.

———. "Will She or Won't She?" *Playboy* Jan. 1956: 13, 64.

Armour, Richard. "Age of the Chest." *Playboy* July 1958: 57, 65.

Armstrong, George. "Are Actors Sissies?" *Photoplay* Feb. 1953: 52–53, 97.

Arnold, Maxine. "Nobody Asked Him." *Photoplay* Dec. 1953: 52–53, 87–90.

"As It Happened: The Great Debates 1960." A&E Cable Network. 26 Sept. 1990.

Attwood, William. "Why Does He Work So Hard?" *Look* 4 Mar. 1958: 71–75.

———. *The Twilight Struggle: Tales of the Cold War.* New York: Harper, 1987.

Axelrod, George. *The Seven Year Itch: A Romantic Comedy.* 1952. *New Voices in the American Theatre.* New York: Modern Library, 1955. 301–75.

Babington, Bruce and Peter William Evans. *Affairs to Remember: Hollywood Comedy of the Sexes.* Manchester: Manchester UP, 1989.

————. *Biblical Epics: Sacred Narrative in Hollywood Cinema.* Manchester, UK: Manchester UP, 1993.

Babuscio, Jack. "Camp and the Gay Sensibility." *Gays and Film.* Rev. Ed. Richard Dyer. New York: Zoetrope, 1984. 40–57.

Bacall, Lauren. *Lauren Bacall by Myself.* New York: Knopf, 1979.

Bacon, James. "His Conflicting Traits Qualify Brando as Genuine Character." *Los Angeles Times* 11 April 1954: IV8. Brando file, Herrick.

Barton, Sabrina. "'Crisscross': Paranoia and Projection in *Strangers on a Train.*" *Camera Obscura* 25–26 (1991): 74–100.

Behlmer, Rudy, ed. *Memo from Darryl F. Zanuck: The Golden Years at Twentieth Century-Fox.* New York: Grove, 1993.

Bell-Metereau, Rebecca. *Hollywood Androgyny.* 2nd ed. New York: Columbia UP, 1993.

Bentley, Eric. "Pathetic Phalluses." *What Is Theatre? Incorporating the Dramatic Event and Other Reviews, 1944–1967.* New York: Atheneum, 1968. 71–74.

Berg, Louis. "Streetcar to Hollywood." *Los Angeles Times* 16 July 1950: n. pag. *This Week Magazine* supplement. Brando file, Herrick.

Bérubé, Allan. *Coming Out Under Fire: The History of Gay Men and Women in World War Two.* 1990. New York: Plume, 1991.

Bingham, Dennis. *Acting Male: Masculinities in the Films of James Stewart, Jack Nicholson, and Clint Eastwood.* New Brunswick: Rutgers UP, 1994.

"Biography of Humphrey Bogart." Paramount Press Release. Jan. 1955. Bogart file, Herrick.

Biskind, Peter. *Seeing Is Believing: How Hollywood Taught Us to Stop Worrying and Love the Fifties.* New York: Pantheon, 1983.

Bocca, Geoffrey. "William Holden: Hollywood's Golden Boy." *Cosmopolitan* Sept. 1955: 28–33. Holden file, Herrick.

"Bogart's a Tough Guy—Even at Chess Board." *Los Angeles Times* 31 Aug. 1952. Bogart file, Herrick.

"Bombs, H and K." *Newsweek* 31 Aug. 1953: 57.

Bosworth, Patricia. *Montgomery Clift: A Biography.* 1978. New York: Bantam, 1979.

Boyd, Malcolm. *Christ and Celebrity Gods: The Church in Mass Culture.* Greenwich, Ct.: Seabury P, 1958.

Boyer, Paul. *By the Bomb's Early Light: American Thought and Culture at the Dawn of the Atomic Age.* New York: Pantheon, 1985.

Bremner, Robert H. "Families, Children, and the State." *Reshaping America: Society and Institutions, 1945–1960.* Eds. Robert H. Bremner and Gary W. Reichard. Columbus: Ohio State UP, 1982. 3–32.

Brenna, Tony. "Brando's Flings with Gay Lovers Helped Turn Son into a Killer." *National Enquirer* 19 Mar. 1991: 36–37.

Brien, Alan. "Mr. Holden Is the Magnet." London *Evening Standard* 9 Feb. 1956: 7.

Brill, Leslie. *The Hitchcock Romance: Love and Irony in Hitchcock's Films.* Princeton: Princeton UP, 1988.

"British Suez Situation Key to 'Commandments.'" *Hollywood Reporter* 20 May 1953: n. pag. *The Ten Commandments* file, Herrick.

Britton, Andrew. "Cary Grant: Comedy and Male Desire." *Cine-Action!* 7 (Dec. 1986): 36–51.

Brodkey, Harold. "Translating Brando." *New Yorker* 24 Oct. 1994: 78–85.

Brown, Helen Gurley. *Sex and the Single Girl.* 1962. New York: Avon, 1983.

Brown, Peter Harry. *Kim Novak: The Reluctant Goddess.* New York: St. Martin's, 1986.

Brynner, Rock. *Yul: The Man Who Would Be King.* New York: Berkeley, 1991.

Buchwald, Art. "A Real Man on the Screen." *Beverly Hills Citizen* 24 Apr. 1958: n. pag. Brynner file, Herrick.

Butler, Judith. *Bodies that Matter: On the Discursive Limits of "Sex."* New York: Routledge, 1993.

———. "Imitation and Gender Insubordination." *Inside/Out: Lesbian Theories, Gay Theories.* Ed. Diana Fuss. New York: Routledge, 1991. 13–31.

———. *Gender Trouble: Feminism and the Subversion of Identity.* New York: Routledge, 1990.

Byars, Jackie. *All that Hollywood Allows: Re-Reading Gender in 1950s Melodrama.* Chapel Hill: U of North Carolina P, 1991.

———. "Gazes/Voices/Power: Expanding Psychoanalysis for Feminist Film and Television Theory." *Female Spectators: Looking at Film and Television.* Ed. E. Deidre Pribram. London: Verso, 1988. 110–31.

"Can Rock's Marriage Be Saved?" *Photoplay* Feb. 1958: 55, 91–92.

"Cardinal Spellman's Condemnation of 'Baby Doll.'" *Le Monde* 27 Dec. 1956. Trans. in typescript. *Baby Doll* PCA file.

Carrigan, Tim, Bob Connell, and John Lee. "Hard and Heavy: Toward a New Sociology of Masculinity." *Beyond Patriarchy: Essays by Men on Pleasure, Power, and Change.* Ed. Michael Kaufman. Toronto: U of Toronto P, 1987. 139–92.

Cavell, Stanley. "*North by Northwest.*" *Critical Inquiry* 7 (1981): 761–76.

Ceplair, Larry and Steven Englund. *The Inquisition in Hollywood: Politics in the Film Community, 1930–1960.* 1979. Berkeley: U of California P, 1983.

Charles, Arthur L. "Barefoot Boy with Shows On." *Modern Screen* (Feb. 1950). Rpt. *The Best of Modern Screen.* Ed. Mark Bego. New York: St. Martin's, 1986. 136–38.

Chauncey, George. *Gay New York: Gender, Urban Culture, and the Making of the Gay Male World 1890–1940.* New York: Basic, 1994.

Clifford E. Clark, Jr. "Ranch-House Suburbia: Ideals and Realities." *Recasting America: Culture and Politics in the Age of the Cold War.* Ed. Lary May. Chicago: U of Chicago P, 1989. 172–91.

Cohan, Steven and Ina Rae Hark, eds. *Screening the Male: Exploring Masculinities in Hollywood Cinema.* London: Routledge, 1993.

"'Commandments' Tops Commie Pic's B.O. Record in Singapore." *Hollywood Reporter* 19 Aug. 1958: n. pag. *The Ten Commandments* file, Herrick.

Connell, R. W. *Gender & Power: Society, the Person and Sexual Politics.* Oxford, U.K.: Polity, 1987.

———. *Masculinities.* Oxford, U.K.: Polity, 1995.

"The Conquest of Smiling Jim." *Time* 27 Feb. 1956: 62–67.

Corber, Robert J. *In the Name of National Security: Hitchcock, Homophobia, and the Political Construction of Gender in Postwar America.* Durham, N.C.: Duke UP, 1993.

Costello, John. *Virtue Under Fire: How World War II Changed Our Social and Sexual Attitudes.* Boston: Little, 1985.

Coughlan, Robert. "Changing Roles in Modern Marriage." *Life* 24 Dec. 1956: 108–18.

Crowther, Bosley. Rev. of *The Ten Commandments. New York Times* 9 Nov. 1956: 35.

Crowther, Bruce. *Charlton Heston: The Epic Presence.* London: Columbus Books, 1986.

Davis, Melody D. *The Male Nude in Contemporary Photography.* Philadelphia: Temple UP, 1991.

DeMille, Cecil. *The Autobiography of Cecil B. DeMille.* Ed. Donald Hayne. Englewood Cliffs, N.J.: Prentice-Hall, 1959.

"DeMille Directs His Biggest Spectacle." *Life* 24 Oct. 1955: 142–49.

"DeMille Makes Co-Op Film Deal with Egypt." *Daily Variety* Oct. 16, 1953: n. pag. *The Ten Commandments* file, Herrick.

D'Emilio, John. "The Homosexual Menace: The Politics of Sexuality in Cold War America." *Passion and Power: Sexuality in History.* Ed. Kathy Peiss and Christina Simmons. Philadelphia: Temple UP, 1989. 225–40.

———. *Sexual Politics, Sexual Communities: The Making of a Homosexual Minority in the United States, 1940–1970.* Chicago: U of Chicago P, 1983. 23–39.

D'Emilio, John and Estelle B. Freedman. *Intimate Matters: A History of Sexuality in America.* New York: Harper, 1988.

Doane, Mary Ann. *Femmes Fatales: Feminism, Film Theory, Psychoanalysis.* New York: Routledge, 1991.

Douglas, Kirk. *The Ragman's Son: An Autobiography.* 1988. New York: Simon, 1989.

Dutton, Kenneth R. *The Perfectible Body: The Western Ideal of Male Development.* New York: Continuum, 1995.

Dworkin, Martin. "*The Desperate Hours* and the Violent Screen." *Shenandoah* 11 (1960): 39–48.

Dyer, Richard. "Coming Out as Going In: The Image of the Homosexual as a Sad Young Man." *The Matter of Images: Essays on Representation.* London: Routledge, 1993. 73–92.

———. "Don't Look Now: The Male Pin-Up." 1982. *The Sexual Subject: A Screen Reader in Sexuality.* London: Routledge, 1992. 267–76.

———. *Heavenly Bodies: Film Stars and Society.* New York: St. Martin's, 1986.

———. "*A Star Is Born* and the Construction of Authenticity." *Stardom: Industry of Desire.* Ed. Christine Gledhill. London: Routledge, 1991. 132–40.

———. *Stars.* 1979. London: BFI, 1986.

———. "White." *Screen* 29.4 (1988): 44–64.

Easthope, Antony. *What a Man's Gotta Do: The Masculine Myth in Popular Culture.* London: Paladin, 1986.

"Eden's Tragic Blunder." *Life* 12 Nov. 1956: 53.

Ehrenreich, Barbara. *Fear of Falling: The Inner Life of the Middle Class.* New York: Pantheon, 1989.

———. *The Hearts of Men: American Dreams and the Flight from Commitment.* New York: Doubleday, 1983.

Elley, Derek. *The Epic Film: Myth and History.* London: Routledge, 1984.

Ellis, John. *Visible Fictions: Cinema, Television, Video.* London: Routledge, 1982.

"Fan Mags Not Striking Out." *Variety* 29 Dec. 1954: 7, 14.

Filene, Peter G. *Him/Her Self: Sex Roles in Modern America.* 2nd. ed. Baltimore: Johns Hopkins UP, 1986.

Fischer, Lucy. "Mama's Boy: Filial Hysteria in *White Heat.*" Cohan and Hark. 70–84.

"5,940 Women." *Time* 24 Aug. 1953: 51–58.

Fletcher, John. "Versions of Masquerade." *Screen* 29.3 (1988): 43–71.

Foster, Alasdair. *Behold the Man: The Male Nude in Photography.* Edinburgh: Stills Gallery, 1988.

Foucault, Michel. *Discipline and Punish: The Birth of the Prison.* 1975. Trans. Alan Sheridan. New York: Vintage, 1979.

Frank, Lawrence K. "How Much Do We Know about Men?" *Look* 17 May 1955: 52–56.

Freedman, Estelle B. "'Uncontrolled Desires': The Response to the Sexual Psychopath, 1920–1960." *Passion and Power: Sexuality in History.* Eds. Kathy Peiss and Christina Simmons. Philadelphia: Temple UP, 1989. 189–225.

"Freedom—New Style." *Time* 27 Sept. 1954: 22–25.

French, Brandon. *On the Verge of Revolt: Women in American Films of the Fifties.* New York: Ungar, 1978.

Gabler, Neal. *An Empire of Their Own: How the Jews Invented Hollywood.* New York: Doubleday, 1988.

Gallico, Paul. "What We Talked About." *While You Were Gone: A Report on Wartime Life in the United States.* Ed. Jack Goodman. New York: Simon, 1946. 28–63.

Garber, Marjorie. *Vested Interests: Cross-Dressing and Cultural Anxiety.* New York: Routledge, 1992.

———. *Vice Versa: Bisexuality and the Eroticism of Everyday Life.* New York: Simon, 1995.

Gardner, Gerald. *The Censorship Papers: Movie Censorship Letters from the Hays Office, 1934 to 1968.* New York: Dodd, 1987.

Gehman, Richard. "Flight from Fear." *Photoplay* Mar. 1957: 34–36, 108–10.

———. "Monty's Brush with Death." *Photoplay* Apr. 1957: 59, 84–87.

Gerber, David A. "Heroes and Misfits: The Troubled Social Reintegration of Disabled Veterans in *The Best Years of Our Lives.*" *American Quarterly* 46 (1994): 545–74.

Gilbert, James. *A Cycle of Outrage: America's Reaction to the Juvenile Delinquent in the 1950s.* New York: Oxford UP, 1986.

Goffman, Erving. *The Presentation of Self in Everyday Life.* New York: Anchor, 1959.

Goldman, Eric F. *The Crucial Decade—And After, America, 1945–1960.* New York: Random, 1960.

Gorn, Elliot J. *The Manly Art: Bare-Knuckle Prize Fighting in America.* Ithaca, NY: Cornell UP, 1986.

Graves, Janet. Rev. of *Picnic. Photoplay* Mar. 1956: 10.

Gumpert, Martin. "The Kinsey Report." *The Nation* 1 May 1948: 471–72.

Hacker, Helen Mayer. "The New Burdens of Masculinity." *Marriage and Family Living* 19 (1957): 227–33.

Hadleigh, Boze. *Conversations with My Elders.* New York: St. Martin's, 1986.

Halberstam, David. *The Fifties.* New York: Villard, 1993.

Hark, Ina Rae. "Animals or Romans: Looking at Masculinity in *Spartacus.*" Cohan and Hark. 151–72.

Harris, Eleanor. "Rock Hudson: Why He Is No. 1." *Look* 18 1958: 47–56.

Haskell, Molly. *From Reverence to Rape: The Treatment of Women in the Movies.* New York: Penguin, 1974.

Héritier-Augé, Françoise. "Older Women, Stout-Hearted Women, Women of Substance." Trans. Leigh Hafrey. *Fragments for a History of the Human Body, Part Three [Zone 5].* Ed. Michel Feher with Ramona Naddaff and Nadia Tazi. Cambridge, Mass.: MIT P, 1989. 280–99.

Hersey, John. *Into the Valley: A Skirmish of the Marines.* 1943. Rpt. New York: Schocken,

1989.

Higham, Charles. *Brando: The Unauthorized Biography*. New York: New American Library, 1987.

Higham, Charles and Roy Moseley. *Cary Grant: The Lonely Heart*. 1989. New York: Avon, 1990.

"Hollywood's Muscle Men and Pin-Up Pretties." *Movieland* Oct. 1954: 48–55.

Holmlund, Chris. "Masculinity as Multiple Masquerade: The 'Mature' Stallone and the Stallone Clone." Cohan and Hark. 213–29.

Holtzman, Will. *William Holden*. New York: Pyramid, 1976.

"Honesty of 'Pitfall' Wins N.Y. Reviewers' Bouquets." *Hollywood Reporter* 23 Aug. 1948: n. pag. *Pitfall* file, Herrick.

Hooven, F. Valentine III. *Beefcake: The Muscle Magazines of America 1950–1970*. Cologne: Benedikt Taschen, 1995.

Hopper, Hedda. "Big Man from Winnetka!" *Chicago Tribune Magazine* 13 Mar. 1955: n. pag. Hudson file, Herrick.

———. "Hollywood's New Sex-boat." *Photoplay* July 1952: 62–63, 108–109.

———. "Never a Bad Show." *Chicago Sunday Tribune Magazine* 6 Apr. 1958: n. pag. Holden file, Herrick.

Hotchner, A. E. *Doris Day: Her Own Story*. New York: Morrow, 1976.

Houston, Penelope and John Gillet. "The Theory and Practice of Blockbusting." *Sight and Sound* Spring 1963: 68–74.

Hudson, Rock and Sara Davidson. *Rock Hudson: His Story*. New York: Morrow, 1986.

Hyams, Joe. *Bogie: The Humphrey Bogart Story*. 1966. New York: Signet, 1967.

———. "The Rock Hudson Story." *Photoplay* Feb. 1957: 43–45, 90–93.

———. "Why Women Are in Love with Rock Hudson." *McCall's* Feb. 1957: 52, 85–88.

"In the Money." *Time* 18 Nov. 1957: 112.

Institute for Sex Research [Alfred C. Kinsey and others]. *Sexual Behavior in the Human Female*. Philadelphia: W.B. Saunders, 1953.

Irigaray, Luce. *This Sex Which Is Not One*. 1977. Trans. Catherine Porter. Ithaca: Cornell UP, 1985.

Ives, Rosalind. "The Great Topic." *Good Housekeeping* (May 1948): 33, 302.

Jacobi, Ernst. "A Character—But Still Brando." *Photoplay* June 1955: 62–63, 83–91.

Jessup, Saul. "Rebel in a Button-Down Collar?" *Photoplay* May 1957: 55, 92. Curtis file, NY Public.

Kael, Pauline. *5001 Nights at the Movies: A Guide from A to Z*. New York: Holt, 1982.

Kaplan, E. Ann. *Women and Film: Both Sides of the Camera*. New York: Methuen, 1983.

Kapsis, Robert E. *Hitchcock: The Making of a Reputation*. Chicago: U of Chicago P, 1992.

Kardiner, Abram. "The Flight from Masculinity." *The Problem of Homosexuality in Modern Society*. Ed. Hendrik M. Ruitenbeek. New York: Dutton, 1963. 17–39.

Kimmel, Michael S. "The Cult of Masculinity: American Social Character and the Legacy of the Cowboy." *Beyond Patriarchy: Essays by Men on Pleasure, Power, and Change*. Ed. Michael Kaufman. Toronto: U of Toronto P, 1987. 235–49.

Kinsey, Alfred C., Wordell B. Pomeroy, and Clyde E. Martin. *Sexual Behavior in the Human Male*. Philadelphia: W. B. Saunders, 1948.

"Kinsey Report on the Air." *Newsweek*. 8 Mar. 1948: 52.

Klapp, Orrin E. *Heroes, Villains, and Fools: The Changing American Character*. Englewood Cliffs, N.J.: Prentice-Hall, 1962.

Klinger, Barbara. *Melodrama and Meaning: History, Culture, and the Films of Douglas Sirk*.

Bloomington: Indiana UP, 1994.

Kolker, Robert P. "The Man of Feeling, or the Vulnerability of the Fifties Male." Paper presented at the Melodrama Conference, British Film Institute, London 1992.

Korman, Seymour. "Meet the Real Marlon Brando!" *Chicago Tribune Magazine* 17 Apr. 1955: n. pag. Brando file, Herrick.

Kroll, Gerry. "Master Harold." *Advocate* 22 Aug. 1995: 38–43.

Krutnik, Frank. "The Faint Aroma of Performing Seals: The 'Nervous' Romance and the Comedy of the Sexes." *Velvet Light Trap* 26 (1990): 57–71.

———. *In a Lonely Street: Film Noir, Genre, Masculinity.* London: Routledge, 1991.

Kuhn, Annette. "The Body and Cinema: Some Problems for Feminism." *Wide Angle* 11 (October 1989): 52–60.

LaGuardia, Robert. *Monty: A Biography of Monty Clift.* 1977. New York: Avon, 1978.

"Land." Rev. of *Camelot.* 25 Oct. 1967. Rpt. *Variety Film Reviews 1964–1967.* New York: Garland, 1983. N. pag.

———. Rev. of *The Seven Year Itch. Variety* 8 June 1955: 6. *The Seven Year Itch* PCA file.

Lane, John Francis. "The Money in Muscles." *Films and Filming* July 1960: 9, 33.

Lane, Laura. "From Brando to Presley: Why the 'Rebel' Craze Is Here to Stay." *Photoplay* Nov. 1956: 56–61, 121–22.

Laro, Frank. "Actor Stays Optimistic Until the End." *Los Angeles Mirror-News* 14 Jan. 1957: 1, 8–9. Bogart file, Herrick.

Larson, Allen. "'There was something (different) about the boy . . .': On the Search for a 'Gay Look' in Classical Hollywood Cinema." *Antithesis* 5 (1992): 21–34.

Lasky, Jesse L. Jr. *Whatever Happened to Hollywood?* New York: Funk & Wagnalls, 1975.

"A Leap Year's Guide to 8 Types of Bachelors." *Photoplay* Mar. 1960: 46–48, 87.

Lears, Jackson. "A Matter of Taste: Corporate Cultural Hegemony in a Mass-Consumption Society." *Recasting America: Culture and Politics in the Age of Cold War.* Ed. Lary May. Chicago: U of Chicago P, 1989. 38–57.

Leff, Leonard J. "Hitchcock at Metro." *Western Humanities Review* 37 (1983): 97–124.

Lehman, Ernest. *North by Northwest.* New York: Viking, 1972.

Lehman, Peter. *Running Scared: Masculinity and the Representation of the Male Body.* Philadelphia: Temple UP, 1993.

Leiser, Ernest. "No Time for Company." *Photoplay* Jan. 1950: 42–45, 89.

Leonard, George B. Jr. "Why Is He Afraid to Be Different?" *Look* 18 Feb. 1958: 95–102.

Lippe, Richard. "Montgomery Clift: A Critical Disturbance." *CineAction!* 17 (1989): 36–42.

Logan, Joshua. *Josh: My Up and Down, In and Out Life.* New York: Delacorte, 1976.

———. *Movie Stars, Real People, and Me.* New York: Delacorte, 1978.

Lyndon, Louis. "Uncertain Hero: The Paradox of the American Male." *Woman's Home Companion* Nov. 1956: 41–43, 107.

Malone, Michael. *Heroes of Eros: Male Sexuality in the Movies.* New York: Dutton, 1979.

"The Man in the Gray Flannel Suit." *Look* 1 May 1956: 104, 106. *The Man in the Gray Flannel Suit* file, Herrick.

"Man in a Gray Flannel Trap." *Life* 9 April 1956: 111–14. *The Man in the Gray Flannel Suit* file, Herrick.

Mann, Roderick. "Curtis Remembers Bernie Schwartz." *New York World Telegram & Sun* 20 Oct. 1962: n. pag. Curtis file, NY Public.

Manners, Dorothy. "Bald Men Find Hero in Yul Brynner." *Los Angeles Examiner* 25 Mar. 1956: 12, 15. Brynner file, Herrick.

Marchand, Roland. "Visions of Classlessness, Questions for Dominion: American Popular Culture, 1945–1960." *Reshaping America: Society and Institutions, 1945–1960.* Eds. Robert H. Bremner and Gary W. Reichard. Columbus: Ohio State UP, 1982. 163–90.

Marling, Karal Ann. *As Seen on TV: The Visual Culture of Everyday Life in the 1950s.* Cambridge, Mass.: Harvard UP, 1994.

Marling, Karal Ann and John Wetenhall. *Iwo Jima: Monuments, Memories, and the American Hero.* Cambridge, Mass.: Harvard UP, 1991.

"MARRIAGE Is What Every Man Needs, Even Rock Hudson." *Movieland* Sept. 1957: 38–39, 70–71.

Marsh, Margaret. "Suburban Men and Masculine Domesticity, 1870–1915." *American Quarterly* 40 (1988): 165–86.

Mast, Gerald. *Howard Hawks, Storyteller.* New York: Oxford UP, 1982.

May, Elaine Tyler. *Homeward Bound: American Families in the Cold War Era.* New York: Basic, 1988.

McArthur, Colin. "The Real Presence." *Sight and Sound* 36.3 (1967): 142–43.

McCann, Graham. *Rebel Males: Clift, Brando and Dean.* London: Hamish Hamilton, 1991.

McCormick, Thomas J. *America's Half-Century: United States Foreign Policy in the Cold War.* Baltimore: Johns Hopkins UP, 1989.

"Meet the Champs." *Photoplay* Oct. 1953: 40–43, 102.

Mellen, Joan. *Big Bad Wolves: Masculinity in the American Film.* New York: Pantheon, 1977.

Meyer, Richard. "Rock Hudson's Body." *Inside/Out: Lesbian Theories, Gay Theories.* Ed. Diana Fuss. New York: Routledge, 1991. 259–88.

Miller, Douglas T. and Marion Nowak. *The Fifties: The Way We Really Were.* New York: Doubleday, 1977.

"Modern Films Unfair to He Men Says John Wayne." *Beverly Hills Citizen* 20 May 1960: n. pag. Wayne file, Herrick.

Modleski, Tania. *Feminism without Women: Culture and Criticism in a "Postfeminist" Age.* New York: Routledge, 1991.

———. *The Women Who Knew Too Much: Hitchcock and Feminist Theory.* 1988. New York: Routledge, 1989.

Moffitt, Jack. Rev. of *The Man in the Gray Flannel Suit. Hollywood Reporter.* 30 March 1956. *The Man in the Gray Flannel Suit* PCA file.

———. Rev. of *North by Northwest. Hollywood Reporter* 30 June 1959: 3.

———. Rev. of *The Seven Year Itch. Hollywood Reporter.* 3 June 1955: n. pag. *The Seven Year Itch* PCA file.

Morella, Joe and Edward Z. Epstein. *Rebels: The Rebel Hero in Films.* Secaucus: Citadel P, 1971.

Mosby, Aline. "Yul Brynner Shaves Head Every Day." *Hollywood Citizen-News* Dec. 10, 1955: n. pag. Brynner file, Herrick.

Moskin, J. Robert. "Why Do *Women* Dominate Him?" *Look* 4 Feb. 1958: 77–80.

"Mount Sinai to Main Street." *Time* 19 Nov. 1956: n. pag. *The Ten Commandments* file, Herrick.

Mourlet, Michel. "In Defense of Violence." 1960. Trans. David Wilson. *Stardom: Industry of Desire,* Ed. Christine Gledhill. London: Routledge, 1991. 233–36.

"Movie of the Week: *A Streetcar Named Desire.*" *Life* 24 Sept. 1951: n. pag. *A Streetcar*

Named Desire file, Herrick.

Mulvey, Laura. "Visual Pleasure and Narrative Cinema." 1975. *Visual and Other Pleasures.* Bloomington: Indiana UP, 1989. 14–26.

Musel, Robert. "Charlton Heston Bound to Task." *Hollywood Citizen-News* 18 Aug. 1959: n. pag. Heston file, Herrick.

Nadel, Alan. *Containment Culture: American Narratives, Postmodernism, and the Atomic Age.* Durham: Duke UP, 1995.

"Naguib Ok's DeMille Film." *Los Angeles Examiner* Oct. 1953: n. pag. *The Ten Commandments* file, Herrick.

Naremore, James. *Acting in the Cinema.* Berkeley: U of California P, 1988.

———. *The Films of Vincente Minnelli.* New York: Cambridge UP, 1993.

Neale, Steve. "Masculinity as Spectacle." 1983. Cohan and Hark. 9–20.

Neibaur, James L. *Tough Guy: The American Movie Macho.* Jefferson, NC: McFarland, 1989.

"The New American Domesticated Male." *Life* 4 Jan. 1954: 42–45.

"New Films on View." *Cue* 31 Aug. 1948: 20. *Pitfall* file, Herrick.

"News from Sam Spiegel Productions' *The Bridge on the River Kwai.*" 1957. Holden file, Herrick.

Noerdlinger, Henry S. *Moses and Egypt: The Documentation to the Motion Picture* The Ten Commandments. Los Angeles: U of California P, 1956.

Noriega, Chon. "'Something's Missing Here!': Homosexuality and Film Reviews During the Production Code Era, 1934–1962." *Cinema Journal* 30 (1990): 20–41.

Oakley, J. Ronald. *God's Country: America in the Fifties.* New York: Dembner, 1990.

"Opulence in Plain Rooms." *Life* Oct. 19, 1959: 76–79.

Packard, Vance. *The Status Seekers.* 1959. Harmondsworth, Eng.: Pelican, 1960.

"Pakistan Bans 'Ten Commandments.'" *Hollywood Reporter* 29 Oct. 1958: n. pag. *The Ten Commandments* file, Herrick.

Palmer, James W. "*In a Lonely Place:* Paranoia in the Dream Factory." *Literature/Film Quarterly* 13 (1985): 200–207.

Paramount press release. c. October 1956. *The Ten Commandments* file, Herrick.

Parsons, Louella. "Marlon Brando: The Strange Case of the Strange Boy." *Los Angeles Examiner* 24 Sept. 1954: n. pag. Brando file, Herrick.

———. "Rock Hudson: 'Marriage Is Not for Me.'" *Los Angeles Examiner* 25 Oct. 1959: n. pag. Pictorial Living section. Hudson file, Herrick.

"Pay Last Tribute to 'Tough Guy' Bogart." *Los Angeles Herald-Express* 17 Jan. 1957: n. pag. Bogart file, Herrick.

"People." *Time* 9 Aug. 1954: 40.

Perchuk, Andrew and Helaine Posner, eds. *The Masculine Masquerade: Masculinity and Representation.* Cambridge: MIT P, 1995.

Peterson, Wayne D. Letter to Editor. *Playboy* Aug. 1958: 4.

Pettigrew, Terence. *Raising Hell: The Rebel in the Movies.* New York: St. Martin's, 1986.

Philips, Dee. "Average Score: Terrific!" *Photoplay* Apr. 1955: 36–37, 109–12.

"The Playboy Reader." *Playboy* Sept. 1955: 36.

"Playboy's Party Jokes." *Playboy* Nov. 1954: 33.

"Playboy's Penthouse Apartment," *Playboy* Sept. 1956: 53–60 (Part I), Oct. 1956: 65–70 (Part II).

Polan, Dana. *In a Lonely Place.* London: BFI, 1993.

————. *Power and Paranoia: History, Narrative, and the American Cinema, 1940–1950.* New York: Columbia UP, 1986.

"Powe." Rev. of *North by Northwest. Daily Variety* 30 June 1959: 3.

Pressbook for *North by Northwest. North by Northwest* file, Herrick.

Pressbook for *Pillow Talk.* NY Public.

Pryor, Thomas S. "Hollywood Clicks: M-G-M Solves its 'Tea and Sympathy' Script Problems." *New York Times* 25 Sept. 1955: n. pag. *Tea and Sympathy* PCA file.

Psychology for the Fighting Man: What You Should Know About Yourself and Others, Prepared for the Fighting Man Himself by a Committee of the National Research Council with the Collaboration of Science Service as a Contribution to the War Effort. Washington: The Infantry Journal [Penguin Books], 1943.

Rabkin, Leslie Yale. Letter. *New York Times* 31 May 1959: X5.

Rappaport, Mark, dir. *Rock Hudson's Home Movies.* Videocassette. Couch Potato Films, 1992.

"Rebels or Psychopaths?" *Time* 16 Dec. 1954: 64–65.

Reed, Donald. "Solved! The Mystery of Kinsey's Strange European Junket." *Hush-Hush* (May 1956): 12–13, 57–59.

Reisman, David in collaboration with Reuel Denney and Nathan Glazer. *The Lonely Crowd: A Study of the Changing American Character.* New Haven: Yale UP, 1950.

Rev. of *Dead Reckoning. Hollywood Reporter.* 17 Jan. 1947: n. pag. *Dead Reckoning* PCA file.

Richards, Jeffrey. "Heston's Heroes." *Movies of the 1950s.* Ed. Ann Lloyd. London: Orbis, 1982. 49–51.

Riviere, Joan. "Womanliness as a Masquerade." 1929. *Formations of Fantasy.* Ed. Victor Burgin, James Donald, and Cora Kaplan. London: Methuen, 1986. 35–44.

Robbins, Jhan. *Yul Brynner: The Inscrutable King.* New York: Dodd, 1987.

"Rock Hudson: What Kind of Romance *Does* He Want?" *Screen Album* Aug.-Oct. 1958: 21–23.

"Rock, the New Giant." *Movieland* April 1955: 38–39, 64–66.

Rogin, Michael Paul. *Ronald Reagan, the Movie and Other Episodes in Political Demonology.* Berkeley: U of California P, 1987.

"Rollicking Role for Rock." *Life* 21 Sept. 1959: 73–75.

Rothman, William. *The "I" of The Camera: Essays in Film Criticism, History, and Aesthetics.* New York: Cambridge UP, 1988.

Rotundo, E. Anthony. *American Manhood: Transformations from the Revolution to the Modern Era.* New York: Basic Books, 1993.

Ruitenbeek, Hendrik M. "Men Alone: The Male Homosexual and the Disintegrated Family." *The Problem of Homosexuality in Modern Society.* Ed. Hendrik M. Ruitenbeek. New York: Dutton, 1963. 80–93.

Russell, Rosalind and Chris Chase. *Life Is a Banquet.* New York: Random House, 1977.

Russo, Vito. *The Celluloid Closet: Homosexuality in the Movies.* New York: Harper, 1981.

Ryan, Martin. "Portrait of *Playboy.*" *Studies in Public Communication* 1 (1957): 11–21.

Saunders, Gil. *The Nude: A New Perspective.* London: Herbert P, 1989.

Sayre, Nora. *Running Time: Films of the Cold War.* New York: Dial, 1982.

Scheuer, Philip K. "'Pitfall' Realistic Underworld Drama." *Los Angeles Times* 27 Aug. 1948: n. pag. *Pitfall* file, Herrick.

Schickel, Richard. *Cary Grant: A Celebration.* Boston: Little, 1983.

Schumach, Murray. *The Face on the Cutting Room Floor: The Story of Movie and Television*

Censorship. 1964. New York: Da Capo, 1975.

Scott, Martin, "John Wayne." *Cosmopolitan* Nov. 1954: 26–32. Wayne file, Herrick.

Scott, Vern. "Glamour Boys Now: Bubble Bath for Tony Curtis." Source unintelligible. c. Oct 1958. Curtis file, NY Public. The article has a UPI syndication credit.

Scott, Vernon. "Charlton Heston Looks Epic." *Citizen-News* 29 Mar. 1959: n. pag. Heston file, Herrick.

———. "2nd Banana Roles Enrich Tony Curtis." *New York World Telegram & Sun* 4 Dec. 1957: n. pag. Curtis file, NY Public.

———. "Yul Brynner Discusses His True Nationality." *Hollywood Citizen-News* 5 July 1958: n. pag. Brynner file, Herrick.

Sedgwick, Eve Kosofsky. *Between Men: English Literature and Male Homosocial Desire*. New York: Columbia UP, 1985.

———. *Epistemology of the Closet*. Berkeley: U of California P, 1990.

———. *Tendencies*. Durham, N.C.: Duke UP, 1993.

Segal, Lynn. "Look Back in Anger: Men in the Fifties." *Male Order: Unwrapping Masculinity*. Eds. Rowena Chapman and Jonathan Rutherford. London: Lawrence & Wishart, 1988. 68–96.

Shearer, Lloyd. "Hero: John 'Duke' Wayne." *Pageant* June 1952: 155–63. Wayne file, Herrick.

Shipman, David. *Marlon Brando*. London: Sphere, 1989.

Shipp, Cameron. "Hollywood's Most Shocking Rumor." *Photoplay* Aug. 1958: 74–75, 86–87.

"The Shoulder Trade." *Time* 2 Aug. 1954: 62–68.

"Sigh Guy Monty Clift." *Movie Glamour Guys* 1949: 4–5.

Sikov, Ed. *Laughing Hysterically: American Screen Comedy of the 1950s*. New York: Columbia UP, 1994.

Silverman, Kaja. *Male Subjectivity at the Margins*. New York: Routledge, 1992.

"The Simple Life of a Busy Bachelor." *Life* 3 Oct. 1955: 128–32.

"6 Ways to Rope in that Summer Romance." *Photoplay* Sept. 1958: 27–30, 95–97.

Sklar, Robert. *City Boys: Cagney, Bogart, Garfield*. Princeton: Princeton UP, 1992.

Skolsky, Sidney. "Hollywood Is My Beat." *Hollywood Citizen-News* 26 Feb. 26, 1953: n. pag. Wayne file, Herrick.

———. "Hollywood Is My Beat." *Hollywood Citizen-News* 17 Mar. 1955: n. pag. Heston file, Herrick.

———. "The New Look in Hollywood Men." *Photoplay* July 1957: 41–43, 111–12.

———. "That's Hollywood for You." *Photoplay* May 1956: 18.

Sloan, Lloyd C. "Leading Ladies? Kisses? 'Phooey,' Says Bogie." *Hollywood Citizen-News* 19 Nov. 1949: 8. Bogart file, Herrick.

Slotkin, Richard. *Gunfighter Nation: The Myth of the Frontier in Twentieth-Century America*. 1992. New York: Harper, 1993.

Smith, Frankenstein. "Virginity: An Important Treatise on a Very Important Subject." *Playboy* Sept. 1954: 9, 40, 50.

Smith, Lou. "Synopsis, *In a Lonely Place*." 28 Oct. 1949. *In a Lonely Place* PCA file.

Sobchack, Vivian. *Screening Space: The American Science Fiction Film*. 2nd ed. New York: Ungar, 1987.

———. "'Surge and Splendor': A Phenomenology of the Hollywood Historical Epic." *Representations* 29 (1990): 24–49.

Souvenir program. *The Ten Commandments* file, Herrick.

Spigel, Lynn. *Make Room for TV: Television and the Family Ideal in Postwar America.* Chicago: U of Chicago P, 1992.

Spoto, Donald. *Camerado: Hollywood and the American Man.* New York: New American Library, 1978.

———. *The Dark Side of Genius: The Life of Alfred Hitchcock.* 1983. New York: Ballantine, 1993.

Staiger, Janet. *Interpreting Films: Studies in the Historical Reception of American Cinema.* Princeton: Princeton UP, 1992.

Stearns, Peter N. "Men, Boys and Anger in American Society, 1860–1940." *Manliness and Morality: Middle-Class Masculinity in Britain and America, 1800–1940.* Eds. J. A. Mangan and James Walvin. Manchester: Manchester UP, 1987. 75–91.

Steele, Joseph. "Restless Rebel." *Photoplay* (July 1950): 48–49, 78.

Strasberg, Susan. *Bittersweet.* New York: Putnam's, 1980.

"The Stronger Sex Makes Strong Box Office." *Life* 31 May 1954: 93–96.

Susman, Warren. "Did Success Spoil the United States? Dual Representations in Postwar America." *Recasting America: Culture and Politics in the Age of Cold War.* Ed. Lary May. Chicago: U of Chicago P, 1989. 19–37.

"Tall, Dark, and Dignified." *Look* 24 July 1956: 81–85.

Taradash, Daniel. *Picnic.* Revised Final Draft. 2 May, 1955. Author's copy.

Telotte, J. P. "Film Noir at Columbia: Fashion and Innovation." *Columbia Pictures: Portrait of a Studio.* Ed. Bernard F. Dick. Lexington, Ky.: UP of Kentucky, 1992. 106–17.

"Temporary Truce?" *Movieland* Nov. 1954: 41–43, 70–71.

"'10 Commandments' As Pic Seen Envoy of Peace Abroad." *The Hollywood Reporter* 20 May 1953. *The Ten Commandments* file, Herrick.

"'10 Commandments' Much More Sexy Than 'Baby Doll' Clergyman Declares." *Los Angeles Times* 24 Dec. 1956. Typescript. *Baby Doll* PCA file.

Terkel, Studs. *"The Good War": An Oral History Of World War Two.* 1984. New York: Ballantine, 1991.

Thomas, Bob. *Golden Boy: The Untold Story of William Holden.* New York: St. Martin's, 1983.

Thompson, Jack. "Triumph of an Average Guy." *New York Mirror Magazine* 31 July 1957: 10. Holden file, Herrick.

"A Tiger in the Reeds." *Time* (11 Oct. 1954): 58–66.

Tompkins, Jane. *West of Everything: The Inner Life of Westerns.* New York: Oxford UP, 1992.

Townsend, Pauline Swanson. "Bachelor Daze." *Photoplay* May 1955: 52–53, 117–18.

Truffaut, François. *Hitchcock.* New York: Simon, 1984.

Vernet, Marc. "Wings of the Desert; or, The Invisible Superimpositions." *Velvet Light Trap.* 28 (Fall 1991): 65–72.

"Volume I, Number I." *Playboy* Dec. 1953: 3.

Walters, Margaret. *The Nude Male: A New Perspective.* London: Penguin, 1978.

Warner Bros. Press Release. c. 1945. Bogart file, Herrick.

Warner, Mrs. R. C. Letter to Editor. *Life* 25 June 1954: n. pag. Lancaster file, NY Public.

Waterbury, Ruth. "He Lost His Shirt and Became a Star." *Photoplay* May 1955: 62–63, 121–22.

———. "The Jury Chooses Male Pin Ups." *Photoplay* Nov. 1951: 38–39, 70.

"Wayne Testifies in Private Life He Was 'Woman-Handled.'" *L.A. Daily News* 2 June 1953: n. pag. Wayne file, Herrick.

Weeks, Jeffrey. *Sexuality*. London: Tavistock P, 1986.

Wexman, Virginia Wright. *Creating the Couple: Love, Marriage, and Hollywood Performance*. Princeton: Princeton UP, 1993.

Whitehall, Richard. "Days of Strife and Nights of Orgy." *Film and Filming* Mar. 1963: 17–31.

"Why the Young Kill: Prowling the Juvenile Jungles of the Big Cities." *Newsweek* 19 Aug. 1957: 25–28.

Whyte, William H. Jr. *The Organization Man*. New York: Simon, 1956.

Williams, Tennessee. *A Streetcar Named Desire*. 1947. *New Voices in the American Theatre*. New York: Modern Library, 1955. 1–110.

Wilson, Earl. "Come Out of the Closet! . . ." *New York Post* 17 Oct. 1968: n. pag. Curtis file, NY Public.

Wilson, George M. *Narration in Light: Studies in Cinematic Point of View*. Baltimore: Johns Hopkins UP, 1986.

Wilson, Liza. "Bill Holden: He Lives with Danger." *American Weekly* 8 Dec., 1957: 20, 22. Holden file, Herrick.

———. "How a Hollywood Bachelor Lives." *American Weekly* 23 May 1954: 13. Hudson file, Herrick.

Wilson, Sloan. *The Man in the Gray Flannel Suit*. New York: Simon, 1955.

Wood, Michael. *America in the Movies or "Santa Maria, It Had Slipped My Mind."* New York: Basic, 1975.

Wood, Robin. *Hitchcock's Films Revisited*. New York: Columbia UP, 1989.

"Would You Marry One of These Men?" *Movieland* Oct. 1954: 17–31.

Yergin, Daniel. *The Prize: The Epic Quest for Oil, Money, and Power*. New York: Simon and Schuster, 1991.

"The Younger Generation." *Time* 5 Nov. 1951: 46–52.

Zollo, Burt. "Open Season on Bachelors." *Playboy* June 1954: 37–38.

Zolotov, Maurice. "Brando—The Real Story." *Los Angeles Examiner* 6 Jan. 1957: 14–17; 20 Jan. 1957: 18–21; 27 Jan. 1957: 22–25. The 13 Jan. 1957 installment is incomplete. *The American Weekly* magazine supplement. Brando file, Herrick.

Zunser, Jesse. "Tony Curtis: Boy into Man." *Cue* 2 Aug. 1958: 10–15. Curtis file, NY Public.

INDEX

STEVEN COHAN is Professor of English at Syracuse University, where he teaches film, gender studies, and narrative theory. He is co-author of *Telling Stories: A Theoretical Analysis of Narrative Fiction*, and co-editor of *Screening the Male: Exploring Masculinities in Hollywood Cinema* and *The Road Movie Book*. His articles on film have appeared in *Camera Obscura, Screen, The Masculine Masquerade, Stud: Architectures of Masculinity*, and *Out Takes: Essays on Queer Theory and Film*.

CPSIA information can be obtained at www.ICGtesting.com
Printed in the USA
BVOW11s0832040815

411724BV00011B/55/P